New Perspectives on

Microsoft®

Excel 7

for Windows® 95

INTRODUCTORY

The New Perspectives Series

The New Perspectives Series consists of texts and technology that teach computer concepts and the programs listed below. Both Windows 3.1 and Windows 95 versions of these programs are available. You can order these New Perspectives texts in many different lengths, software releases, bound combinations, and CourseKits™. Contact your CTI sales representative or customer service representative for the most up-to-date details.

The New Perspectives Series

Computer Concepts

dBASE

Internet and the World Wide Web

Lotus 1-2-3

Microsoft Access

Microsoft Excel

Microsoft Office Professional

Microsoft PowerPoint

Microsoft Windows 3.1

Microsoft Windows 95

Microsoft Word

Microsoft Works

Novell Perfect Office

Paradox

Presentations

Quattro Pro

WordPerfect

New Perspectives on
Microsoft®
Excel 7
for Windows® 95

INTRODUCTORY

June Jamrich Parsons
University of the Virgin Islands

Dan Oja
GuildWare, Inc.

A Susan Solomon Book

COURSE TECHNOLOGY, INC.

A DIVISION OF COURSE TECHNOLOGY

COMMUNICATIONS GROUP

ONE MAIN STREET, CAMBRIDGE MA 02142

AN INTERNATIONAL THOMSON PUBLISHING COMPANY

I(T)P

Albany • Bonn • Boston • Cincinnati • London • Madrid • Melbourne • Mexico City
New York • Paris • San Francisco • Singapore • Tokyo • Toronto • Washington

New Perspectives on Microsoft Excel 7 for Windows 95 — Introductory is published by Course Technology, Inc.

Managing Editor	Mac Mendelsohn
Series Consulting Editor	Susan Solomon
Senior Product Manager	Barbara Clemens
Production Editor	Catherine D. Griffin
Text and Cover Designer	Ella Hanna
Cover Illustrator	Nancy Nash

© 1996 by Course Technology, Inc.
A Division of International Thomson Publishing, Inc.

For more information contact:

Course Technology, Inc.
One Main Street
Cambridge, MA 02142

International Thomson Publishing Europe
Berkshire House 168-173
High Holborn
London WCIV 7AA
England

Thomas Nelson Australia
102 Dodds Street
South Melbourne, 3205
Victoria, Australia

Nelson Canada
1120 Birchmount Road
Scarborough, Ontario
Canada M1K 5G4

International Thomson Editores
Campos Eliseos 385, Piso 7
Col. Polanco
11560 Mexico D.F. Mexico

International Thomson Publishing GmbH
Königswinterer Strasse 418
53227 Bonn
Germany

International Thomson Publishing Asia
211 Henderson Road
#05-10 Henderson Building
Singapore 0315

International Thomson Publishing Japan
Hirakawacho Kyowa Building, 3F
2-2-1 Hirakawacho
Chiyoda-ku, Tokyo 102
Japan

ISBN 0-7600-3541-5

Printed in the United States of America

10 9 8 7 6 5 4 3 2

At Course Technology, Inc., we have one foot in education and the other in technology. We believe that technology is transforming the way people teach and learn, and we are excited about providing instructors and students with materials that use technology to teach about technology.

Our development process is unparalleled in the higher education publishing industry. Every product we create goes through an exacting process of design, development, review, and testing.

Reviewers give us direction and insight that shape our manuscripts and bring them up to the latest standards. Every manuscript is quality tested. Students whose backgrounds match the intended audience work through every keystroke, carefully checking for clarity and pointing out errors in logic and sequence. Together with our own technical reviewers, these testers help us ensure that everything that carries our name is error-free and easy to use.

We show both *how* and *why* technology is critical to solving problems in college and in whatever field you choose to teach or pursue. Our time-tested, step-by-step instructions provide unparalleled clarity. Examples and applications are chosen and crafted to motivate students.

As the New Perspectives Series team at Course Technology, our goal is to produce the most timely, accurate, creative, and technologically-sound product in the entire college publishing industry. We strive for consistent high quality. This takes a lot of communication, coordination, and hard work. But we love what we do. We are determined to be the best. Write us and let us know what you think. You can also e-mail us at info@course.com.

The New Perspectives Series Team

Joseph Adamski	Kathy Finnegan	Karla Mitchell
Judy Adamski	Robin Geller	Dan Oja
Roy Ageloff	Chris Greacen	June Parsons
David Auer	Roger Hayen	Sandra Poindexter
Rachel Bunin	Charles Hommel	Ann Shaffer
Joan Carey	Chris Kelly	Susan Solomon
Patrick Carey	Terry Ann Kremer	John Zeanchock
Barbara Clemens	Melissa Lima	Beverly Zimmerman
Kim Crowley	Mac Mendelsohn	Scott Zimmerman
Jessica Evans		

Preface The New Perspectives Series

What is the New Perspectives Series?

Course Technology, Inc.'s **New Perspectives Series** combines text and technology products that teach computer concepts and microcomputer applications. Users consistently praise this series for its innovative pedagogy, creativity, supportive and engaging style, accuracy, and use of interactive technology. The first New Perspectives text was published in January of 1993. Since then, the series has grown to more than thirty titles and has become the best-selling series on computer concepts and microcomputer applications. Others have imitated the New Perspectives features, design, and technologies, but none have replicated its quality and its ability to consistently anticipate and meet the needs of instructors and students.

How is the New Perspectives Series different from other microcomputer applications series?

The **New Perspectives Series** distinguishes itself from other series in at least four substantial ways: sound instructional design, consistent quality, innovative technology, and proven pedagogy. The texts in this series consist of two or more tutorials, which are based on sound instructional design. Each tutorial is motivated by a realistic case that is meaningful to students. Rather than learn a laundry list of features, students learn the features in the context of solving a problem. This process motivates all concepts and skills by demonstrating to students *why* they would want to know them.

Instructors and students have come to rely on the the high quality of the New Perspectives Series and to consistently praise its accuracy. This accuracy is a result of Course Technology's unique multi-step quality assurance process that incorporates student testing at three stages of development, using hardware and software configurations appropriate to the product. All solutions, test questions, and other CourseTools (see below) are tested using similar procedures. Instructors who adopt this series report that students can work through the tutorials independently, with a minimum of intervention or "damage control" by instructors or staff. This consistent quality has meant that if instructors are pleased with one product from the series, they can rely on the same quality with any other New Perspectives product.

The **New Perspectives Series** distinguishes itself with its innovative technology. This series innovated truly *interactive* learning applications—CTIWinApps and Interactive CourseLabs. These applications have set the standard for interactive learning.

How do I know that the New Perspectives Series will work?

Some instructors who use this series report a significant difference between how much their students learn and retain with this series as compared to other series. With other series, instructors often find that students can work through the book and do well on homework and tests, but still not demonstrate competency when asked to perform particular tasks outside the context of the text's sample case or project. With the **New Perspectives Series**, however, instructors report that students have a complete, integrative learning experience that stays with them. They credit this high retention and competency to the fact that this series incorporates critical thinking and problem solving with the computer skills mastery.

How does the book I'm holding fit into the New Perspectives Series?

New Perspectives microcomputer applications books are available in seven categories—**Brief, Introductory, Intermediate, Comprehensive, Advanced, Four-in-One**, and **Five-in-One**.

Brief books are about 100 pages long and are intended to teach only the essentials of the particular microcomputer application.

Introductory books are about 300 pages long and consist of 6 or 7 tutorials. An Introductory book is designed for a short course on a particular application or for a one-term course to be used in combination with other introductory books.

Four-in-One books and **Five-in-One** books combine a Brief book on Windows with 3 or 4 Introductory books. For example, *New Perspectives on Microsoft Office* is a Five-in-One book—it combines Brief Windows with Introductory Word, Excel, Access, and PowerPoint.

Comprehensive books consist of all of the tutorials in the Introductory book, plus 3 or 4 more tutorials on more advanced topics. They also include the Brief Windows tutorials, 3 or 4 Additional Cases, and a Reference Section.

Intermediate books take the 3 or 4 tutorials at the end of three Comprehensive books and combine them. Reference Sections and Additional Cases are also included.

Advanced books begin by covering topics similar to those in the Comprehensive books, but cover them in more depth. Advanced books then go on to present the most high-level coverage in the series.

Finally, as the name suggests, **Concepts and Applications** books combine the New *Perspectives on Computer Concepts* book with various Brief and Introductory microcomputer applications books.

New Perspectives Series Applications Titles

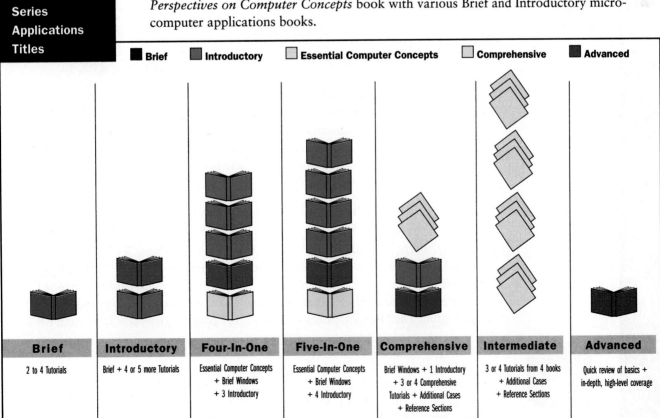

■ **Brief**   ■ **Introductory**   □ **Essential Computer Concepts**   □ **Comprehensive**   ■ **Advanced**

Brief	Introductory	Four-In-One	Five-In-One	Comprehensive	Intermediate	Advanced
2 to 4 Tutorials	Brief + 4 or 5 more Tutorials	Essential Computer Concepts + Brief Windows + 3 Introductory	Essential Computer Concepts + Brief Windows + 4 Introductory	Brief Windows + 1 Introductory + 3 or 4 Comprehensive Tutorials + Additional Cases + Reference Sections	3 or 4 Tutorials from 4 books + Additional Cases + Reference Sections	Quick review of basics + in-depth, high-level coverage

In what kind of course could I use this book?

This book can be used in any course in which you want students to learn all the most important topics of Microsoft Excel 7 for Windows 95—including worksheet planning and creation, functions, formulas, charts, data management, and integration with other programs. This book assumes that students have learned basic Windows 95 navigation and file management skills from *New Perspectives on Microsoft Windows 95 — Brief* or an *equivalent* book.

How do the Windows 95 editions differ from the Windows 3.1 editions?

Larger Page Size   If you've used a *New Perspectives* text before, you'll immediately notice that the book you're holding is larger than the Windows 3.1 series books. We've responded to user requests for a larger page, which allows for larger screen shots and associated callouts. Look on page EX 76 for an example of how we've made the screen shots easier to read.

SESSION 1.5

Sessions   We've divided the tutorials into sessions. Each session is designed to be completed in about 45 minutes to an hour (depending, of course, upon student needs and the speed of your lab equipment). With sessions, learning is broken up into more easily-assimilated chunks. You can more accurately allocate time in your syllabus. Students can more easily manage the available lab time. Each session begins with a "session box," which quickly describes what skills the student will learn in the session. Furthermore, each session is numbered, which makes it easier for you and your students to navigate and communicate about the tutorial. Look on page EX 25 for the session box that opens Session 1.2.

Quick Check

Quick Checks   Each session concludes with meaningful, conceptual questions—called Quick Checks—that test students' understanding of what they learned in the session. The answers to all of the Quick Check questions are at the back of the book preceding the Index. You can find examples of Quick Checks on pages EX 24 and EX 40.

New Design   We have retained a design that helps students easily differentiate between what they are to *do* and what they are to *read*. The steps are easily identified by their shaded background and numbered steps. Furthermore, this new design presents steps and screen shots in a larger, easier-to-read format. Some good examples of our new design are on pages EX 38 and EX 52.

What features are retained in the Windows 95 editions of the New Perspectives Series?

"Read This Before You Begin" Page   This page is consistent with Course Technology's unequaled commitment to helping instructors introduce technology into the classroom. Technical considerations and assumptions about hardware and software are listed in one place to help instructors save time and eliminate unnecessary aggravation. The "Read This Before You Begin" page for this book is on page EX 2.

Tutorial Case   Each tutorial begins with a problem presented in a case that is meaningful to students. The problem turns the task of learning how to use an application into a problem-solving process. The problems increase in complexity with each tutorial. These cases touch on multicultural, international, and ethical issues—so important to today's business curriculum

Step-by-Step Methodology   This unique Course Technology methodology keeps students on track. They click or press keys always within the context of solving the problem posed in the tutorial case. The text constantly guides students, letting them know where they are in the course of solving the problem. In addition, the numerous screen shots include labels that direct students' attention to what they should look at on the screen. On almost every page in this book, you can find an example of how steps, screen shots, and callouts work together.

TROUBLE?

TROUBLE? Paragraphs   TROUBLE? paragraphs anticipate the mistakes that students are likely to make and help them recover from these mistakes. By putting these paragraphs in the book, rather than in the instructor's manual, we facilitate independent learning and free the instructor to focus on substantive conceptual issues rather than on common procedural errors. Two representative examples of Troubles? are on pages EX 172 and EX 224.

Reference Windows   Reference Windows appear throughout the text. They are short, succinct summaries of the most important tasks covered in the tutorials. Reference Windows are specially designed and written so students can refer to them for their reference value when doing the Tutorial Assignments and Case Problems, and after completing the course. Page EX 70 contains the Reference Window for Using AutoFormat.

Task Reference   The Task Reference is a summary of how to perform commonly-used tasks using the most efficient method, as well as helpful shortcuts. It appears as a table at the end of the book. In this book the Task Reference is on pages EX 296–304.

Tutorial Assignments, Case Problems, and Lab Assignments   Each tutorial concludes with Tutorial Assignments, which provide students with additional hands-on practice of the skills they learned in the tutorial. The Tutorial Assignments are followed by four Case Problems that have approximately the same scope as the tutorial case. In the Windows 95 applications texts, there is always one Case Problem in the book and one in the Instructor's Manual that do not use a presupplied student file, requiring students to solve from scratch. Finally, if a Lab (see below) accompanies the tutorial, Lab Assignments are included. Look on pages EX 124 through EX 125 for the Tutorial Assignments for Tutorial 3. An example of a Lab Assignments is on page EX 44.

Exploration Exercises   The Windows environment allows students to learn by exploring and discovering what they can do. Exploration Exercises can be Tutorial Assignments or Case Problems that might challenge students to explore the capabilities of the program they are using, and extend their knowledge using the Windows Help facility and other reference materials. Page EX 203 contains Exploration Exercises for Tutorial 5.

The New Perspectives Series is known for using technology to help instructors teach and administer, and to help students learn. What CourseTools are available with this textbook?

All of the teaching and learning materials available with the **New Perspectives Series** are known as CourseTools.

CourseLabs   Computer skills and concepts come to life with the New Perspectives CourseLabs—highly-interactive tutorials that guide students step by step, present them with Quick Check questions, allow them to explore on their own, and test them on their comprehension. Lab Assignments are also included in the book at the end of each relevant tutorial. The lab available with this book and the tutorial in which it appears is:

Spreadsheet Tour -
Tutorial 1

Course Test Manager   Course Test Manager is a cutting-edge Windows-based testing software that helps instructors design and administer pre-tests, practice tests, and actual examinations. The full-featured program provides random test generation of practice tests, immediate on-line feedback, and generation of detailed study guides for questions that are incorrectly answered. Online pre-tests help instructors assess student skills and plan instruction. Also, students can take tests at the computer; tests can be automatically graded and generate statistical information for the instructor on individual and group performance. Instructors can also use Course Test Manager to produce printed tests.

Course Presenter   Course Presenter is a CD ROM-based presentation tool that provides instructors with a wealth of resources for use in the classroom, replacing traditional overhead transparencies with computer-generated screenshows. Presenter gives instructors the flexibility to create custom presentations, complete with matching student notes and lecture notes pages. The presentations integrate closely with the New Perspectives book and other CourseTools, and provide instructors with another resource to use so they can teach the way they want to teach.

Online Companions   When you use a New Perspectives product you are able to access Course Technology's Online Companion. Instructors may use the Faculty Online Companion for additional instructors' materials. Please see your Instructor's Manual or call your Course Technology customer service representative for more information. Students may access their Online Companion in the Student Center on the World Wide Web at http://www.vmedia.com/cti/.

Instructor's Manual   Instructor's Manuals are written by the authors and are quality-assurance tested. Each Instructor's Manual includes some or all of the following items:

- Answers and solutions to all of the Tutorial Assignments and Case Problems. Suggested solutions are also included for the Exploration Exercises. This is available in both hardcopy and digital form.
- A Setup Disk, which contains all of the data files that students will use for the Tutorials, the Tutorial Assignments, and the Case Problems. A README file includes other technical tips for lab management. These files are also available online. See the inside covers of this book and the "Read This Before You Begin" page before Tutorial 1 for more information on Setup Disk files.
- A CourseLabs Setup Disk, which contains the interactive CourseLabs.
- Troubleshooting Tips, which anticipate commonly-encountered problems.
- Extra Problems, to augment teaching options.
- Instructor's Notes, prepared by the authors and based on their teaching experience.

Acknowledgments

We would like to thank all the members of the New Perspectives team who helped with this revision, particularly Ann Shaffer, whose insight and skill helped shape this book. Our appreciation goes to reviewers Ed Fisher, Central Michigan University; Wanda Grabow, College of DuPage; and John Zales, Harrisburg Area Community College. Thanks also to the unequaled quality assurance and technology support from Jeff Goding and Jim Valente, as well as QA testers Chris Hall, Mike Mitchell, and Lenny Emma; to Catherine Griffin and all the staff at Gex for the pull-out-all-the-stops production work; and the demand-the-best-quality editorial support of Barbara Clemens, Susan Solomon, and Mac Mendelsohn.

June Jamrich Parsons
Dan Oja

Table of Contents

TUTORIAL 6
Managing Data with Excel

TUTORIAL 7
Integrating Excel with Other Windows Programs

New Perspectives on

Microsoft® Excel 7 for Windows® 95

INTRODUCTORY

TUTORIALS

Read This **Before You Begin**

STUDENT DISKS

To complete the tutorials, Tutorial Assignments, and Cases in this book, you need four Student Disks. Your instructor will either provide you with Student Disks or ask you to make your own.

If you are supposed to make your own Student Disks, you will need four blank, formatted disks. You will need to copy a set of folders from a file server or standalone computer onto your disks. Your instructor will tell you which computer, drive letter, and folders contain the folders you need. The following table shows you which folders go on each of your disks, so that you will have enough disk space to complete all the tutorials, Tutorial Assignments, and Cases:

Disk	Write this on the disk label	Put these folders on the disk
1	Student Disk 1: Tutorials 1-4	Tutorial.01, Tutorial.02
		Tutorial.03, Tutorial.04
2	Student Disk 2: Tutorials 5 & 6	Tutorial.05, Tutorial.06
3	Student Disk 3: Tutorial 7 and Tutorial Assignments	Tutorial.07
4	Student Disk 4: Tutorial 7 Cases	Tutorial.07

When you begin each tutorial, be sure you are using the correct Student Disk. See the inside front or inside back cover of this book for more information on Student Disks, or ask your instructor or technical support person for assistance.

COURSE LAB: SPREADSHEETS

This book features an interactive Course Lab to help you understand spreadsheet concepts. There is a Lab Assignment at the end of Tutorial 1 that relates to this Lab. To start the Lab, click the Start button on the Windows 95 taskbar, point to Programs, point to Course Labs, point to New Perspectives Applications, and click Spreadsheets.

USING YOUR OWN COMPUTER

If you are going to work through this book using your own computer, you need:

- **Computer System** Microsoft Windows 95 and Microsoft Excel 7 for Windows 95 must be installed on your computer. This book assumes a complete installation of Excel.

- **Student Disks** Ask your instructor or lab manager for details on how to get the Student Disks. You will not be able to complete the tutorials or exercises in this book using your own computer until you have Student Disks.

- **Course Lab** See your instructor or lab manager to obtain the Course Lab for use on your own computer.

VISIT OUR WORLD WIDE WEB SITE

Additional materials designed especially for you are available on the World Wide Web. Go to http://www.vmedia.com/cti/.

To complete the tutorials in this book, your students must use a set of Student Files. These files are stored on the Student Files Disks that are included with the Instructor's Manual. Follow the instructions on the disk labels and the Readme.doc file to copy them to your server or standalone computer. You can view the Readme.doc file using WordPad.

Once the files are copied, you can make Student Disks for the students yourself, or tell students where to find the files so they can make their own Student Disks. Make sure the files get correctly copied by following the instructions in the Student Disks section above, which will ensure that students have enough disk space to complete all the tutorials, Tutorial Assignments, and Cases.

SPREADSHEET COURSE LAB SOFTWARE

Tutorial 1 features an online Course Lab that introduces basic spreadsheet concepts. This software is distributed on the Course Labs Setup Disk, included in the Instructor's Manual. To install the Lab software, follow the setup instructions on the disk label and in the Readme.doc file. Once you have installed the Course Lab software, your students can start the lab from the Windows 95 desktop by clicking Start, pointing to Programs/Course Labs/New Perspectives, and clicking Spreadsheet Lab.

CTI SOFTWARE AND DATA FILES

You are granted a license to copy the Student Files and Spreadsheet Course Lab to any computer or computer network used by students who have purchased this book. The files and software are included with the Instructor's Manual and may also be obtained electronically over the Internet. See the inside front or inside back cover of this book for more details.

Spreadsheets

Using Worksheets to Make Business Decisions

Evaluating Sites for an Inwood Design Group Golf Course

CASE

Inwood Design Group

In Japan, golf is big business. Spurred by the Japanese passion for the sport, golf enjoys unprecedented popularity. But that small mountainous country of 12 million golfers has fewer than 2,000 courses; fees for 18 holes on a public course average between $200 and $300; and golf club memberships are bought and sold like stock shares. The market potential is phenomenal, but building a golf course in Japan is expensive because of inflated property values, difficult terrain, and strict environmental regulations.

Inwood Design Group plans to build a world-class golf course, and one of the four sites under consideration is Chiba Prefecture, Japan. Other possible sites are Kauai, Hawaii; Edmonton, Canada; and Scottsdale, Arizona. You and Mike Mazzuchi are members of the Inwood Design Group site selection team. The team is responsible for collecting information on the sites, evaluating that information, and recommending the best site for the new golf course.

Your team identified five factors likely to determine the success of a golf course: climate, competition, market size, topography, and transportation. The team collected information on these factors for each of the four potential golf course sites. The next step is to analyze the information and recommend a site to management.

Using Microsoft Excel 7 for Windows 95, Mike created a worksheet that the team can use to evaluate the four sites. He's bringing the worksheet to the next meeting to help the team evaluate the sites and reach a decision.

In this tutorial you learn how to use Excel as you work along with the Inwood team to select the best site for the golf course.

LABS

Spreadsheets

Using the Tutorials Effectively

These tutorials will help you learn about Excel 7 for Windows 95. The tutorials are designed to be used at a computer. Each tutorial is divided into sessions. Watch for the session headings, such as Session 1.1 and Session 1.2. Each session is designed to be completed in about 45 minutes, but take as much time as you need. It's also a good idea to take a break between sessions.

Before you begin, read the following questions and answers. They are designed to help you use the tutorials effectively.

Where do I start?

Each tutorial begins with a case, which sets the scene for the tutorial and gives you background information to help you understand what you will be doing in the tutorial. Ideally, you should read the case before you go to the lab. In the lab, begin with Session 1.1.

How do I know what to do on the computer?

Each session contains steps that you will perform on the computer to learn how to use Excel. Read the text that introduces each series of steps. The steps you need to do at a computer are numbered and are set against a colored background. Read each step carefully and completely before you try it.

How do I know if I did the step correctly?

As you work, compare your computer screen with the corresponding figure in the tutorial. Don't worry if your screen display is somewhat different from the figure. The important parts of the screen display are labeled in each figure. Check to make sure these parts are on your screen.

What if I make a mistake?

Don't worry about making mistakes—they are part of the learning process. Paragraphs labeled "TROUBLE?" identify common problems and explain how to get back on track. Follow the steps in a TROUBLE? paragraph *only* if you are having the problem described. If you run into other problems:

- Carefully consider the current state of your system, the position of the pointer, and any messages on the screen.

- Complete the sentence, "Now I want to... ." Be specific, because you are identifying your goal.

- Develop a plan for accomplishing your goal, and put your plan into action.

How do I use the Reference Windows?

Reference Windows summarize the procedures you learn in the tutorial steps. Do not complete the actions in the Reference Windows when you are working through the tutorial. Instead, refer to the Reference Windows while you are working on the assignments at the end of the tutorial.

How can I test my understanding of the material I learned in the tutorial?

At the end of each session, you can answer the Quick Check questions. The answers for the Quick Checks are at the end of the book.

After you have completed the entire tutorial, you should complete the Tutorial Assignments. The Tutorial Assignments are carefully structured so you will review what you have learned and then apply your knowledge to new situations.

What if I can't remember how to do something?

You should refer to the Task Reference at the end of the tutorial; it summarizes how to accomplish tasks using the most effective method. The Notes column includes shortcuts or additional information.

Now that you've seen how to use the tutorials effectively, you are ready to begin.

SESSION

1.1

In this session you learn about the Excel window and how to open a workbook, how important documentation sheets are, how to use a decision-support worksheet, how to change values and undo mistakes, how to split the worksheet window into panes, and how to save a workbook.

Starting Excel

Mike arrives at the meeting a few minutes early so he can open his laptop computer and connect it to the large screen monitor in the company conference room. In a few moments Windows 95 is up and running. Mike starts Excel and the meeting is about to begin.

Let's start Excel and follow along with Mike as he works with the design team to decide about the golf course site.

To start Excel:

1. Make sure your computer and monitor are on and that the Windows 95 desktop is on your screen.
2. Locate the taskbar, which contains the Start button ![Start]. The taskbar is probably at the bottom of your screen, as in Figure 1-1.

Figure 1-1 ◀
Windows 95 desktop

your desktop might look different, depending on the programs installed on your computer

Start button

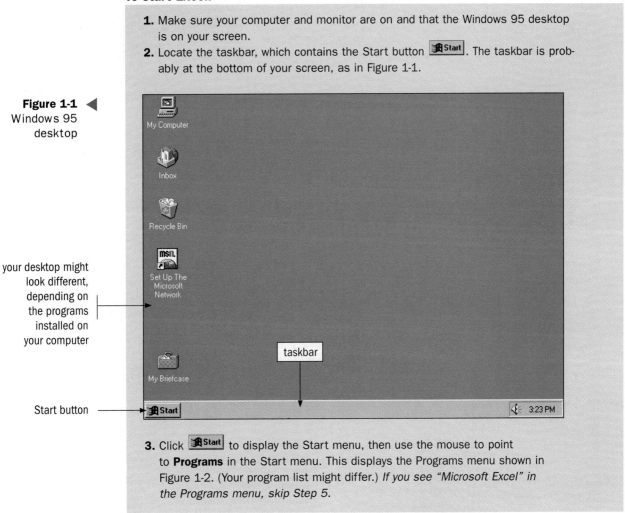

3. Click ![Start] to display the Start menu, then use the mouse to point to **Programs** in the Start menu. This displays the Programs menu shown in Figure 1-2. (Your program list might differ.) *If you see "Microsoft Excel" in the Programs menu, skip Step 5.*

Figure 1-2
Programs menu ◀

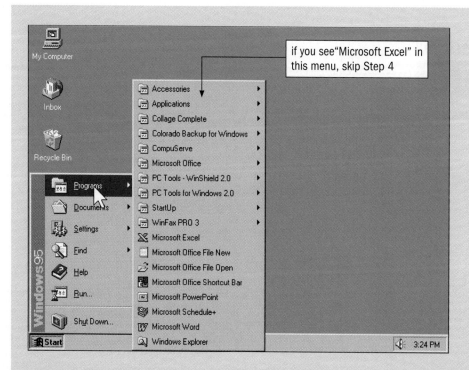

4. Point to **Microsoft Office** to display that menu. "Microsoft Excel" appears in the menu of Microsoft Office programs.

> **TROUBLE?** If you don't see "Microsoft Office" or "Microsoft Excel" on any of the menus, look for similar names. If you still can't find anything like "Microsoft Excel," ask your technical support person for help on how to start Excel. If you are using your own computer, make sure the Excel software has been installed.

5. Click **Microsoft Excel**. Excel opens and a blank worksheet appears. See Figure 1-3.

Figure 1-3 ◀
Microsoft Excel
window

Microsoft Excel
title bar

Microsoft Excel
menu bar

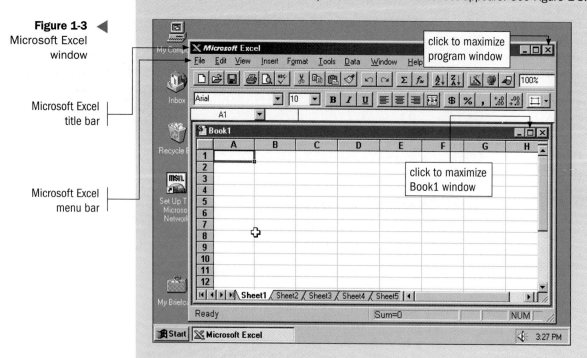

6. Click the **program window Maximize** button if your Microsoft Excel program window is not maximized.

7. If necessary, click the **workbook window Maximize** button to maximize the Book1 window. Figure 1-4 shows the maximized Microsoft Excel and Book1 windows.

Figure 1-4 ◀
Maximized
MIcrosoft Excel
and Book1
windows

grid

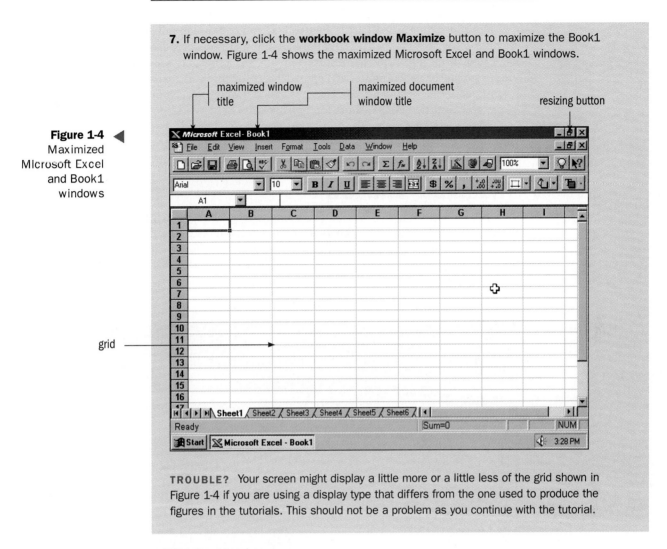

TROUBLE?   Your screen might display a little more or a little less of the grid shown in Figure 1-4 if you are using a display type that differs from the one used to produce the figures in the tutorials. This should not be a problem as you continue with the tutorial.

Spreadsheets

What Is Excel?

Excel is a computerized spreadsheet. A **spreadsheet** is an important business tool that helps you analyze and evaluate information. Spreadsheets are often used for cash flow analysis, budgeting, decision making, cost estimating, inventory management, and financial reporting. For example, an accountant might use a spreadsheet like the one in Figure 1-5 for a budget.

Figure 1-5 ◀
Budget
spreadsheet

Cash Budget Forecast		
	January	*January*
	Estimated	*Actual*
Cash in Bank (Start of Month)	$1,400.00	$1,400.00
Cash in Register (Start of Month)	100.00	100.00
Total Cash	$1,500.00	$1,500.00
Expected Cash Sales	$1,200.00	$1,420.00
Expected Collections	400.00	380.00
Other Money Expected	100.00	52.00
Total Income	$1,700.00	$1,852.00
Total Cash and Income	$3,200.00	$3,352.00
All Expenses (for Month)	$1,200.00	$1,192.00
Cash Balance at End of Month	$2,000.00	$2,160.00

To produce the spreadsheet in Figure 1-5, you could manually calculate the totals and then type your results, or you could use a computer and spreadsheet program to perform the calculations and print the results. Spreadsheet programs are also referred to as electronic spreadsheets, computerized spreadsheets, or just spreadsheets.

In Excel 7 the document you create is called a **workbook**. Notice that the document on your screen is titled Book1, short for Workbook #1. Each workbook is made up of individual worksheets, or **sheets**, just as a spiral-bound notebook is made up of sheets of paper. You'll learn more about using multiple sheets later in this tutorial. For now, just keep in mind that the terms "worksheet" and "sheet" are often used interchangeably.

The Excel Window

If you have used other Windows programs, you probably recognize many of the Excel window controls. Figure 1-6 shows the main components of the Excel window. Let's look at these components so you know their locations.

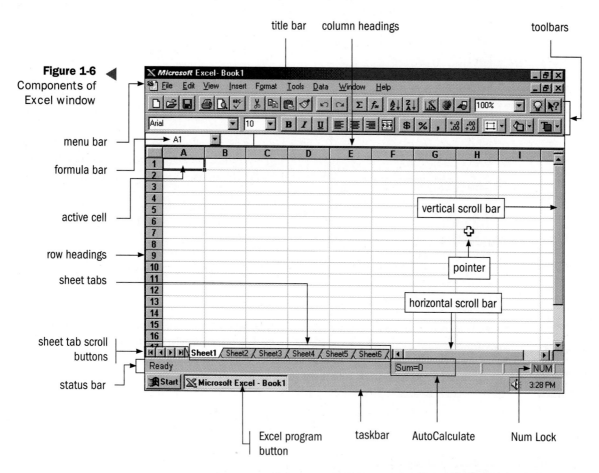

Figure 1-6
Components of
Excel window

Title Bar

The **title bar** at the top of a window identifies the window. On your screen and in Figure 1-6, you see "Microsoft Excel - Book1" in the title bar. The title of the program window is "Microsoft Excel." Because the document window is maximized, the title of the document window, "Book1," also appears on the title bar.

Menu Bar

The **menu bar** is located directly below the title bar. Each word in the menu bar is the title of a menu you can open to see a list of commands and options. The menu bar gives you easy access to all features of the Excel spreadsheet program.

Toolbars

Two rows of square buttons (or tools) and list boxes, located below the menu bar, make up the **toolbars**. These buttons and boxes offer shortcuts for accessing Excel's most commonly used features.

Formula Bar

The **formula bar**, located immediately below the toolbars, displays the data you type or edit.

Worksheet Window

The document window, usually called the **worksheet window** or **workbook window,** contains the sheet you are creating, editing, or using. The worksheet window includes a series of vertical columns identified by lettered **column headings** and a series of horizontal rows identified by numbered **row headings**.

A **cell** is the rectangular area where a column and a row intersect. Each cell is identified by a **cell reference**, which is its column and row location. For example, the cell reference B6 indicates the cell where column B and row 6 intersect. The column letter is always first in the cell reference. B6 is a correct cell reference; 6B is not.

In Figure 1-6 the active cell is A1. The **active cell**, indicated by a black border, is the cell you select to work with. You can change the active cell when you want to work elsewhere in the worksheet.

Pointer

The **pointer** is the indicator that moves on your screen as you move your mouse. The pointer changes shape to reflect the type of task you can perform at a particular location. When you click a mouse button, something happens at the pointer's location. In Figure 1-6 the pointer looks like a white plus sign. Let's see what other shapes the pointer can assume.

To explore pointer shapes:

1. Move the pointer slowly down the row numbers on the far left of the workbook window. Then move it slowly, from left to right, across the formula bar. Notice how the pointer changes shape as you move it over different parts of the window. Do not click the mouse button yet. You'll do that later in the tutorial. You can also use the pointer to display the name of each button in the tool bar. This is helpful when you can't remember what a button does.

2. Move the pointer to the Cut button ✂. After a short pause, a tooltip showing the name of the button—Cut—appears just below the pointer. You see the message "Cuts selection and places it onto Clipboard" in the status bar.

Scroll Bars

The **vertical scroll bar** (on the far right side of the workbook window) and the **horizontal scroll bar** (in the lower-right corner of the workbook window) let you move quickly around the worksheet.

Sheet Tabs

The **sheet tabs** let you move quickly between sheets by simply clicking the sheet tab. You can also use the **sheet tab scroll buttons** to see sheet tabs hidden from view. Let's try moving to a new sheet now.

To move to the blank Sheet2:

1. Click the **Sheet2** tab. (Look at Figure 1-6 again if necessary.) Sheet2, which is blank, appears in the worksheet window.

2. On your own, try clicking the various sheet tab scrolling buttons to display all sheet tabs in the workbook.

3. Click the **Sheet1** tab to return to the first sheet in the workbook.

Status Bar

The status bar is near the bottom of the Excel window. The left side of the status bar briefly describes the current command or task in progress. The right side of the status bar shows the status of important keys such as Caps Lock and Num Lock. In Figure 1-6 the status bar shows that Num Lock mode is in effect, which means you can use your numeric keypad to type numbers. The AutoCalculate box is useful for checking a calculation quickly. You'll learn how to use it later in this tutorial.

Taskbar

The **Windows taskbar** at the bottom of the screen contains a program button for every program currently running. To access a program, simply click its program button. (Figure 1-6 shows only the Excel program button, but you may see others such as the My Computer button.) You could also use the Start button to start a new program or to access any Windows 95 options.

Opening a Workbook

When you want to use a workbook you previously created, you must first open it. Opening a workbook transfers a copy of the workbook file to the random access memory (RAM) of your computer and displays it on your screen. Figure 1-7 shows that when you open the Inwood workbook, Excel copies the file from the hard drive or disk into RAM. When the workbook is open, Inwood is both in RAM and on the disk.

Figure 1-7 ◄
Opening a
workbook

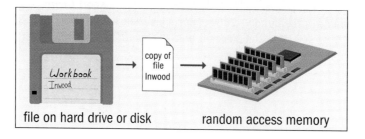

file on hard drive or disk   random access memory

After you open a workbook, you can view, edit, print, or save it again on your disk.

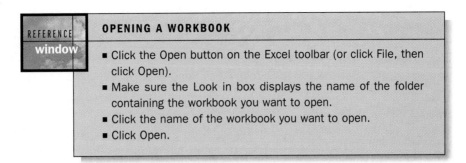

REFERENCE window

OPENING A WORKBOOK

- Click the Open button on the Excel toolbar (or click File, then click Open).
- Make sure the Look in box displays the name of the folder containing the workbook you want to open.
- Click the name of the workbook you want to open.
- Click Open.

Mike created a worksheet to help the site selection team evaluate the four potential locations for the golf course. The workbook, Inwood, is on your Student Disk.

To open the Inwood workbook:

1. Make sure your Excel Student Disk is in drive A.

TROUBLE? If you don't have a Student Disk, you need to get one. Your instructor will either give you one or ask you to make your own following the steps described earlier in this tutorial in "Making Your Excel Student Disk." See your instructor or technical support person for information.

TROUBLE? If your Student Disk won't fit in drive A, try drive B. If it fits in drive B, substitute "drive B" for "drive A" throughout these tutorials.

2. Click the **Open** button 🖰. You see the Open File dialog box shown in Figure 1-8.

Figure 1-8 ◀
Open dialog box

your list of documents and folders may differ

selected filename appears here

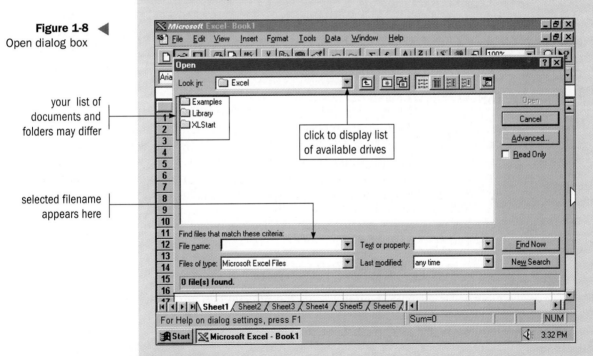

click to display list of available drives

3. Click the **Look in** list arrow. A list of available drives appears. Locate the drive containing your Student Disk. In this text, we assume your Student Disk is a 3 ½ inch floppy in drive A.

4. Click **3 ½ Floppy [A]** to select drive A. A list of documents and folders on your Student Disk appears in the list box.

5. In the list of document and folder names, double-click **Tutorial.01** to display that folder in the Look in box, then click **Inwood**. Finally click the **Open** button in the dialog box. (You could also double-click the filename to open the file.) The **Inwood** workbook opens. See Figure 1-9.

TROUBLE? If you do not see Inwood listed, use the scroll bar to see additional names.

Figure 1-9 ◀
Inwood Design
Group workbook

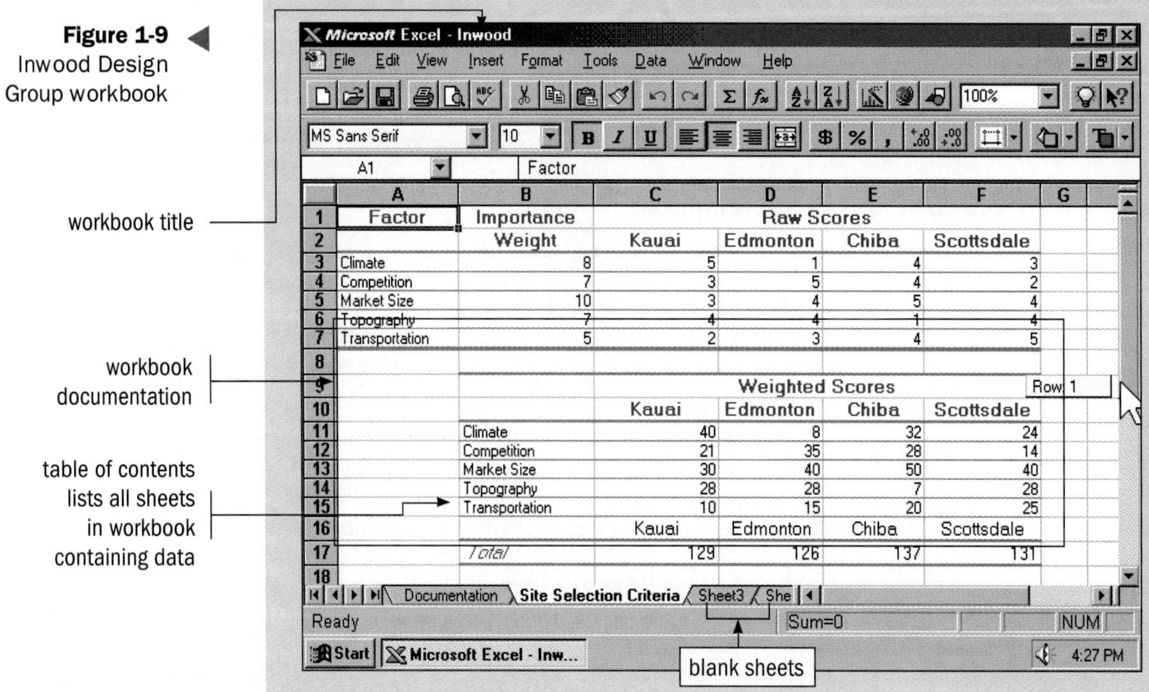

workbook title

workbook
documentation

table of contents
lists all sheets
in workbook
containing data

blank sheets

Workbook Documentation

The first worksheet, Documentation, contains information about the workbook. The **documentation sheet** tells who created the workbook, the date when it was created, and its purpose. Most importantly, the table of contents tells you what's in each sheet in the workbook. Notice that the table of contents does not list blank sheets, such as Sheet3.

Mike explains that whenever he creates a new workbook he makes sure he documents it carefully. This information is especially useful if he returns to a workbook after a long period of time (or if a new user opens it) because it provides a quick review of the workbook's contents and purpose.

Scrolling the Worksheet

Now Mike wants to show the group the site selection criteria worksheet.

To move to the next worksheet:

1. Click the **Site Selection Criteria** tab. The Site Selection Criteria worksheet shown in Figure 1-10 appears.

Figure 1-10 ◀
Site Selection
Criteria
Worksheet

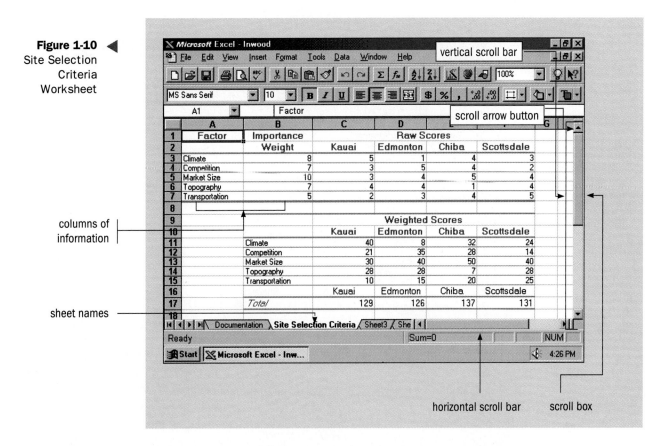

Mike's worksheet contains columns of information and a chart. To see the chart you must scroll the worksheet.

The worksheet window has a horizontal scroll bar and a vertical scroll bar, as shown in Figure 1-10 The **vertical scroll bar** at the right edge of the worksheet window moves the worksheet window up and down. The **horizontal scroll bar** in the lower-right corner of the worksheet window moves the worksheet left and right.

You click the scroll arrow buttons on the scroll bar to move the window one row or column at a time. You drag the **scroll box** to move the window more than one row or column at a time. When you click the scroll bar, a **scrolltip** appears telling you where you will scroll to. Let's scroll the worksheet to view the chart.

To scroll the worksheet to view the chart:

1. Click the vertical scroll box to display the scrolltip, as shown in Figure 1-11. The scrolltip indicates which row (in this case Row 1) will be at the top of the screen when you release the mouse button. You haven't moved the scroll box at all, so it makes sense that Row 1 remains at the top of the screen when you release the mouse button.

Figure 1-11 ◄
Scrolltip

indicates which
row will be at the
top of the screen
when you release
the mouse button

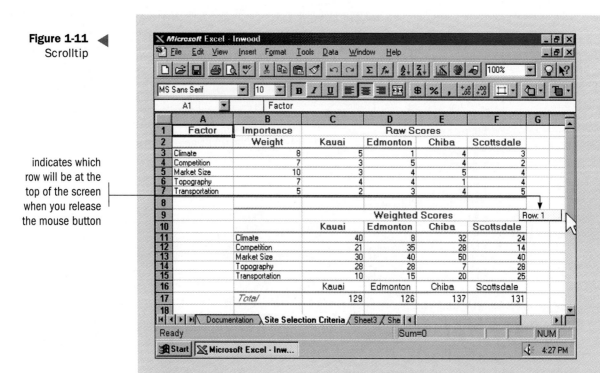

2. Drag the scroll box on the vertical scroll to the bottom of the scrollbar, then release the mouse button. The worksheet window displays the section of the worksheet containing the chart. See Figure 1-12.

Figure 1-12 ◄
Scrolling the
worksheet to
view the chart

chart

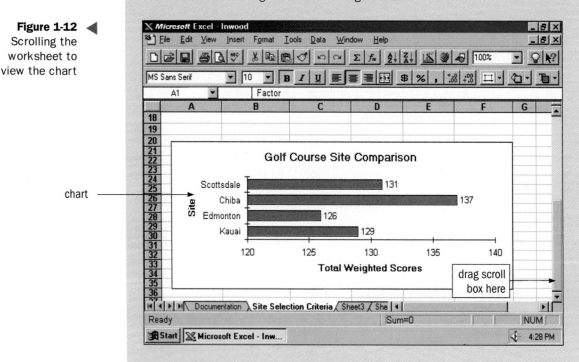

TROUBLE? If your chart is not positioned like the one in Figure 1-12, use the scroll arrow buttons or scroll box until your screen matches Figure 1-12.

3. After you look at the chart, scroll the worksheet until you can see rows 1 through 17.

How many rows and columns you see in your worksheet window depends on your computer's display type. If your screen displays fewer rows than the screens shown in the figures, you can simply scroll the worksheet whenever you need to see an area of the worksheet that is not in the worksheet window.

Using a Decision-support Worksheet

Mike explains the general layout of the decision-support worksheet to the rest of your team. Cells A3 through A7 in Figure 1-13 contain the five factors on which the team's decision is based: climate, competition, market size, topography, and transportation. The team assigned an importance weight to each factor according to its relative importance to the success of the golf course. The team assigned importance weights using a scale from 1 to 10; Mike entered the weights in cells B3 through B7. Market size, weighted 10, is the most important factor. The least important factor is transportation.

Figure 1-13
Layout of decision-support worksheet

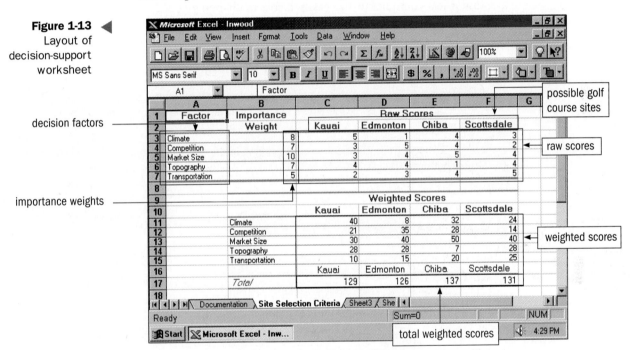

Cells C2 through F2 list the four sites under consideration. The team used a scale of 1 to 5 to assign a raw score to each location for climate, competition, market size, topography, and transportation. Larger raw scores indicate strength. Smaller raw scores indicate weakness. For example, the raw score for Kauai's climate is 5. Other locations have scores of 1, 4, and 3, so Kauai, with warm, sunny days all year, has the best climate for the golf course. Edmonton, on the other hand, has cold weather and only received a climate raw score of 1.

The raw scores do not reflect the importance of each factor. Climate is important but the team considers market size most important. Therefore, they do not use the raw scores to make a final decision. Instead, they multiply the raw scores by the importance weight to produce weighted scores. Which site has the highest weighted score for any factor? If you look at the scores in cells C11 through F15, you see that Chiba's score of 50 for market size is the highest weighted score for any factor.

Cells C17 through F17 contain the total weighted scores for each location. With the current weighting and raw scores, Chiba is the most promising site, with a total score of 137.

As the team examines the worksheet, you ask if the raw scores take into account recent news that a competing design group announced plans to build a $325 million golf resort just 10 miles away from Inwood's Chiba site. Mike admits that he assigned the values before the announcement, so they do not reflect the increased competition in the Chiba market. You suggest revising Chiba's raw score for competition to reflect this market change.

Changing Values and Observing Results

When you change a value in a worksheet, Excel recalculates the worksheet and displays updated results. This feature makes Excel an extremely useful decision-making tool because it lets you quickly and easily factor in changing conditions.

Another development group has announced plans to construct a new golf course in the Chiba area, so the team decides to lower Chiba's competition raw score from 4 to 2.

To change Chiba's competition raw score from 4 to 2:

1. Click cell **E4**. The black border around cell E4 indicates it is the active cell. The formula bar shows E4 is the active cell and shows that the current value of cell E4 is 4.

2. Type **2**. Notice that 2 appears in the cell and in the formula bar, along with three new buttons. The buttons shown in Figure 1-14—the Cancel box, the Enter box, and the Function Wizard button—offer shortcuts for entering data and formulas.

Figure 1-14 ◀
Changing a cell's contents

formula bar shows active cell and your entry

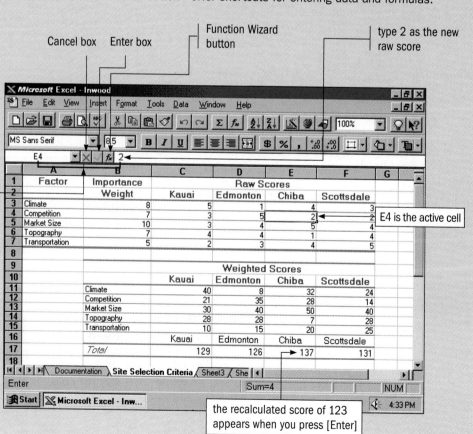

3. Press **Enter**. Excel recalculates the total weighted score for Chiba and displays it in cell E17. Cell E5 is now the active cell.

The team takes another look at the total weighted scores in row 17. Scottsdale just became the top ranking site, with a total weighted score of 131.

As the team continues to discuss the worksheet, several members express concern over the importance weight used for transportation. On the current worksheet, transportation is weighted 5. You remember the group agreed to use an importance weight of 2 at its last meeting. You ask Mike to change the importance weight for transportation.

To change the importance weight for transportation:

1. Click cell **B7** to make it the active cell.

2. Type **2** and press **Enter**. Cell B7 now contains the value 2 instead of 5. Cell B8 becomes the active cell.

The change in the transportation importance weight puts Kauai ahead as the most favorable site, with a total weighted score of 123.

Mike explains that the most commonly made mistake on a worksheet is a typing error. Typing mistakes are easy to correct, so Mike asks the group if he can take a minute to demonstrate.

Correcting Mistakes

It is easy to correct a mistake as you are typing information in a cell, before you press the Enter key. If you need to correct a mistake as you are typing information in a cell, press the Backspace key to back up and delete one or more characters. When you are typing information in a cell, don't use the cursor arrow keys to edit because they move the cell pointer to another cell. Mike demonstrates how to correct a typing mistake by starting to type the word "Faktors" instead of "Factors."

To correct a mistake as you type:

1. Click cell **B9** to make it the active cell.

2. Type **Fak**, intentionally making an error, but don't press **Enter**.

3. Press **Backspace** to delete **k**.

4. Type **ctors** and press **Enter**.

Now the word "Factors" is in cell B9, but Mike really wants the word "Factor" in the cell. He explains that after you press the Enter key, you use a different method to change a cell's contents. Double-clicking a cell or pressing the F2 key puts Excel into Edit mode, which lets you use the Backspace key, Left Arrow key, Right Arrow key, and the mouse to change the text in the formula bar.

REFERENCE window

CORRECTING MISTAKES USING EDIT MODE

- Double-click the cell you want to edit to begin Edit mode and display the contents of the cell in the formula bar (or click the cell you want to edit, then press [F2]).
- Use Backspace, Delete, →, ←, or the mouse to edit the cell's contents either in the cell or in the formula bar.
- Press Enter when you finish editing.

Mike uses Edit mode to demonstrate how to change "Factors" to "Factor" in cell B9.

To change the word "Factors" to "Factor" in cell B9:

1. Double-click cell **B9** to begin Edit mode. Note that "Edit" appears in the status bar, reminding you that Excel is currently in Edit mode.

2. Press **End** if necessary to move the cursor to the right of the word "**Factors**," then press **Backspace** to delete the **s**.

3. Press **Enter** to complete the edit.

Mike points out that sometimes you might inadvertently type the wrong value in a cell. To correct that type of error, you can use the Undo button.

Undo Button

Excel's **Undo button** lets you cancel the last change—and only the last change—you made to the worksheet. You can use Undo not only to correct typing mistakes but to correct almost anything you did to the worksheet that you wish you hadn't. For example, Undo cancels formatting changes, deletions, and cell entries. If you make a mistake, use Undo to put things back the way they were. But remember: Excel can't reverse an entire series of actions. It can only reverse your most recent change to the worksheet.

Mike changes **font size** (the size of the characters) of the label in cell B9. Then he uses the Undo button to cancel his font size change.

To change and then restore the font size using the Undo feature:

1. Click cell **B9** if it is not the active cell.

2. Click the **Font Size** list arrow. Figure 1-15 shows the list of font sizes that appears.

click here to open the font size list

horizontal split bar

Figure 1-15
Font size mistake

your font size options may differ

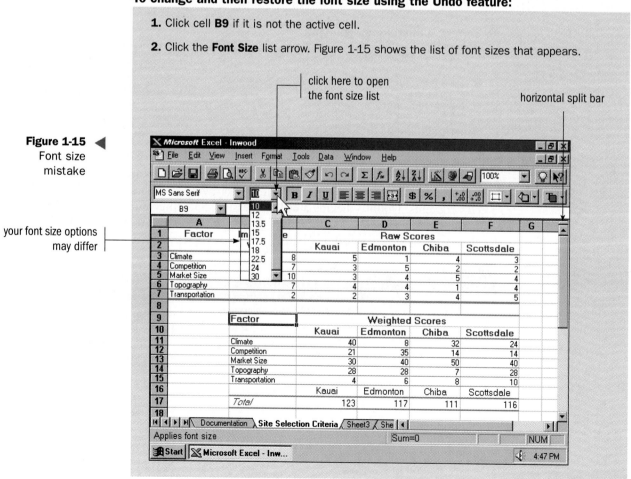

3. Click **24** in the list. The characters' size increases in cell B9.

4. To undo the font size change, click the **Undo** button 🔙.

> **TROUBLE?** If the fonts size does not change, make sure that you did not click the similar-looking Repeat button 🔁.

Now that you know how to correct typing mistakes and use the Undo button to cancel your last entry or command, you can apply these skills whenever you need them.

Mike says the team must continue working on golf course site selection. The team wants to see the chart and the scores at the same time. Mike can do that by splitting the worksheet window.

Splitting the Worksheet Window

The worksheet window displays only a section of the entire worksheet. Although you can scroll to any section of the worksheet, you might want to view two different parts of the worksheet at the same time. To do this, you can split the window into two or more separate window panes using the split bar, shown in Figure 1-16.

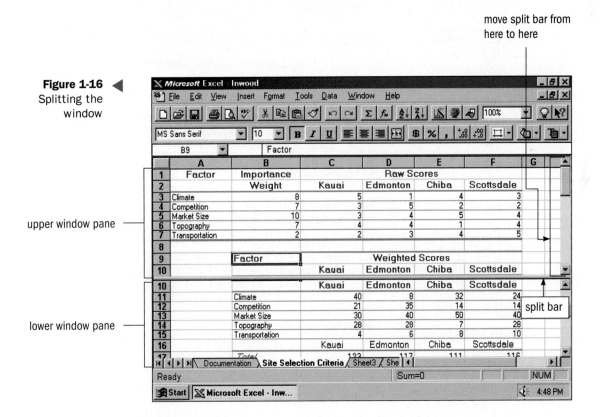

Figure 1-16 ◀
Splitting the window

A **window pane** is a part of the worksheet window that you can scroll separately to display a section of the worksheet. This is handy when you want to change some worksheet values and immediately see how your changes affect such things as totals or, in this case, a chart.

Mike decides to split the worksheet window into two window panes. When he does this the top pane will show rows 3 through 9 of the worksheet. Then Mike needs to scroll the lower pane to display the chart.

To split the screen into two horizontal windows:

1. Move ⬚ over the horizontal split bar (shown in Figure 1-15) until it changes to ⬍. Drag the split bar just under row 10, then release the mouse button. Figure 1-16 shows the screen split into two horizontal windows.

   Next you display the chart using the scroll bar on the lower window pane.

2. Drag the scroll box on the lower window pane about half way down the vertical scroll bar, then release the left mouse button. The lower window pane displays the chart. See Figure 1-17. Don't worry if your worksheet displays fewer rows than the figure shows. Just make sure you can see row 7 in the upper window pane and the four bars of the chart in the lower window pane.

Figure 1-17 ◀
Chart displayed in lower window pane

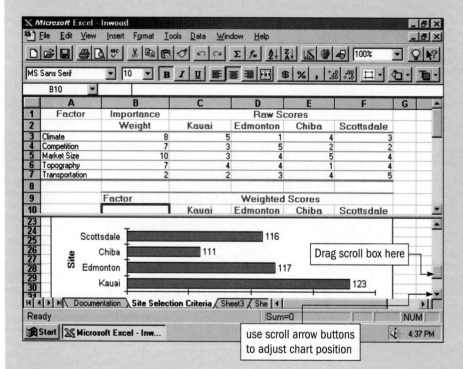

TROUBLE? If your screen does not look like Figure 1-17, click the scroll arrow buttons or drag the scroll box to adjust the chart's position.

3. Take a moment to study the chart, noting that Kauai has the highest weighted score.

Reviewing your notes from the previous meetings, you find that after a long discussion about the importance of transportation, the team eventually agreed to use 5 (instead of 2) as the importance weight. Mike needs to restore the original importance weight for transportation. The team immediately sees its effect on the chart.

To see the chart change when you change the weight in the worksheet:

1. Click cell **B7** to make it the active cell.

2. Type **5** and, as you press **Enter**, watch the chart change to reflect the new scores for all four sites.

Scottsdale once again ranks highest with a weighted score total of 131. Kauai ranks second with a total score of 129. Edmonton is third with a total score of 126. Chiba comes in last with a total score of 123.

Mike asks if everyone is satisfied with the current weightings and scores. The team agrees that the current worksheet reasonably represents the factors that need consideration for each site. Mike decides to remove the split screen so everyone can see all the scores and results on the worksheet.

Removing the Split Window

There are two ways to remove a split from your worksheet window. You can drag the split bar back to the top of the scroll bar, or you can use the Remove Split command on the Window menu. Use whichever method you prefer. If you are using a mouse, it is probably easier to use the split bar.

Mike drags the split bar to remove the split window.

To remove the split window:

1. Move the pointer over the split bar until it changes to $\frac{\textbf{+}}{\textbf{+}}$.

2. Drag the split bar to the top of the scroll bar, then release the mouse button.

3. If necessary, scroll the worksheet so you can see rows 1 through 17.

Making and Documenting the Decision

You ask if the team is ready to recommend a final site. Mike wants to recommend Scottsdale as the primary site and Kauai as an alternative. You ask for a vote, and the team unanimously agrees with Mike's recommendation.

Mike suggests saving the modified worksheet under a different name. This helps document the decision-making process because it preserves the original sheet showing Chiba with the highest score and it saves the current sheet showing Scottsdale with the highest score.

Saving the Workbook

When you save a workbook, you copy it from RAM onto your disk. Excel has more than one Save command on the File menu. Most often you'll use the Save and Save As commands. The Save command copies the workbook onto a disk using its current filename. If an old version of the file exists, the new version replaces the old one. The Save As command asks for a filename before copying the workbook onto a disk. When you enter a new filename, you save the current file under that new name. The previous version of the file remains on the disk under its original name. The flowchart in Figure 1-18 helps you decide whether to use the Save or the Save As command.

Figure 1-18 ◄
Deciding
whether to
use Save or
Save As

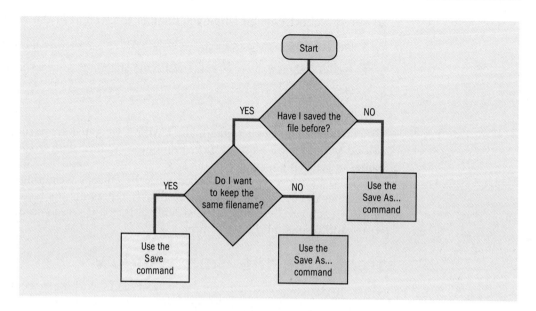

You can type either uppercase or lowercase letters in a filename. You do not need to type the .XLS extension. Excel automatically adds the extension when it saves the file.

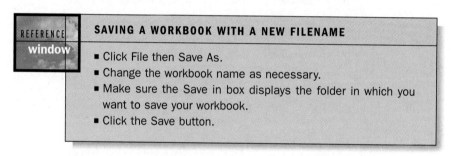

REFERENCE window

SAVING A WORKBOOK WITH A NEW FILENAME

- Click File then Save As.
- Change the workbook name as necessary.
- Make sure the Save in box displays the folder in which you want to save your workbook.
- Click the Save button.

As a general rule, use the Save As command the first time you save a file or whenever you modify a file and want to save both the old and new versions. Use the Save command when you modify a file and want to save only the current version.

It is a good idea to use the Save As command to save and name your file soon after you start a new workbook. Then, as you continue to work, periodically use the Save command to save the workbook. That way, if the power goes out or the computer stops working, you're less likely to lose your work. Because you use the Save command frequently, the toolbar has a Save button, a single mouse-click shortcut for saving your workbook.

Mike's workbook is named Inwood. On your screen is a version of Inwood that you modified during this work session. The original version—the one that shows Chiba with the highest score—is still on Mike's disk. Mike decides to save the modified workbook as Inwood 2 on the disk in drive A. Then he has two versions of the workbook on the disk—the original version Inwood and the revised version Inwood 2.

To save the modified workbook as Inwood 2:

1. Click **File** then click **Save As**. The Save As dialog box appears with the current workbook name in the file name text box.

2. Click at the end of the current workbook name, press **Spacebar**, then type **2**. (*Do not press Enter.*)

   Before you proceed, check the other dialog box specifications to ensure that you save the workbook on your Student Disk.

3. When your Save As dialog box looks like the one in Figure 1-19, click the **Save** button to close the dialog box. The new workbook title, Inwood 2, appears in the title bar.

Figure 1-19
Saving the
worksheet with
a new file name

save in the
Tutorial.01
folder on your
student disk

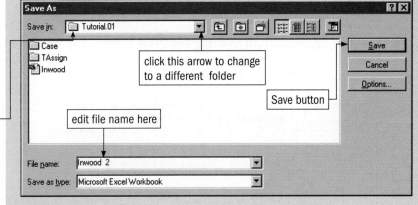

Quick Check

1. List three uses of spreadsheets in business.

2. In your own words describe what a spreadsheet program does.

3. A(n) —————— is the rectangular area where a column and a row intersect.

4. When you —————— a workbook, the computer copies it from your disk into RAM.

5. The cell with a black border around it is called the ——————.

6. To view more than one window pane, use the —————— bar.

7. Use the —————— command the first time you want to save a file.

8. To reverse your most recent action, which button should you click?
   a. 🖫
   b. 🗅
   c. ⤳
   d. ↺

Now that you've completed Session 1.1, you can exit Excel (by clicking File, and then Exit) or continue on to the next session.

SESSION 1.2

In this session you learn how to print an entire worksheet or a specific page and how to create a chart. You'll also become familiar with some basic spreadsheet concepts such as values, text, formulas, and functions. Finally, you learn how to use the Excel Help system, and how to close a worksheet and exit Excel.

Printing the Worksheet and Chart

You want to have complete documentation for the team's written recommendation to management, so you ask Mike to print the worksheet and chart.

You can start the Print command using the File menu or the Print button. If you start printing with the Print command on the File menu, a dialog box lets you specify which worksheet pages you want to print, the number of copies you want to print, and the print quality (resolution). If you use the Print button, you do not have these options; Excel prints one copy of the entire worksheet with the default resolution, usually the highest quality your printer can produce.

REFERENCE window

PRINTING A WORKSHEET

- Click the Print button (or click File then click Print).
- Adjust any settings you want in the Print dialog box.
- Click the OK button.

Mike wants to print the entire worksheet and chart. He decides to select the Print command from the File menu instead of using the Print button because he wants to check the Print dialog box settings.

To check the print settings and then print the worksheet and chart:

1. Make sure your printer is turned on and contains paper.

2. Click **File** then click **Print** to display the Print dialog box.

3. Make sure your Print dialog box settings for Print What, Copies, and Page Range are the same as those in Figure 1-20.

Figure 1-20
Printing the
worksheet

Print button

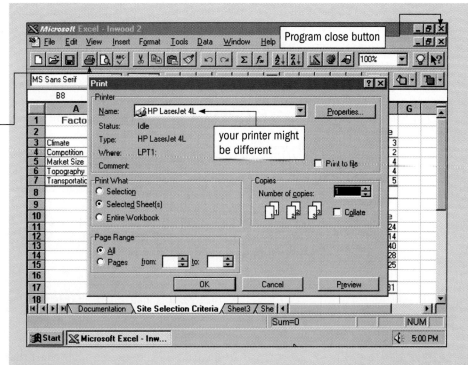

4. Click the **OK** button to print the worksheet and chart. See Figure 1-21.

   TROUBLE? If the worksheet and chart do not print, see your technical support person for help.

Figure 1-21 ◄
Printed
worksheet
and chart

Inwood 2

	A	B	C	D	E	F
1	Factor	Importance		Raw Scores		
2		Weight	Kauai	Edmonton	Chiba	Scottsdale
3	Climate	8	5	1	4	3
4	Competition	7	3	5	2	2
5	Market Size	10	3	4	5	4
6	Topography	7	4	4	1	4
7	Transportation	5	2	3	4	5
8						
9		Factor		Weighted Scores		
10			Kauai	Edmonton	Chiba	Scottsdale
11		Climate	40	8	32	24
12		Competition	21	35	14	14
13		Market Size	30	40	50	40
14		Topography	28	28	7	28
15		Transportation	10	15	20	25
16			Kauai	Edmonton	Chiba	Scottsdale
17		*Total*	129	126	123	131
18						
19						
20						

Golf Course Site Comparison

Scottsdale 131
Chiba 123
Edmonton 126
Kauai 129

Site

118   120   122   124   126   128   130   132

Total Weighted Scores

You ask Mike if it's possible to create a chart that illustrates the weighted scores for every factor for each site. Mike says he can do that easily with Excel's ChartWizard.

Creating a Chart

ChartWizard guides you through five steps to create a chart. You can select from a variety of chart types, including bar charts, column charts, line charts, and pie charts. After you create a chart using ChartWizard, you can change it, move it to a new location, or save it.

REFERENCE window	**CREATING A CHART WITH CHARTWIZARD**
	■ Position the pointer in the upper-left corner of the area you want to chart. ■ Drag the pointer to highlight all the cells you want to chart. Make sure to include row and column titles. ■ Click the ChartWizard button. ■ Drag the pointer to outline the area in the worksheet where you want the chart to appear. ■ Follow the ChartWizard's instructions to complete the chart.

Mike is ready to use the ChartWizard to create a bar chart that shows weighted scores for each of the four sites. First he highlights the cells that contain the data he wants to chart. Then he activates the ChartWizard and follows the five steps to outline the area where he wants the chart to appear and to specify how he wants his chart to look.

A rectangular block of cells is a **range**. For example, you can refer to cells B4, B5, and B6 as "the range B4 through B6." Excel displays this range in the formula bar as B4:B6. The colon in the notation B4:B6 indicates the range B4 through B6, that is, cells B4, B5, and B6.

When Mike highlights the range of cells for the chart, he begins by positioning the pointer on the cell that will be the upper-left corner of the range. Next, he holds the mouse button down while he drags the pointer to the cell in the lower-right corner of the range. This **highlights**, or selects, all the cells in the range; that is, they change color, usually becoming black. The cell in the upper-left corner of the range is the active cell, so it does not appear highlighted, but it is included in the range. Let's see how this works.

To highlight the data in the range B10:F15 for the chart:

1. Position the pointer on cell **B10**, the upper-left corner of the range you want to highlight.

2. Hold the mouse button down while you drag the pointer to cell F15.

3. Release the mouse button. The range of cells from B11 to F15 is highlighted. Cell B10 does not appear highlighted because it is the active cell, but it is still included in the selected range. See Figure 1-22.

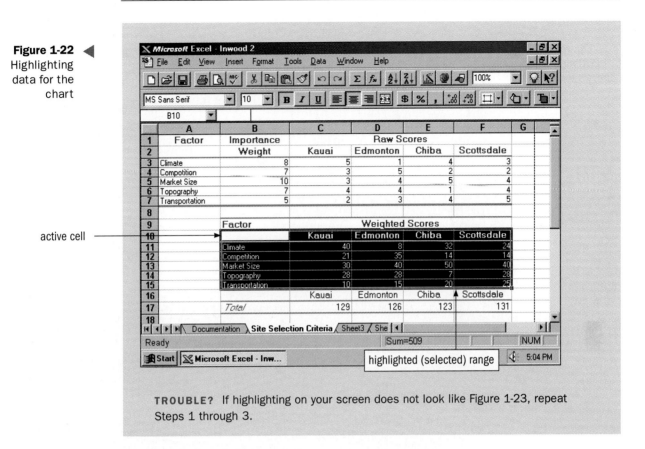

Figure 1-22
Highlighting data for the chart

active cell

highlighted (selected) range

TROUBLE? If highlighting on your screen does not look like Figure 1-23, repeat Steps 1 through 3.

Next, Mike clicks the ChartWizard button and gives the chart's location. He wants the new chart positioned between rows 45 and 61 on the worksheet, so he outlines that location by dragging the pointer from cell A45 to cell F61.

To activate ChartWizard and give the chart's location:

1. Click the **ChartWizard** button. The prompt "Drag in document to create a chart" appears in the status bar, and the pointer changes to.

2. Use the vertical scroll bar to scroll the worksheet so you can view rows 43 through 62. (Note that the pointer becomes when it's over the scroll bar.)

3. Drag from cell A45 to cell F61 to outline the chart's location. See Figure 1-23.

Figure 1-23 ◀
Outlining the
chart's location

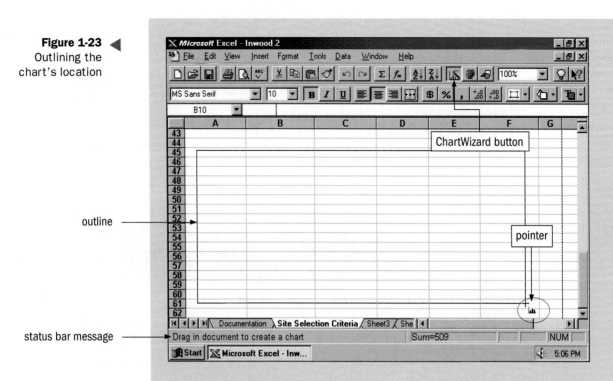

outline

status bar message

4. Release the mouse button.

5. When the ChartWizard - Step 1 of 5 dialog box appears, make sure the Range box shows =$B$10:$F$15. See Figure 1-24. Don't be concerned about the dollar signs ($) in the cell references. You'll learn what these dollar signs mean as you gain more experience with Excel.

TROUBLE? If the Range box does not display $B$10:$F$15, you highlighted the wrong cells for the chart's location. With the dialog box still on the screen, scroll back through the worksheet, drag the pointer from B10 to F15, and then release the mouse button.

Figure 1-24 ◀
ChartWizard 1 of
5 dialog box

range box

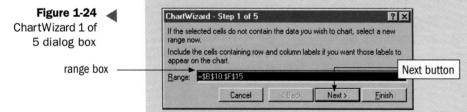

6. Click the **Next >** button to display the ChartWizard - Step 2 of 5 dialog box.

7. Double-click the chart type labeled **Bar**. The ChartWizard - Step 3 of 5 dialog box appears.

8. Double-click the box for format **6** to select a horizontal chart with gridlines. The ChartWizard - Step 4 of 5 dialog box appears, showing you a preview of your chart. Don't worry if the titles are not formatted correctly.

9. You do not want to make any additional changes to your chart at this point, so click the **Next >** button to display the ChartWizard - Step 5 of 5 dialog box.

PRINTING A SPECIFIC PAGE

10. Click the **Chart Title** text box, type **Weighted Scores**, then click the **Finish** button. The chart and the Chart Toolbar appear in the worksheet. You can use the Chart Toolbar to change the chart quickly. (Don't worry if you do not see the Chart Toolbar.) See Figure 1-25.

Figure 1-25 ◄
Weighted
Score chart

dashed line
represents a page
break

use this square
handle to make the
chart taller or shorter

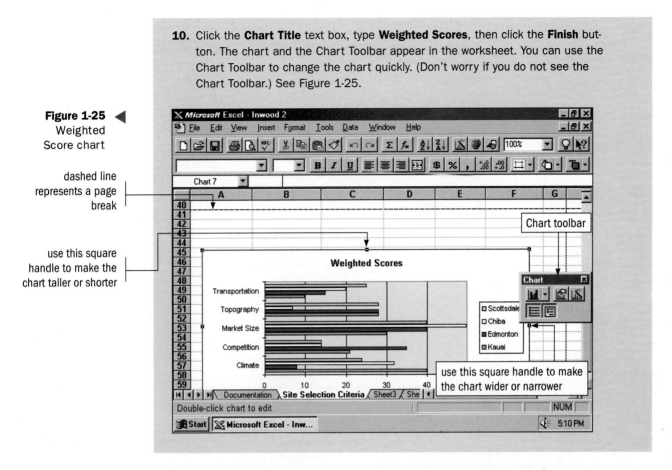

Mike's Weighted Scores chart impresses the entire team. They want to see it printed.

Printing a Specific Page

The Weighted Scores chart is on page 2 of the worksheet. On your screen and in Figure 1-25, the dashed line between row 40 and row 41 represents a page break. To print the Weighted Scores chart, Mike must print page 2 of the worksheet. The Print dialog box setting for Page(s) from:__ to:__ lets you specify the first and last pages of the pages you want to print. To print page 2 only, Mike prints from page 2 to page 2.

To print page 2 of the worksheet containing the Weighted Scores chart:

1. Click **File** then click **Print** to use the Print dialog box.

2. Click the **Pages** radio button in the Page Range box.

3. Type **2** in the from box, then press **Tab**.

4. Type **2** in the to box.

5. Make sure your settings are the same as those in Figure 1-26. Note that because you are only printing one copy, it doesn't matter whether the Collate check box is selected.

Figure 1-26 ◀
Printing page 2
of the worksheet

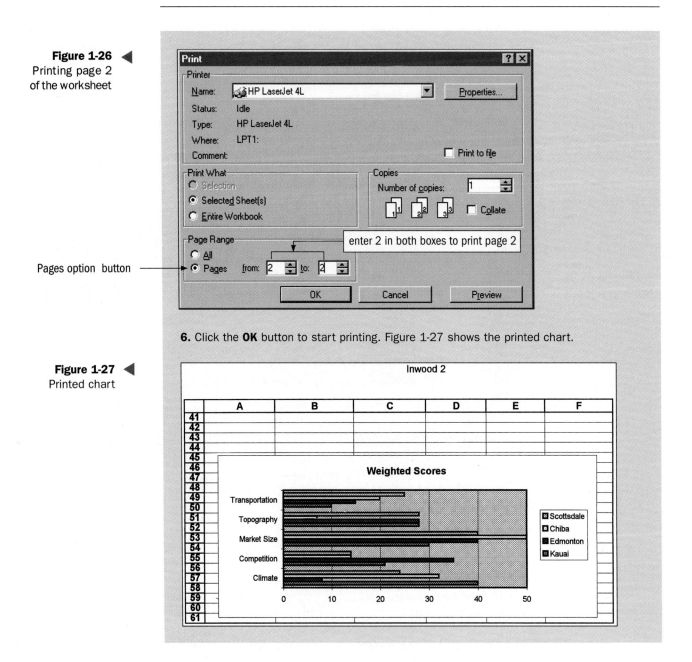

Pages option button —

6. Click the **OK** button to start printing. Figure 1-27 shows the printed chart.

Figure 1-27 ◀
Printed chart

You suggest saving the worksheet and the Weighted Scores chart under its current name, Inwood 2. The new version, which includes the Weighted Scores chart, replaces the old version of Inwood 2.

To save the workbook with the same filename:

1. Click the **Save** button 🖫 to replace the old version of the workbook with the new version.

Mike volunteers to put together the report with the team's final recommendation, and the meeting adjourns. After the meeting you tell Mike how impressed you are with the way the spreadsheet program helped the team analyze data and make a decision. Mike offers to explain some basic spreadsheet concepts.

Values, Text, Formulas, and Functions

Mike explains that an Excel worksheet is a grid of 256 columns and 16,384 rows. As you know, the rectangular areas at the intersections of each column and row are called cells. A cell can contain a value, text, or a formula. Mike tells you that to understand how the spreadsheet program works, you must understand how Excel manipulates values, text, formulas, and functions.

Values

Values are numbers, dates, and times that Excel can use for calculations. Examples of values are 378, 11/29/94, and 4:40:31. As you type information in a cell, Excel determines if the characters you're typing can be used as values. For example, if you type 456, Excel recognizes it as a value and displays it on the right side of the cell. Mike shows you that cells B3 through B7 contain values.

To examine the contents of cells B3 through B7:

1. Use the vertical scroll bar to scroll up the worksheet until you can see rows 1 through 18.

2. Click cell **B3** to make it the active cell. The formula bar at the top of the screen displays B3 and its contents. See Figure 1-28.

Figure 1-28 ◄
Examining cell B3's contents

formula bar shows active cell and contents

cell B3 is active

values

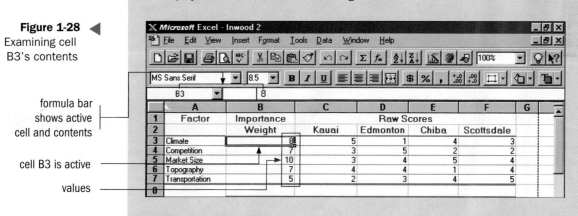

3. Press ↓ to make B4 the active cell. Note the contents of the cell appear in the formula bar.

4. Press ↓ to look at the contents of cells B5, B6, and B7.

Text

Text is any character set that Excel does not interpret as a value. Text is often used to label columns and rows in a worksheet. Examples of text are Total Sales, Acme Co., and Eastern Division.

Text entries cannot be used for calculations. Excel treats some data commonly referred to as "numbers" as text. For example, Excel treats a telephone number (227-1240) or a social security number (372-70-9654) as text that cannot be used for calculations. Mike shows you that cells A3 through A7 contain text.

To examine the contents of cells A3 through A7:

1. Click cell **A3** to make it the active cell. The formula bar displays the cell reference A3 and the cell contents, Climate. See Figure 1-29.

Figure 1-29
Examining cell
A3's contents

formula bar
shows active
cell and contents

cell A3 is active

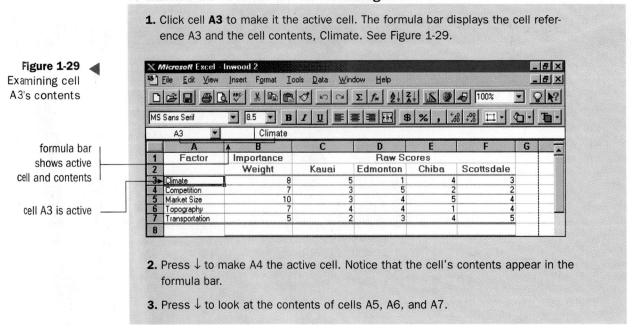

2. Press ↓ to make A4 the active cell. Notice that the cell's contents appear in the formula bar.

3. Press ↓ to look at the contents of cells A5, A6, and A7.

Formulas

Formulas specify the calculations you want Excel to perform. Formulas always begin with an equal sign (=), and most contain **mathematical operators** such as + - * / to tell Excel how to manipulate the numbers in the calculation. When you type a formula, use an asterisk (*) for multiplication and a slash (/) for division.

Formulas can contain numbers or cell references. Some examples are =20+10, =G9/2, and =C5*B5. The formula =C5*B5 instructs Excel to multiply cell C5's contents by cell B5's contents.

The result of the formula appears in the cell where you entered the formula. To see the formula in a cell, you must first make the cell active, then look at the formula bar. Mike shows you how to view formulas and their results.

To view the formula in cell C11:

1. Click cell **C11** to make it the active cell. The formula bar shows =C3*B3, the formula for cell C11. This formula multiplies cell C3's contents by cell B3's contents. See Figure 1-30.

Figure 1-30
Viewing cell C11's contents

formula displayed in formula bar

result displayed in cell

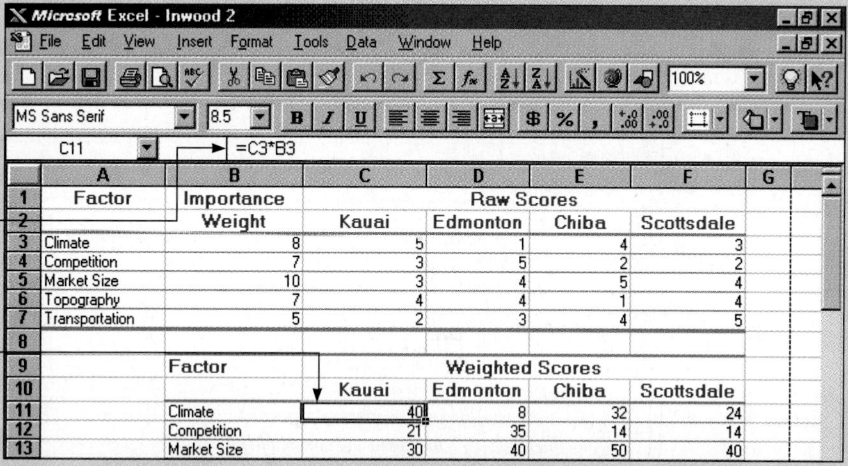

2. Look at cell C3. The number in this cell is 5.

3. Look at cell B3. The number in this cell is 8.

4. Look at the formula bar. Multiplying the contents of C3 by B3 means to multiply 5 by 8. The result of this formula, 40, appears in cell C11.

Functions

A **function** is a special prewritten formula that's a shortcut for commonly used calculations. For example, you can use the SUM function to create the formula =SUM(D14:D18) instead of typing the longer formula =D14+D15+D16+D17+D18. The SUM function in this example adds the range D14:D18. (Recall that D14:D18 refers to the rectangular block of cells beginning at D14 and ending at D18.) Other functions include AVERAGE, which calculates the average value; MIN, which finds the smallest value; and MAX, which finds the largest value.

To view the function in the formula in cell C17:

1. Click cell **C17** to make it the active cell. See Figure 1-31.

Figure 1-31 ◄
Viewing the
function in
the formula
in cell C17

function displayed
in formula bar

result displayed
in cell

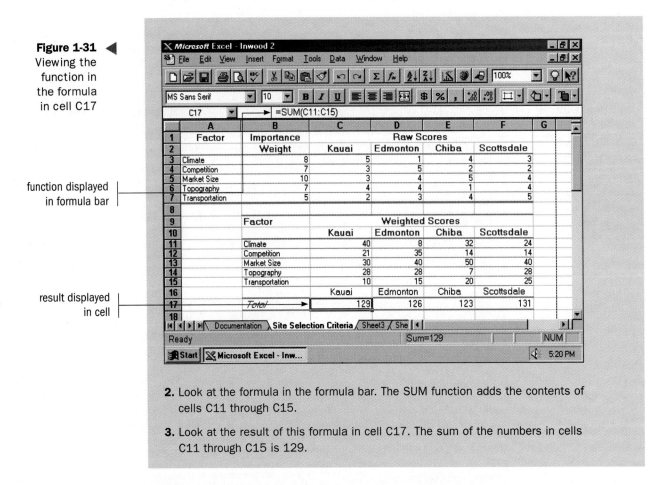

2. Look at the formula in the formula bar. The SUM function adds the contents of cells C11 through C15.

3. Look at the result of this formula in cell C17. The sum of the numbers in cells C11 through C15 is 129.

Remember that the formula bar shows the cell's contents, the formula =SUM(C11:C15). The worksheet cell shows the result of the formula. *To determine the source of a number in a cell, you must make that cell active and look at the formula bar.*

AutoCalculate

Sometimes you may want to do a quick calculation on a range, without actually entering a formula or function. You can use the AutoCalculate indicator in the status bar to do so.

Mike shows you how easy AutoCalculate is to use by summing all the Scottsdale weighted scores except tranportation.

To sum the values in a range automatically:

1. Click cell **F11** and drag the pointer to **F14** to highlight the range F11:F14. The sum of the four values in this range, 106, appears in the status bar, as shown in Figure 1-32.

Figure 1-32 ◀
Using
AutoCalculate

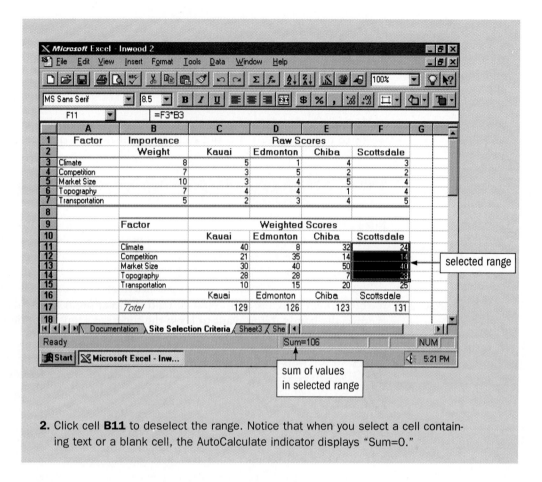

2. Click cell **B11** to deselect the range. Notice that when you select a cell containing text or a blank cell, the AutoCalculate indicator displays "Sum=0."

Mike says you can easily perform other calculations placing the pointer over the AutoCalculate indicator, clicking the right mouse button, and selecting a different function from the AutoCalculate menu. For example, you could average the numbers in the highlighted range by selecting Average.

Worksheet Recalculation

Mike explains that any time a value in a worksheet cell changes, Excel automatically recalculates all the formulas. Changing a number in a single cell might result in many changes throughout the worksheet. Mike demonstrates by changing the importance weight for climate from 8 to 2.

To change the importance weight for climate:

1. Note the current importance weight for climate (8), the weighted scores for climate in each location (Kauai 40, Edmonton 8, Chiba 32, and Scottsdale 24), and the total weighted scores for each location (Kauai 129, Edmonton 126, Chiba 123, and Scottsdale 131).

> **2.** Click cell **B3** to make it the active cell.
>
> **3.** Type **2** and press **Enter**. Watch Excel update the results of the formulas in cells C11 through F11 and cells C17 through F17.

Note the updated results for the climate weighted scores (10, 2, 8, and 6) and the weighted totals (99, 120, 99, and 113). Remember, when a value in a worksheet changes, Excel recalculates every cell that depends on that value.

Excel Help

Mike explains that many spreadsheet programs are available, but he prefers Excel because it is one of the easiest to use. He especially likes the on-line Help system that Excel provides.

Located on the far right side of the toolbar, the Help button provides information about any object you point to in the Excel window. When you click the Help button, the pointer changes to ⌖? indicating that you are in Help mode. In Help mode, you can move the Help pointer to a screen object to read its description in a window. The Help button is especially handy if you want to learn the function of menu options.

REFERENCE window	**USING THE HELP BUTTON**
	■ Click the Help button to enter Help mode and display the Help pointer ⌖? .
	■ Position ⌖? on the screen object or menu item you want to know more about.
	■ Click the mouse button to display a window that briefly describes the object.
	■ When you finish, click anywhere in the worksheet outside the window, or press [Esc].
	■ If you still see the Help pointer and want to exit Help mode, click the Help button again.

Mike shows you how to use the Help button to learn how the Cells command on the Format menu works.

To use the Help button to learn how the Cells command on the Format menu works:

> **1.** Click the **Help** button ⌖? . The pointer changes to ⌖? .
>
> **2.** Click the vertical scroll bar. A window opens describing the scroll bar's function. See Figure 1-33.

Figure 1-33 ◀
Using the Help
button

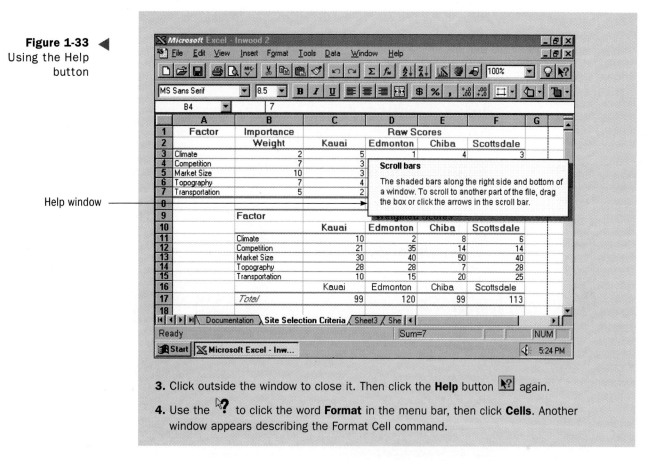

Help window ——

3. Click outside the window to close it. Then click the **Help** button 🔲 again.

4. Use the 🔲 to click the word **Format** in the menu bar, then click **Cells**. Another window appears describing the Format Cell command.

Use the Help button when you need quick information on a particular topic. For more detailed information, you can use the Help command on the menu bar to see the Help topics dialog box. This dialog box contains several tabs that let you search for information in a number of ways. Usually, you'll find the Index tab easiest to use.

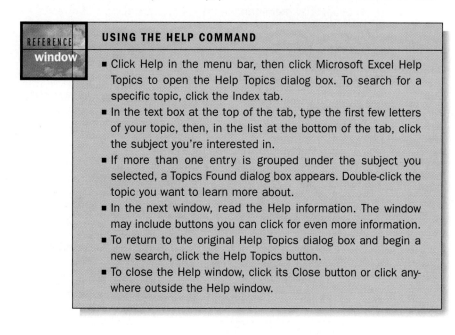

REFERENCE window

USING THE HELP COMMAND

- Click Help in the menu bar, then click Microsoft Excel Help Topics to open the Help Topics dialog box. To search for a specific topic, click the Index tab.
- In the text box at the top of the tab, type the first few letters of your topic, then, in the list at the bottom of the tab, click the subject you're interested in.
- If more than one entry is grouped under the subject you selected, a Topics Found dialog box appears. Double-click the topic you want to learn more about.
- In the next window, read the Help information. The window may include buttons you can click for even more information.
- To return to the original Help Topics dialog box and begin a new search, click the Help Topics button.
- To close the Help window, click its Close button or click anywhere outside the Help window.

Mike shows you how to use the Help command to get more details on formatting cells.

To get detailed information on formatting cells:

1. Click **Help** in the menu bar, then click **Microsoft Excel Help Topics**. The Help Topics: Microsoft Excel dialog box opens.

2. If necessary, click the **Index** tab shown in Figure 1-34.

Figure 1-34 ◄
Help Topics
dialog box

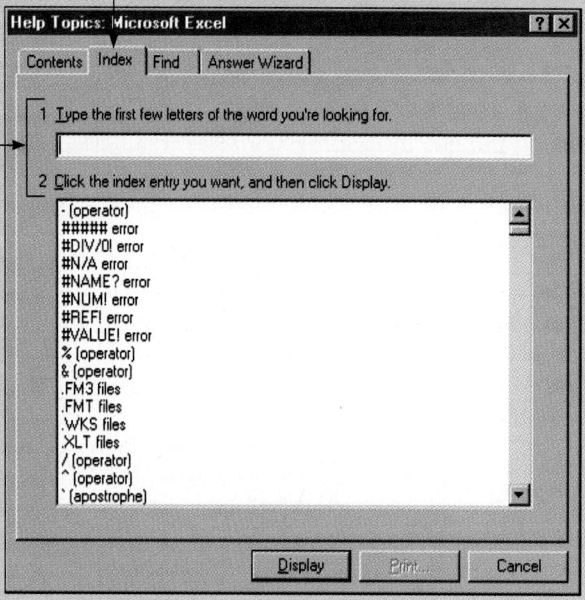

follow these
directions

use the Index tab to search
for a specific topic

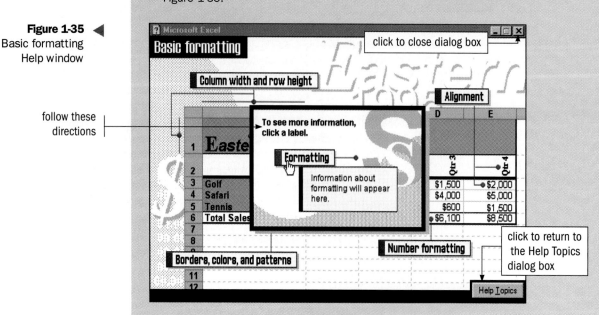

3. Type **Cells** in the text box at the top of the tab, then notice how the list of topics scrolls to display topics beginning with the word "Cells." Under "cells" is a list of subtopics.

4. Double-click **formatting** in the list of index entries. The Topics Found dialog box opens.

5. Double-click **Basic formatting** to open the Basic formatting window. See Figure 1-35.

Figure 1-35 ◄
Basic formatting
Help window

follow these
directions

6. Click the **Borders, colors, and patterns** label to see more information in a small yellow window. Click outside the yellow Help window to close it.

7. On your own, click any of the labels to display more information. If you like, you can click the Help Topics button to return to the Help Topics dialog box to begin a new search. When you finish, click the **Help Window** close button to return to the worksheet.

Mike says you can also click the TipWizard button to display the TipWizard box. (The TipWizard button is the button with the lightbulb, next to the Help button.) This TipWizard box tells you about quicker, more efficient ways to perform actions you just completed. Mike doesn't have time to explain all these features, but he assures you that you can easily explore the options on your own.

Closing the Worksheet

Mike closes the worksheet window. He does not want to save the changes that he made while demonstrating, so he does not use the Save or Save As. When he tries to close the worksheet window, a message asks if he wants to save his changes. Mike clicks the No button in response.

To close the Inwood 2 workbook without saving changes:

1. Click **File** then click **Close**. A dialog box displays the message "Save changes in Inwood 2.xls?"

2. Click the **No** button to exit without saving changes.

The Excel window stays open so Mike can open or create another workbook. He does not want to, so his next step is to exit Excel.

Exiting Excel

To exit Excel, you can double-click the Close button, or you can use the Exit command on the File menu. Mike generally uses the Close button.

To exit Excel using the File menu:

1. Click the **Close** button in the upper-right corner of the Excel window to exit Excel and return to the Windows desktop. If Excel asks if you want to save changes for Book1, click No.

Exiting Windows 95

If you want to exit Windows 95, remember that it's important to do so properly. Ask your instructor or technical support person to explain the correct method.

The Inwood site selection team has completed its work. Mike's decision-support worksheet helped the team analyze the data and recommend Scottsdale as the best site for Inwood's next golf course. Although the Japanese market was a strong factor in favor of locating the course in Japan's Chiba Prefecture, the mountainous terrain and competition from nearby courses reduced the site's desirability.

Quick Check

1 Explain how to create a chart using ChartWizard.

2 If you want to save the new version of a file, replacing the old version, use the _____ command.

3 The colon in the notation B4:B6 indicates a(n) _____.

4 What do dashed lines on the worksheet indicate?

5 In a few sentences, describe how to print a specific worksheet page.

6 Identify each numbered component of the Excel window shown in Figure 1-36.

Figure 1-36

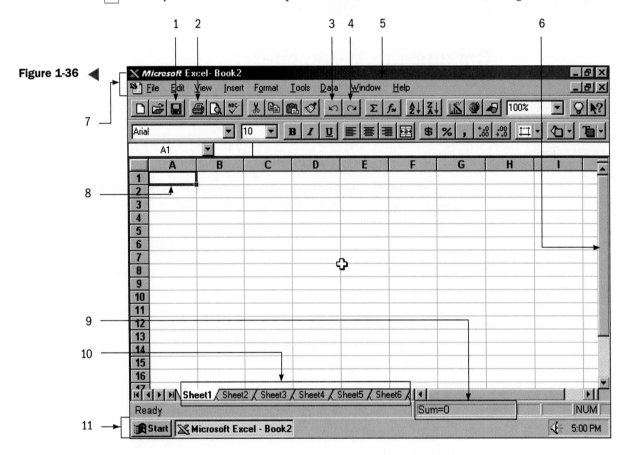

7 Any character set that Excel does not use for calculations is called _____.

8 Numbers, dates, and times that Excel uses for calculations are called _____.

9 A(n) _____ is a special prewritten formula that provides a shortcut for commonly used calculations.

10 A(n) _____ specifies the calculations you want Excel to make.

11 In the formula =B5*125, B5 is a(n) _____.

12 Identify each of these mathematical operators:
a. *
b. -
c. +
d. /

13 Indicate whether Excel treats these cell entries as a value, text, or a formula:
   a. Profit
   b. 11/09/95
   c. February 10, 1996
   d. =AVERAGE(B5:B20)
   e. 11:01:25
   f. =B9*225
   g. =A6*D8
   h. 227-1240
   i. =SUM(C1:C10)
   j. 372-80-2367
   k. 123 N. First St.

14 Describe how to sum the values in a range quickly without using a formula or function.

Tutorial Assignments

The other company that had planned a golf course in Chiba, Japan, has run into financial difficulties. Rumors are that the project may be canceled. A copy of the final Inwood Design team workbook is on your Student Disk. Do the Tutorial Assignments to change this worksheet to show the effect of the other project's cancellation on your site selection. Print your results for Tutorial Assignment 14. Write your answers to Tutorial Assignments 15 through 18.

1. Start Excel. Make sure your Student Disk is in the disk drive.
2. Open the Inwood3 file in the TAssign folder for Tutorial 1 on your Student Disk.
3. Use the Save As command to save the workbook as Inwood 4 in the TAssign folder for Tutorial 1. That way you won't change the original workbook.
4. Click the TipWizard button to see the TipWizard box. As you complete your Tutorial Assignments notice how the information in the TipWizard box changes.
5. In the Inwood 4 worksheet change the competition raw score for Chiba from 2 to 3.
6. Use the vertical scroll bar to view the effect on the chart showing weighted scores.
7. Enter the text "Scores if the Competing Project in Chiba, Japan, is Canceled" in cell B2.
   The importance weight assigned to each factor is a critical component in the site selection worksheet. Create a bar chart showing the weights assigned to each factor.
8. Highlight cells A4 through B9.
9. Activate ChartWizard.
10. Locate the chart in cells A67 through F83.
11. Use ChartWizard - Steps 1 through 4 to select a bar chart using format 6.
12. For ChartWizard - Step 5 of 5, enter "Importance Weights" as the chart title and indicate that you do not want to use a legend in the chart.
13. Save the worksheet and chart as Inwood 4.
14. Print the entire worksheet, including the charts.
15. Practice using the AutoCalculate indicator to sum the values in four different ranges instantly. Right-click the AutoCalculate indicator to see a list of other possible calculations. What other options are available?
16. Use the Help button to learn how the four buttons shown in Figure 1-37 work.

Figure 1-37 ◀

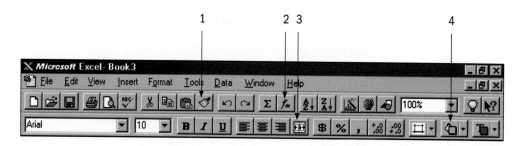

17. Use the Help command to learn more about printing documents. How do you print more than one copy at a time?

18. Use the scroll arrows to scroll through the tips in the TipWizard box. What new information did you learn? Click the TipWizard button in the toolbar to close the TipWizard box.

19. Close the workbook and exit Excel.

20. Use the resources in your library to find information on decision-support systems. Write a one- or two-page paper describing a decision-support system and how one might be used in a business. Also include your ideas on the relationship between spreadsheets and decision-support systems.

Case Problems

1. Selecting a Hospital Laboratory Computer System for Bridgeport Medical Center David Choi is on the Laboratory Computer Selection Committee for the Bridgeport Medical Center. After an extensive search, the committee identified three vendors whose products appear to meet its needs. The Selection Committee prepared an Excel worksheet to help evaluate the three potential vendors' strengths and weaknesses. The raw scores for two of the vendors, LabStar and Health Systems, have already been entered. Now raw scores must be entered for the third vendor, MedTech. Which vendor's system is best for the Bridgeport Medical Center? Complete these steps to find out:

1. If necessary, start Windows and Excel. Make sure your Student Disk is in the disk drive.

2. Open the workbook Medical in the Case folder for Tutorial 1.

3. Use the Save As command to save the workbook as Medical 2 in the Case folder for Tutorial 1. That way you won't change the original workbook for this case.

4. Take a moment to examine the documentation sheet. Then, in the Evaluation Scores worksheet, type the following raw scores for MedTech: Cost = 6, Compatibility = 5, Vendor Reliability = 5, Size of Installed Base = 4, User Satisfaction = 5, Critical Functionality = 9, Additional Functionality = 8.

5. Use ChartWizard to create a column chart showing the total weighted scores for the three vendors. Hint: The chart will include cells C24 to E25. Position the chart below the worksheet in cells A28 to E45. Use a column chart with format 2. Type "Total Weighted Scores" as the chart title.

6. Use the Save command to save the modified worksheet and chart.

7. Print the worksheet and chart.

2. Market Share Analysis at Aldon Industries Helen Shalala is assistant to the regional director for Aldon Industries, a manufacturer of corporate voice mail systems. Helen analyzed the market share of the top vendors with installations in the region. She's on her way to a meeting with the marketing staff where she will use her worksheet to plan a new marketing campaign. Help Helen and her team evaluate the options and plan the best advertising campaign for Aldon Industries. Write your responses to questions 4 through 10, then create the chart and print it.

1. If necessary, start Excel. Make sure your Student Disk is in the disk drive.
2. Open the workbook Aldon in the Case folder for Tutorial 1.
3. Use the Save As command to save the workbook as Aldon 2 in the Case folder for Tutorial 1. That way you won't change the original workbook for this case.
4. Take a moment to look over the Documentation sheet, then look at the Market Share worksheet. Do the following ranges contain text, values, or formulas?
   a. G13:F13
   b. C3:C10
   c. A3:A10
   d. G3:G10
5. What is Aldon Industries' overall market share?
6. Examine the worksheet to determine in which state Aldon Industries has the highest market share.
7. Aldon Industries runs local marketing campaigns in each state.
   a. In which state does Aldon Industries' marketing campaign appear to be most successful?
   b. In which state does Aldon Industries' marketing campaign appear to be least successful?
8. Which company leads the overall market?
9. What is Aldon Industries' overall ranking in total market share (1st, 2nd, 3rd, etc.)?
10. Which companies rank ahead of Aldon Industries in total market share?
11. Michigan is the state in which Aldon Industries' market share is lowest. Use ChartWizard to create a column chart showing the number of installations in Michigan for each company. Hint: The chart will include the range A2 through B10. Place the chart in cells A15 through F50. Select format 2 for the column chart. Type "Installations in Michigan" as the chart title.
12. Save the workbook on your Student Disk.
13. Print the worksheet and chart.

3. Completing Your Own Decision Analysis Think of a decision that you are trying to make. It might be choosing a new car, selecting a major, deciding where to vacation, or accepting a job offer. Use the Personal workbook to evaluate up to three options on the basis of up to five factors. Write your responses to questions 10 through 13, and print the worksheet and chart.

1. If necessary, start Excel. Make sure your Student Disk is in the disk drive.
2. Open the Personal workbook in the Case folder for Tutorial 1.
3. Use the Save As command to save the workbook as Personal 2 in the Case folder for Tutorial 1.
4. In the Documentation sheet, click cell B5 and type your name. Then click cell B6 and type the current date. Type the workbook's purpose in cell B9.
5. Click the Decision Analysis sheet tab to go to that sheet.
6. Click cell A1 and type the worksheet title.
7. Type the titles for up to three choices in cells C4, D4, and E4.
8. Type the titles for up to five factors in cells A6 to A10.
9. Type the importance weights for each of the five factors in cells B6 to B10.
10. Type the raw scores for each of your choices in columns C, D, and E.
11. Use ChartWizard to create a column chart showing the total weighted scores for each choice.
12. Write a paragraph explaining your choice of factors and assignment of importance weights.
13. On the basis of the current importance weights and raw scores, which option appears most desirable?
14. How confident are you that the worksheet shows the most desirable choice?
15. Write a paragraph explaining your reaction to the worksheet's results.
16. Save the worksheet and chart on your Student Disk.
17. Print the worksheet and chart.

Lab Assignment

Spreadsheets

This Lab Assignment is designed to accompany the interactive CourseLab called Spreadsheets. To start the Spreadsheets Lab, click the Start button on the Windows 95 taskbar, point to Programs, point to CourseLabs, point to New Perspectives Applications, and click Spreadsheets. If you do not see CourseLabs on your Programs menu, see your instructor or lab manager.

Spreadsheet software is used extensively in business, education, science, and the humanities to simplify tasks that involve calculations. In this Lab you will learn how spreadsheet software works. You will use spreadsheet software to examine and modify worksheets, as well as to create your own worksheets.

1. Click the Steps button to learn how spreadsheet software works. As you proceed through the Step, answer all of the Quick Check questions that appear. After you complete the Steps, you will see a Quick Check Report. Follow the instructions on the screen to print this report.

2. Click the Explore button to begin this assignment. Click OK to display a new worksheet. Click File, then click Open to display the Open dialog box. Click the file INCOME.XLS, then press the Enter key to open the Income and Expense Summary worksheet. Notice that the worksheet contains labels and values for income from consulting and training. It also contains labels and values for expenses such as rent and salaries. The worksheet does not, however, contain formulas to calculate Total Income, Total Expenses, or Profit. Do the following:
   a. Calculate the Total Income by entering the formula =sum(C4:C5) in cell C6.
   b. Calculate the Total Expenses by entering the formula =sum(C9:C12) in cell C13.
   c. Calculate Profit by entering the formula =C6-C13 in cell C15.
   d. Manually check the results to make sure you entered the formulas correctly.
   e. Print your completed worksheet showing your results.

3. You can use a spreadsheet to keep track of your grade in a class. Click the Explore button to display a blank worksheet. Click File, then click Open to display the Open dialog box. Click the file GRADES.XLS to open the Grades worksheet. This worksheet contains all the labels and formulas necessary to calculate your grade based on four test scores.

   Suppose you receive a score of 88 out of 100 on the first test. On the second test, you score 42 out of 48. On the third test, you score 92 out of 100. You have not taken the fourth test yet. Enter the appropriate data in the GRADES.XLS worksheet to determine your grade after taking three tests. Print out your worksheet.

4. Worksheets are handy for answering "what if" questions. Suppose you decide to open a lemonade stand. You're interested in how much profit you can make each day. What if you sell 20 cups of lemonade? What if you sell 100? What if the cost of lemons increases?

   In Explore, open the file LEMONS.XLS and use the worksheet to answer questions a through d, then print the worksheet for item e:
   a. What is your profit if you sell 20 cups a day?
   b. What is your profit if you sell 100 cups a day?
   c. What is your profit if the price of lemons increases to $.07 and you sell 100 cups?
   d. What is your profit if you raise the price of a cup of lemonade to $.30? (Lemons still cost $.07 and assume you sell 100 cups.)
   e. Suppose your competitor boasts that she sold 50 cups of lemonade in one day and made exactly $12.00. On your worksheet adjust the cost of cups, water, lemons, and sugar, and the price per cup to show a profit of exactly $12.00 for 50 cups sold. Print this worksheet.

5. It is important to make sure the formulas in your worksheet are accurate. An easy way to test this is to enter 1's for all the values on your worksheet, then check the calculations manually. In Explore, open the worksheet RECEIPT.XLS, which calculates sales receipts. Enter 1 as the value for Item 1, Item 2, and Item 3. Enter .01 for the Sales Tax rate. Now, manually calculate what you would pay for three items that cost $1.00 each in a state where sales tax is 1% (.01). Do your manual calculations match those of the worksheet? If not, correct the formulas in the worksheet and print out a formula report of your revised worksheet.

6. In Explore, create your own worksheet showing your household budget for one month. Make sure you put a title on the worksheet. Use formulas to calculate your total income and your total expenses for the month. Add another formula to calculate how much money you were able to save. Print a formulas report of your worksheet. Also, print your worksheet showing realistic values for one month.

Planning, Building, Testing, and Documenting Worksheets

Creating a Standardized Income and Expense Template for Branch Offices

SGL Business Training and Consulting

CASE   SGL Business Training and Consulting, headquartered in Springfield, Massachusetts, provides consulting services and management training for small businesses. SGL has 12 regional branch offices throughout the United States. Branch office managers prepare a quarterly report called "Income and Expense Summary" and send it to you, the staff accountant at SGL headquarters.

Each quarter you must compile the income and expense information from the 12 reports. This task is not easy because branch managers do not use the same categories for income and expenses. For example, some managers have money for advertising, and so they list advertising as an expense; other managers do not have money for advertising, and, therefore, advertising is not an expense on their reports.

You know that you can simplify the task of consolidating the branch office information if you can convince branch managers to use a standard form for their reports. Management gives you approval to create an Excel template as the standard form that branch managers will use to report income and expenses.

A **template** is a preformatted worksheet that contains labels and formulas but no values. You will send the template to branch managers. Each manager will fill in the template with income and expense information, then return it to you. With all the information in a standard format, you will be able to consolidate it easily in a company-wide report.

You begin by studying the branch managers' reports. Then you plan how to create a standard worksheet template for reporting income and expenses. In this tutorial, you will plan, build, test, and document the worksheet template for the SGL branch managers.

SESSION 2.1

In this session you will learn how to plan the four steps necessary to build effective worksheets. You will also learn how to enter labels and formulas, change column width, use AutoComplete, create a series with AutoFill, rename a sheet, save a new workbook, and use the Fill handle to copy a formula. Finally, you will learn about relative and absolute cell references and the SUM function, and how to use the mouse to select cell references.

Developing Effective Worksheets

An effective worksheet is well planned, carefully built, thoroughly tested, and comprehensively documented. Therefore, when you develop a worksheet you do each of these activities:

- *Plan* the worksheet by identifying the overall project goal; listing requirements for input, output, and calculations; and sketching the worksheet's layout.

- *Build* the worksheet by entering labels, values, and formulas; then format the worksheet so it has a professional appearance.

- *Test* the worksheet to make sure that it provides correct results.

- *Document* the worksheet by recording information others need to understand, use, and revise it.

Although planning is generally the first activity of the worksheet development process, the four development activities are not necessarily sequential. After you begin to enter labels, values, and formulas for the worksheet, you might need to return to the planning phase and revise your original plan. You are also likely to return to the building phase to change some values or formulas after you test the worksheet. And it is important to note that documentation activities can and should take place throughout the process of worksheet development. For example, you might jot down some documentation notes as you plan the worksheet, or you might enter documentation on the worksheet itself as you build it.

Planning the Worksheet

To create a plan for the SGL worksheet template, you first study the content and format of the branch managers' reports. You notice that although there are 12 branches, there are only three different report formats.

Reports from four branch managers look similar to the sample report in Figure 2-1. On these reports the labels for each quarter appear on the left side of the report. The column titles, arranged across the top of the report, are Income, Expenses, and Profit. Profit for each quarter is calculated by subtracting expenses from income. Annual totals appear at the bottom of the report.

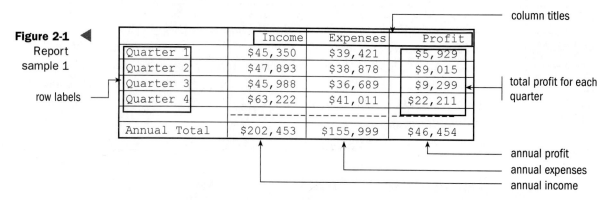

Figure 2-1
Report
sample 1

row labels

Reports from five branch managers look similar to the sample report in Figure 2-2. The format of report sample 2 is very different from that of report sample 1. On report sample 2, quarters are listed across the top as Q1, Q2, Q3, and Q4, rather than down the side. The income and expense categories, referred to as Revenue and Expenses, are listed down the left side of the report. This report has one revenue category and six expense categories. For each revenue or expense category, the sum of the amounts for each quarter produces the year-to-date totals shown on the right side of the report. The profit, shown at the bottom of the worksheet, is calculated by subtracting total expenses from total revenue.

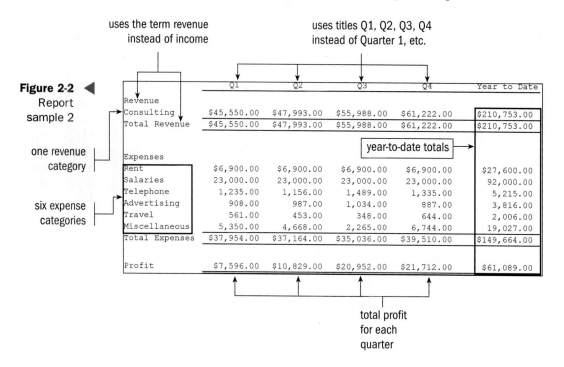

Figure 2-2
Report
sample 2

one revenue
category

six expense
categories

Reports from remaining branch managers look similar to the sample report in Figure 2-3. Notice the two income categories and eight expense categories. Titles for each quarter are listed across the top of the report. For each income or expense category, the sum of the amounts for each quarter produces the year-to-date totals shown on the right side of the report. The total profit for each quarter is shown in the last row of the report.

Figure 2-3
Report sample 3

two income
categories

eight expense
categories

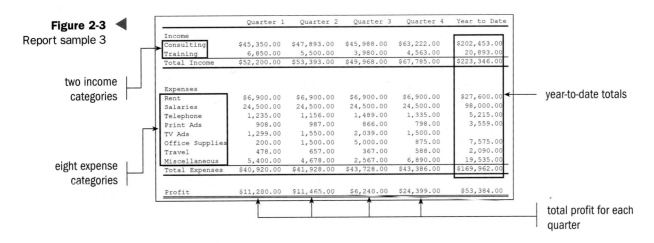

year-to-date totals

total profit for each
quarter

After studying the report, you write a worksheet plan that

- lists the goal(s) for the worksheet development project
- identifies the results, or **output**, that the worksheet must produce
- lists the information, or **input**, required to construct the worksheet
- specifies the calculations that use the input to produce the required output

You develop the worksheet plan as you build and test the worksheet. Figure 2-4 shows the worksheet plan.

Figure 2-4
Worksheet plan

Worksheet Plan for Loan Management Worksheet

<u>My Goal:</u>
To develop an Excel template that all branch managers can use to submit income
and expense reports.

<u>What results do I want to see?</u>
Income categories for consulting and training.
Expense categories for rent, salaries, telephone, advertising, office supplies, travel, and
miscellaneous.
Income and expenses for each quarter.
Total income for each quarter.
Total expenses for each quarter.
Total profit for each quarter.

<u>What information do I need?</u>
The amount for each income and expense category.

<u>What calculations will I perform?</u>
Total income = consulting income + training income
Total expenses = rent+salaries+telephone+advertising+office supplies+travel+miscellaneous
Profit = total income − total expenses

After you complete the worksheet plan, you sketch the worksheet template, showing the worksheet titles, row labels, column titles, and formulas. See Figure 2-5. You decide to list income and expense categories down the left side of the worksheet and list quarters across the top.

Figure 2-5 ◀
Worksheet
sketch

	Quarter 1	Quarter 2	Quarter 3	Quarter 4
Branch Office Name				
Income and Expense Summary				
Income				
Consulting	$9,999,999.99	$9,999,999.99	$9,999,999.99	$9,999,999.99
Training	:	:	:	:
Total Income	${total income formula}	${total income formula}	${total income formula}	${total income formula}
Expenses				
Rent	$9,999,999.99	$9,999,999.99	$9,999,999.99	$9,999,999.99
Salaries	:	:	:	:
Telephone	:	:	:	:
Advertising	:	:	:	:
Office Supplies	:	:	:	:
Travel	:	:	:	:
Miscellaneous	:	:	:	:
Total Expenses	${total expenses formula}	${total expenses formula}	${total expenses formula}	${total expenses formula}
Profit	${profit formula}	${profit formula}	${profit formula}	${profit formula}

Dollar signs indicate that you will format these cells for currency. The number 9,999,999.99 indicates the largest number these cells can hold and specifies how wide these columns must be on the final worksheet.

You indicate which cells will contain formulas by using curly brackets like these: {}. The calculation section of the worksheet plan in Figure 2-4 describes the formulas. For example, the {total income formula} in the sketch is described in the worksheet plan as

total income = consulting income + training income

Look at the calculation section of the worksheet plan in Figure 2-4 to find descriptions of the other formulas.

Now that you have completed the worksheet plan and the worksheet sketch, you are ready to build the worksheet.

To start Excel and maximize the worksheet:

1. Start Excel as usual.

2. Make sure your Student Disk is in the disk drive.

3. Make sure the Microsoft Excel and Book1 windows are maximized.

Building the Worksheet

A worksheet generally contains values, labels that describe the values, and formulas that perform calculations. When you build a worksheet, you usually enter the labels first. What you enter next depends on how you intend to use the worksheet. If you intend to use the worksheet as a template, you enter formulas, then enter values. If you are not creating a template, you generally enter values before you enter formulas.

In addition to entering labels, formulas, and perhaps values, when you build a worksheet you should format it so the information displayed is clear and understandable.

You intend to create a template to send to branch managers, so you enter labels, enter formulas, then format the worksheet. The branch managers enter the values later.

Entering Labels

When you build a worksheet, you first enter the labels you defined in the planning stage. When you type a label in a cell, Excel aligns the label at the left side of the cell. Labels too long to fit in a cell spill over into the cell or cells to the right, if those cells are empty. If the cells to the right are not empty, Excel displays only as much of the label as fits in the cell.

AutoComplete

Whenever you enter a series of labels in consecutive cells in a column, Excel's **AutoComplete** facility automatically makes suggestions based on labels you already entered. For example, suppose you have already typed the word "Baker" in the column, and then further down the column, you begin typing the word "Basket." After you type the first two letters, "Ba" Autocomplete detects a potential match in the column ("Baker") and displays that label in the active cell. To accept Excel's suggestion ("Baker"), you can simply press Enter. To ignore it, simply continue typing the new label (in this case, "Basket").

AutoComplete is especially useful when you're using a worksheet that requires you to enter the same label repeatedly. For example, in a checkbook register worksheet, you might enter the name of your favorite grocery store (where you write checks regularly) several times a month. In that case, when you type the first few letters of the store's name, AutoComplete automatically enters the rest of the store's name. The homework assignments at the end of this tutorial give you a chance to practice using AutoComplete.

To start, enter the worksheet title.

To enter the worksheet title:

1. If necessary, click cell **A1** to make it the active cell.

2. Type **Income and Expense Summary** and press **Enter**. The title in cell A1 spills over into cells B1 and C1. Cell A2 is now the active cell.

You continue working in column A, typing labels for the income and expense categories defined on the worksheet sketch in Figure 2-5.

To enter labels for income categories:

1. Click cell **A3** to make it the active cell.

2. Type **Income** and press **Enter** to complete the entry and move to cell A4.

TROUBLE? If you make a mistake while typing, remember that you can correct errors with the Backspace key.

3. In cell A4 type **Consulting** and press **Enter**.

4. In cell A5 type **Training** and press **Enter**.

5. In cell A6 type **T**. Notice that after you type the letter "T," AutoComplete automatically displays the word "Training." To ignore the AutoComplete suggestion, simply continue typing.

6. Continue typing **otal Income** and then press **Enter**.

Next, you type labels for expense categories.

To enter labels for expense categories:

1. Click cell **A8** to make it the active cell.

2. Type **Expenses** and press **Enter** to complete the entry and move to cell A9.

3. Refer to Figure 2-6 and type the labels for cells A9 through A16: **Rent, Salaries, Telephone, Advertising, Office Supplies, Travel, Miscellaneous,** and **Total Expenses.**

Figure 2-6 ◄
Income and
expense labels

worksheet title ⎯

income categories ⎯

expense categories ⎯

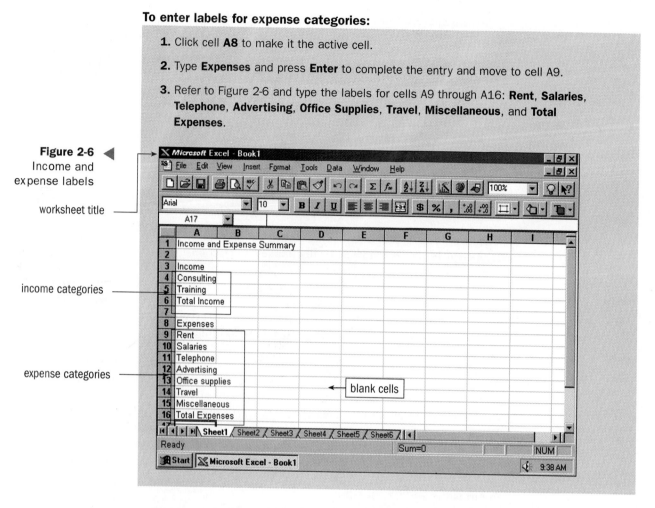

You want to leave a blank row after the "Total Expenses" label and type the label "Profit" in cell A18.

To type the label "Profit" in cell A18:

1. Press ↓ until the active cell is A18.

2. Type **Profit** and press **Enter**.

Notice that text in some cells spills over into column B. To fix this, you need to increase column A's width.

Changing Column Width

How many letters or numbers Excel displays in a cell depends on the size and style of the lettering, or font, you are using and the column width. If you do not change the columns' width on your worksheet, Excel automatically uses a column width that displays about eight and one-half digits. To see the exact column width in the formula bar, simply move the pointer over the right-hand border of the column header, then press and hold the mouse button down.

Figure 2-7 shows that Excel provides several methods for changing column width. For example, you can click a column heading or drag the pointer to highlight a series of column headings and then use the Format menu. You can also use the dividing line between column headings. When you move the pointer over the dividing line between two column headings, the pointer changes to ╬. You can use the pointer to drag the dividing line to a new location. You can also double-click the dividing line to make the column as wide as the longest text label or number in the column.

Figure 2-7 ◄
Changing
column width

click a column
heading, then click
the Format menu to
access the Column
Width dialog box

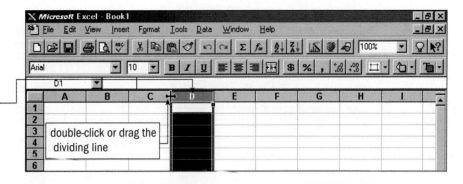

double-click or drag the dividing line

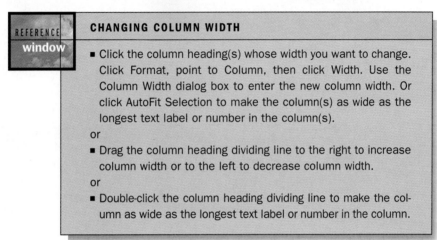

REFERENCE
window

CHANGING COLUMN WIDTH

- Click the column heading(s) whose width you want to change. Click Format, point to Column, then click Width. Use the Column Width dialog box to enter the new column width. Or click AutoFit Selection to make the column(s) as wide as the longest text label or number in the column(s).

or

- Drag the column heading dividing line to the right to increase column width or to the left to decrease column width.

or

- Double-click the column heading dividing line to make the column as wide as the longest text label or number in the column.

You want to change column A's width so that all the labels fit within it. You decide to double-click the column heading dividing line.

To change the width of column A:

1. Position the pointer on the box that contains the column heading for column A.

2. Move the pointer slowly to the right until it is over the dividing line between column A and column B. Notice how the pointer changes to ++.

3. Double-click the dividing line. Column A automatically adjusts to the appropriate width, and the complete worksheet title fits in cell A1. See Figure 2-8.

Figure 2-8 ◀
Changing
column A's
width

column A adjusts
to width of longest
label

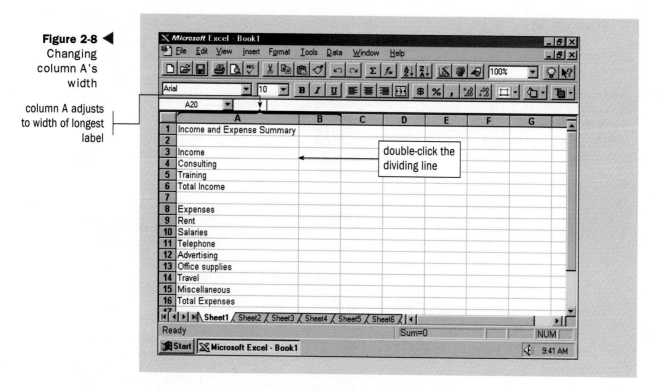

Next, you enter the column titles for each quarter. You start by entering the label "Quarter 1" in cell B2.

To enter the label "Quarter 1" in cell B2:

1. Click cell **B2** to make it the active cell.

2. Type **Quarter 1** and press **Enter**.

Is there any way to avoid typing the names of the next three quarters across the top of the worksheet? Yes there is. You can use AutoFill.

Creating a Series with AutoFill

The **AutoFill** feature automatically fills areas of a worksheet with a series of values or text. To use this feature you type one or two initial values or text entries, then AutoFill does the rest. AutoFill evaluates the initial entry or entries, determines the most likely sequence to follow, and completes the remaining entries in the range of cells you specify.

AutoFill recognizes series of numbers, dates, times, and certain labels. Figure 2-9 shows a series that AutoFill recognizes and completes.

Figure 2-9 ◀
Series
completed
by AutoFill

Initial Entry	Completed With
Monday	Tuesday, Wednesday, etc.
Mon	Tue, Wed, etc.
January	February, March, etc.
Jan	Feb, Mar, etc.
Quarter 1	Quarter 2, Quarter 3, etc.
Qtr1	Qtr2, Qtr3, etc.
11:00 AM	12:00 PM, 1:00 PM, etc.
Product 1	Product 2, Product 3, etc.
1992, 1993	1994, 1995, etc.
1, 2, 3, 4	5, 6, 7, etc.
1, 3, 5	7, 9, 11, etc.

If you use a repeating series such as months or days of the week, you can begin any-where in the series. If some cells need to be filled after the series ends, AutoFill repeats the series again from the beginning. For example, if you enter "October," AutoFill completes the series by entering "November" and "December," then it continues the series with "January," "February," and so on.

When you use AutoFill, you drag the fill handle to outline your initial entry and the cells you want to fill. Figure 2-10 shows the **fill handle**, a small black square in the lower-right corner of the active cell's border.

Figure 2-10 ◀
Fill handle

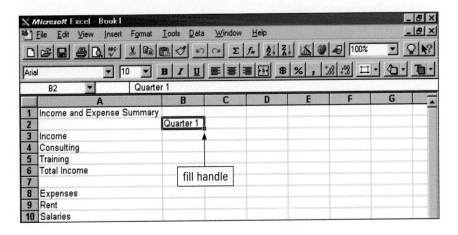

You can use AutoFill now to enter labels for the remaining quarters.

To fill in labels for the other quarters using AutoFill:

1. Click cell **B2** to make it the active cell. Look closely at the black border around the cell. Notice the fill handle, the small black square in the lower-right corner of the border.

2. Move the pointer over the fill handle until the pointer changes to **+**.

3. Click and drag the pointer across the worksheet to outline cells B2 through E2. See Figure 2-11.

Figure 2-11 ◄
Using AutoFill
to fill in labels
for cells B2
through E2

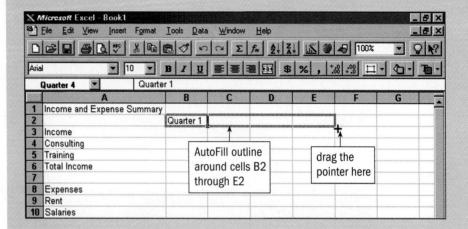

4. Release the mouse button. The label for each quarter appears in row 2 at the top of each column.

5. Click any cell to remove the highlighting from cells B2 through E2.

Renaming the Sheet

Look at the lower-left corner of the worksheet window: the sheet is currently named "Sheet1"—the name Excel uses automatically when it opens a new workbook. Now that your worksheet is taking shape, you give it a more specific name: Income and Expense. This way, if you use other sheets in the workbook in the future you can quickly and easily find the Income and Expense Summary.

To rename Sheet1:

1. Double-click the **Sheet1** tab in the lower-left corner of the worksheet to open the Rename Sheet dialog box. See Figure 2-12.

Figure 2-12 ◄
Rename Sheet
dialog box

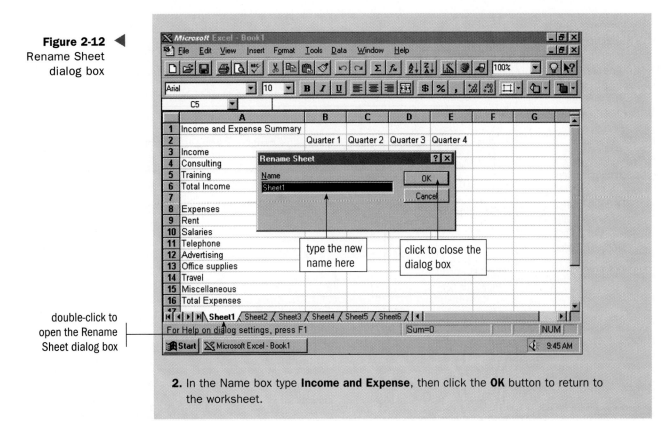

double-click to
open the Rename
Sheet dialog box

2. In the Name box type **Income and Expense**, then click the **OK** button to return to the worksheet.

Saving the New Workbook

You decide to save the workbook so you won't lose your work if power goes out. Because this is the first time you save the workbook, you use the Save As command and name the workbook SGL Income and Expense Summary.

Excel workbook names can contain up to 255 characters. These characters can be letters, numbers, or any symbols except for / \ < > * ? " | : ;. Excel automatically adds the .XLS extension to the workbook name, although you don't normally see it as part of the title.

The best way to organize your workbooks (also called files) is to store them in folders. For example, on your Student Disk you'll find a different folder for each tutorial listed in Figure 2-13. Within each tutorial folder are two subfolders, TAssign and Cases. Each time you open a new file in a tutorial, you save it with new name in the main folder for that tutorial. You save the Tutorial Assignment workbooks in the TAssign folder. Likewise, you save the Case Problem workbooks in the Cases folder.

Figure 2-13 ◀
Organization of
folders and
workbooks on
your Student
Disk

each tutorial folder
contains tutorial files
(if any), a Tutorial
Assignments
folder, and a Case
Problems folder.

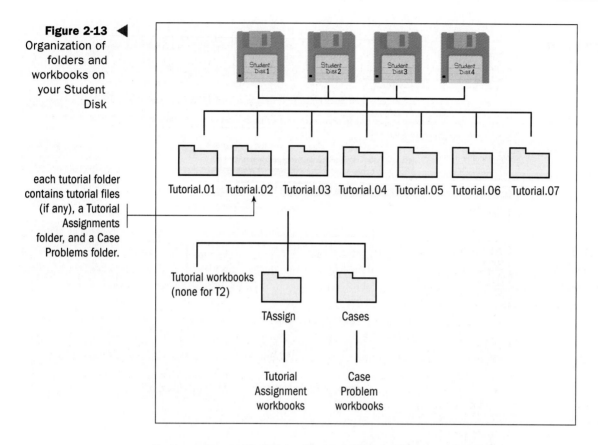

To save the workbook as SGL Income and Expense Summary:

1. Click **File** then click **Save As** to display the Save As dialog box.

2. Type **SGL Income and Expense Summary** but don't press Enter because you need to check some other settings.

3. Click the **Save in** list arrow, then click **3½ Floppy [A:]** to select the drive containing your Student Disk.

4. In the folder list, double-click the **Tutorial.02** folder to select the folder you want to save the workbook in. Your Save As dialog box should look like the dialog box in Figure 2-14.

Figure 2-14 ◀
Saving the
workbook as
SGL Income and
Expense
Summary

type workbook name
here

new sheet name

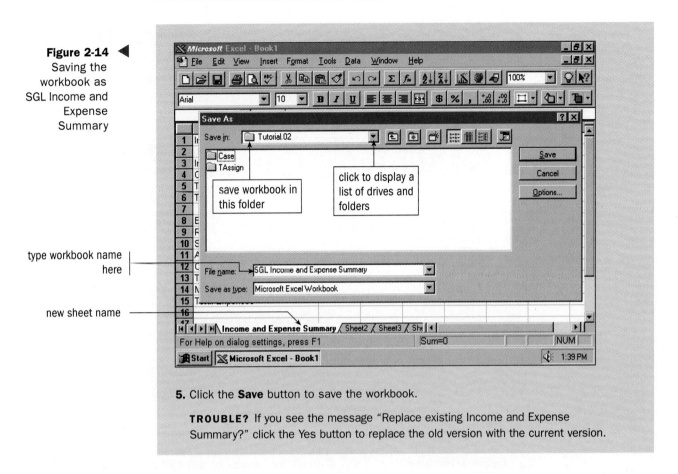

5. Click the **Save** button to save the workbook.

TROUBLE? If you see the message "Replace existing Income and Expense Summary?" click the Yes button to replace the old version with the current version.

Now you have entered the labels for the worksheet template. Your next step is to enter the formulas.

Entering Formulas

Formulas tell Excel what to calculate. When you enter a formula in a cell, type an equal sign (=) first. It tells Excel that the numbers or symbols that follow it constitute a formula, not just data. Formulas can contain cell references such as A1 and G14, operators such as * and +, and numbers such as 30 or 247. Figure 2-15 shows some examples of numbers, operators, and references you can include in a formula.

Figure 2-15 ◄
Examples of
numbers,
operators, and
references
used in
formulas

Example	Description	Example	Description
30	a number	<	less than sign
+	addition operator	>=	greater than or equal to sign
–	subtraction operator	<=	less than or equal to sign
/	division operator	<>	not equal to sign
*	multiplication operator	A1	reference to cell
%	percentage operator	(A1:A5)	reference to a range of cells
^	exponentiation operator	(A:A)	reference to entire column A
&	connects two text labels	(1:1)	reference to entire row 1
=	equal sign	(1:3)	reference to entire rows 1–3
>	greater than sign		

Figure 2-16 shows that Excel displays the results of a formula in the cell where you typed the formula. To see the formula itself, you must look at the formula bar.

Figure 2-16 ◄
Viewing a
formula and
its result

formula bar shows
the formula that is
in cell B6

cell displays result
of formula

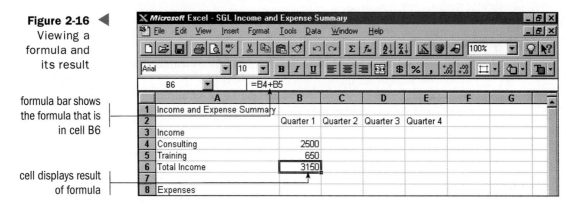

When Excel calculates the results of a formula that contains more than one operator, it follows the standard order of operations shown in Figure 2-17.

Figure 2-17 ◀
Order of
operations

Order	Operator	Description
1.	( )	parentheses
2.	^	exponentiation
3.	* /	multiplication or division
4.	+ –	addition or subtraction
5.	= <> > < >= <=	comparison

Following the order of operations, Excel calculates by doing any operations contained in parentheses first, then exponentiation, then multiplication or division, and so on. For example, the result of the formula 3+4*5 is 23 because Excel completes multiplication before the addition. The result of the formula (3+4)*5 is 35 because Excel calculates the operation in parentheses first.

REFERENCE window

ENTERING A FORMULA

- Click the cell where you want the result to appear.
- Type = and then type the rest of the formula.
- For formulas that include cell references, such as B2 or D78, you can type the cell reference or you can use the mouse or arrow keys to select each cell.
- When the formula is complete, press Enter.

You decide to enter the formula to calculate total income:

total income = consulting income + training income

The worksheet does not yet contain any values because you are building a template that branch managers will fill. You know that they will enter consulting income in cell B4 and training income in cell B5. Therefore, the total income formula must add the contents of cells B4 and B5. You type this formula as =B4+B5.

You want the total income displayed in cell B6, so you enter the formula in this cell.

To enter the formula for total income:

1. Click cell **B6** because this is where you want the total income displayed.

2. Type **=B4+B5** and press **Enter**. (You can use either uppercase or lowercase.) The result 0 appears in cell B6.

The result of the formula =B4+B5 is zero because cells B4 and B5 contain no values.

You want to enter the total income formulas for Quarters 2, 3, and 4. You could type the formula =C4+C5 in cell C6, then type the formula =D4+D5 in cell D6, and finally type the formula =E4+E5 in cell E6. Instead, you can use a shortcut to copy the formula you entered for Quarter 1.

Using the Fill Handle to Copy a Formula

Earlier in this tutorial you used the fill handle in the lower-right corner of the active cell to fill the series that began with Quarter 1. You can also use the fill handle to copy one cell's contents to other cells. Using the fill handle, you can copy formulas, values, and labels from one cell or from a group of cells.

REFERENCE window	**COPYING CELL CONTENTS WITH THE FILL HANDLE**
	■ Click the cell that contains the label, value, or formula you want to copy. If you want to copy the contents of more than one cell, highlight the cells you want to copy.
	■ Drag the fill handle to outline the cells where you want the copy or copies to appear.
	■ Release the mouse button.

You want to copy the formula from cell B6 to cells C6, D6, and E6.

To copy the formula from cell B6 to cells C6, D6, and E6:

1. Click cell **B6** to make it the active cell.

2. Position the pointer over the fill handle (in the lower-right corner of cell B6) until the pointer changes to .

3. Drag the pointer across the worksheet to outline cells B6 through E6.

4. Release the mouse button. Zeros now appear in cells B6 through E6.

5. Click any cell to remove the highlighting.

The formula in B6 is =B4+B5. Because you copied this formula to cells C6, D6, and E6, you are concerned that Quarters 2, 3, and 4 will show the same total income as Quarter 1 when branch managers enter their data. Take a moment to look at the formulas in cells C6, D6, and E6.

To examine the formulas in cells C6, D6, and E6:

1. Click cell **C6**. The formula =C4+C5 appears in the formula bar.

   When Excel copied the formula from cell B6 to cell C6, the cell references changed. The formula =B4+B5 became =C4+C5 when Excel copied it to column C.

2. Click cell **D6**. The formula =D4+D5 appears in the formula bar. When Excel copied the formula to column D, the cell references changed from B to D.

3. Click cell **E6**. The formula =E4+E5 appears in the formula bar.

When you copied the formula from cell B6, Excel automatically changed the cell references in the formulas to reflect the formula's new position in the worksheet.

Relative and Absolute References

You just learned how Excel uses relative references. A **relative reference** tells Excel which cell to use based on its location *relative* to the cell containing the formula. When you copy or move a formula that contains a relative reference, Excel changes cell references so they refer to cells located in the same position relative to the cell that contains the new copy of the formula. Figure 2-18 shows how this works.

Figure 2-18 ◄
Relative
references

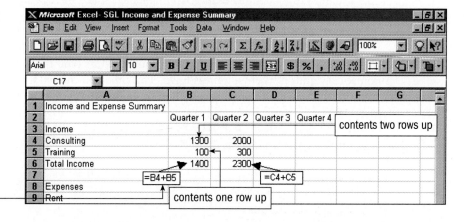

formulas add the
contents of the cell
two rows up to the
contents of the cell
one row up

Your original formula =B4+B5 contains relative references. Excel interpreted this formula to mean "add the value from the cell two rows up (B4) to the cell one row up (B5) and display the result in the current cell (B6)."

When you copied this formula to cell C6, Excel created the new formula to perform the same calculation, but starting at cell C6 instead of B6. The new formula means to add the value from the cell two rows up (C4) to the cell one row up (C5) and display the result in the current cell (C6).

All references in formulas are relative references unless you specify otherwise. Usually you want to use relative references because you can then easily copy and move formulas to different worksheet cells.

From time to time, you might need to create a formula that refers to a cell in a fixed location on the worksheet. A reference that always points to the same cell is an **absolute reference**. Absolute references contain a dollar sign before the column letter, the row number, or both. Examples of absolute references include $A$4, $C$27, $A17, and D$32.

Now you continue to enter the other formulas you planned for the worksheet template, starting with the formula to calculate total expenses.

SUM Function

The **SUM function** is a shortcut for entering formulas that total values in rows or columns. You can use the SUM function to replace a lengthy formula such as =B9+B10+B11+B12+B13+B14+B15 with the more compact formula =SUM(B9:B15).

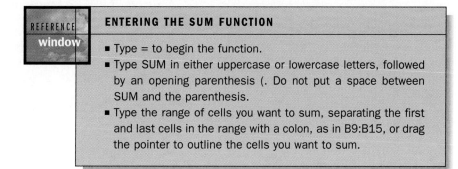

REFERENCE
window

ENTERING THE SUM FUNCTION

- Type = to begin the function.
- Type SUM in either uppercase or lowercase letters, followed by an opening parenthesis (. Do not put a space between SUM and the parenthesis.
- Type the range of cells you want to sum, separating the first and last cells in the range with a colon, as in B9:B15, or drag the pointer to outline the cells you want to sum.

You want to enter a formula in cell B16 that calculates total expenses by summing expenses such as rent, salaries, and so forth. You use the SUM function to do this.

To calculate total expenses using the SUM function:

1. Click cell **B16** because this is where you want to display the result of the formula.

2. Type **=SUM(** to begin the formula. Don't forget to include the open parenthesis.

3. Type **B9:B15)** and press **Enter**. Don't forget to include the closing parenthesis. The result 0 appears in cell B16.

Normally when typing a formula, you don't need to type the closing parenthesis. Excel automatically adds it when you press Enter. This time you entered it yourself just for practice.

Now you can copy the formula in B16 to cells C16, D16, and E16.

To copy the formula from cell B16 to cells C16, D16, and E16:

1. Click cell **B16**.

2. Drag the fill handle (in the lower-right corner of cell B16) to outline cells B16 through E16, then release the mouse button. Zeros appear in cells B16 through E16.

3. Click any cell to remove the highlighting.

Reviewing your worksheet plan and sketch, you realize that you need to enter the profit formula next.

Using the Mouse to Select Cell References

Excel provides several ways for entering cell references in a formula. One is to type the cell references directly, as you did to create the formula =B4+B5. Recall that you typed the equal sign, then typed B4, a plus sign, and finally B5. Another way to put a cell reference in a formula is to select the cell using the mouse or arrow keys. To use this method to enter the formula =B4+B5, you type the equal sign, then click cell B4, type the plus sign, then click cell B5. You may prefer to use the mouse to select cell references because it minimizes typing errors.

You want to calculate the profit for the first quarter:

profit = total income - total expenses

First look at the worksheet to locate cell references for the profit formula. Cell B6 contains total income and cell B16 contains total expenses, so you know that the formula should be =B6–B16. You create the formula to calculate profit by selecting the cell references with the mouse.

To create the formula to calculate profit by selecting cell references:

1. Click cell **B18** because this is where you want the result of the formula displayed.

2. Type **=** to begin the formula.

3. Click cell **B6**. Notice the dashed box around cell B6. Also notice that Excel added B6 to the formula in the formula bar and in cell B18. See Figure 2-19.

Figure 2-19 ◀
Selecting cell
references with
the mouse

after you type = click
cell B6 to add it to
the formula

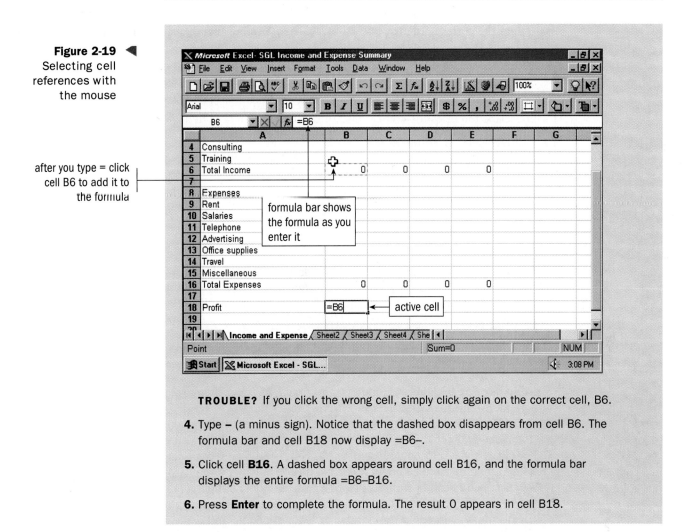

TROUBLE? If you click the wrong cell, simply click again on the correct cell, B6.

4. Type – (a minus sign). Notice that the dashed box disappears from cell B6. The formula bar and cell B18 now display =B6–.

5. Click cell **B16**. A dashed box appears around cell B16, and the formula bar displays the entire formula =B6–B16.

6. Press **Enter** to complete the formula. The result 0 appears in cell B18.

Now you can copy the formula in B18 to cells C18, D18, and E18.

To copy the formula from B18 to cells C18, D18, and E18:

1. Click cell **B18** because it contains the formula you want to copy.

2. Drag the fill handle to outline cells B18 through E18. Release the mouse button. Zeros appear in cells B18 through E18.

3. Click any cell to remove the highlighting.

   Now that you have entered all the formulas, you decide to save the workbook.

4. Click the **Save** button ▨.

Quick Check

1. What command do you use to name a worksheet and save it?

2. Describe how AutoComplete works.

3. What four activities are required to create an effective worksheet?

4 Using the correct order of operations, calculate the results of the formulas:
   a. 2+3*6
   b. (4/2)*5
   c. 2^2+5
   d. 10+10/2

5 Describe the methods you can use to enter cell references in a formula.

6 All references in formulas are ——————— unless you specify otherwise.

7 When you copy a formula, what happens to the relative references?

8 Describe how to quickly complete a series such as Jan, Feb, Mar?

SESSION

2.2

In this session you will learn how to test a new worksheet, insert rows or columns, use AutoFormat, use the AutoSum button, and clear cells. You'll also learn the meaning of number symbols (###) in a cell and what to do about them.

Testing the Worksheet

You have entered labels, formulas, and functions for each quarter. Before proceeding, you decide to test the worksheet by entering test values.

Test values are numbers that generate a known result. You enter the test values in your worksheet to determine if your formulas are accurate. After you enter the test values, you compare the results on your worksheet with the known results. If the results on your worksheet don't match the known results, you probably made an error.

Test values can be numbers from a real sample or simple numbers that make it easy to determine if the worksheet is calculating correctly. As an example of test values from a real sample, you could use numbers from an income and expense report that you know has been calculated correctly. As an example of simple numbers, you could enter the value 1 in all cells. Then it would be easy to do the calculations in your head to verify the formulas' accuracy.

You decide to use the number 100 as a test value because you can easily check the accuracy of the formulas you entered in the worksheet.

To enter the test value 100 in cells B4 and B5:

1. Click cell **B4** to make it the active cell.

2. Type **100** and press **Enter** to move to cell B5.

3. Type **100** and press **Enter**. The value 200 appears in cells B6 and B18.

You know that 100 plus 100 equals 200. Because this result is displayed as total income in cell B6, the formula seems to be correct. You decide to copy the test values from cells B4 and B5 to columns C, D, and E.

To copy the test values to cells C4 through E5:

1. Drag the pointer to highlight cells B4 and B5, then release the mouse button.

2. Drag the fill handle to outline cells B4 through E5. See Figure 2-20.

Figure 2-20 ◀
Copying test
values

outline around
cells B3
through C5

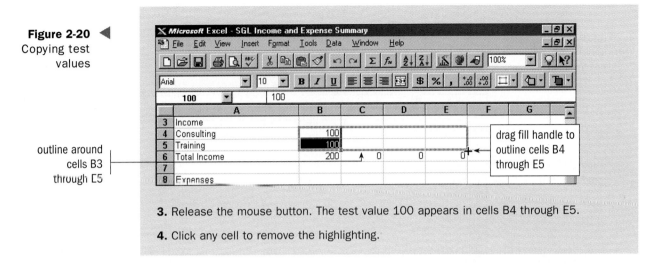

3. Release the mouse button. The test value 100 appears in cells B4 through E5.

4. Click any cell to remove the highlighting.

Notice that the formulas in cells B6, C6, D6, and E6 display 200, the result of the formula that calculates total income. In addition, the formulas that calculate profit in cells B18, C18, D18, and E18 also display the value 200. This makes sense. The formula for profit is total income – total expenses. On the worksheet the total income is 200 and the total expenses are 0.

Now you enter the test value 100 for each expense category. First you type the test value in cell B9, and then copy it to cells B10 through B15. Then you can copy the test values from column B to columns C, D, and E.

To enter a test value in cell B9, then copy it to cells B10 through B15:

1. Click cell **B9** to make it the active cell.

2. Type **100** and press **Enter**.

3. Press ↑ to make cell B9 the active cell again.

4. Drag the fill handle to outline cells B9 through B15, then release the mouse button. Do not remove the highlighting from the fill area. As a result the test value 100 appears in cells B9 through B15.

5. Drag the fill handle again to outline cells B9 through E15, then release the mouse button. The test value 100 appears in cells B9 through E15.

6. Click any cell to remove the highlighting. See Figure 2-21.

Figure 2-21 ◀
Worksheet with
test values

formula for
total income
produces 200

formula for
total expenses
produces 700

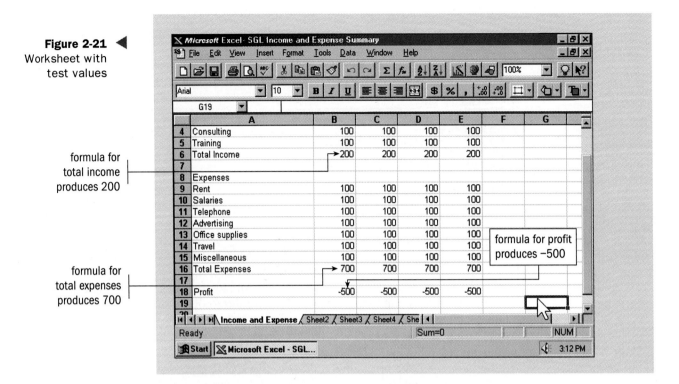

Next, take a moment to make sure that the formulas produced the results you expected. The formulas for total expenses in cells B16, C16, D16, and E16 display 700. This looks correct because the seven expense categories each contain the test value 100.

The formulas for profit in cells B18, C18, D18, and E18 display –500. This also looks correct. Total income is 200, total expenses are 700, and 200 minus 700 equals –500.

Compare this worksheet to your worksheet sketch (Figure 2-5). Notice that on the worksheet sketch you left row 1 blank for branch managers to type their branch office names. You didn't leave row 1 blank when you entered the labels on the worksheet, and now there isn't space for the branch office name. Do you need to start over? No, you can use the Insert command to insert a blank row.

Inserting a Row or Column

You can insert a row or column in a worksheet to make room for new data or to make the worksheet easier to read. When you insert rows or columns, Excel repositions other rows and columns in the worksheet and automatically adjusts cell references in formulas to reflect the new location of values used in calculations. Using the **Insert command** you can insert an entire row or many rows. You can insert an entire column or many columns.

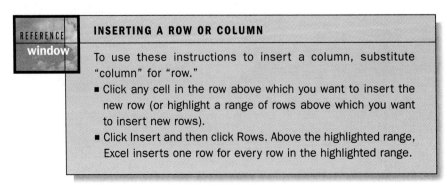

REFERENCE
window

INSERTING A ROW OR COLUMN

To use these instructions to insert a column, substitute "column" for "row."
■ Click any cell in the row above which you want to insert the new row (or highlight a range of rows above which you want to insert new rows).
■ Click Insert and then click Rows. Above the highlighted range, Excel inserts one row for every row in the highlighted range.

You decide to use the Insert menu to insert a row at the top of the worksheet. You cannot type a branch name in the new row because 12 branch offices will use this template. Instead, you decide to enter "SGL Branch Office Name" in the new row. The branch managers can then type their branches' names when they use the worksheet.

To insert a row at the top of the worksheet:

1. Click cell **A1** because you want to insert one new row above row 1.

2. Click **Insert** and then click **Rows**. Excel inserts a blank row at the top of the worksheet. All other rows shift down one row.

3. Make sure cell A1 is still active, then type **SGL Branch Office Name** and press **Enter**.

Adding a row changed the location of the data in the worksheet. For example, the consulting income originally in cell B4 is now in cell B5. Did Excel adjust the formulas to compensate for the new row?

You originally entered the formula =B4+B5 in cell B6 to calculate total income. Now the consulting income value is in cell B5, and the training income value is in cell B6. Let's look at the formula for total income, now located in cell B7.

To examine the contents of cell B7:

1. Click cell **B7**. The formula =B5+B6 appears in the formula bar.

Clearly, Excel did adjust the formula to compensate for the new location of the data. Take a moment to check a few more formulas, just to make sure that they have also been adjusted.

To check the formulas in B17 and B19:

1. Click cell **B17**. The formula =SUM(B10:B16) appears in the formula bar. The original formula was =SUM(B9:B15). Excel adjusted this formula to compensate for the new location of the data.

2. Click cell **B19**. The formula =B7-B17 appears in the formula bar. This formula used to be =B6-B16.

After you examine the formulas in your worksheet, you conclude that Excel automatically adjusted all the formulas when you inserted the new row.

Now, you want to use Excel's AutoFormat feature to improve the worksheet's appearance by emphasizing the titles and displaying dollar signs in cells that contain currency data.

Using AutoFormat

The **AutoFormat** command lets you change your worksheet's appearance by selecting from a collection of predesigned worksheet formats. Each worksheet format in the AutoFormat collection gives your worksheet a more professional appearance by using attractive fonts, borders, colors, and shading. AutoFormat also manipulates column widths, row heights, and the alignment of text in cells.

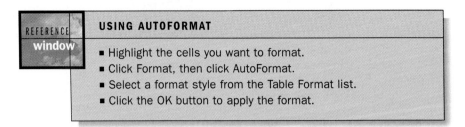

REFERENCE window

USING AUTOFORMAT

- Highlight the cells you want to format.
- Click Format, then click AutoFormat.
- Select a format style from the Table Format list.
- Click the OK button to apply the format.

Now you'll use AutoFormat's Financial 3 format to improve the worksheet's appearance.

To apply AutoFormat's Financial 3 format:

1. Highlight cells A1 through E19, then release the mouse button.

2. Click **Format** then click **AutoFormat**. The AutoFormat dialog box appears. See Figure 2-22.

Figure 2-22 ◀
AutoFormat
dialog box

list of formats

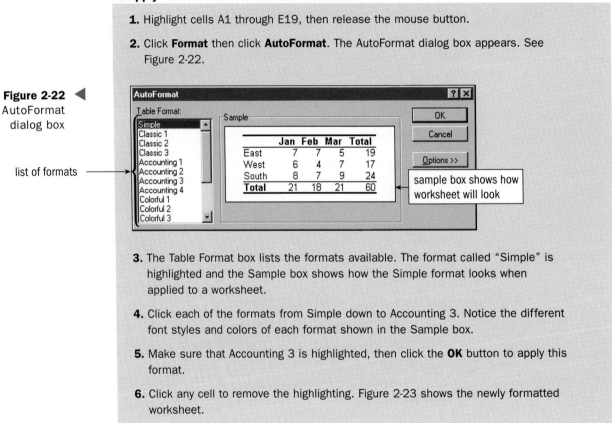

3. The Table Format box lists the formats available. The format called "Simple" is highlighted and the Sample box shows how the Simple format looks when applied to a worksheet.

4. Click each of the formats from Simple down to Accounting 3. Notice the different font styles and colors of each format shown in the Sample box.

5. Make sure that Accounting 3 is highlighted, then click the **OK** button to apply this format.

6. Click any cell to remove the highlighting. Figure 2-23 shows the newly formatted worksheet.

Figure 2-23 ◀
Worksheet
formatted using
Accounting 3

bold titles ──────

bold major row
labels

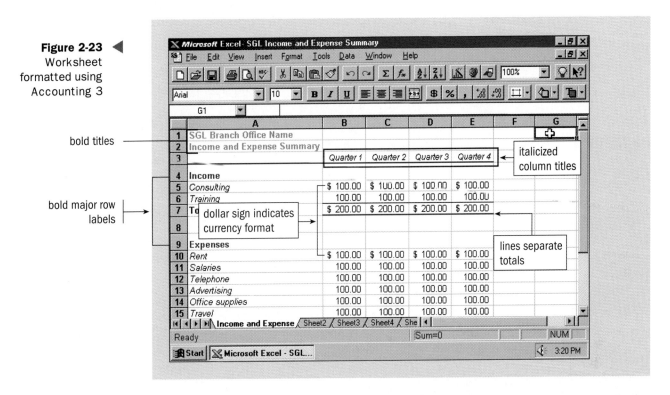

Your worksheet looks great so far. Referring back to your worksheet plan, you see that you didn't include a column to display year-to-date totals. You revise your worksheet plan, as shown in Figure 2-24.

Figure 2-24 ◀
Revised
worksheet plan

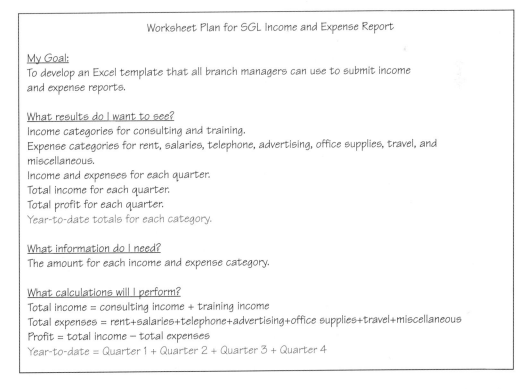

You also revise your worksheet sketch (Figure 2-25) to show column titles, formulas, and formats for the Year to Date column.

SGL Branch Office Name

Income and Expenses Summary

	Quarter 1	Quarter 2	Quarter 3	Quarter 4	Year to Date
Income					
Consulting	$9,999,999.99	$9,999,999.99	$9,999,999.99	$9,999,999.99	${year-to-date formula}
Training	:	:	:	:	:
Total Income	${total income formula}	${total income formula}	${total income formula}	${total income formula}	${year-to-date formula}
Expenses					
Rent	$9,999,999.99	$9,999,999.99	$9,999,999.99	$9,999,999.99	${year-to-date formula}
Salaries	:	:	:	:	:
Telephone	:	:	:	:	:
Advertising	:	:	:	:	:
Office Supplies	:	:	:	:	:
Travel	:	:	:	:	:
Miscellaneous	:	:	:	:	:
Total Expenses	${total expenses formula}	${total expenses formula}	${total expenses formula}	${total expenses formula}	${year-to-date formula}
Profit	${profit formula}	${profit formula}	${profit formula}	${profit formula}	${year-to-date formula}

Figure 2-25 ◄
Revised
worksheet
sketch

You begin by entering the title for the Year to Date column in cell F3.

To enter the title for column F:

1. Click cell **F3** to make it the active cell.

2. Type **Year to Date** and press **Enter**.

Next, you need to enter a formula in cell F5 to calculate the year-to-date consulting income. You could type the formula =SUM(B5:E5), but you decide to use the AutoSum button to eliminate extra typing.

AutoSum Button

The **AutoSum button**, the Σ button on the toolbar, automatically creates formulas that contain the SUM function. To do this, Excel looks at the cells adjacent to the active cell, guesses which cells you want to sum, and displays a formula based on its best guess about the range you want to sum. You can press the Enter key to accept the formula, or you can drag the mouse over a different range of cells to change the range in the formula.

To enter the formula in cell F5 using the AutoSum button:

1. Click cell **F5** because this is where you want to put the formula.

2. Click the **AutoSum** button ⟨Σ⟩. See Figure 2-26. Excel guesses that you probably want to sum the contents of the range B5 through E5. That's exactly what you want to do.

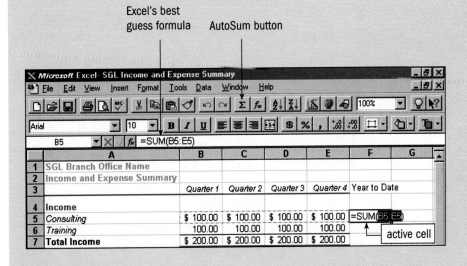

Figure 2-26 ◀
Using the
AutoSum tool

3. Press **Enter** to complete the formula. The result $400.00 appears in cell F5.

Note that AutoSum assumed that you wanted to use the same format in cell F5 as you used in the cells containing the values for the sum. Therefore, cell F5 is formatted for currency with two decimal places.

You can use the same formula to calculate the year-to-date totals for all income and expense categories as well as the totals. You use the fill handle to copy the formula from cell F5 to cells F6 through F19.

To copy the formula from cell F5 to cells F6 through F19:

1. If necessary, scroll the worksheet so you can see rows 5 through 19.

2. Click cell **F5** because this cell contains the formula you want to copy.

3. Drag the fill handle to outline cells F5 through F19, then release the mouse button.

4. Click any cell to remove the highlighting and see the results of the copy. See Figure 2-27.

Figure 2-27 ◄
Result of
copying formula
from F5

these cells should
display values

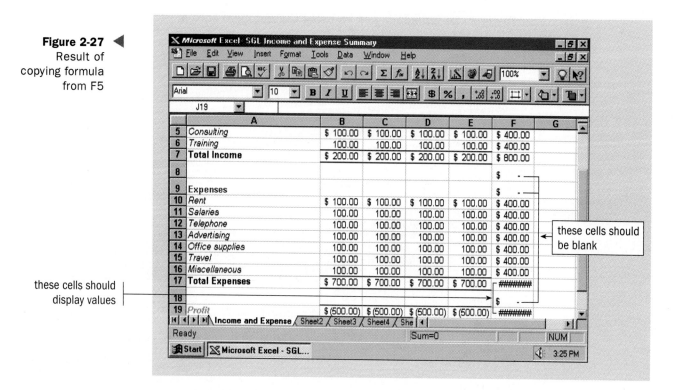

You copied the formula from cell F5 to the range F6 through F19, but there are a few problems, as shown in Figure 2-27. Cells F8, F9, and F18 should be blank. Instead they contain a dollar sign and a hyphen because of the SUM function now located in those cells. Another problem is that number signs (###) appear in cells F17 and F19 instead of a value for the year-to-date total expenses and year-to-date profit.

Next, you clear the formulas from cells in column F that should be blank.

Clearing Cells

To erase the contents or the formats of a cell, you use either the Delete key or the Clear dialog box. Erasing the *contents* of a cell is known as **clearing a cell**. Keep in mind that clearing a cell differs from deleting the entire cell. When you *delete* a cell, the entire cell is removed from the worksheet and adjacent cells move to fill the space the deleted cell left.

When clearing a cell you have three choices. You can clear only the cell contents (i.e., the values or text in the cell), you can clear the formats in the cell, or you can clear both the cell's contents and formats. To do this, use the Delete key or the Clear dialog box on the Edit menu.

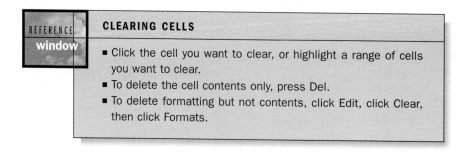

REFERENCE
window

CLEARING CELLS

- Click the cell you want to clear, or highlight a range of cells you want to clear.
- To delete the cell contents only, press Del.
- To delete formatting but not contents, click Edit, click Clear, then click Formats.

You decide to clear the formula from cell F18 first. Then you highlight cells F8 and F9 and clear both formulas with one command.

To clear the formulas from cells F18, F8, and F9:

1. Click cell **F18** because this is the first cell you want to clear.

2. Press **Del**.

3. Highlight cells F8 through F9, then release the mouse button.

4. Press **Del**.

Now that you have cleared unwanted formulas from the cells, your attention turns to the number signs in cells F17 and F19.

Number Sign (###) Replacement

If a value is too long to fit within a cell's boundaries, Excel displays a series of number signs (###) in the cell. The number signs signal that the number of digits in the value exceeds the cell's width. It would be misleading to display only some digits of the value. For example, suppose you enter the value 5129 in a cell wide enough to display only two digits. Should Excel display the first two digits or the last two digits? Either choice would be misleading, so Excel displays number signs (###) instead. The values, formats, and formulas have *not* been erased from the cell. To display the value, you just need to increase the column width.

For example, on your worksheet cell F19 displays a maximum of eight full digits. Because Excel formatted this cell for currency as a result of the AutoSum operation, Excel must have space in the column to display the dollar sign, the comma indicating thousands, the decimal point, two numbers after the decimal, and the parentheses for negative numbers. The value in this cell, ($2,000.00), requires an 11-digit cell width.

You need to widen cells F17 and F19. You also want a double underline in cell F19, a thick single underline in cells F7 and F17, and single underlines in cells F3 and F16 so column F looks like other columns in the worksheet. Rather than applying these formats separately, you decide to use AutoFormat again to reapply the Accounting 3 format to the entire worksheet. Reapplying the format also widens column F because AutoFormat determines column width based on the numbers in the cells at the time you apply the format.

To reapply the Accounting 3 format to the entire worksheet:

1. If necessary, scroll the worksheet to display row 1.

2. Highlight cells A1 through F19, then release the mouse button.

   TROUBLE? If you don't see row 19 on the screen when you highlight the worksheet, move the pointer below the bottom of the window and the worksheet scrolls.

3. Click **Format** then click **AutoFormat**. The AutoFormat dialog box appears.

4. Click the **Accounting 3** format, then click the **OK** button to apply the format.

5. Click any cell to remove the highlighting.

Excel reformats the entire worksheet. Column F contains the same format as columns A through E. Next, make sure that column F's width increased enough to display the value for year-to-date total expenses in cell F17 and year-to-date profit in cell F19.

To verify that cells F17 and F19 display values rather than number signs:

1. If necessary, scroll the worksheet until you see rows 17 and 19. Cell F17 displays $2,800.00 instead of number signs.

2. Cell F19 displays $(2,000.00) instead of number signs.

Can you still be certain that the columns are wide enough? For example, what if a branch manager reports consulting income of $1 million for the first quarter? Will that value fit in cell B5? Try it now.

To enter $1 million in cell B5:

1. Click cell **B5** to make it the active cell.

2. Type **1000000** and press **Enter**. Number signs appear in cells B5, B7, B19, F5, F7, and F19, as shown in Figure 2-28.

Figure 2-28 ◄
After entering
$1,000,000 in
cell B5

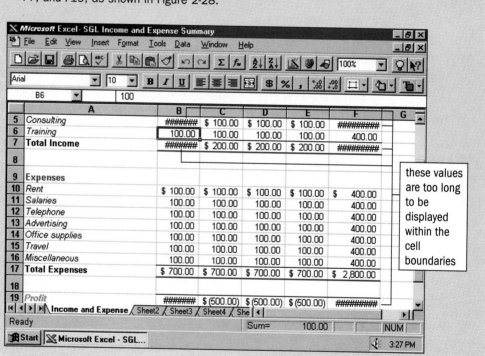

It looks like columns B through F need to display at least 13 digits. Because you used small test values, AutoFormat did not make the cells as wide as they need to be when branch managers enter their data. You decide to change column width using the Column Width command.

To change the width of columns B through F using the Column Width command:

1. Click the **column heading** box at the top of column B. This highlights column B.

2. Drag the pointer to column F, then release the mouse button. Columns B through F are highlighted.

3. Position the pointer over the selected range, then click the right mouse button to display a menu.

4. Click **Column Width** to display the Column Width dialog box. The insertion point is flashing in the Column Width box.

5. Type **13** in the Column Width box, then click the **OK** button.

6. Click any cell to remove the highlighting and view the new column widths.

Column A is too wide because the longest income or expense category label, "Total Expenses," is only 14 characters. You decide to allow the titles "SGL Branch Office Name" and "Income and Expense Summary" to spill over into adjacent columns. You adjust column A, making it just wide enough for the "Total Expenses" label.

To adjust the width of column A:

1. Make sure you can see cell A17, which contains the "Total Expenses" label.

2. Position the pointer on the column heading box at the top of column A.

3. Move the pointer slowly to the right until it is positioned over the dividing line between columns A and B and changes to ↔.

4. Drag the dividing line to the left, just to the right of the last "s" in the label "Total Expenses."

5. Release the mouse button. Column A adjusts to the new width.

This is a good time to save the workbook.

To save the workbook:

1. Click the **Save** button 🖫 to save the workbook on your Student Disk.

Quick Check

1. Describe how AutoSum works.

2. Why would you use 1 as a test value?

3. To clear a cell's contents (but not its formatting) click the cell and then click _____.

4. _____ is a command that lets you change your worksheet's appearance by selecting from a collection of predesigned worksheet formats.

5. What is the difference between clearing a cell and deleting a cell?

6. Describe how to insert a row or column.

7. _____ are numbers that generate a known result.

8. Why does Excel display number signs (###) in a cell?

SESSION 2.3

In this session you learn how to perform a final check on a new worksheet with realistic data, how to document a worksheet, how to add a text note to a cell, how to check spelling in a worksheet, how to protect a worksheet's cells, and how to save a worksheet as an Excel Template.

Testing the Worksheet with Realistic Data

Before trusting a worksheet and its results, you should test it to make sure you entered the correct formulas and specified appropriate formats. You want the worksheet to produce accurate results, and you want the results clearly displayed.

Earlier you used the simple value 100 because you could make the calculations in your head and verify the worksheet formulas. So far, the formulas appear to be correct, but you are still not satisfied.

You know that this worksheet is extremely important. Branch managers will enter values into it, assuming the worksheet calculates the correct results. Your reputation, the reputations of branch managers, and the success of the corporation could depend on the worksheet's providing correct results. So you are determined to test the worksheet thoroughly before you distribute it to branch offices.

You want to test the worksheet using realistic data, so you decide to enter last year's values from the Littleton, North Carolina, branch office report shown in Figure 2-29.

Figure 2-29 ◀
Littleton, North
Carolina, branch
office data

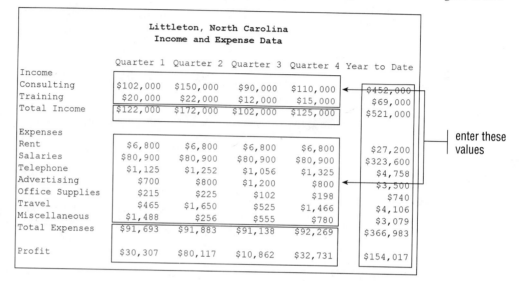

To enter the Littleton test values:

1. Enter the test values shown in the blue-boxed area of Figure 2-29. Do not enter values in any cells that contain formulas. Because you have already formatted your worksheet, enter the test values without dollar signs or decimal places. Excel automatically adds the dollar signs and decimal places where appropriate.

TROUBLE? If you enter a number in a cell that contains a formula, and you notice it right away, click ⟳. If you don't notice the problem until after you make other entries, retype the formula in the appropriate cell.

Next, you compare the results displayed on your worksheet with the results for the North Carolina branch values shown in the yellow-boxed area of Figure 2-29. The values your worksheet formulas produced match the Littleton results. Now, you feel more confident that the worksheet will provide correct results.

Clearing Test Values from the Worksheet

The worksheet contains test values that must not be included in the final worksheet template, so you clear the test values from the worksheet.

To clear the test values from the worksheet:

1. Highlight cells B5 through E6, then release the mouse button. *Do not drag to column F.* Column F contains formulas and you don't want to clear them.

TROUBLE? If you highlight column F, drag the pointer from B5 to E6 again.

2. Press **Del**.

3. Highlight cells B10 through E16, then release the mouse button. *Do not drag to column F.*

4. Press **Del**.

5. Click any cell to remove the highlighting.

Documenting the Worksheet

Documenting a worksheet provides the information needed to use and modify the worksheet. Documentation can take many forms; if you work for a company that does not have documentation standards or requirements, you must choose the type of documentation most effective for your worksheets.

Your worksheet plan and worksheet sketch offer one type of worksheet documentation. As you know, the worksheet plan and sketch give you a blueprint to follow as you build and test the worksheet. This information is useful to someone who needs to modify your worksheet because it states your goals, specifies the required input, describes the output, and indicates the calculations you used to produce the output. Excel provides a way to print all the formulas you entered in the worksheet. This is also a very useful form of documentation.

Because the worksheet plan, the worksheet sketch, and the formula printout are not part of the workbook, they might not be readily available to the person using it. For this reason, it's a good idea to include some form of documentation *within* the workbook. If you like, you can make the first sheet in the workbook a documentation sheet, in which you state who created the workbook and when, what the workbook is used for, and, finally, what each workbook sheet contains.

If you prefer, you can include documentation in each sheet of the workbook. This documentation might simply be a header with your name and the date you created the worksheet. You can also include documentation by adding a cell note to your worksheet.

Adding a Cell Note

A **cell note** is text attached to a cell. The note does not appear on the worksheet unless you place the mouse pointer over the attached cell. Cells that contain text notes always display a small square in the upper-right corner. On a color monitor this square is red. You can attach cell notes to a cell even if it contains data.

REFERENCE window	ADDING A CELL NOTE
	▪ Click the cell to which you want to attach a note.
	▪ Click Insert then click Note.
	▪ Type your note in the Text Note box. The insertion point automatically moves down when you reach the end of a line. If you need to type a short line and then move down, press Enter.
	▪ When you finish typing the note, click the OK button.

SGL management recommends that anyone who creates a worksheet attach a note to cell A1 with this information:

- ▪ who created the worksheet

- ▪ the date the worksheet was created or revised

- ▪ a brief description of the worksheet

You add a cell note to your worksheet to provide the required documentation.

To add a text note to cell A1:

1. Click cell **A1** because this is the cell to which you want to attach the text note.

2. Click **Insert** then click **Note** to display the Cell Note dialog box.

3. Click in the Text Note box to make sure the insertion point is active, then type **Income and Expense Summary**.

4. Press **Enter** to move the insertion point to the next line.

5. Type **Created by**, type your first and last names, and then press **Enter**.

6. Type today's date and press **Enter**.

7. Type the rest of the note you see in Figure 2-30 without pressing Enter. Because the rest of the note is a paragraph, you do not need to press Enter; the words automatically wrap to the next line.

Figure 2-30 ◀
Adding a cell note

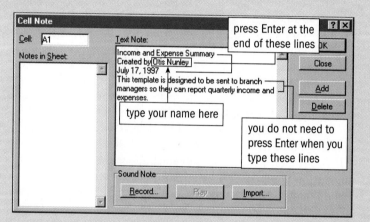

8. When you finish typing the note, click the **OK** button. Notice a small red square in the upper-right corner of cell A1.

9. Move the mouse pointer over cell A1. The cell note shown in Figure 2-31 appears. When you move the mouse pointer to another cell, the cell note disappears.

Figure 2-31 ◀
Displaying a cell note

cell note appears only when pointer is on cell A1

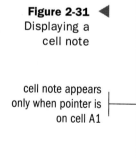
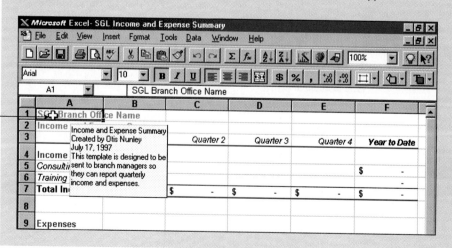

Now that the worksheet is almost done, you want to make sure you haven't misspelled any words.

Checking Spelling in the Worksheet

Excel's **Spelling command** helps you find misspelled words in your worksheets. When you choose this command, Excel compares the words in your worksheet to the words in its dictionary. When it finds a word in your worksheet that is not in its dictionary, it shows you the word and provides options for correcting it or leaving it as is.

REFERENCE window	**USING THE SPELLING BUTTON**
	■ Click cell A1 so you begin to check spelling from the top of the worksheet.
	■ Click the Spelling button.
	■ Excel shows you any word that is in your worksheet but not in its dictionary. If the Excel dictionary includes similar words, you see alternatives in the Suggestions list. Your options are
	■ If the word is correct and you do not want to change this one occurrence, click the Ignore button.
	■ If the word is correct and you want Excel to ignore all future occurrences of the word, click the Ignore All button.
	■ If you want Excel to corrrect the spelling automatically using its best guess from Suggestions box, click the AutoCorrect button.
	■ If you want to change the word to one listed in the Suggestions box, click the correct word, then click the Change button.
	■ If Excel does not provide an acceptable alternative, you can edit the word in the Change To box, then click the Change button.

To check spelling in the entire worksheet:

1. Click cell **A1** so Excel's spelling check begins at the first cell in the worksheet.

2. Click the **Spelling** button to check the spelling in the entire worksheet. Excel finds the word SGL, the name of the company you work for. See Figure 2-32. This acronym is correctly spelled, but it is not in Excel's dictionary.

   TROUBLE? Don't worry if your list of suggested alternatives differs; simply continue to Step 3.

Figure 2-32 ◀
Checking
spelling in the
worksheet

this word is not in
Excel's dictionary

suggested
alternatives

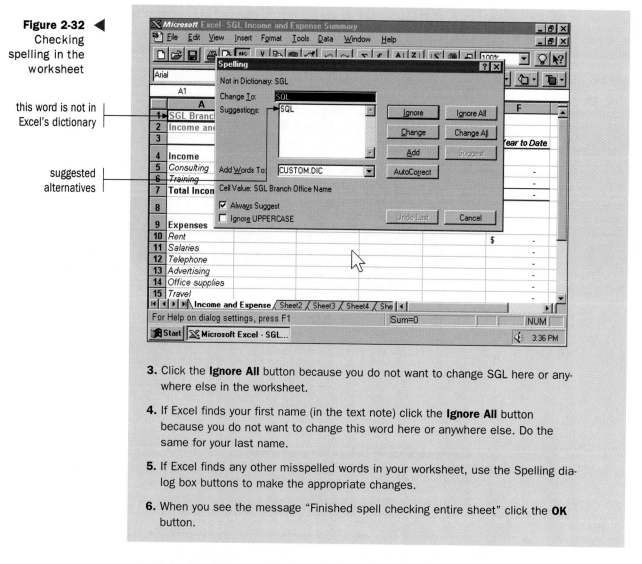

3. Click the **Ignore All** button because you do not want to change SGL here or anywhere else in the worksheet.

4. If Excel finds your first name (in the text note) click the **Ignore All** button because you do not want to change this word here or anywhere else. Do the same for your last name.

5. If Excel finds any other misspelled words in your worksheet, use the Spelling dialog box buttons to make the appropriate changes.

6. When you see the message "Finished spell checking entire sheet" click the **OK** button.

You look at the completed worksheet and think about how it will be used. Branch managers will receive your template—a version of the worksheet with titles and formulas, but no values. At the start of each year, each branch manager will open a copy of the template and save it under a name that indicates the branch office name.

At the end of each quarter, branch managers will retrieve the worksheet, enter the values for that quarter, then save and print the worksheet. They will send a printed copy to you, along with a disk containing a copy of the worksheet.

You foresee one problem with the template. What if a branch manager types a value over a cell containing a formula? The formula would be erased, the cell would not recalculate to reflect changes, and the worksheet would be unreliable. You need some way to protect the worksheet.

Protecting Cells in the Worksheet

Excel lets you protect cells from changes while still allowing users to enter or change values in unprotected cells. Cells that are protected so that their contents cannot be changed are **locked cells**.

Two commands protect or unprotect cells: the Cell Protection command and the Protect Document command. The **Cell Protection command** lets you specify the protection status of any cell in the worksheet. In the worksheet you are currently building, the protection status of all cells is locked. How, then, can you change the cell contents in the worksheet when you build it? Here's where the Protect Document command comes into play. Protection status does not go in effect until you use the **Protect Document command** to put the worksheet into protected mode.

When you want to protect some worksheet cells, you first unlock the cells in which you want users to make entries. Then you use the Protection command on the Tools menu to protect those cells you left locked.

When you protect the worksheet, Excel lets you enter a password. If you use a password, you must make sure to remember so you can unlock the worksheet in the future. Unless you are working on confidential material, it's probably easier not to use a password at all. You use one in this tutorial just for practice.

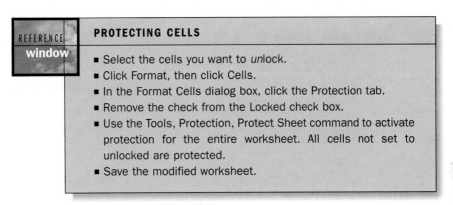

REFERENCE window	**PROTECTING CELLS**
	▪ Select the cells you want to *unlock*.
	▪ Click Format, then click Cells.
	▪ In the Format Cells dialog box, click the Protection tab.
	▪ Remove the check from the Locked check box.
	▪ Use the Tools, Protection, Protect Sheet command to activate protection for the entire worksheet. All cells not set to unlocked are protected.
	▪ Save the modified worksheet.

You start by unlocking the range of cells where managers can enter data. Then, you activate document protection for the rest of the worksheet.

To unlock the cells for data entry:

1. Highlight cells B5 through E6, then release the mouse button.

2. Click **Format** then click **Cells**. The Format Cells dialog box appears.

3. Click the **Protection** tab. Notice that the Locked box contains a check. See Figure 2-33.

Figure 2-33 ◀
Unlocking cells

click Locked to
remove the check

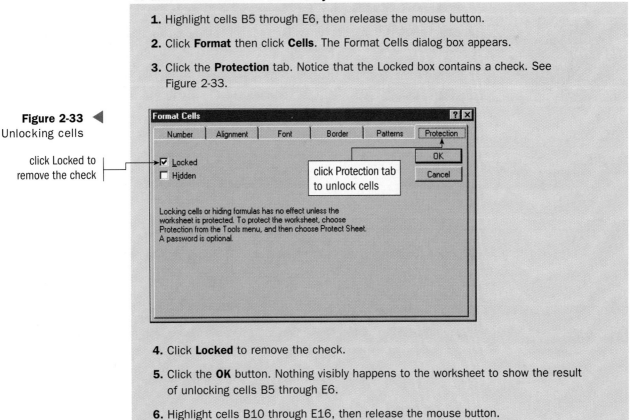

4. Click **Locked** to remove the check.

5. Click the **OK** button. Nothing visibly happens to the worksheet to show the result of unlocking cells B5 through E6.

6. Highlight cells B10 through E16, then release the mouse button.

7. Click **Format** then click **Cells**. The Format Cells dialog box appears.

8. If necessary, click the **Protection** tab. Notice that the Locked box contains a check.

9. Click **Locked** to remove the check.

10. Click the **OK** button.

In addition to entering data in the cells, branch managers will type the appropriate branch office name in row 1. You unlock cell A1 to let them do so.

To unlock cell A1:

1. Click **A1** to make it the active cell.

2. Click **Format** then click **Cells**. The Format Cells dialog box appears.

3. If necessary, click the **Protection** tab, then click **Locked** to remove the check.

4. Click the **OK** button.

Now that you have unlocked the cells for data entry, you turn on protection for the entire worksheet to protect every cell that you didn't unlock.

To turn protection on:

1. Click **Tools**, point to **Protection**, then click **Protect Sheet**. The Protect Sheet dialog box appears.

2. Type the password **bluesky**. The letters appear as x's or *'s in the text box.

3. Click the **OK** button. Excel prompts you to enter the password again to make sure that you remember it and that you entered it correctly the first time.

4. Type **bluesky** again then click the **OK** button. Nothing visibly happens to show that you protected the worksheet.

You decide to test worksheet protection.

To test worksheet protection:

1. Click **A8** then type **5**. A dialog box displays the message "Locked cells cannot be changed."

2. Click the **OK** button to continue.

3. Click **B10**, then type **3**. The number 3 appears in the formula bar and in the cell.

4. Press **Enter**. You can make an entry in cell B10 because you unlocked it before protecting the worksheet.

5. If you like, continue testing the other cells in your worksheet until you are satisfied that the cell protection will prevent managers from overwriting formulas.

Now you need to delete the entry you made in cell B10 when you tested cell protection.

To clear cell B10:

1. Click **B10** then press **Del**.

Now the worksheet is complete, and you are ready to save it as a template.

Saving the Worksheet as an Excel Template

Excel templates are stored with an .XLT extension rather than the .XLS extension used for workbooks. In the Open dialog box, a thin yellow line at the top of the icon (the small picture next to the filename) for a template differentiates it from a workbook icon.

Figure 2-34 shows what happens when you open a template. (1) Excel copies it from the disk to RAM and displays the template on your screen. (2) You fill the template with values, as you would any worksheet. (3) When you save this workbook, Excel prompts you for a new filename so you do not overwrite the template. Excel then saves the completed workbook under the new filename.

Figure 2-34 ◀
How a
template works

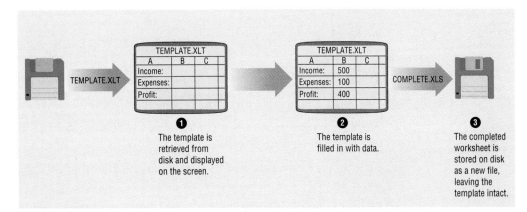

You use the Save As command to save the Income and Expense Summary worksheet as a template.

To save the worksheet as a template:

1. Click **File** then click **Save As.** to display the Save As dialog box.

2. Click the **Save as type** box list arrow to display a list of file types.

3. Click **Template**.

4. Click the **Save in** list arrow and click the drive containing your Student Disk.

5. In the list of folders, double-click **Tutorial.02**.

6. Change the filename to SGL Income and Expense Summary Template. See Figure 2-35.

Figure 2-35 ◀
Saving the
workbook as a
template

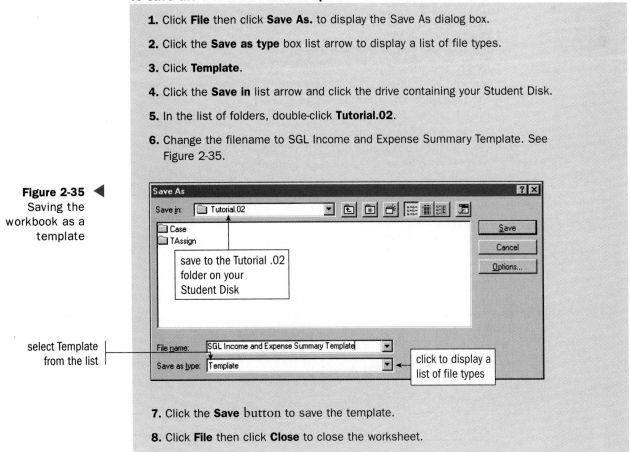

7. Click the **Save** button to save the template.

8. Click **File** then click **Close** to close the worksheet.

You are ready to send your finished template to branch managers. If you are not going to the Tutorial Assignment now, you can exit Excel.

Quick Check

[1] To protect a worksheet, you must first unlock those cells that the user can change and then activate —————————.

[2] Explain the function of these toolbar buttons:

a. Σ

b. (spelling button)

c. (undo button)

d. (redo button)

[3] How does a template differ from a worksheet?

[4] What are your options when you're using the Spelling command and Excel finds a word that is not in its dictionary?

[5] Cells that are protected so that their contents cannot be changed are called —————————.

[6] Explain why it is important to document your worksheet, and list four forms of documentation.

[7] Explain how to add a cell note to a worksheet.

Tutorial Assignments

You are branch manager for the Duluth, Minnesota, branch of SGL. The home office just sent you a copy of the new quarterly income and expense summary template. You need to test the template by filling in the information for the first two quarters of this year and returning a printed copy of the worksheet.

To complete the Tutorial Assignments:

1. Open the template SGL (located in the TAssign folder for Tutorial 2). Notice how a thin yellow line at the top of the icon for a template (next to the filename in the Open dialog box) differentiates it from the workbook icon. (This may be hard to see if the filename is highlighted.)
2. Enter your name in cell A1 in place of the branch office name.
3. Enter the values for Quarter 1 and Quarter 2 as shown in Figure 2-36.

Figure 2-36 ◀

Duluth Branch Office					
Income and Expense Summary					
	Quarter 1	*Quarter 2*	*Quarter 3*	*Quarter 4*	**Year to Date**
Income					
Consulting	$27,930.00	$33,550.00			$61,480.00
Training	11,560.00	13,520.00			25,080.00
Total Income	$39,490.00	$47,070.00	$0.00	$0.00	$86,560.00
Expenses					
Rent	$2,300.00	$2,300.00			$4,600.00
Salaries	7,200.00	7,200.00			14,400.00
Telephone	547.00	615.00			1,162.00
Advertising	1,215.00	692.00			1,907.00
Office Supplies	315.00	297.00			612.00
Travel	1,257.00	1,408.00			2,665.00
Miscellaneous	928.00	802.00			1,730.00
Total Expenses	$13,762.00	$13,314.00	$0.00	$0.00	$27,076.00
Profit	$25,728.00	$33,756.00	$0.00	$0.00	$59,484.00

4. Compare your results with those in Figure 2-36 to verify that the formulas are correct.

5. Practice using AutoCalculate by selecting the range containing Rent for Quarter 1 and Quarter 2. What is the sum of these two values, as displayed in the status bar? Right-click the AutoCalculate indicator to open the menu, then click Average. What is the average of these two values? Right-click the AutoCalculate indicator again, then click Sum to redisplay the sum in the status bar.

6. Save the file as an Excel workbook in the TAssign folder for Tutorial 2 on your Student Disk. (Do not save it as a template.) Name the workbook SGL - Duluth Branch Office.

7. Print the worksheet.

You show the Quarterly Income and Expense Summary template to your boss, Joan LeValle. She suggests several additions to the template. Joan mentions that some branch offices have started long-term employee education programs, so she wants you to add a separate expense category for education.

8. Open the template SGL - Income and Expense Summary Template 2 in the TAssign folder for Tutorial 2 on your Student Disk.

9. Deactivate document protection by clicking Tools, pointing to Protection, then selecting Unprotect Sheet. Type the password "bluesky" then click the OK button.

10. Insert a row above the current row 14.

11. Begin entering the row label "Education" in cell A14. Notice how, after you type the first letter, AutoComplete suggests the word "Expenses." Would this have happened if you were typing the label in cell D14 instead? Why or why not? Ignore the AutoComplete suggestion in cell A14 and finish typing the label.

12. Use the fill handle to copy the formula from cell F13 to cell F14.

13. Use the Protection command to reactivate document protection, using the password bluesky.

14. Save the workbook as the template SGL Income and Expense Summary Template 3, and then close the workbook.

15. Open the template SGL Income and Expense Summary Template 3, and test it by entering 1 as the test value for each of the income and expense categories for each quarter. Make any revisions necessary to formulas, formats, or cell protection so it works according to your plan.

16. Save the file as an Excel workbook with the test values as SGL Test Values, then print it.

Case Problems

1. Tracking Ticket Sales for the Brookstone Dance Group Robin Yeh is the ticket sales coordinator for the Brookstone Dance Group, a community dance company. Brookstone sells five types of tickets: season tickets, reserved seating, general admission, student tickets, and senior citizen tickets.

Robin needs to track sales of each ticket type. After doing the initial planning for an Excel worksheet to track ticket sales, she asks you to create the worksheet.

Study Robin's worksheet plan in Figure 2-37 and her worksheet sketch in Figure 2-38, then build, test, and document a template Robin can use to enter ticket sales data.

Figure 2-37 ◀

Worksheet Plan for Brookstone Dance Group

Goal:
To create a worksheet to track monthly ticket sales.

What results do I want to see?
Total ticket sales for each month.
Total annual sales for each of the five ticket types.
Total annual sales for all ticket types.

What information do I need?
The monthly sales for each type of ticket

What calculations will I perform?
Total ticket sales = season tickets + reserved seating + general admission + student tickets + senior citizen tickets

Season ticket annual sales = sum of each month's sales of season tickets
Reserved seating annual sales = sum of each month's sales of reserved seating
General admission annual sales = sum of each month's sales of general admission
Student ticket annual sales = sum of each month's sales of student tickets
Senior citizen ticket annual sales = sum of each month's sales of senior citizen tickets

Figure 2-38 ◀

Brookstone Dance Group Ticket Sales

	April	May	June	July	YTD
Season tickets	:	:	:	:	{season ticket annual sales formula}
Reserved seating	:	:	:	:	{reserved seating annual sales formula}
General admission	:	:	:	:	{general admission annual sales formula}
Student tickets	:	:	:	:	{student ticket annual sales formula}
Senior citizen tickets	:	:	:	:	{senior citizen ticket annual sales formula}
Total ticket sales	{total ticket sales formula}	{total ticket sales formula}	{total ticket sales formula}	{total ticket sales formula}	{total ticket sales formula}

1. Start Excel and make sure a blank worksheet is on your screen. If the Excel window is open and you do not have a blank worksheet, click the New Workbook button ☐.
2. Enter the labels for the title for the first column as shown in Figure 2-38. Does AutoComplete automatically suggest any labels? Why or why not?
3. Use AutoFill to fill in month names automatically.
4. Enter YTD in the cell to the right of the cell containing the label July.
5. Create formulas to calculate total ticket sales and year-to-date sales for each ticket type.
6. Use the AutoFormat Classic 3 style for the worksheet's format. Adjust column widths as necessary.
7. Add a note to cell A1 that includes your name, the date, and a short description of the template.
8. Rename Sheet1 "Ticket Sales."
9. Test the template using 1000 as the test value, then make any changes necessary for the template to work correctly.
10. Clear the test values from the cells.
11. Unprotect the cells where Robin will enter data; then protect the document using bluesky as the password.

12. Save the workbook as a template named Brookstone Dance Group Template in the Cases folder for Tutorial 2.

13. Print and close the template.

14. Open the template Brookstone Dance Group Template and enter some realistic test data for April, May, and June. You can make up this data, keeping in mind that Brookstone typically sells about 500 tickets per month.

15. Print the worksheet with the realistic test data, then close the workbook without saving it.

2. Tracking Customer Activity at Brownie's Sandwich Shop Sherri McWilliams is the assistant manager of Brownie's Sandwich Shop. She is responsible for scheduling waitresses and cooks. To plan an effecient schedule, Sherri wants to know the busiest days of the week and the busiest hours of the day. She started to create a worksheet to help track customer activity in the shop, and she asked if you could help her complete the worksheet. Open the workbook Brownie (in the Cases folder for Tutorial 2) and do the following.

1. Save the workbook as Brownie's Sandwich Shop (in the Cases folder for Tutorial 2) so you will not modify the original file if you want to do this case again.

2. Use AutoFill to complete the column titles for days of the week.

3. Use AutoFill to complete the labels showing open hours from 11:00 AM to 10:00 PM.

4. Use the AutoSum button to create a formula to calculate the total number of customers in cell B15.

5. Copy the formula in cell B15 to cells C15 through H15.

6. Enter the column title "Hourly" in cell I1, and the title "Average" in cell I2. Sherri plans to use column I to display the average number of customers for each one-hour time period.

7. Enter the formula =AVERAGE(B3:H3) in cell I3, then copy it to cells I4 through I15.

8. Type the worksheet title, "Sandwich Shop Activity," in cell A1.

9. Add a text note to cell A1 that includes your name, the date, and a brief description of the worksheet.

10. Rename Sheet1 "Customer Activity."

11. Save the workbook as Brownie's Sandwich Shop.

12. Print the worksheet.

13. On your printout, circle the busiest day of the week and the hour of the day with the highest customer traffic.

3. Reporting Activity for Magazines Unlimited Norm McGruder was just hired as a fulfillment driver for Magazines Unlimited. He is responsible for stocking magazines in supermarkets and bookstores in his territory. Each week Norm goes to each store in his territory, removes outdated magazines, and delivers current issues.

Plan, build, test, and document a template that Norm can use to track the number of magazines he removes from and replaces at the Safeway supermarket during one week. Although Norm typically handles 100 to 150 different magazine titles at the Safeway store, for this Case Problem, create the template for only 11 of them: *Entertainment Weekly, Auto News, Harpers, Time, Entertainment News, Newsweek, Ebony, PC Week, The New Republic, The New Yorker,* and *Vogue.*

Your worksheet should contain:

- a column that lists the magazine names

- a column that shows the number of magazines delivered

- a column that shows the number of magazines removed

- a column that holds a formula to calculate the number of magazines sold by subtracting the number of magazines removed from the number of magazines delivered

- a cell that displays the total number of magazines delivered

- a cell that displays the total number of magazines removed

- a cell that shows the total number of magazines sold during the week

To complete this Case Problem:

1. Create a worksheet plan similar to the one in Figure 2-4 at the beginning of the tutorial. Describe the worksheet goal, list results you want to see, list input information you need, and describe calculations that must be performed.
2. Draw a worksheet sketch showing the layout for the template.
3. Build the worksheet by entering the title, the row labels, the column titles, and the formulas. When possible, use AutoComplete to minimize the typing necessary to enter the labels.
4. Format the worksheet using a format of your choice from the AutoFormat list.
5. Test the worksheet using 1 as the test value. Make any changes necessary for the worksheet to work according to plan.
6. Add a text note to cell A1 to document the worksheet.
7. Rename Sheet1 with an appropriate name.
8. Clear the test values from the worksheet.
9. Unprotect the cells where you will enter the number of magazines delivered and removed; then protect the entire document using the password bluesky.
10. Save the workbook as a template called Magazines Unlimited Template in the Cases folder for Tutorial 2 on your student disk.
11. Print the template, then enter some realistic test data and print it again. Close the template without saving it as a workbook and without saving the realistic data.
12. Submit your worksheet plan, your worksheet sketch, the printout of the template, and the printout with the realistic test data.

4. Tracking Monthly Invoices for Your Freelance Consulting Business You are a freelance computer consultant, specializing in assisting small business owners in purchasing, installing and maintaining software and hardware to suit their special needs. To ensure prompt payment from your customers, you need to keep careful track of your monthly invoices. You charge an hourly rate for your services. In addition, you bill your clients for long distance phone and Internet connection charges.

Plan and build a worksheet template that tracks your total monthly invoices. Invent your own data. Include data for 12 invoices, divided among four different clients.

1 Think about how you want to organize your data. Your worksheet should include columns for: Invoice Number, Date, Client, Services, Expenses, Total Amount Due. Be sure to assign each invoice a unique number.
2 Sketch a sample worksheet on a piece of paper, indicating how your labels and formulas should be arranged. The worksheet design should make it easy for you to add rows to accommodate more invoices.
3 Build the worksheet by entering a title, column titles, labels and formulas. Whenever possible use AutoComplete to minimize the typing necessary to enter the labels.
4 Test the template using 1 as the test value. Make any changes necessary for the worksheet to work according to your plan.
5 Test the template again using realistic values. Make any changes necessary for the worksheet to work according to your plan.
6 Add a text note to cell A1 to document the worksheet.
7 Format the worksheet using a format of your choice from the AutoFormat list.
8 Rename Sheet1 with an appropriate name.
9 Save the workbook as a template called 1996 Invoices in the Case folder for Tutorial 2.
10 Preview and print the worksheet with the realistic data, then clear the data from the worksheet and print it again.
11 Save the template again (do not save it as a workbook).
12 Submit your plan, your worksheet sketch, and your printouts.

Formatting and Printing

Producing a Projected Sales Impact Report

Pronto Authentic Recipe Salsa Company

CASE

Anne Castelar owns the Pronto Authentic Recipe Salsa Company, a successful business located in the heart of Tex-Mex country. She is working on a plan to add a new product, Salsa de Chile Guero Medium, to Pronto's gourmet salsa line.

Anne wants to take out a bank loan to purchase additional food processing equipment to handle the production increase the new salsa requires. She has an appointment with her bank loan officer at 2:00 this afternoon. To prepare for the meeting, Anne creates a worksheet to show the projected sales of the new salsa and the expected effect on profits.

Although the numbers and formulas are in place on the worksheet, Anne has no time to format the worksheet for the best impact. She planned to do that now, but an unexpected problem with today's produce shipment requires her to leave the office for a few hours. Anne asks you, her office manager, to complete the worksheet. She shows you a printout of the unformatted worksheet and explains that she wants the finished worksheet to look very professional—like those you see in business magazines. She also asks you to make sure that the worksheet emphasizes the profits expected from sales of the new salsa.

SESSION 3.1

In this session you will learn how to make your worksheets easier to understand through various formatting techniques. You will change font styles, and font sizes, and change the alignment of data within cells and across columns. You will also format values using currency formats, number formats, and percentage formats. Finally, you will add borders, colors, and patterns for emphasis. As you perform all these tasks, you'll find the Format Painter button an extremely useful tool.

Opening the Workbook

After Anne leaves, you develop the worksheet plan in Figure 3-1 and the worksheet format plan in Figure 3-2.

Figure 3-1
Worksheet plan

> Worksheet Plan for Projected Sales Report
>
> My Goal:
> To format the worksheet so it produces a professional-looking printout.
>
> What results do I want to see?
> The profits that are expected from sales of the new salsa product.
>
> What information do I need?
> The unformatted worksheet.
>
> What calculations will I perform?
> None. Formulas have already been entered.

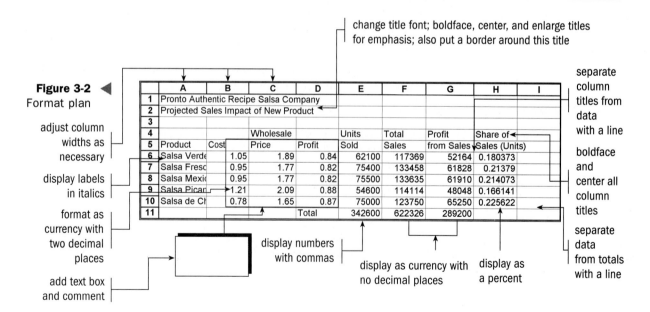

Figure 3-2
Format plan

change title font; boldface, center, and enlarge titles for emphasis; also put a border around this title

separate column titles from data with a line

boldface and center all column titles

separate data from totals with a line

adjust column widths as necessary

display labels in italics

format as currency with two decimal places

add text box and comment

display numbers with commas

display as currency with no decimal places

display as a percent

	A	B	C	D	E	F	G	H	I
1	Pronto Authentic Recipe Salsa Company								
2	Projected Sales Impact of New Product								
3									
4			Wholesale		Units	Total	Profit	Share of	
5	Product	Cost	Price	Profit	Sold	Sales	from Sales	Sales (Units)	
6	Salsa Verde	1.05	1.89	0.84	62100	117369	52164	0.180373	
7	Salsa Fresc	0.95	1.77	0.82	75400	133458	61828	0.21379	
8	Salsa Mexic	0.95	1.77	0.82	75500	133635	61910	0.214073	
9	Salsa Picar	1.21	2.09	0.88	54600	114114	48048	0.166141	
10	Salsa de Ch	0.78	1.65	0.87	75000	123750	65250	0.225622	
11				Total	342600	622326	289200		

Now you are ready to start Excel and open the workbook. To begin, you need to start Excel.

To start Excel and organize your desktop:

1. Start Excel following your usual procedure.

2. Make sure your Student Disk is in the disk drive.

3. Make sure the Microsoft Excel and Book1 windows are maximized.

Anne stored the workbook as Pronto. Now you need to open this file.

To open the Pronto workbook:

1. Click the **Open** button  to display the Open dialog box.

2. Open the Pronto workbook in the Tutorial.03 folder on your Student Disk. See Figure 3-3.

Figure 3-3 ◀
Pronto Salsa
Company
workbook

workbook title

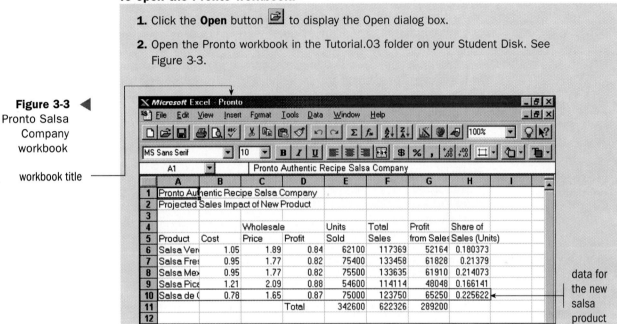

data for
the new
salsa
product

Before you begin to change the workbook, let's save it using the long filename Pronto Salsa Company so you can work on a copy of the workbook. The original workbook, Pronto Salsa Company, remains unchanged in case you want to do this tutorial again.

To save the workbook as Pronto Salsa Company:

1. Click **File**, then click **Save As** to display the Save As dialog box.

2. Change the filename to **Pronto Salsa Company**.

3. Click the **Save** button to save the workbook under the new filename. You should see the new filename, **Pronto Salsa Company**, in the title bar.

TROUBLE? If you see the message "Replace existing file?" click the Yes button to replace the old version of Pronto Salsa Company with your new version.

Studying the worksheet, you notice that the salsa names do not fit in column A. It is easy to widen column A, but if you do, some of the worksheet will scroll off the screen. Other formatting tasks are easier if you can see the entire worksheet, so you decide to do these tasks first.

Formatting Worksheet Data

Formatting is the process of changing the appearance of the data in worksheet cells. Formatting can make your worksheets easier to understand and draw attention to important points.

Formatting changes only the appearance of the worksheet; it does not change the text or numbers stored in the cells. For example, if you format the number .123653 using a percentage format that displays only one decimal place, the number appears on the worksheet as 12.4%; however, the original number .123653 remains stored in the cell.

When you enter data in cells, Excel applies an automatic format, referred to as the General format. The **General format** aligns numbers at the right side of the cell and displays them without trailing zeros to the right of the decimal point. You can change the General format by using AutoFormat, the Format menu, the Shortcut menu, or toolbar buttons.

AutoFormat applies a predefined format to your entire workbook. AutoFormat is easy to use, but its predefined format might not suit every worksheet. If you decide to customize a workbook's format, you can use Excel's extensive array of formatting options. When you select your own formats, you can format an individual cell or a range of cells.

There are many ways to access Excel's formatting options. The Format menu provides access to all formatting commands. See Figure 3-4.

Figure 3-4 ◀
Format menu

The Shortcut menu provides quick access to the Format dialog box. See Figure 3-5. To display the Shortcut menu, make sure the pointer is on one of the cells in the range you have highlighted to format, then click the right mouse button.

Figure 3-5 ◀
Shortcut menu

click here to open
the Format Cells
dialog box

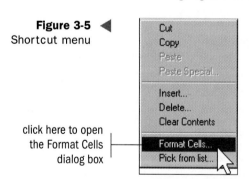

The formatting toolbar contains formatting buttons, including the style and alignment buttons, and the Font Style and Font Size boxes. See Figure 3-6.

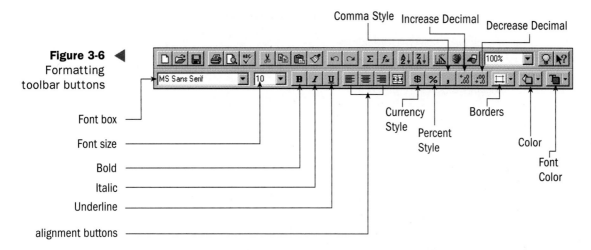

Figure 3-6
Formatting
toolbar buttons

Font box

Font size

Bold

Italic

Underline

alignment buttons

Most experienced Excel users develop a preference for which menu or buttons they use to access Excel's formatting options; however, most beginners find it easy to remember that all formatting options are available from the Format menu.

You decide to use the Bold button to change some titles on the worksheet to boldface.

Changing the Font, Font Style, and Font Size

A **font** is a set of letters, numbers, punctuation marks, and symbols with a specific size and design. Figure 3-7 shows some examples. A font can have one or more of the following **font styles**: regular, italic, bold, and bold italic.

Figure 3-7
Selected fonts

Font	Regular Style	Italic Style	Bold Style	Bold Italic Style
Times	AaBbCc	AaBbCc	**AaBbCc**	**AaBbCc**
Courier	AaBbCc	AaBbCc	**AaBbCc**	**AaBbCc**
Garamond	AaBbCc	AaBbCc	**AaBbCc**	**AaBbCc**
Helvetica Condensed	AaBbCc	AaBbCc	**AaBbCc**	**AaBbCc**

Most fonts are available in many sizes, and you can also select font effects, such as strikeout, underline, and color. The toolbar provides tools for boldface, italics, underline, changing font style, and increasing or decreasing font size. To access other font effects, you can open the Cells dialog box from the Format menu.

You begin by formatting the word "Total" in cell D11 in boldface letters.

To change the font style for cell D11 to boldface:

1. Click cell **D11**.

2. Click the **Bold** button **B** to set the font style to boldface. See Figure 3-6 for the location of the Bold button.

You also want to display the worksheet titles and the column titles in boldface letters. To do this, first highlight the range you want to format, then click the Bold button to apply the format.

To display the worksheet titles and column titles in boldface:

1. Highlight cells A1 through H5.

2. Click the **Bold** button **B** to apply the bold font style.

3. Click any cell to remove the highlighting.

Next, you decide to display the salsa products' names in italics.

To italicize the row labels:

1. Highlight cells A6 through A10.

2. Click the **Italic** button *I* to apply the italic font style. Figure 3-6 shows the location of the Italic button.

3. Click any cell to remove the highlighting and view the formatting you have done so far. For now, don't worry that the entire labels aren't visible. You will widen the columns later. See Figure 3-8.

Figure 3-8 ◀
Bold and italic
formats applied

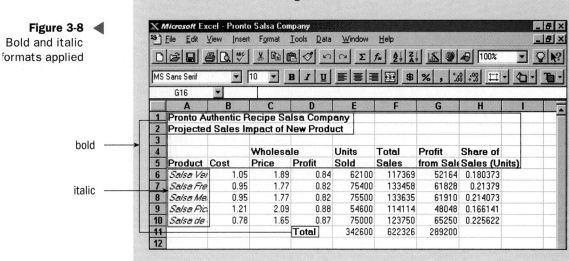

Next, you change the font and size of the worksheet titles for emphasis. You use the Font dialog box (instead of the toolbar) so you can preview your changes. Remember, although the worksheet titles appear to be in columns A through E, they are just spilling over from column A. To format the titles, you need to highlight only cells A1 and A2— the cells where the titles were originally entered.

To change the font and font size of the worksheet titles:

1. Highlight cells A1 through A2.

2. Click **Format**, then click **Cells** to display the Format Cells dialog box.

3. Click the **Font** tab.

4. Use the Font box scroll bar to find the Times New Roman font. Click the **Times New Roman** font to select it.

5. Make sure **Bold** is selected in the Font Style list box.

6. Click **14** in the Size list box. A sample of the font appears in the Preview box. See Figure 3-9.

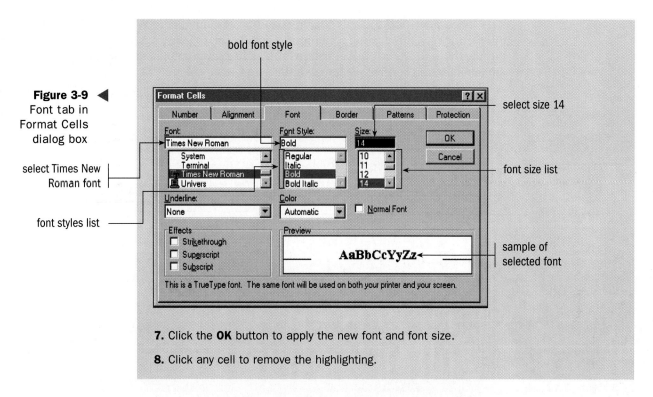

Figure 3-9
Font tab in
Format Cells
dialog box

select Times New
Roman font

font styles list

bold font style

select size 14

font size list

sample of
selected font

7. Click the **OK** button to apply the new font and font size.

8. Click any cell to remove the highlighting.

Times New Roman font is a good choice because it looks like the font on the Pronto salsa jar labels. Your next step is to adjust alignment of column titles.

Aligning Cell Contents

The **alignment** of data in a cell is the position of the data relative to the right and left edges of the cell. Cell contents can be aligned on the left side or right side of the cell, or centered in the cell. When you enter numbers and formulas, Excel automatically aligns them on the cell's right side. Excel automatically aligns text entries on the cell's left side.

Excel's automatic alignment does not always create the most readable worksheet. Figure 3-10 shows a worksheet with the column titles left aligned and the numbers in the columns right aligned.

Figure 3-10
Poorly
formatted
worksheet

column titles
left aligned

numbers
right aligned

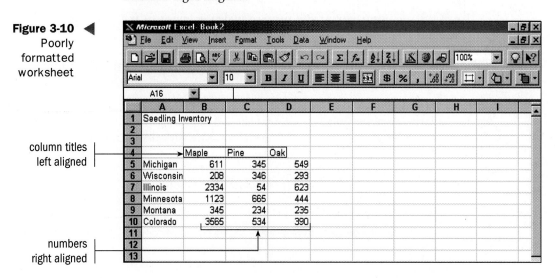

Notice how difficult it is to figure out which numbers go with each column title. Centering or right-aligning column titles would improve the readability of the worksheet in Figure 3-10. As a general rule, you should center column titles, format columns of numbers so the decimal places are in line, and leave columns of text aligned on the left.

The Excel toolbar provides the four alignment tools shown in Figure 3-11. You can access additional alignment options by selecting the Alignment tab in the Format Cells dialog box.

Figure 3-11 ◀
Toolbar
alignment
buttons

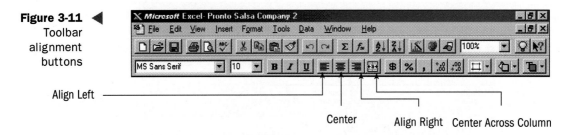

Align Left ————

Center   Align Right   Center Across Column

To center the column titles:

1. Highlight cells A4 through H5.

2. Click the **Center** button 🔳 on the toolbar to center the cell contents.

3. Click any cell to remove the highlighting and view the centered titles. See Figure 3-12.

Figure 3-12 ◀
Worksheet with
centered
column titles

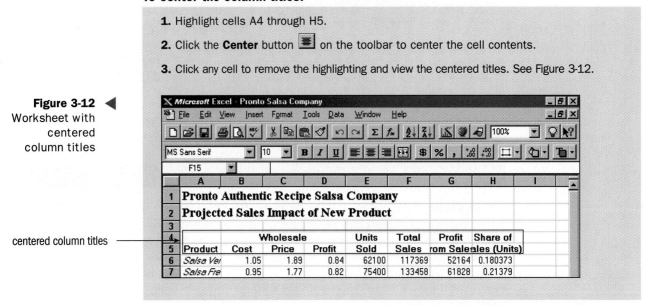

centered column titles ————

Notice that eventually you will need to widen columns G and H to display the entire column titles, but for now you will center the main worksheet titles.

Centering Text Across Columns

Sometimes you might want to center a cell's contents across more than one column. This is particularly useful for centering titles at the top of a worksheet. Now you use the Center Across Columns button to center the worksheet titles in cells A1 and A2 across columns A through H.

To center the worksheet titles across columns A through H:

1. Highlight cells A1 through H2.

2. Click the **Center Across Columns** button 🔳 to center the titles across columns A through H.

3. Click any cell to remove the highlighting.

Looking at your plan, you see that you need to display the cost, price, profit, and total sales figures as currency.

Currency Formats

You have several options when formatting values as currency. You need to decide the number of decimal places you want displayed; whether or not you want see the dollar sign; and how you want negative numbers to look. Keep in mind that if you want the currency symbols and decimal places to line up within a column, you should choose the Accounting format, rather than the Currency format.

In the Pronto Salsa Company worksheet, you want to format the amounts in columns B, C, and D as currency with two decimal places. You also decide to display negative numbers in parentheses.

To format columns B, C, and D as currency:

1. Highlight cells B6 through D10.

2. Click **Format**, then click **Cells** to display the Format Cells dialog box.

3. Click the **Number** tab.

4. Click **Currency** in the Category list. The Currency tab appears, as in Figure 3-13. Notice that a sample of the selected format appears in the center of the dialog box. As you make further selections, the sample automatically changes to reflect your choices.

Figure 3-13 ◀
Selecting a currency format

Number tab
select Currency

default decimal place setting

dollar sign displayed by default

select negative number format

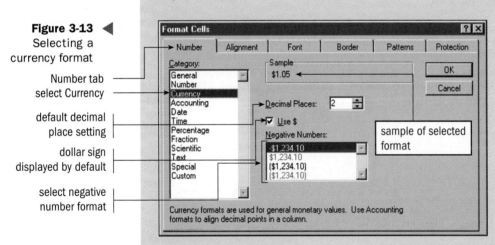

Notice that 2 decimal places is the default setting. The Use $ checkbox is already selected, too, indicating that the dollar sign is displayed by default. That means you only need to select a format for negative numbers.

5. Click the third option (**$1,234.10**) in the Negative Numbers list box.

6. Click the **OK** button to format the selected range.

7. Click any cell to remove the highlighting and view the new formatting. See Figure 3-14.

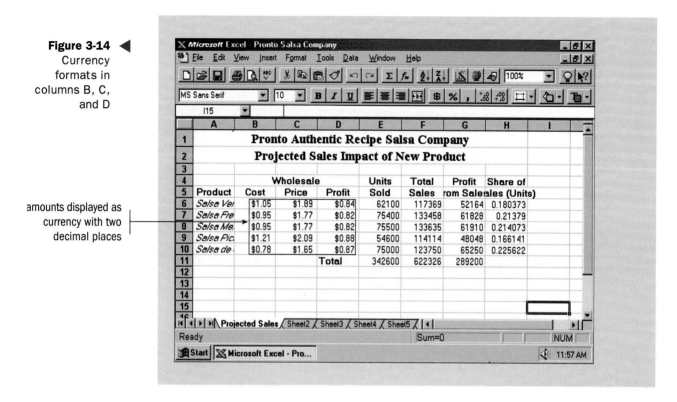

Figure 3-14 ◀
Currency
formats in
columns B, C,
and D

amounts displayed as
currency with two
decimal places

When your worksheet has large dollar amounts, you might want to use a currency format that does not display any decimal places. To do this use the Decrease Decimal button on the Formatting toolbar, or change the decimal place setting in the Cell Format dialog box. Currency values displayed with no decimal places are rounded to the nearest dollar: $15,612.56 becomes $15,613, $16,507.49 becomes $16,507, and so on.

You decide to format the Total Sales column as currency rounded to the nearest dollar.

To format cells F6 through F11 as currency rounded to the nearest dollar:

1. Highlight cells F6 through F11.

2. Click **Format**, then click **Cells** to display the Format Cells dialog box.

3. If necessary, click the **Number** tab.

4. Click **Currency** in the Category box.

5. Click the **Decimal Places** down arrow twice to change the setting to 0. Notice the sample format changes to reflect the new settings.

6. Click the **OK** button to apply the format.

7. Click any cell to remove the highlighting.

After formatting the Total Sales figures in column F, you realize you should have used the same format for the numbers in column G. To save time, you simply copy the formatting from column F to column G.

The Format Painter Button

The Format Painter button lets you copy formats quickly from one cell or range to another. You simply click a cell containing the formats you want to copy, click the Format Painter button, and then drag through the range to which you want to apply the formats.

To copy the format from cell F6:

1. Click cell **F6** because it contains the format you want to copy.

2. Click the **Format Painter** button ⬚. The pointer turns into ⬚.

3. Highlight cells G6 through G11. When you release the mouse button, the cells appear in the proper format.

Now the cells containing cost, price, profit, and total sales data are formatted as currency. Next, you want to apply formats to the numbers in columns E and H so they are easier to read.

Number Formats

Like Currency formats, Excel's Number formats offer many options. You can select Number formats to specify

- the number of decimal places displayed

- whether to display a comma to delimit thousands, millions, and billions

- whether to display negative numbers with a minus sign, parentheses, or red numerals

To access all Excel Number formats, you can use the use the Number tab in the Format Cells dialog box. You can also use the Comma Style button and the Increase and Decrease Decimal buttons on the Formatting toolbar to change some formats.

To format the contents in column E with a comma and no decimal places:

1. Highlight cells E6 through E11.

2. Click **Format**, then click **Cells** to display the Format Cells dialog box.

3. If necessary, click the **Number** tab.

4. Click **Number** in the Category list.

5. Click the **Use Thousand Separator (,)** check box to select it.

6. Change the decimal place setting to 0.

7. Click the third option, **(1,234)**, in the Negative Numbers box, then look at the sample format in the center of the dialog box.

8. Click the **OK** button to apply the format.

9. Click any cell to remove the highlighting and view the format results. See Figure 3-15.

Figure 3-15
Cells formatted
with Number
format

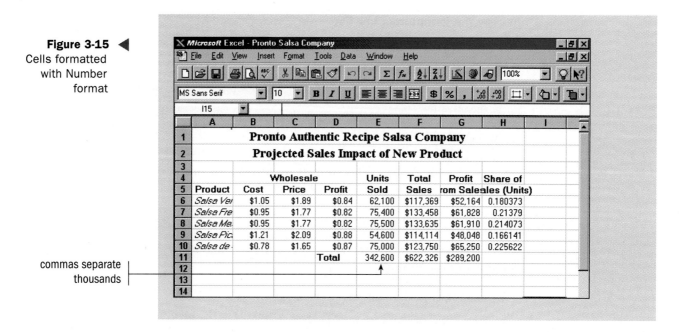

commas separate
thousands

Looking at the numbers in column H, you realize they are difficult to interpret and decide that you do not need to display so many decimal places. What are your options for displaying percentages?

Percentage Formats

When formatting values as percentages, you need to select how many decimal places you want displayed. The percent format with no decimal places displays the number 0.18037 as 18%. The percent format with two decimal places displays the same number as 18.04%.

Your format plan specifies a percentage format with no decimal places for the values in column H. You could use the Number tab to choose this format. But it's faster to use the Percent Style button. (Note that if you want to use the percent style with two decimal places, you select it using the Number tab in the Format Cells dialog box. Or, you can use the Percent Style button, and then click the Increase Decimal button twice to add two decimal places.)

To format the values in column H as a percentage with no decimal places:

1. Highlight cells H6 through H10.

2. Click the **Percent Style** button %.

3. Click any cell to remove the highlighting and view the percentage format.

You check your plan once again and confirm that you selected formats for all worksheet cells. You delayed changing the width of column A because you knew that doing so would cause some columns to scroll off the screen, forcing you to scroll around the worksheet to format all the labels and values. Now that you have finished formatting labels and values, you can change all columns to appropriate widths to best display the information in them.

To do this, you can double-click the right column heading border for each column you want to widen. But because you need to widen several columns, using the Format menu is easier.

To change the column width using the Format menu:

1. Highlight cells A4 through H11.

2. Click **Format**, point to **Column**, then click **AutoFit Selection**.

3. Click any cell to remove the highlighting and view the results of the column width change. See Figure 3-16.

Figure 3-16 ◄
Results of changing column width

column titles fit in cells

column H scrolls out of the window

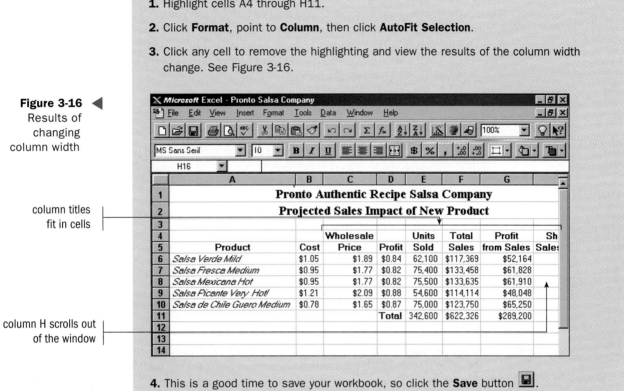

4. This is a good time to save your workbook, so click the **Save** button 🖫.

As you expected, the worksheet is now too wide to fit on the screen. You might need to scroll from side to side to complete additional formatting tasks. Keep in mind that if you want to see part of the worksheet that is not displayed, you can use the scroll bars. If you are highlighting a range, but some of the range is not visible, drag the pointer to the edge of the screen to make the worksheet scroll. You will see how this works next when you add borders.

Adding and Removing Borders

A well-constructed worksheet is clearly divided into zones that visually group related information. Figure 3-17 shows the zones on your worksheet. Lines, called borders, can help to distinguish different zones of the worksheet and add visual interest.

Figure 3-17 ◄
Information zones

title zone

column title zone

data label zone

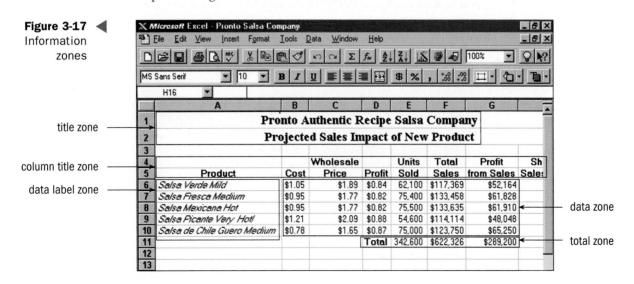

data zone

total zone

You can create lines and borders using either the Borders button or the Border tab in the Format Cells dialog box. You can put a border around a single cell or a group of cells using the Outline option. To create a horizontal line, you create a border at the top or bottom of a cell. To create a vertical line, you create a border on the right or left of a cell.

The Border tab lets you choose from numerous border styles, including different line thicknesses, double lines, dashed lines, and colored lines. With the Border Styles button, your choice of border styles is limited.

REFERENCE window

ADDING A BORDER

- Select the cell to which you want to add the border.
- Click Format, click Cells, then click Border.
- Click the Outline, Top, Bottom, Left, and/or Right border box to indicate where you want the border.
- Select the border style and color.
- Click the OK button.

or

- Select the cell to which you want to add the border.
- Click the Borders list arrow, then click the type of border you want.

To remove a border from a cell or group of cells, you can use the Border dialog box. To remove all borders from a selected range of cells, make sure the Outline, Top, Bottom, Left, and Right border boxes are blank. Excel shades in a border box to show that some cells in the selected range contain a border but others do not. If a border box is gray and you want to remove the border, click the box to remove the gray shading.

REFERENCE window

REMOVING A BORDER

- Select the cell or cells that contain the border you want to remove.
- Click Format, click Cells, then click Border.
- Look for the border box that contains a border or shading, then click this box until it is empty.
- Click the OK button.

You want a thick line under all column titles. To do this, you use the Borders button.

To underline column titles:

1. Highlight cells A5 through H5.

> **TROUBLE?** If cell H5 is not visible on your screen, drag the pointer from cell A5 to G5, then without releasing the mouse button, continue moving the pointer right. The worksheet window scrolls so you can include cell H5 in the highlighted range. If the worksheet scrolls too fast and you highlight I, J, K, L, and M, move the mouse left—without releasing the mouse button—until H5 is the rightmost cell in the highlighted range. If you release the mouse button too soon, use the scroll bars to scroll column A back on the screen, then go back to Step 1.

2. Click the **Borders** button list arrow. The Borders palette appears.

3. Click the thick underline button in the second row. See Figure 3-18.

Figure 3-18 ◀
New border

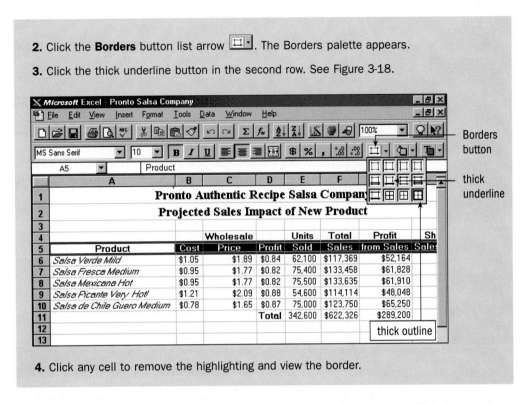

Borders button

thick underline

thick outline

4. Click any cell to remove the highlighting and view the border.

You also want a line to separate the data from the totals in row 11. This time you use the Border tab in the Format Cells dialog box. First you highlights cells A11 through H11, then you select a thick top border from the Border tab. Why would you use a top border here, when you used a bottom border for the column titles? It is good practice not to attach borders to the cells in the data zone because when you copy cells, you also copy cell formats. If you attach borders to the wrong cells, you can end up with borders in every cell, or you can end up erasing borders you wanted when you copy cell contents down a column.

To add a line separating the data and the totals:

1. Highlight cells A11 through H11.

2. Click **Format**, click **Cells**, then click the **Border** tab.

3. Click **Top** to select a top border.

4. Click the thickest line in the Style box.

5. Click the **OK** button to apply the border.

6. Click any cell to remove the highlighting and view the border.

You consult your format sketch and see that you planned a border around the title zone to add a professional touch. Let's add this border now.

To place an outline border around the title zone:

1. Highlight cells A1 through H2.

2. Click the **Borders** button list arrow.

3. Click the thick outline button. See Figure 3-18.

4. Click any cell to remove the highlighting and view the border. See Figure 3-19.

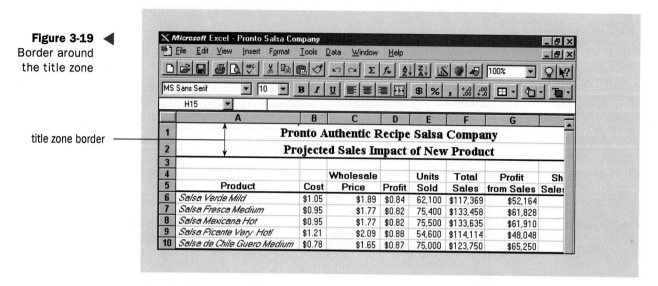

Figure 3-19
Border around
the title zone

title zone border

In addition to a border around the title zone, you want to add color and shading in the title zone.

Using Patterns and Color for Emphasis

Patterns and colors provide visual interest, emphasize worksheet zones, or indicate data-entry areas. Base the use of patterns or colors on the way you intend to use the worksheet. If you print the worksheet in color and distribute a hardcopy of it, or if you plan to use a color projection device to display your worksheet on screen, you can take advantage of Excel's color formatting options. On the other hand, if you do not have a color printer you can use patterns. It is difficult to predict how colors you see on your screen will be translated into gray shades on your printout.

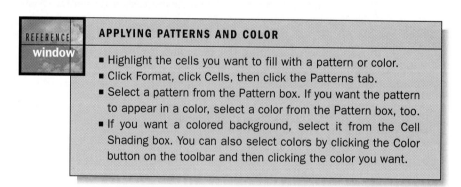

REFERENCE window

APPLYING PATTERNS AND COLOR

- Highlight the cells you want to fill with a pattern or color.
- Click Format, click Cells, then click the Patterns tab.
- Select a pattern from the Pattern box. If you want the pattern to appear in a color, select a color from the Pattern box, too.
- If you want a colored background, select it from the Cell Shading box. You can also select colors by clicking the Color button on the toolbar and then clicking the color you want.

You want your worksheet to look good when you print it in black and white on the office laser printer, but you also want it to look good on the screen when you show it to Anne. You decide on a yellow background with a light dot pattern because it matches the color on Pronto Salsa labels and looks fairly good on the screen and the printout. You apply this format to the title zone using the Patterns tab.

To apply a pattern and color to the title zone:

1. Highlight cells A1 through H2.

2. Click **Format**, click **Cells**, then click the **Patterns** tab.

3. Click the **Pattern** box list arrow to display the patterns palette.

To move the Drawing toolbar to the bottom of the worksheet window:

1. Position the pointer on the title bar of the Drawing toolbar.

2. Drag the toolbar to the bottom of the screen. The toolbar's outline changes to the long, narrow rectangle shown Figure 3-22.

Figure 3-22 ◄
Positioning the Drawing toolbar

position the pointer on the title bar of the Drawing toolbar

drag outline here until it changes to a long rectangle

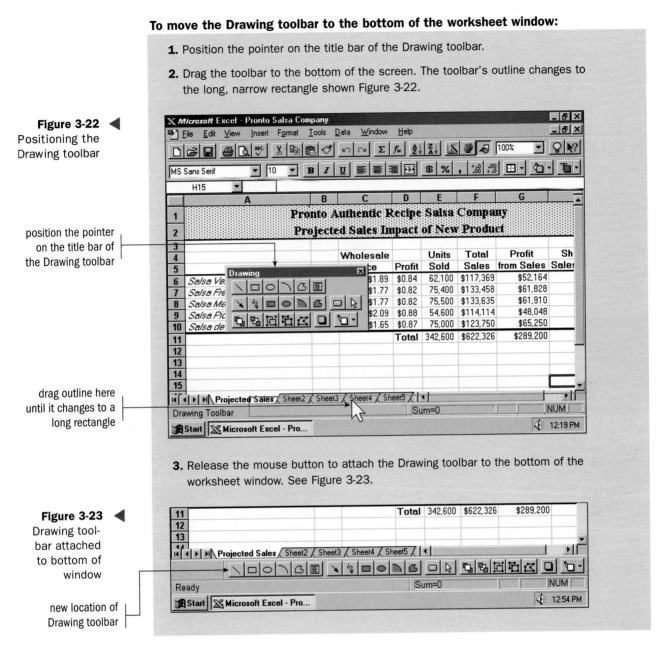

3. Release the mouse button to attach the Drawing toolbar to the bottom of the worksheet window. See Figure 3-23.

Figure 3-23 ◄
Drawing toolbar attached to bottom of window

new location of Drawing toolbar

Now that the Drawing toolbar is where you want it, you proceed with your plan to add a comment to the worksheet.

Adding Comments to the Worksheet

Excel's text box feature lets you display a comment on a worksheet. Unlike the cell note (such as the one in cell A1), which only appears when you place the pointer over the cell it is attached to, a comment is like an electronic Post-it note that you paste inside a rectangular text box on the worksheet. You do not need to position the pointer over a cell to see a comment as you do to see a text note.

To add a comment to your worksheet, you create a text box using the Text Box tool. Then you simply type the text in the box.

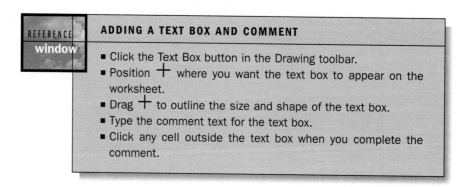

REFERENCE window

ADDING A TEXT BOX AND COMMENT

- Click the Text Box button in the Drawing toolbar.
- Position ✛ where you want the text box to appear on the worksheet.
- Drag ✛ to outline the size and shape of the text box.
- Type the comment text for the text box.
- Click any cell outside the text box when you complete the comment.

A text box is one example of an Excel object. Excel objects include shapes, arrows, and text boxes. If you need to move, modify, or delete an object, you select it first. To select an object, you move the pointer over the object until the pointer changes to ⬉, then click. Small square handles indicate that the object is selected. Use these handles to adjust an object's size, change its location, or delete it.

You want to draw attention to the new salsa product's low price and high profit margin. To do this, you plan to add a text box that contains a comment about expected profits. Refer to Figure 3-2 to see where you planned to place the text box.

To add a comment in a text box:

1. Click the **Text Box** button 🔲 on the Drawing toolbar. The pointer changes to ✛.

2. Scroll the worksheet so you can see rows 11 through 19. Then position the pointer in cell A13 to mark the upper-left corner of the text box.

3. Click and drag ✛ to cell C18, then release the mouse button to mark the lower-right corner of the text box. See Figure 3-24.

Figure 3-24 ◀
Creating a text box

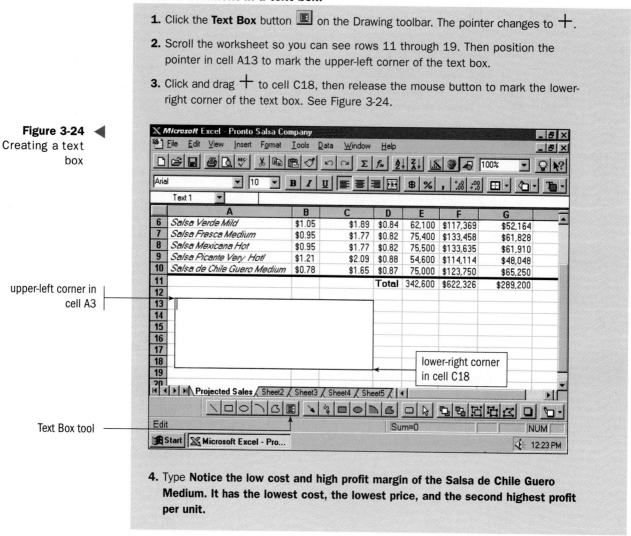

upper-left corner in cell A3

lower-right corner in cell C18

Text Box tool

4. Type **Notice the low cost and high profit margin of the Salsa de Chile Guero Medium. It has the lowest cost, the lowest price, and the second highest profit per unit.**

You want to use a different font style to emphasize the name of the new salsa product in the text box.

To italicize the name of the new salsa product:

1. Position I in the text box just before the word "Salsa."

2. Drag I to the end of the word **Medium**, then release the mouse button. See Figure 3-25.

Figure 3-25 ◄
Italicizing text
in the text box

Italic tool

highlight the name
of the new salsa
product

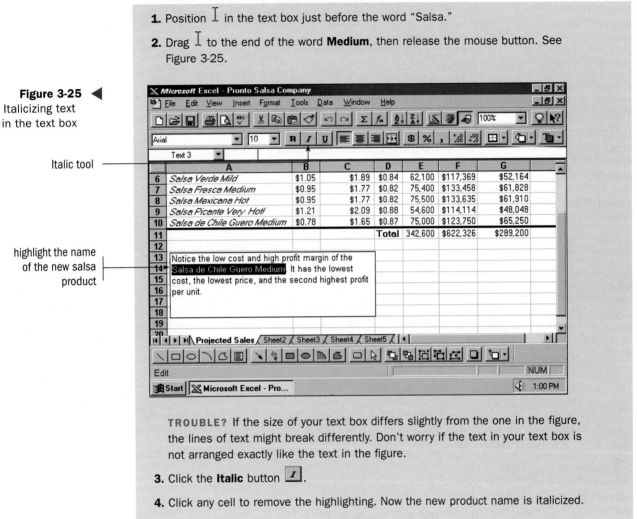

TROUBLE? If the size of your text box differs slightly from the one in the figure, the lines of text might break differently. Don't worry if the text in your text box is not arranged exactly like the text in the figure.

3. Click the **Italic** button I.

4. Click any cell to remove the highlighting. Now the new product name is italicized.

You decide to change the text box size so there is no empty space at the bottom.

To change the text box size:

1. Click the **text box** to select it and display the thick border with handles.

2. Position the pointer on the center handle at the bottom of the box. The pointer changes to $\updownarrow$. See Figure 3-26.

Figure 3-26 ◄
Changing text
box size

when text box is
selected, a thick
border with
handles appears

position pointer on
handle and drag up

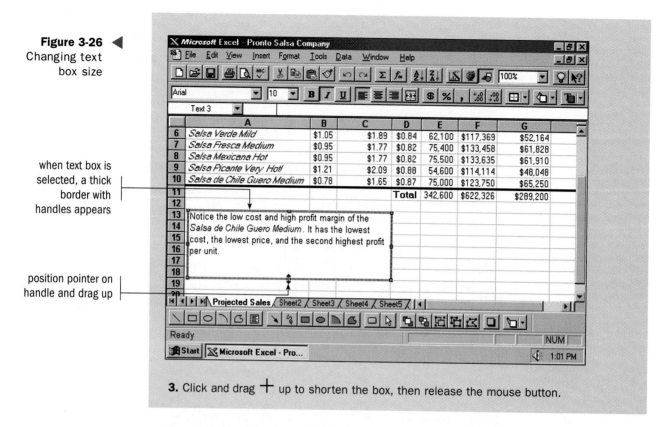

3. Click and drag ✛ up to shorten the box, then release the mouse button.

You want to change the text box a bit more. First you add a 3-D drop shadow.

To add a drop shadow:

1. Make sure the text box is still selected. (Look for the thick border and handles.)

2. Click the **Drop Shadow** button 🔲 in the Drawing toolbar.

Next you want to make the text border thicker.

To modify the text box border:

1. Make sure the text box is still selected.

2. Click **Format**, click **Object** to display the Format Object dialog box, then click the **Patterns** tab.

3. Click the **Weight** box list arrow to display the border thicknesses.

4. Click the third border weight in the list, as shown in Figure 3-27. Notice that the Shadow box contains a check. That's because you used the Drop Shadow button to add a shadow.

Figure 3-27 ◀
Selecting
border
weight

shadow checkbox
should already be
selected

select third
weight in list

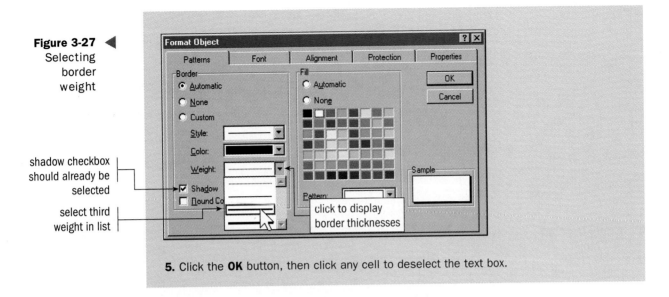

5. Click the **OK** button, then click any cell to deselect the text box.

Adding an Arrow

You decide to add an arrow pointing from the text box to the row with information on the new salsa.

To add an arrow:

1. Click the **Arrow** button ◣ the Drawing toolbar. The pointer changes to $+$.

2. Position the pointer on the top edge of the text box in cell B12. Drag the pointer to cell **B10**, then release the mouse button. See Figure 3-28.

Figure 3-28 ◀
Creating an
arrow

position pointer here,
then drag to cell B10

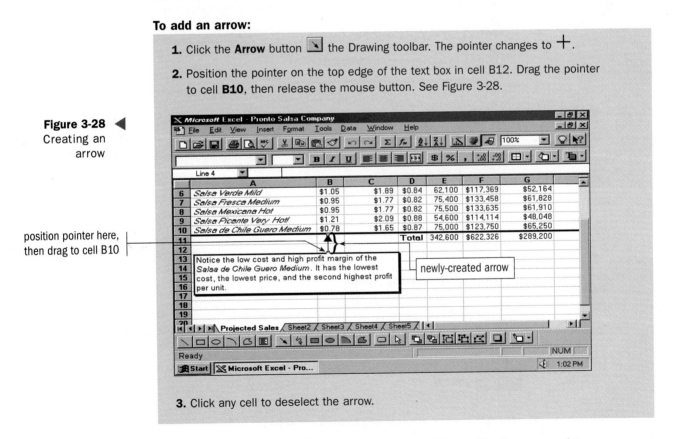

3. Click any cell to deselect the arrow.

Like a text box, an arrow is an Excel object. To modify the arrow object, you must select it. When you do so, two small square handles appear on it. You can reposition either end of the arrow by dragging one of the handles.

You want the arrow to point to cell D10 instead of B10. Let's see how to reposition the arrow.

To reposition the arrow:

1. Move the pointer over the arrow object. The pointer changes to ⬉.

2. Click the mouse button to select the arrow. Handles appear at each end of the arrow.

3. Move the pointer to the top handle on the arrowhead until the pointer changes to ✛.

4. Drag ✛ to cell **D10**, then release the mouse button.

5. Click any cell to deselect the arrow object. See Figure 3-29.

Figure 3-29 ◄
Moving
the arrow

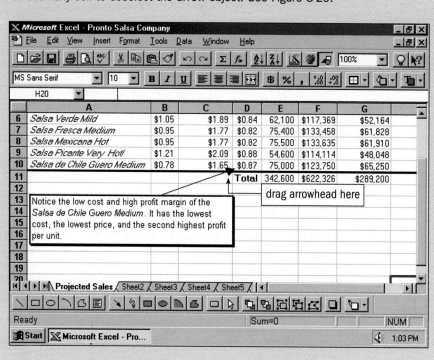

Now that the text box is finished, you can remove the Drawing toolbar from the worksheet.

To remove the Drawing toolbar:

1. Click the **Drawing** button 🔲 on the Standard toolbar.

2. This is a good time to save your workbook, so click the **Save** button 🔲

Quick Check

1. Describe how to activate the Drawing toolbar.

2. Describe how to remove the Drawing toolbar.

3. Describe how to activate and remove any other toolbar.

4. What is the difference between a text box and a cell note?

5. Give three examples of Excel objects.

6. To move, modify or delete an object, you must _____ it first.

SESSION

3.3

In this session you learn how to improve the appearance of your printed worksheet using the Print Preview window, display formulas in the worksheet, and use a macro (also called a Visual Basic module).

Print Preview

The text box and arrow effectively call attention to the profits expected from the new salsa product. Now you are ready to print the worksheet.

Before you print a worksheet, you can use Excel's print preview window to see how it will look when printed. The Print Preview window shows you margins, page breaks, headers, and footers that are not always visible on the screen.

To preview the worksheet before you print it:

1. Click the **Print Preview** button ⬚. After a moment Excel displays the first worksheet page in the Print Preview window. See Figure 3-30.

Figure 3-30 ◄
Print preview

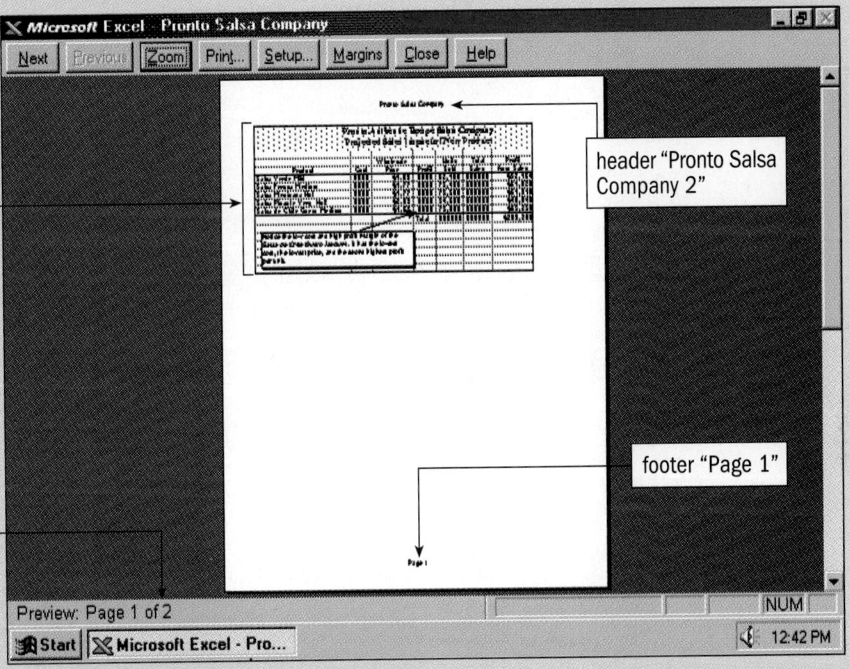

worksheet

header "Pronto Salsa Company 2"

footer "Page 1"

number of pages required for printout

2. Click the **Next** button to preview the second worksheet page. Only one column appears on this page.

3. Click the **Previous** button to preview the first page again.

When Excel displays a full page on the print preview screen, you might have difficulty seeing the text of the worksheet because it is so small. If you want to read the text, you can use the Zoom button.

To display an enlarged section of the print preview:

1. Click the **Zoom** button to display an enlarged section of the print preview.

2. Click the **Zoom** button again to return to the full-page view.

The print preview screen contains several other buttons. The Print button lets you access the Print dialog box directly from the preview screen. The Setup button lets you change the page layout by adjusting margins, creating headers and footers, adding page numbers, changing paper size, or centering the worksheet on the page. The Margins button lets you adjust the margins and immediately see the result. The Close button returns you to the worksheet window.

Looking at the print preview, you see that the worksheet is too wide to fit on a single page. You realize that if you print the worksheet sideways, it fits on a single sheet of paper.

Portrait and Landscape Orientations

Excel provides two print orientations, portrait and landscape. **Portrait** orientation prints the worksheet with the paper positioned so it is taller than it is wide. **Landscape** orientation prints the worksheet with the paper positioned so it is wider than it is tall. Because many worksheets are wider than they are tall, landscape orientation is used frequently.

You can specify print orientation using the Page Setup command on the File menu or using the Setup button on the print preview screen. Let's use the landscape orientation for your worksheet.

To change the print orientation to landscape:

1. Click the **Setup** button to display the Page Setup dialog box. If necessary, click the Page tab.

2. Click **Landscape** in the Orientation options. The Landscape icon—the sheet of paper with the large "A" on it—shows that the page is wider than it is tall. See Figure 3-31.

Figure 3-31 ◄
Selecting landscape orientation

Landscape icon

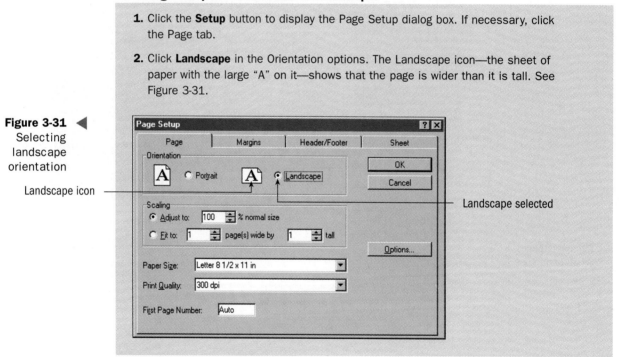

Landscape selected

While the Page Setup dialog box is open, let's use the Header/Footer tab to document the worksheet.

Headers and Footers

A **header** is text printed in the top margin of every worksheet page. A **footer** is text printed in the bottom margin of every worksheet page. Headers and footers are not displayed in the worksheet window. To see them, you must preview or print a worksheet.

A header or footer provides basic documentation about your worksheet, such as the name of the person who created the worksheet, the date it was created, and its filename. Excel automatically creates a centered header with the worksheet filename and a centered footer with the page number, unless you specify otherwise. Look back at Figure 3-30 to see the headers and footers in the print preview window.

Excel uses formatting codes in headers and footers. **Formatting codes** produce dates, times, and filenames that you might want a header or footer to include. You can type these codes, or you can click a formatting code button to insert the code. Figure 3-32 shows the formatting codes and the tools for inserting them.

Figure 3-32 ◀
Header
and footer
formatting

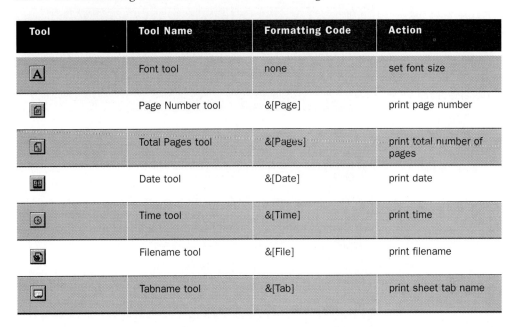

Tool	Tool Name	Formatting Code	Action
A	Font tool	none	set font size
	Page Number tool	&[Page]	print page number
	Total Pages tool	&[Pages]	print total number of pages
	Date tool	&[Date]	print date
	Time tool	&[Time]	print time
	Filename tool	&[File]	print filename
	Tabname tool	&[Tab]	print sheet tab name

You want to change the header and footer that Excel added automatically.

To change the worksheet header:

1. Make sure the Page Setup dialog box is still open, then click the **Header/Footer** tab.

2. Click the **Custom Header** button to display the Header dialog box.

3. Double-click **&[File]** in the Center Section box to highlight it. See Figure 3-33.

Figure 3-33 ◀
Deleting a
header

highlight &[File] ———

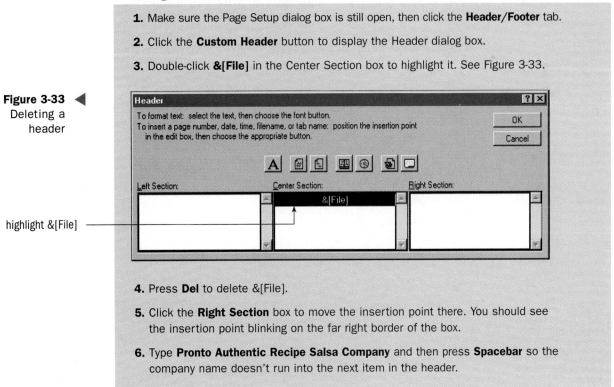

4. Press **Del** to delete &[File].

5. Click the **Right Section** box to move the insertion point there. You should see the insertion point blinking on the far right border of the box.

6. Type **Pronto Authentic Recipe Salsa Company** and then press **Spacebar** so the company name doesn't run into the next item in the header.

7. Click the **Date** button 🔳 to add &[Date] to the header, then press **Spacebar**.

8. Click the **Filename** button 🔳 to add &[File] to the header. See Figure 3-34.

Figure 3-34 ◄
Adding a right-
justified header.

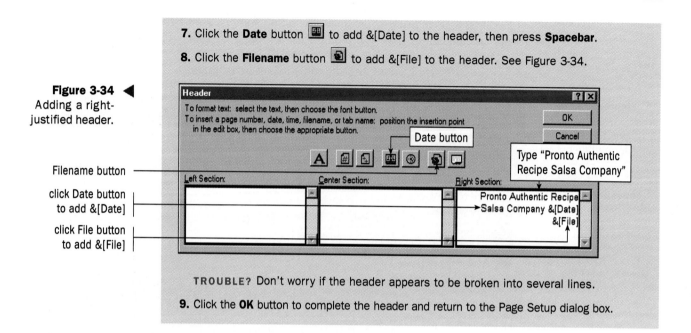

Filename button

click Date button
to add &[Date]

click File button
to add &[File]

TROUBLE? Don't worry if the header appears to be broken into several lines.

9. Click the **OK** button to complete the header and return to the Page Setup dialog box.

Centering the Printout and Removing Cell Gridlines and Row/Column Headings

Worksheet printouts generally look more professional without gridlines and row/column headings. The row/column headings—the letters A, B, C, and so forth that identify the columns—are useful when you design and create the worksheet but are distracting on the printout. Worksheets also look better centered on the printed page. Let's make those changes now.

To center the printout and remove the row/column headings and gridlines:

1. Make sure the Page Setup dialog box is still open.

2. Click the **Margins** tab.

3. If the Horizontally box does not contain a check, click the Horizontally box to place a check in it.

4. If the Vertically box does not contain a check, click the Vertically box to place a check in it.

5. Click the **Sheet** tab.

6. If the Gridlines box contains a check, click the **Gridlines** box to remove the check.

7. Make sure the Row & Column Headings box is empty.

8. Click the **OK** button to complete the Page Setup changes and display a print preview showing the effect of changes you made. See Figure 3-35.

Figure 3-35 ◄
Previewing
printed
worksheet

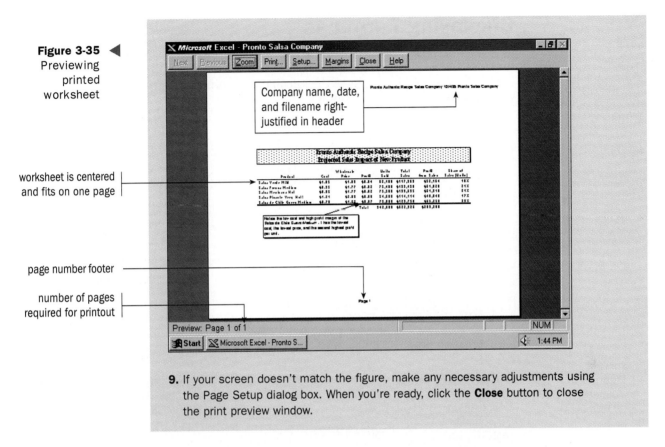

Company name, date,
and filename right-
justified in header

worksheet is centered
and fits on one page

page number footer

number of pages
required for printout

9. If your screen doesn't match the figure, make any necessary adjustments using the Page Setup dialog box. When you're ready, click the **Close** button to close the print preview window.

The worksheet is ready to print, but you always save your work before printing.

To save your page setup settings and print the worksheet:

1. Click the **Save** button 🖫.

2. Click the **Print** button 🖨.

TROUBLE? If you see a message that indicates you have a printer problem, click the Cancel button to cancel the printout. Check your printer to make sure it is turned on and is on line; also make sure it has paper. Then go back and try Step 2 again. If you have no printer available, click the Cancel button.

Figure 3-36 ◄
Your printed
worksheet

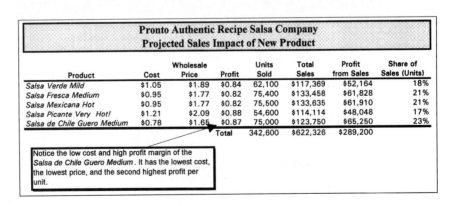

		Wholesale		Units	Total	Profit	Share of
Product	Cost	Price	Profit	Sold	Sales	from Sales	Sales (Units)
Salsa Verde Mild	$1.05	$1.89	$0.84	62,100	$117,369	$52,164	18%
Salsa Fresca Medium	$0.95	$1.77	$0.82	75,400	$133,458	$61,828	21%
Salsa Mexicana Hot	$0.95	$1.77	$0.82	75,500	$133,635	$61,910	21%
Salsa Picante Very Hot!	$1.21	$2.09	$0.88	54,600	$114,114	$48,048	17%
Salsa de Chile Guero Medium	$0.78	$1.65	$0.87	75,000	$123,750	$65,250	23%
			Total	342,600	$622,326	$289,200	

Pronto Authentic Recipe Salsa Company
Projected Sales Impact of New Product

Notice the low cost and high profit margin of the
Salsa de Chile Guero Medium. It has the lowest cost,
the lowest price, and the second highest profit per
unit.

You have a few minutes before your boss returns, so you decide to add some documentation for the worksheet.

Displaying Formulas

You can document formulas you entered in a worksheet by displaying and printing the formulas. When you display formulas, Excel shows the formulas you entered in each cell instead of showing the results of the calculations. You want a printout of the formulas in your worksheet for documentation.

To display formulas:

1. Click **Tools**, then click **Options** to open the Options dialog box.

2. Click the **View** tab, then click **Formulas** in the Windows Option box to place a check in the Formulas box.

3. Click the **OK** button to return to the worksheet.

   The worksheet columns are excessively wide, but you aren't concerned about worksheet format right now. You simply want to make sure the formulas display properly in the worksheet. (If you wanted to readjust column width, you would repeat the AutoFit Selection command you used earlier.)

4. Scroll the worksheet to look at columns D, E, F, G, and H—the columns with formulas. See Figure 3-37. (Don't be concerned if the columns on your screen are wider than those in the figure.)

Figure 3-37 ◀
Displaying
formulas

formulas displayed
instead of results

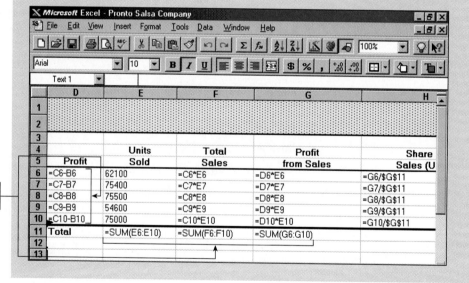

You could manually make the settings to print the worksheet with the formulas displayed, but doing so is time consuming because you have to change column widths and make the appropriate settings in the Page Setup dialog box to show the gridlines and the row/column headings, center the worksheet on the page, and fit the printout on a single page. To avoid doing all this work every time you want to print formulas, you'll use a macro, or Visual Basic module, to automate this printing task.

Before you look at the macro, let's turn off the formulas display.

To turn off the formulas display:

1. Click **Tools**, then click **Options** to open the Options dialog box.

2. Click the **View** tab if necessary, then click **Formulas** to remove the check.

3. Click the **OK** button to return to the worksheet. The formulas are no longer displayed.

4. Scroll the worksheet so you can see column A.

A Macro to Print Formulas

A **macro**, also called a **Visual Basic module**, automatically performs a sequence of tasks or commands such as menu selections, dialog box selections, or keystrokes. You create macros to automate Excel tasks that you perform frequently and that require a series of steps. To create a macro you can record the series of steps as you perform them, or you can enter a series of commands (in the Visual Basic programming language) that tell Excel how to do the task.

In this section of the tutorial, you will have the opportunity to use a prewritten macro that prints formulas. You will learn how to run the macro and you will look at the commands in the module. As you will discover, the Formulas macro is very useful for documenting worksheets you complete as course assignments.

Opening a Macro

Your Student Disk contains a copy of a macro that:

- Makes a copy of the worksheet in a separate sheet
- Displays formulas
- Adjusts column width for best fit
- Turns on cell gridlines and row/column headings
- Fits the printout on a single page in landscape orientation
- Prints the worksheet
- Erases the copy of the worksheet and returns to the original worksheet

To use the print formulas macro, you first need to open the workbook where it is stored. Let's open the Formulas workbook and look at the commands.

To open the Formulas workbook:

1. Click the **Open** button  to display the Open dialog box.

2. Open the workbook Formulas in the Tutorial.03 folder on your Student Disk. The macros and the Visual Basic toolbar appear. See Figure 3-38.

Figure 3-38 ◄
Some commands in the Print Formulas Macro

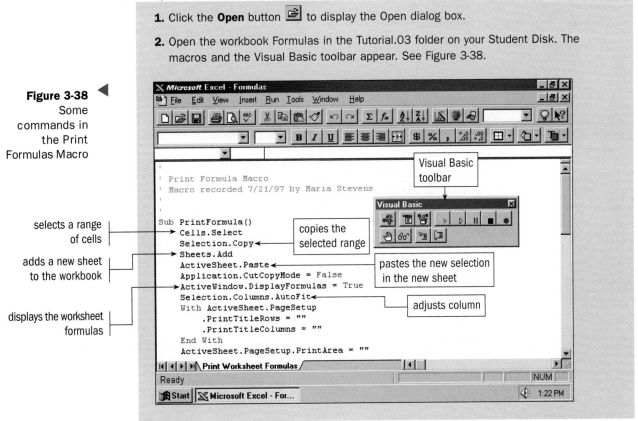

selects a range of cells

adds a new sheet to the workbook

displays the worksheet formulas

copies the selected range

pastes the new selection in the new sheet

adjusts column

Visual Basic toolbar

The easiest way to create a macro is to perform a series of steps while Excel records what you do. When you complete the steps, Excel translates your actions into the commands you see on the screen. Each row of the module displays one command. The Visual Basic toolbar lets you adjust the macro simply by clicking the proper toolbar button.

Although the commands may seem difficult to understand at first, you can probably decipher a few just by taking a close look. For example, Sheets.Add tells Excel to add a new sheet to the workbook. Then, as you might expect, the next command, ActiveSheet.Paste, tells Excel to paste something into the active sheet. Figure 3-38 explains other commands.

Running a Macro

To run the Print Formulas Macro, you need to return to the worksheet whose formulas you want to print. Then you can use the Macro command on the Tools menu to run the macro.

To run the module:

1. Click **Window**, then click **2 Pronto Salsa Company**. You return to your Projected Sales worksheet.

2. Click **Tools**, then click **Macro** to display the Macro dialog box. See Figure 3-39. The list box displays the names of all available macros. In this case, there's only one: Formulas.xls PrintFormula. The first part of the macro name is the workbook where the macro is stored (Formulas.xls). The second part is the name of the macro itself (PrintFormula).

Figure 3-39 ◀
Macro dialog box

available macros ⟶

workbook where
macro is stored ⟶

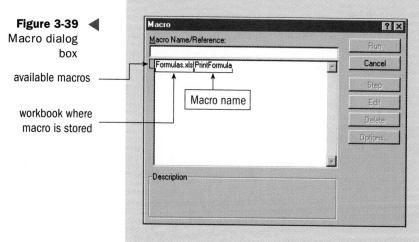

3. Click **'Print Formulas Macro.xls'!PrintFormulas** to display it in the Macro Name/Reference box.

4. Click the **Run** button.

5. After a moment, you see the message "Selected sheets will be permanently deleted. Continue?" Click the **OK button** because you do not want to save the copy of the worksheet that the macro created. As a result, you return to your Projected Sales worksheet. Excel prints the worksheet formulas.

Now that you're finished with the macro, you can close both workbooks.

To close the workbooks:

1. Use the **File** menu to close the Pronto Salsa Company workbook and then the Formulas workbook. Do not save changes for either workbook.

2. Exit Excel if you are not going to do the Tutorial Assignments right away.

Now you have a printout of the formulas in your worksheet (Figure 3-40), in addition to the printout showing the results of the formula calculations.

Figure 3-40
Worksheet formulas printed by macro

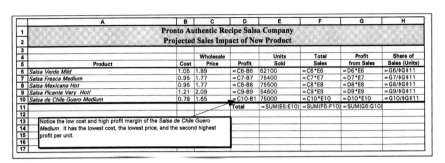

	A	B	C	D	E	F	G	H
1		Pronto Authentic Recipe Salsa Company						
2		Projected Sales Impact of New Product						
3								
4			Wholesale			Units	Total	Profit	Share of
5	Product	Cost	Price	Profit	Sold	Sales	from Sales	Sales (Units)
6	Salsa Verde Mild	1.05	1.89	=C6-B6	62100	=C6*E6	=D6*E6	=G6/$G$11
7	Salsa Fresca Medium	0.95	1.77	=C7-B7	75400	=C7*E7	=D7*E7	=G7/$G$11
8	Salsa Mexicana Hot	0.95	1.77	=C8-B8	75500	=C8*E8	=D8*E8	=G8/$G$11
9	Salsa Picante Very Hot!	1.21	2.09	=C9-B9	54600	=C9*E9	=D9*E9	=G9/$G$11
10	Salsa de Chile Guero Medium	0.78	1.65	=C10-B1	75000	=C10*E10	=D10*E10	=G10/$G$11
11					Total	=SUM(E6:E10)	=SUM(F6:F10)	=SUM(G6:G10)	
12								
13	Notice the low cost and high profit margin of the Salsa de Chile Guero							
14	Medium. It has the lowest cost, the lowest price, and the second highest							
15	profit per unit.							
16								
17								

Tips for Using the Print Formulas Macro

The print formulas macro you used in this tutorial helped you print the formulas for your worksheet. In the Tutorial Assignments you will modify this macro to create a customized print formulas macro called My Macro. Your customized macro automatically prints your name in the header of the formulas printout. You can use your customized macro to print the formulas for any worksheet you create.

Many Tutorial Assignments and Case Problems require you to print your worksheet formulas, in addition to printing the results of the formula calculations. When you complete worksheets for the Tutorial Assignments and Case Problems, follow these general steps:

1. Create the worksheet and format it as required.

2. When you are ready to print the worksheet, use the Print Preview command to see how the worksheet fits on the printed page. Adjust column widths on the worksheet if necessary.

3. Use the Page Setup dialog box to center the printout on the page and turn off the cell gridlines and row/column headings. Add your name to the header, and include the date and filename.

4. Print the worksheet.

5. Save the workbook at this point to save your print specifications.

6. Open your customized workbook, My Macro.

7. Display the workbook and worksheet containing the formulas you want to print.

8. Use the Macro command on the Tools menu to open the Macro dialog box and select the print formula macro. Then click the Run button.

9. When the macro asks if you want to continue, click the OK button.

10. If you are not going to print any other worksheets during your computing session, use the Window menu to activate the macro workbook, then close it.

As you look over the worksheet and formula printouts, Anne returns and asks to see the formatted worksheet. She examines the printouts and briefly checks the accuracy of the formulas shown on the formulas printout. Anne praises you for your excellent work before rushing off to her appointment with the loan officer.

Quick Check

1 Define the following terms in your own words:
   a. column titles
   b. font style
   c. Visual Basic module
   d. formatting
   e. formatting codes
   f. font effects
   g. headers
   h. footers
   i. column headings

2 A macro is also known as a _____.

3 Before you can use a macro, you need to _____.

4 Explain the steps you need to follow to run a macro.

5 Make a list of things to look for in the Print Preview window to make sure that your printed worksheets look professional.

6 _____ orientation prints the worksheet with the paper positioned so it is taller than it is wide.

7 A _____ is text that is printed in the top margin of every worksheet page.

8 List and explain three formatting codes you might insert into a worksheet footer.

9 Explain how to center a worksheet on the page.

10 Why would you want to print the formulas in a worksheet?

Tutorial Assignments

Start Windows and Excel, if necessary. Insert your Student Disk in the disk drive. Make sure the Excel and Book1 windows are maximized. Complete these steps to customize the print formulas macro so it automatically places your name in the header.
   1. Open the workbook Formulas.
   2. Move the pointer I to the line that reads .RightHeader = "&D."
   3. Position I after the first quotation mark and click.
   4. Type your own name and make sure there is a space between your name and the &D formatting code.
   5. Scroll back to the line "Sub PrintFormula ()." Replace "PrintFormula" with "MyMacro." The modified line should now read: Sub MyMacro ( ).
   6. Change the first line of text from "Print Formula Macro" to "My Macro."
   7. Edit the second line of text, changing "7/21/97" to the current date, and "Maria Stevens" to your name. Then click at the very beginning of the line to place the insertion point before the apostrophe.
   8. Save the revised workbook as My Macro in the TAssign folder on your Student Disk.
   9. Test the macro. Open the Pronto2 workbook in the TAssign folder on your Student Disk.

10. Use the Macro command on the Tools menu to open the Macro dialog box and run your macro. Your name, the date, and the filename should appear in the header of the printed worksheet.

Next, revise the Pronto2 workbook.

11. Make the text box narrower so it fits in columns A and B.
12. Move the tail-end of the arrow that goes from the top of the text box to cell D10, so that it comes from the right side of the text box.
13. Center the percentages displayed in column H.
14. Make the contents of cells A10 through H10 bold to emphasize the new product. Make any necessary column width adjustments.
15. Add shading to cells A10 through H10 using the same dot pattern and color you used for the titles.
16. Put your name in the header so it appears on the printout of the worksheet. Make sure the header also prints the date and worksheet filename.
17. Make sure the Page Setup menu settings are for landscape orientation, centered horizontally and vertically, no row/column headings, and no cell gridlines.
18. Preview the printout to make sure it fits on one page.
19. Print the worksheet.
20. Save your workbook as Pronto Salsa Company 2, in the TAssign folder on your Student Disk.

Case Problems

1. Fresh Air Sales Incentive Program Carl Stambaugh is assistant sales manager at Fresh Air Inc., a manufacturer of outdoor and expedition clothing. Fresh Air sales representatives contact retail chains and individual retail outlets to sell the Fresh Air line.

This year, to spur sales Carl has decided to run a sales incentive program for sales representatives. Each sales representative has been assigned a sales goal 15% higher than his or her total sales last year. All sales representatives who reach this new goal will be awarded with an all-expense paid trip for two to Cozumel, Mexico.

Carl has been tracking the results of the sales incentive program with an Excel worksheet. He asked you to format the worksheet so it looks professional. He also wants a printout before he presents the worksheet at the next sales meeting. Complete these steps to format and print the worksheet:

1. Start Windows and Excel as usual.
2. Open the workbook Fresh (in the Case folder for Tutorial 3 on your student disk). Maximize the worksheet window and save the workbook as Fresh Air Sales Incentives in the Case folder for Tutorial 3.
3. Make the formatting changes shown in Figure 3-41.
4. Use the Page Setup dialog box to scale the worksheet to fit on one page printed in landscape orientation.
5. Center the worksheet horizontally and vertically.
6. Add an appropriate header and delete the formatting code &[File] from the Center Section of the header.
7. Save the workbook.
8. Preview the worksheet and adjust page setup as necessary for the printed results you want.
9. Print the worksheet.
10. Use the macro (stored in the workbook My Macro) that you created in the Tutorial Assignments to print your worksheet formulas.

Figure 3-41 ◄

center title across columns, enlarge font using Increase Font Size tool

right justify this label

format regions in bold italics

	A	B	C	D	E	F	G	H	I	J
1	Fresh Air Sales Representative Incentive Program									
2										
3										
4		Goal % Increase	0.15							
5										
6			1994	1st Qtr	2nd Qtr	3rd Qtr	4th Qtr	1994	1994	% Goal
7	Territory	Name	Sales	Actual	Actual	Actual	Actual	Actual	Goal	Reached
8	Western	Delman, Amy	142789	47899	41567	81266	96782	267514	164207.4	1.649123
9	Western	Trout, Patricia	152402	35008.2	68909	66328	91344	261589.2	175262.3	1.492558
10	Western	Valentino, Elizabeth	163284	33567	70929.7	63213	99345	267054.7	187776.6	1.422194
11	Southern	Schuda, Jay	156782	56893	62332	89547	45877	254649	180299.3	1.412368
12	Central	Oliver, Deby	182018	66897	56874	66345	93234	283350	209320.7	1.353664
13	Western	Chu, Johnathon	166324	41889	75892	87445	51678	256904	191272.6	1.34313
14	Western	Shalala, Donna	161300	36221.5	71563	62341	76432	246557.5	185495	1.329187
15	Western	Leatherman, Courtney	136589	34327	37899	64333	67894	204453	157077.4	1.301607
16	Southern	Epstein, Lee	159778	33258	65700	65789	44661	209408	183744.7	1.139668
17	Western	Cook, Pamela	157896	42339	45233	58566	45328	191466	181580.4	1.054442
18	Southern	Rose, Ann C.	155840	33258	61788	46777	42215	184038	179216	1.026906
19	Western	Vagelos, Paul	155329	43667	39086	68733	31566	183052	178628.4	1.024765
20	Central	Richstone, Ellen	176900	43658	65223	59087	38900	206868	203435	1.016875
21	Central	Azevedo, Tricia	179385	53278	47895	53334	43445	197952	206292.8	0.959568
22	Eastern	Gyorog, Mike	211408	55789	65996	69023	42215	233023	243119.2	0.958472
23	Southern	Dufallo, Basil	166805	46899	48912	45687	38999	180497	191825.8	0.940942
24	Central	Johnson, Carole	145823	34122	34557	39700	46789	155168	167696.5	0.925291
25	Central	Crawford, Lori	226050	56821	72100	66872	44122	239915	259957.5	0.922901
26	Eastern	Haag, Candee	156877	43677		48043.5	41566	164852.5	180408.6	0.913773
27	Central	Lewis, Kathryn	156998	39800	46772	45687	29876	162135	180547.7	0.898018
28	Southern	Kim, Choong Soon	207630	51233	66721	61788	29878	209620	238774.5	0.877899
29	Southern	Baer, Joachim	206850	56821	55781	51223	38900	202725	237877.5	0.852224
30	Western	Massalska, Angela	172894	35998	41566	44366	38071.1	160001.1	198828.1	0.804721
31	Eastern	Sako, Mari	176504	36221.5	45987	46033.8	33546	161788.3	202979.6	0.797067
32	Central	McChesney, Darlene	189600	37889	56894	45687	32172.2	172642.2	218040	0.791791
33	Southern	Free, Valerie	195365	47822	48900	48043.5	33123	177888.5	224669.8	0.791778
34	Western	Widnall, Sheila	172369	31567	45987	44024.1	33156	154734.1	198224.4	0.780601
35	Eastern	Dupre, William	195887	43223	38900	45789	46877	174789	225270.1	0.775909
36	Western	Lahiri, Nayanjot	238605	61233	72344	41277	32172.2	207026.2	274395.8	0.75448
37	Eastern	Horiuchi, Kotaro	208695	44105	61788	45687	26273.3	177853.3	239999.3	0.741058
38	Eastern	Luck, Steven P.	214689	56821	32678	45789	46877	182165	246892.4	0.737832
39	Southern	Hess, Lisa	212550	32778	65996	42334	37650	178758	244432.5	0.731318
40	Southern	Wertheim, Andrea	193250	42666	35874	34788	47888	161216	222237.5	0.725422
41	Eastern	Catoe, Chris	189560	38766	34566	41555	41233	156120	217994	0.716166
42	Eastern	Bolitho, Jason	215600	42177	56894	49800	20374.4	169245.4	247940	0.682606
43	Eastern	Jansson, Maija	227588	33794.9	55223	46512	29876	165405.9	261726.2	0.631981

format using 0% format

center all headings

add bottom border

format this column using 0.00% format

adjust column widths to best fit

2. Age Group Changes in the U.S. Population Rick Stephanopolous is preparing a report on changes in the U.S. population. Part of his report focuses on age group changes in the population from 1970 through 1980. Rick created a worksheet that contains information from the U.S. Census reports, and he is ready to format it. Complete these steps to format the worksheet:

1. Start Windows and Excel as usual.
2. Open the workbook Census (in the Case folder for Tutorial 3), maximize the worksheet window, then save the workbook as US Population in the Case folder for Tutorial 3.
3. Make the formatting changes shown in Figure 3-42, adjusting column widths as necessary.
4. Use the Page Setup dialog box to modify the header so the Right Section consists of your name, a space, the current date, and the filename. Delete the contents of the Center Section of the header.
5. Save the workbook again.
6. Preview and print the worksheet.
7. Use the macro (stored in the workbook My Print Formulas Macro) that you created in the Tutorial Assignments to print your worksheet formulas.

add your name, date, and filename as header

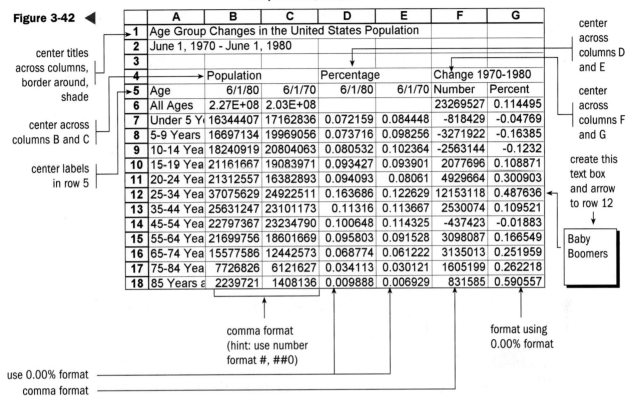

Figure 3-42

center titles across columns, border around, shade

center across columns B and C

center labels in row 5

center across columns D and E

center across columns F and G

create this text box and arrow to row 12

Baby Boomers

	A	B	C	D	E	F	G
1	Age Group Changes in the United States Population						
2	June 1, 1970 - June 1, 1980						
3							
4		Population		Percentage		Change 1970-1980	
5	Age	6/1/80	6/1/70	6/1/80	6/1/70	Number	Percent
6	All Ages	2.27E+08	2.03E+08			23269527	0.114495
7	Under 5 Y(	16344407	17162836	0.072159	0.084448	-818429	-0.04769
8	5-9 Years	16697134	19969056	0.073716	0.098256	-3271922	-0.16385
9	10-14 Yea	18240919	20804063	0.080532	0.102364	-2563144	-0.1232
10	15-19 Yea	21161667	19083971	0.093427	0.093901	2077696	0.108871
11	20-24 Yea	21312557	16382893	0.094093	0.08061	4929664	0.300903
12	25-34 Yea	37075629	24922511	0.163686	0.122629	12153118	0.487636
13	35-44 Yea	25631247	23101173	0.11316	0.113667	2530074	0.109521
14	45-54 Yea	22797367	23234790	0.100648	0.114325	-437423	-0.01883
15	55-64 Yea	21699756	18601669	0.095803	0.091528	3098087	0.166549
16	65-74 Yea	15577586	12442573	0.068774	0.061222	3135013	0.251959
17	75-84 Yea	7726826	6121627	0.034113	0.030121	1605199	0.262218
18	85 Years a	2239721	1408136	0.009888	0.006929	831585	0.590557

comma format (hint: use number format #, ##0)

format using 0.00% format

use 0.00% format
comma format

3. Creating and Formatting Your Own Worksheet Design a worksheet for a problem with which you are familiar. The problem might be a business problem from one of your other business courses, or it could be a mathematical problem from a biology, education, or sociology course. Follow these steps to plan your worksheet, prepare your planning documents, and complete the worksheet.

1. Decide what problem you would like to solve.
2. Create a worksheet plan for the problem you want to solve. State your goal, list the results you want to see and the information needed for the worksheet cells, and describe the formulas you will need for the worksheet calculations.
3. Sketch a plan for your worksheet showing the worksheet title(s), the data labels, column headings, and totals. Indicate the formats for titles, headings, labels, data, and totals.
4. Build the worksheet by entering the titles and labels first and then entering the data and formulas.
5. Test the formulas using simple values such as 1s or 10s.
6. After you are sure the formulas are correct, format the worksheet according to your plan.
7. Save the workbook periodically as you work.
8. When you have formatted the worksheet, use Excel's print preview feature to determine the Page Setup settings you need to make.
9. Make the Page Setup settings needed to:
   a. center the worksheet
   b. print a header containing your name, the date, and the filename
   c. turn off row/column headings and cell gridlines
10. Print your worksheet.

11. Use the macro (stored in the workbook My Macro) that you created in the Tutorial Assignments to print the formulas for your worksheet.
12. Submit to your instructor:
    a. your planning sheet
    b. your planning sketch
    c. a printout of the worksheet
    d. a printout of the worksheet formulas

4. Tracking Payments to Freelance Writers at *The Culture Times* You've just been hired as the business manager of *The Culture Times,* an alternative weekly newspaper specializing in arts coverage and investigative reporting. One of your jobs is to keep track of payments to free-lance writers. These writers are paid by the column inch, at a rate that varies from $4.00 to $6.50 an inch. You created an Excel workbook to keep track of this information. Now you need to format the worksheet and add the newspaper logo by following these steps:

1. Start Windows and Excel as usual.
2. Open the workbook Culture (in the Case folder for Tutorial 3 on your Student Disk). Save the workbook as The Culture Times in the Case folder for Tutorial 3.
3. Finish building the worksheet using your own data and formulas. Save your work.
4. Sketch a plan for your worksheet, showing the formatting changes you plan to make.
5. Format the worksheet according to your plan..

6. Use the Rows command on the Insert menu to insert 9 rows above the worksheet title. Then click Insert on the menu bar and click Picture to open the Picture dialog box. Select the file Star, in the Case folder for Tutorial 3, and then click OK to insert the picture into the worksheet.
7. Preview the worksheet. Adjust the page setup settings as necessary to:
    a. center the worksheet
    b. print a header containing your name, the date, and the filename
    c. turn off row/column headings and cell gridlines
8. Print your worksheet.
9. Use the macro (stored in the workbook My Macro) that you created in the Tutorial Assignments to print the formulas for your worksheet.
10. Save your work before closing the file.
11. Submit the following to your instructor:
    a. your planning sketch
    b. a printout of the worksheet
    c. a printout of the formulas

Functions, Formulas, and Absolute References

Managing Loan Payments

CASE

Superior Sails Charter Company

The Superior Sails Charter Company is based in Sault Sainte Marie, Michigan, on the shores of Lake Superior. It is close to the North Channel, one of the most pristine boating areas in the Northern Hemisphere. The company purchased a large fleet of boats with bank loans. James LaSalle, the company owner, asks you to create some Excel worksheets so he will have better information for managing the business.

James asks you to create a worksheet that contains the following information about each Superior Sails boat loan:

- original amount
- payments left to repay
- interest rate
- payment amount per month

James also wants to see the total monthly amount that Superior Sails pays for all the loans, and he encourages you to include any other information that might be useful for managing the boat loans.

You think about the project and then develop the worksheet plan shown in Figure 4-1 and the sketch shown in Figure 4-2.

OBJECTIVES

In this tutorial you will:

- Use the MAX function to find the largest number in a range of cells
- Use the MIN function to find the smallest number in a range of cells
- Use the AVERAGE function to calculate the average of a column of numbers
- Calculate monthly loan payments using the PMT function
- Create a formula using the IF function
- Use the TODAY function to display today's date
- Learn when to use absolute references in formulas

Figure 4-1 ◄
Worksheet plan

Worksheet Plan for Loan Management Worksheet

My Goal:
To develop a worksheet to help management keep track of loan
payments for boats in the Superior Sails fleet.

What results do I want to see?
Total payments due this month.
The amounts of the largest and smallest loans.
The average loan amount.

What information do I need?
A list of all boats in the Superior Sails fleet.
The amount, interest rate, and number of monthly payments for each loan.
The loan status (paid or due) for each boat.

What calculations will I perform?
largest loan = MAX (all loans)
smallest loan = MIN (all loans)
average loan = AVERAGE (all loans)
monthly payment amount = PMT (interest rate, number of payments, loan amount)
payments due this month = IF (loan is not paid, display the loan payment)
total payments due = SUM (all payments for loans not paid off)
percent of total payment = loan payment/total payments due

Superior Sails Charter Company – Loan Management Worksheet

Boat Type and Length	Loan Amount	Annual Interest Rate	Number of Monthly Payments	Monthly Payment Amount	Current Loan Status	Payments Due this Month	Percent of Total Payment
O'Day 34	$37,700	11.00%	60	${monthly payment amount formula}	xxxx	${payments due this month formula}	{percent of total payment formula}%
:	:	:	:	:	:	:	:
:	:	:	:	:	:	:	:
:	:	:	:	:	:	:	:
:	:	:	:	:	:	:	:
:	:	:	:	:	:	:	:
:	:	:	:	:	:	:	:
:	:	:	:	:	:	:	:

Largest loan: ${largest loan formula}   Total Payments Due ${total payments
                                                                         due formula}
Smallest loan: ${smallest loan formula}

Average loan: ${average loan formula}

Figure 4-2 ◄
Worksheet
sketch

You decide that the worksheet should show the largest loan, the smallest loan, and the average loan amount, in addition to the information James specified. You also decide to add a column that shows what percent each loan payment is of the total payment. This information might be useful if James decides to sell or replace any of his boats.

James approves your plan, then shows you where to find information on the boat loans. You begin to develop the worksheet according to your plan.

SESSION

4.1

In this session you will begin creating a worksheet to help James manage his boat loans. You will use several Excel functions to simplify the worksheet formulas. You will enter those functions by typing them directly in the worksheet and by using the Function Wizard.

Reviewing the Loan Management Worksheet

You've already entered the labels for the worksheet and the loan data James provided. You start Excel and open the workbook Superior to review what you've done.

To open the Superior workbook:

1. Start Excel as usual.

2. Make sure your Student Disk is in the disk drive.

3. Make sure the Microsoft Excel and Book1 windows are maximized.

4. Open the Superior workbook in the Tutorial.04 folder on your Student Disk.

5. Review the documentation sheet, which summarizes the workbook's purpose and contents.

6. Enter your name in cell B5 and the current date in cell B6.

7. Click the **Loan Management** tab to display the sheet shown in Figure 4-3.

Figure 4-3 ◄
Superior Sails
Charter
Company
workbook

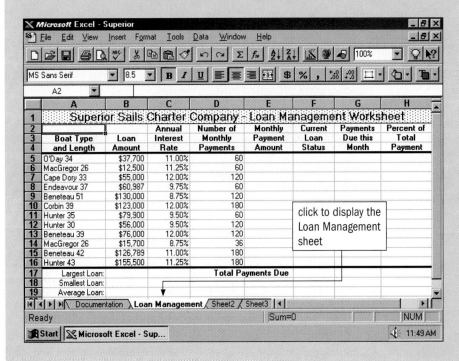

The boats are listed in column A and the loan amounts in column B; for example, Superior Sails purchased the 51-foot Beneteau sailboat with a $130,000 loan. The annual interest rate for each loan is in column C, which is formatted to display percents. Column D contains the number of monthly payments required to pay the loan. The loans are payable in three years (36 months), five years (60 months), 10 years (120 months), or 15 years (180 months). Although columns E through H do not yet contain data, you've already typed titles for these columns and selected appropriate formats.

Now that you have had an opportunity to review the workbook, save it under a different name so your changes will not alter the original file.

To save the workbook under a different filename:

1. Click **File** then click **Save As** to display the Save As dialog box.

2. Change the filename to Superior Sails Charter Company.

3. Click the **Save** button to save the workbook under the new filename on your Student Disk. Notice the new workbook filename, Superior Sails Charter Company, in the title bar.

   TROUBLE? If you see the message "Replace existing Superior Sails Charter Company.xls?" click the OK button to replace the old version of the file with your current version.

To finish creating your worksheet and to simplify the formulas for the Loan Management worksheet, you'll need to use several Excel functions. Keep in mind that when using functions you can also turn to Microsoft Excel On-line Help and the Microsoft Excel users guide for tips. The next section includes information summarized from these references.

Excel Functions

Excel's many functions help you enter formulas for calculations and other specialized tasks, even if you don't know the mathematical details of the calculations. As you probably already know, a function is a calculation tool that performs a predefined operation. You are already familiar with the SUM function, which adds the values in a range of cells. Excel provides hundreds of functions, including a function to calculate the average of a list of numbers, a function to find a number's square root, a function to calculate loan payments, and a function to calculate the number of days between two dates. Figure 4-4 shows how these functions are organized into categories.

Figure 4-4 ◄
Excel function
categories

Function Category	Examples of Functions in This Category
Financial	Calculate loan payments, depreciation, interest rate, internal rate of return
Date & Time	Display today's date and/or time; calculate the number of days between two dates
Math & Trig	Round off numbers; calculate sums, logs, and least common multiple; generate random numbers
Statistical	Calculate average, standard deviation, and frequencies; find minimum, maximum; count how many numbers are in a list
Lookup & Reference	Look for a value in a range of cells; find the row or column location of a reference
Database	Perform crosstabs, averages, counts, and standard deviation for an Excel database
Text	Convert numbers to text; compare two text entries; find the length of a text entry
Logical	Perform conditional calculations
Information	Returns information about the formatting, location, or contents of a range

Each function has a syntax, which tells you the order in which you must type the parts of the function and where to put commas, parentheses, and other punctuation. The general syntax of an Excel function is

NAME(*argument1,argument2,...*)

The syntax of most functions requires you to type the function name followed by one or more arguments in parentheses. Function arguments specify the values that Excel must use in the calculation or the cell references that Excel must include in the calculation. For example, in the function SUM(A1:A20) the function name is SUM and the argument is A1:A20.

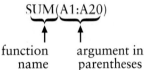

function name   argument in parentheses

You can use a function in a simple formula such as =SUM(A1:A20) or a more complex formula such as =SUM(A1:A20)*26. As with all formulas, you enter the formula that contains a function in the cell where you want the results displayed. The easiest way to enter a function in a cell is to use the Function Wizard, which asks you for the arguments and then enters the function for you.

REFERENCE window

USING THE FUNCTION WIZARD

- Click the cell where you want to display the results of the function. Then click the Function Wizard button to open the Function Wizard - Step 1 of 2 dialog box.
- Click the type of function you want in the Function Category box. (This narrows the possibilities in the Function Name box.)
- Click the function you want in the Function Name box.
- Click the Next button to move to the Step 2 of 2 box.
- Enter values for each argument in the function by either typing in the appropriate cell addresses or using the mouse to click the appropriate cells.
- Press Enter (or click the Finish button) to close the dialog box and display the results of the function in the cell.

If you prefer, you can type the function directly in the cell. Although the function name is always shown in uppercase, you can type it in either uppercase or lowercase. Also, even though parentheses enclose the arguments, you need not type the closing parenthesis if the function ends the formula. Excel automatically adds the closing parenthesis when you press the Enter key to complete the formula.

TYPING FUNCTIONS DIRECTLY IN A CELL

- Click the cell where you want to display the formula's result.
- Type = to begin the formula.
- Type the function name in either uppercase or lowercase.
- Type (, an opening parenthesis.
- Enter the appropriate arguments using the keyboard or mouse.
- When the arguments are complete, press Enter. Excel enters the closing parenthesis and displays the results of the function in the cell.

You can also perform quick calculations on a selected range, without actually entering a function in a cell, by using the AutoCalculate box in the status bar. You'll have a chance to use AutoCalculate in the Tutorial Assignments.

According to your plan, you need to enter a formula to find the largest loan amount. To do this, you'll use the MAX function.

MAX Function

MAX is a statistical function that finds the largest number. The syntax of the MAX function is

$$MAX(number1,number2,...)$$

In the MAX function, *number* can be a constant number such as 345, a cell reference such as B6, or a range of cells such as B5:B16. You can use the MAX function to simply display the largest number or to use the largest number in a calculation.

USING MAX TO DISPLAY THE LARGEST NUMBER IN A RANGE OF CELLS

- Click the cell where you want to display function's result.
- Click the Function Wizard button, then select the statistical function MAX or type =MAX(to begin the formula.
- Drag the pointer to outline the range of cells in which you want to find the largest number.
- Press Enter to complete the function.

You want to find the largest loan amount in the range of cells from B5 through B16. You want to display that amount in cell B17 next to the label "Largest Loan."

To use the MAX function to find the largest loan amount:

1. Click cell **B17** to move to the cell where you want to type the formula that uses the MAX function.

2. Type **=MAX(** to begin the formula.

3. Drag the pointer to outline cells **B5** through **B16**, then release the mouse button. See Figure 4-5.

Figure 4-5
Using the MAX
function

formula appears in
formula bar

cells B5 through
B16 outlined

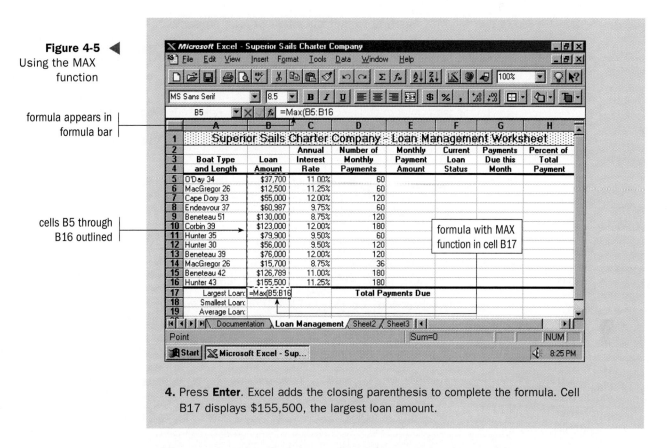

4. Press **Enter**. Excel adds the closing parenthesis to complete the formula. Cell B17 displays $155,500, the largest loan amount.

Next, you need to find the smallest loan amount.

MIN Function

MIN is a statistical function that finds the smallest number. The syntax of the MIN function is

$$MIN(number1, number2,...)$$

You can use the MIN function to simply display the smallest number or to use the smallest number in a calculation.

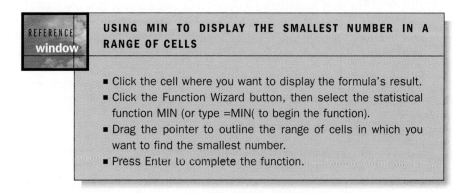

REFERENCE
window

USING MIN TO DISPLAY THE SMALLEST NUMBER IN A RANGE OF CELLS

■ Click the cell where you want to display the formula's result.
■ Click the Function Wizard button, then select the statistical function MIN (or type =MIN(to begin the function).
■ Drag the pointer to outline the range of cells in which you want to find the smallest number.
■ Press Enter to complete the function.

Now you want to find the smallest loan amount and display it in cell B18.

To use the MIN function to find the smallest loan amount:

1. Click cell **B18** to move to the cell where you want to type the formula that uses the MIN function.

2. Type **=MIN(** to begin the formula.

3. Drag the pointer to outline cells **B5** through **B16**. Release the mouse button.

4. Press **Enter**. Cell B18 displays $12,500, the smallest loan amount.

According to your plan, the next step is to calculate the average loan amount.

AVERAGE Function

AVERAGE is a statistical function that calculates the average, or the arithmetic mean. The syntax for the AVERAGE function is

$$\text{AVERAGE}(number1, number2, ...)$$

Generally when you use the AVERAGE function *number* is a range of cells. To calculate the average of a range of cells, Excel sums the values in the range, then divides by the number of *non-blank* cells in the range. Figure 4-6 shows the results of using the AVERAGE function on three ranges.

Figure 4-6 ◄
How the
AVERAGE
function
handles zeros
and blank cells

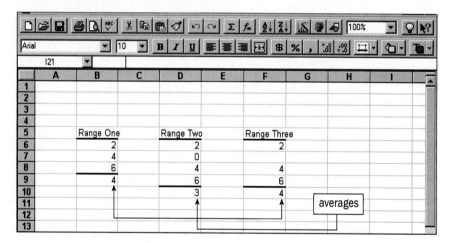

The first range has no blank cells and no cells that contain zeros, so Excel divides the sum of the numbers, 12, by 3 to find the average. In the second range, Excel counts the cells with zeros and divides the sum, 12, by 4 to find the average. In the third range, Excel does not count the blank cells and divides the sum, 12, by 3 to find the average.

> **REFERENCE window**
>
> **USING AVERAGE TO CALCULATE THE AVERAGE OF THE NUMBERS IN A RANGE OF CELLS**
>
> - Click the cell where you want to display the formula's result.
> - Click the Function Wizard button, then select the statistical function AVERAGE (or type =AVERAGE(to begin the function).
> - Drag the pointer to outline the range of cells you want to average.
> - Press Enter to complete the function.

You need to calculate the average of the boat loans listed in cells B5 through B16 and display the average in cell B19. Because you're still not very familiar with the syntax of the AVERAGE function, you'll use the Function Wizard button. The Function Wizard dialog box displays the syntax for the AVERAGE function; you simply fill in the arguments. This way you're sure to use the correct syntax.

To enter the AVERAGE function in cell B19 using the Function Wizard button:

1. Click cell **B19** to move to the cell where you want to enter the AVERAGE function.

2. Click the **Function Wizard** button to display the Function Wizard - Step 1 of 2 dialog box.

3. Click **Statistical** in the Function Category box.

4. Click **AVERAGE** in the Function Name box. You see the syntax of the function, AVERAGE(number1,number2,...), near the bottom of the dialog box and in the formula bar. See Figure 4-7.

Figure 4-7 ◀
Function
Wizard - Step 1
of 2 dialog box

list of function
categories

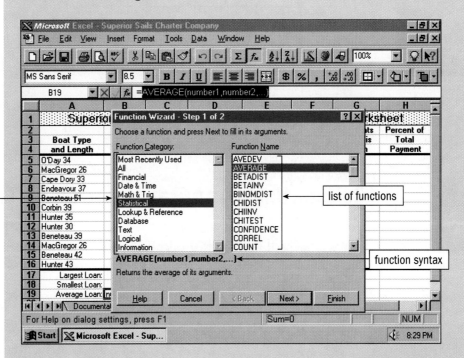

5. Click the **Next >** button to move to the Step 2 of 2 dialog box.

6. Click the **number1** box to make sure the insertion pointer appears there.

7. Drag the pointer to outline cells **B5** through **B16**, then release the mouse button.

   TROUBLE? If the dialog box covers part of cells B5 through B16, click its title bar and drag it to a new location.

8. Click the **Finish** button to close the dialog box and return to the worksheet. Cell B19 displays $77,423, the average loan amount. See Figure 4-8.

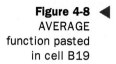

Figure 4-8 ◀
AVERAGE
function pasted
in cell B19

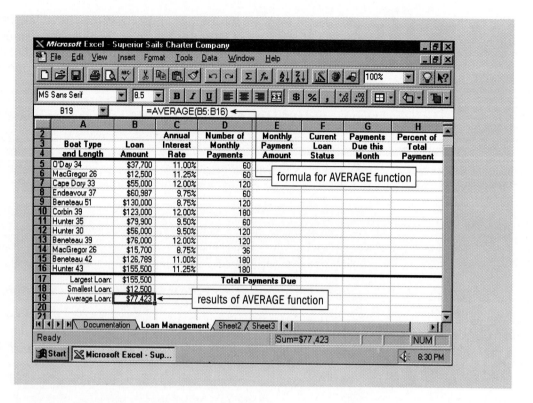

Next, you consult your plan and decide to create a formula to calculate the monthly payment for each loan.

Calculating Loan Payments with the PMT Function

PMT is a financial function that calculates the periodic payment amount for money borrowed. For example, if you want to borrow $5,000 for five years at 11% interest, you can use the PMT function to find your monthly payment—$108.71.

The syntax of the PMT function is

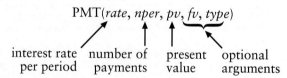

PMT(*rate, nper, pv, fv, type*)

interest rate   number of   present   optional
per period   payments   value   arguments

The last two arguments, *fv* and *type*, are optional; you will not include them in the loan management worksheet. Refer to the Microsoft Excel On-line Help for more information about these two optional arguments.

The *rate* argument is the interest rate per period. Usually interest rates are expressed as annual rates. For example, a 10% interest rate means that if you borrow $1,000 for a year, you must pay back the $1,000 plus $100 interest—that's 10% of 1,000—at the end of the year.

The *nper* argument is the total number of payments required to pay back the loan.

The *pv* argument is the present value; in the case of a loan, this value is the total amount borrowed.

When you enter the arguments for the PMT function, you must be consistent about the units you use for *rate* and *nper*. For example, if you use the number of monthly payments for *nper*, then you must express the interest rate as the percentage per month. Usually, the loan payment period is monthly, but interest is expressed as an annual rate. If you are repaying the loan in monthly installments, you need to divide the annual interest rate by 12 when you enter the rate as an argument for the PMT function.

To illustrate the PMT function, let's say that you want to know the monthly payment for a $5,000, 36-month loan at 11% annual interest. You use the PMT function in the formula:

=PMT(*11%/12, 36, 5000*)

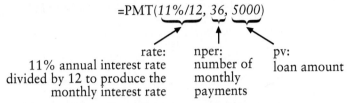

rate:
11% annual interest rate
divided by 12 to produce the
monthly interest rate

nper:
number of
monthly
payments

pv:
loan amount

As another example, suppose you want to know the monthly payment for a $95,000, 30-year loan at 9% (.09) interest. You use the PMT function in the formula:

=PMT(*.09/12, 30*12, 95000*)

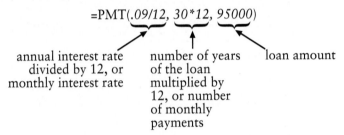

annual interest rate
divided by 12, or
monthly interest rate

number of years
of the loan
multiplied by
12, or number
of monthly
payments

loan amount

Excel displays the PMT function result as a negative number because you must pay it. Think of this as money that you subtract from your checkbook. If you prefer to display the payment amount as a positive number, place a minus sign before the PMT function.

REFERENCE window

USING PMT TO CALCULATE A MONTHLY PAYMENT

These directions assume you are typing the function in a cell. Keep in mind that you can also use the Function Wizard button and then enter the arguments in the Step 2 of 2 dialog box.

- Click the cell where you want to display the monthly payment amount.
- Type =PMT(if you want the result displayed as a negative number (or type = –PMT(if you want the result displayed as a positive number).
- Type the annual interest rate, type %, then type /12 to divide the interest rate by 12 months.
- Type a comma to separate the interest rate from the next argument.
- Type the number of monthly payments required to pay back the loan, then type a comma to separate the number of payments from the next argument.
- Type the loan amount then press Enter.

Instead of typing the arguments, you can click the cells that contain the values you want to use for the arguments.

According to your plan, you need to display the monthly payment for the O'Day 34 loan in cell E5. The annual interest rate in cell C5 must be divided by 12 to obtain the monthly interest rate. The number of periods is in cell D5, and the loan amount is in cell B5. Let's enter the =PMT(C5/12,D5,B5) formula for the O'Day 34 loan.

To calculate the monthly payment for the O'Day 34 loan:

1. Click cell **E5** to move to the cell where you want to enter the formula for the monthly payment.

2. Type **=PMT(** to begin the formula.

3. Click cell **C5** to specify the location of the annual interest rate.

4. Type **/12** to convert the annual interest rate to the monthly interest rate.

5. Type **,** (a comma) to separate the first argument from the second.

6. Click cell **D5** to specify the location of the number of payments.

7. Type **,** (a comma) to separate the second argument from the third.

8. Click cell **B5** to specify the location of the loan amount. See Figure 4-9.

Figure 4-9 ◀
Entering a
formula using
the PMT
function

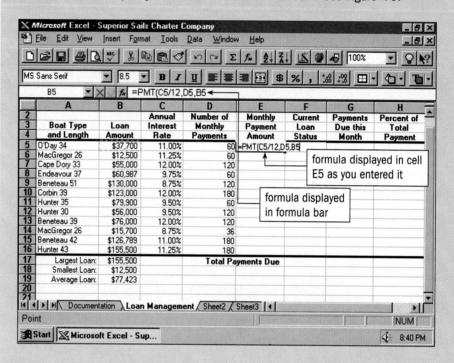

9. Press **Enter** to complete the formula and display ($819.69) in cell E5.

As expected, the PMT function displays the payment as a negative number, in parentheses. (If you are using a color monitor, the number also appears in red.) You decide to change the formula to display the payment as a positive number. You'll use the F2 function key to change the contents of cell E5 to = –PMT(C5/12,D5,B5).

To display the payment as a positive number:

1. Click cell **E5** to make it the active cell.

2. Press **F2** to edit the formula in cell E5.

3. Press **Home** to position the insertion point at the beginning of the formula.

4. Press → to move the insertion point between the equal sign and the "P" in PMT.

5. Type **–** (a minus sign). The formula is now = –PMT(C5/12,D5,B5).

6. Press **Enter** to complete the edit. Cell E5 displays the positive value $819.69. On a color monitor, the value appears in black.

If you like, you can check to see that this formula is correct by comparing the result to a table of loan payment amounts. When you are confident that you used the PMT function correctly, you can copy the formula in cell E5 to calculate the payments for the other loans.

To copy the PMT formula to cells E6 through E16:

1. Click cell **E5** to make it the active cell.

2. Position the pointer over the fill handle in the lower-right corner of cell E5 until it changes to $+$.

3. Drag the pointer to cell **E16**, then release the mouse button.

4. Click any cell to remove the highlighting and view the payment amounts displayed in cells E5 through E16. See Figure 4-10.

    TROUBLE? If your formula did not copy to all the cells, repeat Steps 1 through 4.

Figure 4-10 ◀
Payment formula copied from cell E5 to cells E6 through E16

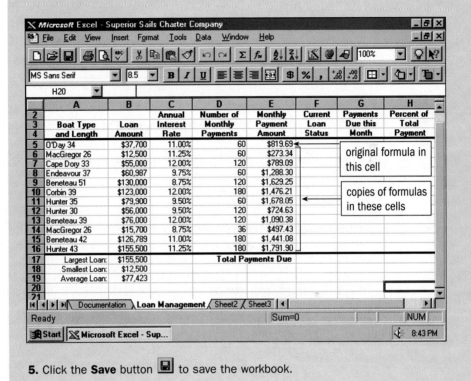

5. Click the **Save** button 🔘 to save the workbook.

Take a moment to review your plan again. James wants a list of all boat loans, but he wants a sum of only those he must pay this month. He doesn't need to make payments on boat loans that he has already paid off; therefore, there is no need to sum the values in column E.

Quick Check

1. List the Excel functions you used so far in this tutorial.
   a. Briefly explain what each function does.
   b. Write the syntax for each function.
   c. Write a sample function that uses cell references or constant numbers for the arguments.

2. Use the Function Wizard or the Excel On-line Help to find one function for each category listed in Figure 4-4.
   a. Indicate the category to which this function belongs.
   b. List the function name.
   c. Write a short description of what this function does.

3. Write the definition of a function. Explain the relationship between functions and formulas.

4 Explain the difference between the way the AVERAGE function handles zeros and the way it handles blank cells included in the range of cells to be averaged.

5 Explain the advantage of using the MAX and MIN functions on large lists that change frequently.

6 What are the advantages of using the Function Wizard dialog box instead of typing a function directly into a cell?

7 Write the formula you would use to calculate the monthly payment for a $150,000, 30-year home loan at 8.75% annual interest.

8 Write the formula you would use to calculate the monthly payment for a $10,000, 48-month loan at 8% annual interest.

SESSION

4.2

In this session you will enter more functions in the worksheet. You'll also learn how to use absolute references and then practice copying formulas and updating the worksheet.

IF Function

You take a look at the loan paperwork and find that the O'Day 34, the Endeavour 37, and the Beneteau 51 loans have been paid in full. According to your plan, you need to type the word "Paid" in column F if a boat loan has been paid.

To enter current loan status:

1. Click cell **F5** because this is where you want to enter "Paid" for the O'Day 34.

2. Type **Paid** and press **Enter**.

3. Click cell **F8** because this is where you want to enter the status of the Endeavour 37.

4. Type and press **Enter**. AutoComplete finishes the entry for you.

5. If necessary, click cell **F9** because this is where you want to enter the status of the Beneteau 51.

6. Type **P** and press **Enter**.

Next, you want to display the payment amounts for the loans that are not paid. To do this you'll use the IF function in column G, which shows payments due this month. The **IF function** provides a way to specify the if-then-else logic required to calculate or display information based on one or more conditions.

Here's an example of an if-then-else condition in the current worksheet: if the loan status is paid, then place a zero in the payment due column, otherwise (else) display the monthly payment amount in the payment due column. See Figure 4-11.

Figure 4-11 ◀
Conditions for
displaying
payments due
this month

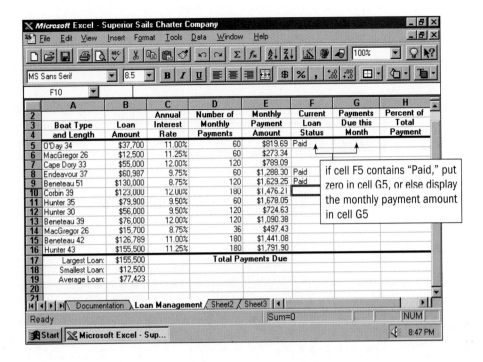

The syntax of the IF function is

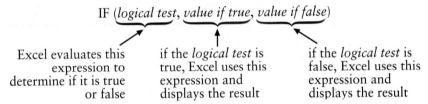

IF (*logical test*, *value if true*, *value if false*)

Excel evaluates this
expression to
determine if it is true
or false

if the *logical test* is
true, Excel uses this
expression and
displays the result

if the *logical test* is
false, Excel uses this
expression and
displays the result

The *logical test* is any value or expression that Excel evaluates as true or false. For example, Excel evaluates the expression 2=2 as true when you use it for a logical test. Excel evaluates the expression 2=1 as false. Most expressions you use for logical tests will contain numbers or cell references separated by one of the comparison operators shown in Figure 4-12.

Figure 4-12 ◀
Comparison
operators

Type of Comparison	Comparison Operator Symbol
less than	<
greater than	>
less than or equal to	<=
greater than or equal to	>=
equal to	=
not equal to	<>

Some examples of expressions are 2>3, B5=C3, and B8<=0. An expression can also include text. Note that you must put quotation marks around any text that you use in the IF function.

The *value if true* argument specifies what to display in the cell if the expression for the logical test is true.

The *value if false* argument specifies what to display in the cell if the expression for the logical test is false.

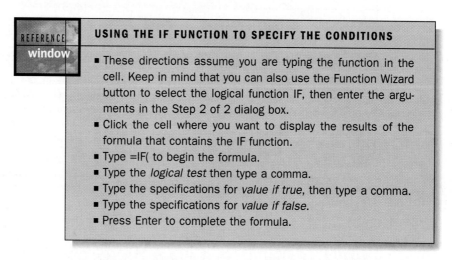

REFERENCE window	**USING THE IF FUNCTION TO SPECIFY THE CONDITIONS**
	■ These directions assume you are typing the function in the cell. Keep in mind that you can also use the Function Wizard button to select the logical function IF, then enter the arguments in the Step 2 of 2 dialog box.
	■ Click the cell where you want to display the results of the formula that contains the IF function.
	■ Type =IF(to begin the formula.
	■ Type the *logical test* then type a comma.
	■ Type the specifications for *value if true*, then type a comma.
	■ Type the specifications for *value if false*.
	■ Press Enter to complete the formula.

Suppose you want Excel to display a warning message if the loan amount in cell B5 is greater than $150,000. You can use the formula:

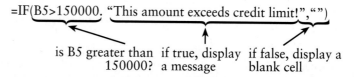

=IF(B5>150000. "This amount exceeds credit limit!","")

is B5 greater than 150000?   if true, display a message   if false, display a blank cell

Notice the quotation marks around the text that contain the credit limit message and the quotation marks without any text, which will leave the cell blank. When you use text as an argument for the IF function, you *must* enclose the text in quotation marks.

As another example, suppose you want to add a $100 bonus to the salary of any salesperson whose sales exceed $10,000. Look at Figure 4-13. The amount of merchandise Sergio Armanti sold is in cell B9. Sergio's base salary is in cell C9.

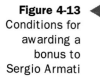

Figure 4-13 ◄
Conditions for
awarding a
bonus to
Sergio Armati

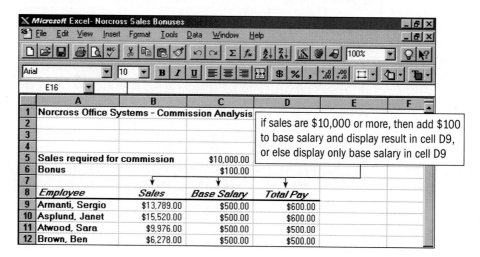

To calculate Sergio's total pay, including the bonus if he earned it, you enter the formula =IF(B9>=10000,C9+100,C9) in cell D9. In this case if the amount sold in cell B9 is at least $10,000, Excel adds $100 to the base salary and displays it in cell D9. If the amount sold in cell B9 is less than $10,000, Excel displays the base salary in cell D9.

Unlike the previous example that displayed text, all arguments for the IF function that calculates Sergio's bonus are numeric, so you do not use quotation marks.

Let's consider the formula you need to use now. In cell G5 you want to display the amount of the payment due. The conditions for this situation: if the current loan status is "Paid," then put a zero in the payments due column; otherwise, put the monthly payment amount in the payments due column. Your formula is

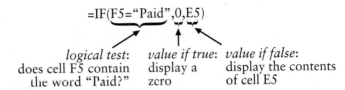

$$=IF(F5="Paid",0,E5)$$

logical test: does cell F5 contain the word "Paid?"   *value if true*: display a zero   *value if false*: display the contents of cell E5

If this formula works, you should see a zero in cell G5 because the O'Day 34 loan is paid. Let's see if the formula produces the expected results. This time you will use the Function Wizard button in the formula bar (instead of the Function Wizard button in the tool bar) to enter the formula.

To enter the formula containing the IF function in cell G5:

1. Double-click cell **G5** to display the Function Wizard button f_x in the formula bar. See Figure 4-14.

Figure 4-14 ◄
Function Wizard button in formula bar

click the Function Wizard button in the formula bar to open the Function Wizard - Step 1 of 2 dialog box

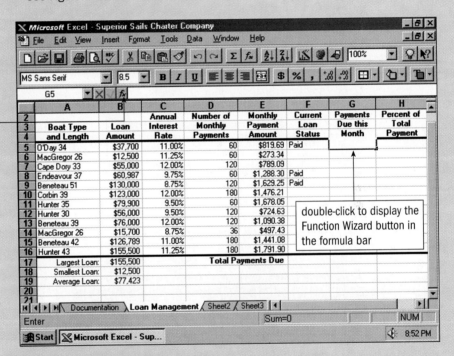

double-click to display the Function Wizard button in the formula bar

2. Click the **Function Wizard** button f_x to open the Function Wizard - Step 1 of 2 dialog box.

3. Click **Logical** in the Function Category box, then click **IF** in the Function Name box. Notice the function syntax displayed in the formula bar.

4. Click the **Next >** button to move to the Function Wizard - Step 2 of 2 dialog box.

5. Type **F5="Paid"** in the logical_test box. Make sure you type the quotation marks. (Notice that you do not have to type commas to separate arguments when using the Function Wizard dialog box.) Excel displays "True" in the box next to the logical_test box because cell F5 *does* contain the entry "Paid."

6. Click the **value_if_true** box and type **0**. Make sure you type the number zero, and not the capital letter "O." The box next to the value_if_true box displays "0."

7. Click the **value_if_false** box and type **E5**. The box next to the value_if_false box displays "819.68935," which is the value in cell E5 displayed without formatting. See Figure 4-15.

Figure 4-15
Function
Wizard - Step 2
of 2 dialog box

make sure your settings
match these

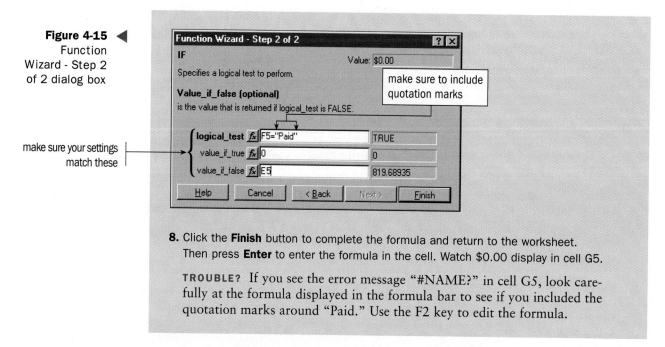

8. Click the **Finish** button to complete the formula and return to the worksheet. Then press **Enter** to enter the formula in the cell. Watch $0.00 display in cell G5.

> **TROUBLE?** If you see the error message "#NAME?" in cell G5, look carefully at the formula displayed in the formula bar to see if you included the quotation marks around "Paid." Use the F2 key to edit the formula.

The formula produced the expected results, so now you can copy it to cells G6 through G16.

To copy the IF formula to cells G6 through G16:

1. Make sure that G5 is the active cell because it contains the formula you want to copy.

2. Move the pointer over the fill handle until it turns into +.

3. Drag the pointer to cell **G16**, then release the mouse button.

4. Click any cell to remove the highlighting and view the results displayed in cells G5 through G16. See Figure 4-16.

Figure 4-16
Results of
copying the IF
formula

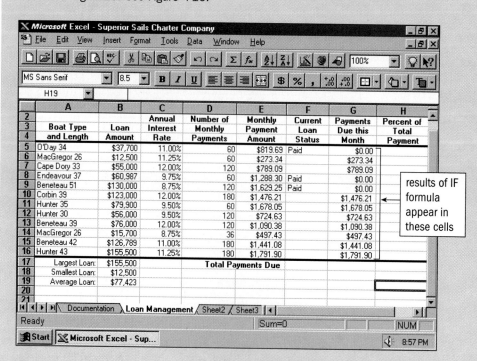

As you review the results of the IF formulas in cells G5 through G16 you see that the formulas produced zeros in cells G5, G8, and G9 because the boat loans are paid. In the other cells the IF formulas have correctly placed the same value as that displayed in column E.

James wants a total of payments due, so next you need to sum the payments in column G. You want to display the sum in cell G17.

To sum the payments due this month:

1. Click cell **G17** to move to the cell where you want the sum displayed.

2. Click the **AutoSum** button Ⲋ.

3. Make sure cells G5 through G16 are outlined.

4. Press **Enter**. The amount $9,762.10 appears in cell G17.

Now take a look at the label for total payments. You want the label to indicate the month and year for which the payment is calculated. You can use Excel's TODAY function to display the date.

Displaying and Formatting the Date with the TODAY Function

The **TODAY function** reads your computer's system clock and displays the current date in the cell that contains the TODAY function. The syntax of the TODAY function is

$$TODAY(\ )$$

The empty parentheses indicate that this function requires no arguments. You enter the function by typing only "TODAY( )." An alternative to typing the TODAY function is using the Function Wizard dialog box. In this case, you want the date to appear in cell F17.

To enter the TODAY function in cell F17:

1. Click cell **F17** to move to the cell where you want to enter the function.

2. Click the **Function Wizard** button *fx* to open the Function Wizard - Step 1 of 2 dialog box.

3. Click **Date & Time** in the Function Category box, then click **Today** in the Function Name box.

4. Click the **Next >** button to move on to the Step 2 of 2 dialog box.

5. Press **Enter** to display the date in the cell.

To display only the month and year, you must change the date format for cell F17. You can format the cell that contains the TODAY function using the Format menu.

To format today's date to show only the month and year:

1. Make sure cell F17 is the active cell.

2. Click **Format** then click **Cells** to display the Format Cells dialog box.

3. Click the **Number** tab.

4. Click **Date** in the Category box.

5. Click **Mar-95** in the Type box to select the month-year format for the date.

6. Click the **OK** button to display the new date format.

The date doesn't look quite right. It would look better if it were bold and aligned on the left side of the cell.

To bold the date and align it on the left side of the cell:

1. Make sure cell F17 is the active cell.

2. Click the **Bold** button B on the toolbar.

3. Click the **Align Left** button on the toolbar. See Figure 4-17.

Figure 4-17 ◄
TODAY function

click to boldface
contents of active cell

result of TODAY
function appears here

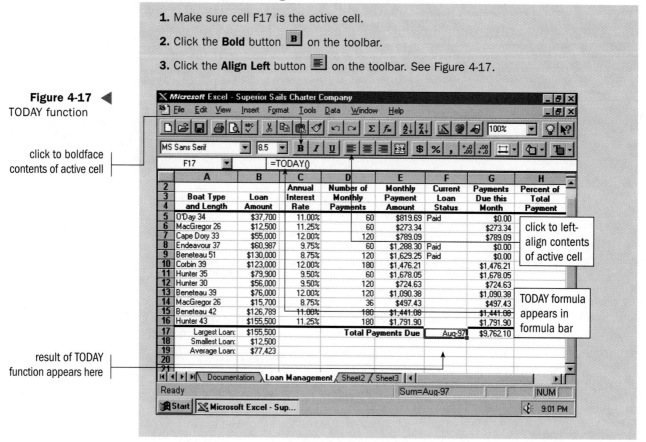

According to your worksheet sketch, you only have one column left to complete the worksheet. You want column H to display the percent of the total payment that each individual loan payment represents. For example, if all loan payments total $10,000 and the O'Day payment is $1,000, the O'Day payment is 10% of the total payment. To do this calculation you need to divide each payment by the total payment, as shown in the equation:

percent of total payment = payment due this month / total payments due

You enter the formula =G5/G17 in cell H5.

To enter the formula to calculate the percent of total payment in cell H5:

1. Click cell **H5** to move to the cell where you want to enter the formula.

2. Type **=G5/G17** and press **Enter** to complete the formula and display 0.00% in cell H5.

Cell H5 seems to display the correct result. James is paying $0 for the O'Day loan, which is 0% of the $9,762.10 total. Next, you decide to copy the formula to cells H6 through H16.

To copy the percent formula to cells H6 through H16:

1. Make **H5** the active cell. Then move the pointer over the fill handle in cell H5 until it changes to **+**.

2. Drag the pointer to cell **H16**. Release the mouse button.

3. Click any blank cell to remove the highlighting and view the message "#DIV/0!" in cells H6 through H16.

Something seems wrong. Cells H6 through H16 display "#DIV/0!," a message that means Excel was instructed to divide by zero, which is not possible. Take a moment to look at the formulas you copied into cells H6 through H16.

To examine the formulas in cells H6 through H16:

1. Click cell **H6** and look at the formula displayed in the formula bar. The first relative reference changed from G5 in the original formula to G6 in the copied formula. That's correct because the loan amount for row 6 is in cell G6. The second reference changed from G17 in the original formula to G18, which is not correct. This formula should be =G6/G17 because the payments total is in cell G17.

2. Look at the formulas in cells H7 through H16 and see how the relative references changed in each.

The problem with these formulas has to do with absolute and relative references. You should have used an absolute reference instead of a relative reference for cell G17 in the percent of total payment formula.

Absolute References

Sometimes when you copy a formula, you don't want Excel to change all cell references automatically to reflect their new positions in the worksheet. If you want a cell reference to point to the same location in the worksheet even when you copy it, you must use an absolute reference. An **absolute reference** is the row and column location of a cell that must not change if it is copied to other cells.

The reference to cell $G$17 is an absolute reference, whereas the reference to cell G17 is a relative reference. If you copy a formula that contains the absolute reference $G$17, the reference to $G$17 does not change. On the other hand, if you copy a formula containing the relative reference G17, the reference to G17 could change to G18, G19, G20, and so forth as you copy it to other cells.

To include an absolute reference in a formula, you can type a dollar sign when you type the cell reference, or you can use the F4 key to change the cell reference type. You can always edit a formula that contains the wrong cell reference type.

REFERENCE window	EDITING CELL REFERENCE TYPES
	■ Click the cell that contains the formula you want to edit.
	■ Press F2 to begin editing in the formula bar.
	■ Use the arrow keys to move the insertion point to the right of the cell reference you want to change.
	■ Press F4 until the reference is correct.
	■ Press Enter to complete the edit.

To correct the problems in your worksheet, you need to change the reference type for the formula in cell H5. In other words, you need to use an absolute reference, instead of a relative reference, to indicate the location of total payments. That is, you need to change the reference G17 to $G$17.

To change the formula in cell H5 from =G5/G17 to =G5/$G$17:

1. Click cell **H5** to move to the cell that contains the formula you want to edit.

2. Double-click the mouse button to edit the formula in the cell.

3. Make sure the insertion point is just to the right of the reference G17. See Figure 4-18.

Figure 4-18 ◄
Error messages produced by copying the formula from cell H5

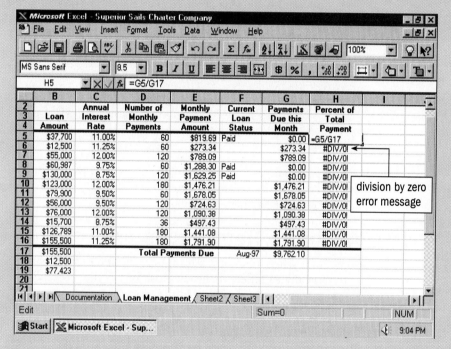

4. Press **F4** to change the reference to $G$17.

5. Press **Enter** to update the formula in cell H5.

Cell H5 still displays 0.00% as the formula's correct result, but the problem in your original formula did not surface until your copied it to cells H6 through H16. So now you need to copy the revised formula and check to see if it produces the correct results.

To copy the revised formula from cell H5 to cells H6 through H16:

1. Click cell **H5** because it contains the revised formula that you want to copy.

2. Move the pointer to the fill handle until it changes to ✛.

3. Drag the pointer to cell **H16**, then release the mouse button.

4. Click any cell to remove the highlighting and view the formula's results. See Figure 4-19.

Figure 4-19 ◄
Results of
copying the
formula with
an absolute
reference

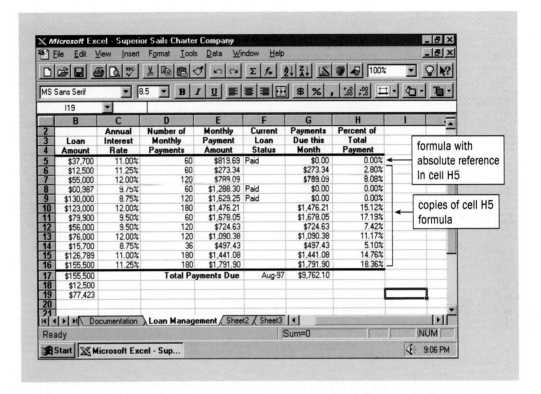

The revised formula works correctly. You're just about to close the worksheet when James stops by your office. He thinks the worksheet looks great, but he notices that the MacGregor 26 loan in row 6 should be marked "Paid" because he made the last payment a month ago. You explain how easy it is to make the change and how the worksheet will recalculate the amount for the total payments due this month.

To change the loan status of the MacGregor 26:

1. Click cell **F6** to make it the active cell.

2. Type **P** and AutoComplete finishes typing "Paid" for you. Then watch cell G17 as you press **Enter**.

As a result of changing the loan status, the amount in cell G6 changes to $0.00, the total payments due in cell G17 changes to $9,488.76, and Excel recalculates the percentages in column H. James is impressed. Now you can save the workbook and then print the Loan Management worksheet.

To produce a good looking printout, you decide to print the worksheet in landscape orientation, center it on the page from left to right and top to bottom, and omit the row and column headings and the cell gridlines.

To save the workbook and print the worksheet:

1. Click the **Save** button 🖫.

2. Click the **Print Preview** button 🔍 to see how the worksheet will look when you print it.

3. Click the **Setup** button to display the Page Setup dialog box. Then click the **Page** tab if it is not already selected.

4. If landscape orientation is not selected, click the **Landscape** button.

5. Click the **Margins** tab. Then click the **Horizontally** and **Vertically** boxes to center the worksheet on the page.

6. Click the **Sheet** tab. Make sure the Gridlines box and the Row and Column Headings box are empty.

7. Click the **OK** button to return to the print preview.

8. Click the **Print** button then click the **OK** button on the Print dialog box to send the worksheet to the printer. Figure 4-20 shows the final printout for the Loan Management worksheet.

Figure 4-20 ◀
Printout of Loan
Management
worksheet

Superior Sails Charter Company - Loan Management Worksheet							
Boat Type and Length	Loan Amount	Annual Interest Rate	Number of Monthly Payments	Monthly Payment Amount	Current Loan Status	Payments Due this Month	Percent of Total Payment
O'Day 34	$37,700	11.00%	60	$819.69	Paid	$0.00	0.00%
MacGregor 26	$12,500	11.25%	60	$273.34	Paid	$0.00	0.00%
Cape Dory 33	$55,000	12.00%	120	$789.09		$789.09	8.32%
Endeavour 37	$60,987	9.75%	60	$1,288.30	Paid	$0.00	0.00%
Beneteau 51	$130,000	8.75%	120	$1,629.25	Paid	$0.00	0.00%
Corbin 39	$123,000	12.00%	180	$1,476.21		$1,476.21	15.56%
Hunter 35	$79,900	9.50%	60	$1,678.05		$1,678.05	17.68%
Hunter 30	$56,000	9.50%	120	$724.63		$724.63	7.64%
Beneteau 39	$76,000	12.00%	120	$1,090.38		$1,090.38	11.49%
MacGregor 26	$15,700	8.75%	36	$497.43		$497.43	5.24%
Beneteau 42	$126,789	11.00%	180	$1,441.08		$1,441.08	15.19%
Hunter 43	$155,500	11.25%	180	$1,791.90		$1,791.90	18.88%
Largest Loan:	$155,500		Total Payments Due		Aug-97	$9,488.76	
Smallest Loan:	$12,500						
Average Loan:	$77,423						

9. Save your file again, so it includes the page setup format you specified.

Next, James wonders how much less his monthly payment would be if he refinanced some loans, so he would pay 11% interest instead of 12%. You show him that this sort of what-if analysis is easy to do.

To change the interest rates and look at the effect on the total payment:

1. Click cell **C7**, which contains one of the 12% interest rates.

2. Type **11** and notice how the percent symbol (%) remains in the cell. You don't have to type it after you format the cell to display percents. Then press **Enter**. The total loan payment in cell G17 changes from $9,488.76 to $9,457.29.

3. Click cell **C10**, which contains another of the 12% interest rates.

4. Type **11** and press **Enter**. The total loan payment in cell G17 changes to $9,379.10.

5. Click cell **C13**, which contains another of the 12% interest rates.

6. Type **11** and press **Enter**. The total loan payment in cell G17 changes to $9,335.62.

James sees that refinancing the three loans with 12% interest saves about $150 each month. Now he wonders "what if" he bought a 19-foot West Wight Potter for $9,000 at 11% interest.

To add another boat to the list, you must insert a row at the current location of row 17. Then you must copy the formulas to calculate the monthly payment amount, the payments due this month, and the percent of total payment to the new row.

To insert a row for the new boat and copy the necessary formulas:

1. Click cell **A17** because you want to insert a new row above this cell.

2. Click **Insert** then click **Rows** to insert a blank row.

3. Highlight cells **A16** through **H17**, then release the mouse button.

4. Click **Edit**, point to **Fill**, then click **Down** to duplicate the formulas and data from row 16 to row 17. Click any cell to remove the highlighting and view the results. See Figure 4-21.

Figure 4-21 ◀
Duplicating
a row

formulas and data
from row 16 copied
to row 17

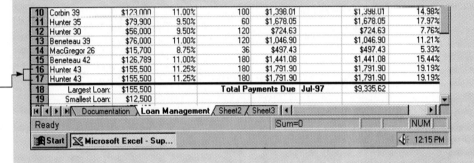

The Fill Down command copied the data and the formulas to row 17. That causes problems because you can easily type data for the West Wight Potter 19 over the copied data. Now you'll fill row 17 with information for the West Wight Potter.

To change the data in row 17:

1. Click cell **A17**, type **W W Potter 19**, and press →.

2. Type **9000** as the loan amount and press →.

3. Type **11** as the interest rate and press →.

4. Type **60** as the number of payments, and press **Enter**. The monthly payment for this loan, $195.68, appears in cell E17.

Looking at the total payments due in cell G18, you see that something is wrong. The amount in this cell did not change to reflect the addition of the West Wight Potter. Look at the formulas in cells G18, B18, B19, and B20 to find out what happened.

To view the contents of cells G18, B18, B19, and B20:

1. Click cell **G18** to make it the active cell. The formula for this cell appears in the formula bar as =SUM(G5:G16). The formula was not updated to include cell G17.

2. Click cell **B18** and look at the formula that appears in the formula bar. The formula =MAX(B5:B16) was not updated to include B17.

3. Click cell **B19** and look at the formula that appears in the formula bar. The formula =MIN(B5:B16) was not updated.

4. Click cell **B20** and look at the formula that appears in the formula bar. The formula =AVERAGE(B5:B16) was not updated after you inserted row 17.

You need to update these formulas to include row 17. You explain to James that if you add a row in the location of any of the current rows in a formula, the formula will be updated automatically. *However, if you add a row that is not included in a formula, you must manually update the formulas to include the new row.*

The original range in these formulas was B5:B16. You could have inserted a row in the current location of row 10, for example, and the range in the total payment formula would have "stretched" to include cells G5 through G17. But, you inserted row 17, which was outside the original range, so you need to manually update the formulas in cells G18, B18, B19, and B20.

To update the formulas in cells G18, B18, B19, and B20:

1. Double-click cell **G18**, which contains the formula you want to change.

2. Place $\mathcal{I}$ at the end of the formula and click. Then press **Backspace** twice to delete the 6.

3. Type **7** and press **Enter**.

4. Repeat Steps 2 through 4 so that the formulas in cells B18, B19, and B20 contain the argument (B5:B17). See Figure 4-22.

Figure 4-22 ◀
Manually updated formulas

updated formulas reflect correct values

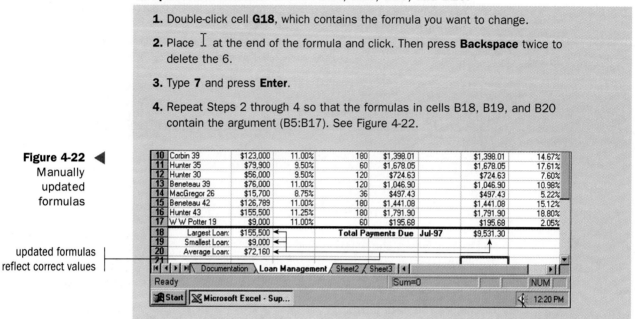

10	Corbin 39	$123,000	11.00%	180	$1,398.01		$1,398.01	14.67%
11	Hunter 35	$79,900	9.50%	60	$1,678.05		$1,678.05	17.61%
12	Hunter 30	$56,000	9.50%	120	$724.63		$724.63	7.60%
13	Beneteau 39	$76,000	11.00%	120	$1,046.90		$1,046.90	10.98%
14	MacGregor 26	$15,700	8.75%	36	$497.43		$497.43	5.22%
15	Beneteau 42	$126,789	11.00%	180	$1,441.08		$1,441.08	15.12%
16	Hunter 43	$155,500	11.25%	180	$1,791.90		$1,791.90	18.80%
17	W W Potter 19	$9,000	11.00%	60	$195.68		$195.68	2.05%
18	Largest Loan:	$155,500 ◀		Total Payments Due	Jul-97	$9,531.30		
19	Smallest Loan:	$9,000 ◀						
20	Average Loan:	$72,160 ◀						

Documentation \ **Loan Management** \ Sheet2 / Sheet3

Ready   Sum=0   NUM

Start   Microsoft Excel - Sup...   12:20 PM

Now James sees that the total loan payment would be $9,531.30 with the loan payment for a new West Wight Potter 19. The largest loan amount, shown in cell B18, did not change. The smallest loan, shown in cell B19, is now $9,000. The amount shown in cell B20 for the average loan changed from $77,423 to $72,160.

James now understands how important it is to check each formula to make sure it works. You explain that there are many ways to test a worksheet to verify its accuracy. For example, you can use test data or compare results with known values, such as those in loan payment tables.

James does not want a printout of the what-if analysis, so you close the workbook without saving it. Because you do not save the current version of the workbook, the version on disk reflects the worksheet before you changed the interest rates from 12% to 11% and added the West Wight Potter.

To close the workbook without saving the what-if analysis:

1. Click the document window **Close** button.

2. Click the **No** button when you see the message "Save changes in Super Sails Charter Company.xls?"

3. Exit Excel if you are not going to do the Tutorial Assignments now.

To complete the Loan Management worksheet, you used many Excel functions to simplify the formulas you entered. You were able to troubleshoot the problem you encountered when you copied the percent of total payment formula and got a column of "#DIV/0!" error messages because you remembered that absolute references don't change when you copy them to other cells.

Quick Check

1. Write the formula you would use to display the value $100 if cell A9 contains the word "Bonus," but display $0 if cell A9 is empty.

2. Write the formula you would use to display the message "Over budget" whenever the amount in cell B5 is greater than or equal to $800,000, but display the message "Budget OK" if the amount in cell B5 is less than $800,000.

3. Give an example of a situation in which you would want to use an absolute reference rather than a relative reference.

4. What do the empty parentheses in the TODAY function mean?

5. Explain what the message #DIV/0! means.

6. Which function key changes the cell reference type from relative to absolute?

Tutorial Assignments

Launch Windows and Excel, if necessary, then complete the Tutorial Assignments, and print the results for Tutorial Assignments Steps 11 and 19.

1. Open the file Sails in the TAssign folder for Tutorial 4 on your student disk, then save it as Superior Sails Charter Company 2 in the same folder.

2. In the Documentation sheet, enter your name in cell B5, and use the TODAY function to display the date in cell B6. Then display the Loan Management sheet.

3. Look at the If formulas in column G. How do they differ from the If formulas you created in the tutorial? Which form do you prefer? Why?
   You've just received some additional paperwork for a new loan. Superior Sails purchased the CSY Gulfstar 42 with a $183,000 loan at 9.75% (.0975) interest for 20 years.

4. On the loan management sheet, insert a blank row between the Hunter 30 and the Beneteau 39 at row 13. Hint: Because you are adding the row in the middle of the range specified for the function arguments, you will not need to adjust the SUM, MAX, MIN, and AVERAGE formulas.

5. Enter the name of the boat, "CSY Gulfstar 42," in column A.

6. Enter the loan amount in cell B13, the interest rate in cell C13, and the number of monthly payments in cell D13.

7. In cell E13 use the PMT function to calculate the monthly payment.

8. In cell F13, enter "Outstanding."

9. In cell G13 use the IF function to display $0.00 if the loan is paid, or the correct payment if the loan is outstanding.

10. Copy the formula from cell H12 to cell H13 to calculate the percent of total payment.

11. Edit the header to insert your name.

12. Save the revised workbook.

13. Print the worksheet in landscape orientation; center it from top to bottom and from left to right. Do not print cell borders or row and column headings.

14. Use a felt marker or pen on your printout to indicate which cells display different results after adding the CSY Gulfstar 42.

15. Return to the worksheet on your screen and enter the label "Largest Payment:" in cell A21; then in cell B21 enter the formula to find the largest loan payment in column G.

16. Enter the label "Smallest Payment:" in cell A22; then in cell B22 enter the formula to find the smallest loan payment in column G.

17. Enter the label "Average Interest Rate:" in cell A23; then in cell B23 enter the formula to calculate the average of the interest rates shown in column C.

18. Format the text in cells A21 through A23 to align on the right side of the cell, and adjust column width, if necessary.

19. Use the AutoCalculate box in the status bar to perform some quick calculations without actually entering any formulas. Select the range containing the loan amounts in column B, then right-click the AutoCalculate box in the status bar to display the menu and select COUNT. (This function counts the number of non-blank cells in a selected range.) How many loans does the worksheet include? Next, use AutoCalculate to calculate the average loan amount. Finally, select SUM again to display the sum of the selected range. Write the COUNT, AVERAGE, and SUM figures on a separate piece of paper and include it with your printouts.

20. Save the revised workbook.

21. Make two printouts:
    a. Print the worksheet in landscape orientation, centered on the page, without cell gridlines or row and column headings.
    b. Print the formulas in landscape orientation, centered on the page, and include cell gridlines and row and column headings.

Case Problems

1. Compiling Data on the U.S. Airline Industry The editor of *Aviation Week and Space Technology* asked you to research the current status of the U.S. airline industry. You collect information on the revenue-miles and passenger-miles for each major U.S. airline. You want to calculate summary information to use in the article:

- total revenue-miles for the U.S. airline industry
- total passenger-miles for the U.S. airline industry
- each airline's share of the total revenue-miles
- each airline's share of the total passenger-miles
- average revenue-miles for U.S. airlines
- average passenger-miles for U.S. airlines

Complete these steps:

1. Open the workbook Aviation in the Case folder for Tutorial 4, then save it as Aviation Week in the same folder.

2. In the Documentation sheet, enter your name in cell B5, and use the TODAY function to display the date in cell B6.

3. On the Mileage Data sheet, use the SUM function to calculate the industry total revenue-miles in cell B14.

4. Use the SUM function to calculate the industry total passenger-miles in cell D14.

5. In cell C7, enter the formula to calculate American Airlines' share of the total industry revenue-miles using the equation:

$$\frac{\text{American's share of total}}{\text{industry revenue-miles}} = \frac{\text{American's revenue-miles}}{\text{industry total revenue-miles}}$$

Hint: You are going to use this formula for the other airlines, so consider which cell reference should be absolute.

6. Copy the formula from cell C7 to calculate each airline's share of the total industry revenue-miles.

7. In cell E7 enter the formula to calculate American Airlines' share of the total industry passenger-miles, then copy this formula for the other airlines.

8. In cell B15 use the AVERAGE function to calculate the average revenue-miles for the U.S. airline industry.

9. In cell D15 use the AVERAGE function to calculate the average passenger-miles for the U.S. airline industry.
10. Use the TODAY function to display the date in cell B3.
11. Edit the header to insert your name.
12. Format the worksheet so it is easier to read:
    a. Bold the titles and column headings.
    b. Center the title across the entire worksheet and center column titles over each column.
    c. Add a border at the bottom of cells A6 through E6, and add a border at the top of cells A14 through E14.
    d. Format columns B and D to display numbers with commas; for example, the revenue-miles for American Airlines will display as 26,851 instead of 26851.
    e. Format columns C and E for percents that display two decimal places.
13. Save your workbook.
14. Make two printouts:
    a. Print the worksheet in portrait orientation, centered on the page, without cell gridlines or row and column headings.
    b. Print the formulas in landscape orientation, centered on the page, and include cell gridlines and row and column headings.

2. Commission Analysis at Norcross Office Systems You are sales manager for Norcross Office Systems, an office supply store. You are thinking about changing the commission structure to motivate sales representatives to increase sales. Currently, sales representatives earn a monthly base salary of $500.00. In addition to the base salary, sales representatives earn a 6% (.06) commission on their sales when their monthly sales volume totals $6,000.00 or more.

To look at some options for changing the commission structure, you collected past payroll information for one employee, Jim Marley. Jim's monthly sales are typical of most of the Norcross sales representatives. You want to design a worksheet that will help you look at how much money Jim would have earned in the past 12 months if the commission structure were different.

To complete the worksheet:

1. Open the workbook Norcross in the Case folder for Tutorial 4 on your Student Disk, then save it as Norcross Sales Bonuses in the same folder.
2. In the Documentation sheet, enter your name in cell B5, and use the TODAY function to display the date in cell B6.
3. In the Commission Analysis sheet, enter the names of the months January through December in column A. Hint: Use the fill handle to automatically fill cells A9 through A20 with the names of months.
4. In cell C9, enter a formula that uses the IF function to calculate Jim's January bonus:
    a. For the *logical test* argument, enter the expression to check if Jim's sales are greater than or equal to sales required for a commission in cell C5.
    b. For the *value if true* argument, multiply Jim's sales by the commission percent in cell C6.
    c. For the *value if false* argument, enter a zero.
5. Copy the formula from cell C9 to cells C10 through C20.
6. If your formulas produce zeros for every month, something is wrong. Examine the formula in cell C9 and determine which references need to be absolute. Edit the formula and then copy it again. Your formulas are correct if cell C18 shows that Jim earned a $433.56 commission.
7. In cell E9, enter a formula to calculate Jim's total pay for January. Calculate Jim's total pay by adding his commission to his base salary.
8. Copy the formula from cell E9 to cells E10 through E20.
9. In cell E21, use the SUM function to total Jim's yearly pay.
10. Edit the header to insert your name, and then save the workbook.

11. Write your answers to these questions:
    a. How much did Jim earn in the last 12 months under the current commission structure?
    b. How much would Jim have earned last year if the commission were 8%?
    c. How much would Jim have earned in the last 12 months if the commission rate were 7%, but he had to make at least $6,500 in sales each month before earning a commission?
12. Print two versions of your worksheet:
    a. Print the worksheet showing what Jim would have earned if he had to sell $6,500 each month to earn a 7% commission. Center the worksheet on the page, but do not print cell gridlines or row and column headings.
    b. Display the formulas for the worksheet and adjust column widths to eliminate extra space. Print the formulas for the worksheet in portrait orientation. Print the entire worksheet on one page; include cell gridlines and row and column headings.

3. Calculating Car Loans at First Federal Bank You are a loan officer in the Consumer Loan Department of the First Federal Bank. Your job is to evaluate customer applications for car loans, and you want to create a worksheet to calculate monthly payments, total payments, and total interest paid on a loan.

To complete the loan worksheet:
1. Open the workbook First in the Case folder for Tutorial 4 on your Student Disk, then save it as First Federal Loan Department in the same folder.
2. In the Documentation sheet, enter your name in cell B5, and use the TODAY function to display the date in cell B6.
3. In the Car Loan Evaluation sheet, enter a formula in cell B10 that uses the PMT function to calculate the monthly payment for the loan amount in cell B5, at the annual interest rate in cell B6, for the term in cell A10. Display the monthly payment as a positive amount.
4. Edit the formula in cell B10 so you use absolute references for any cell references that should not change when you copy the formula.
5. Copy the formula from cell B10 to cells B11 through B14.
6. Enter the formula in cell D10 to calculate the total interest using the following equation:

$$total\ interest = total\ payments - loan\ amount$$

7. Edit the formula in cell D10 so you use absolute references for any cell references that should not change when you copy the formula.
8. Copy the formula from cell D10 to cells D11 through D14.
9. Edit the header to insert your name.
10. Make any formatting changes you consider appropriate for a professional-looking worksheet.
11. Preview the printed worksheet. Change page setup settings as needed to produce a professional-looking printout, then print the worksheet.
12. Save the workbook with formatting changes.
13. Print the formulas in landscape orientation. Include cell gridlines and row and column headings.

4. Tracking Homework Assignments Create a log to track your homework assignments for the current term. Your worksheet should include a column for Assignment, Class, Due Date, Status, and Hours to Complete. The worksheet should also display the current date, as well as the total number of assignments completed. Use the IF function to display "Late" in the Status column whenever the current date is later than the Due Date. When you complete a homework assignment, you can replace the IF function with the word "Finished." To create your homework log, follow these steps:
1. Think about how you want to organize your worksheet, and then create a rough sketch. Indicate which formulas you want to include, and how you want to format the worksheet.

2. Open a new workbook and save it as Homework, in the Case folder for Tutorial 4.

3. Enter a worksheet title in cell A1. Use the TODAY function to enter the date in cell A2.

4. Enter and format the column labels.

5. In the Status column, create a formula that tells Excel to do the following: If the due date is greater than the current date, display the word "Pending," otherwise, display the word "Late." Use absolute values as necessary.

6. Copy the IF formula to ten blank rows, and then enter data for at least ten homework assignments in the Assignment, Class, and Due Date columns. For assignments you have already handed in, enter "finished" in the Status column (replacing the existing IF formula) and then enter a value in the Hours to Complete column.

7. In another area of the worksheet, enter the label "Total Assignments Completed," and then use the COUNT function to count the total number of completed assignments. *Hint*: You'll want to count the nonblank cells in the Hours to Complete column.

8. Add data for four more assignments. Remember to copy the IF function to the new rows as necessary. Do you need to revise any other part of the worksheet to make it work properly?

9. Format your worksheet to make it look professional.

10. Document your worksheet in a text note attached to cell A1, then save your work.

11. Preview the worksheet, adjust the page setup options as necessary, and print it. When you're finished printing, save the workbook again.

12. Print the worksheet formulas.

Charts and Graphing

Charting Sales Information

Cast Iron Concepts

CASE

You are assistant marketing director at Cast Iron Concepts, a distributor of traditional cast iron stoves. You're working on a new product catalog, and your main concern is how much space to allocate for each product. In previous catalogs the Box Windsor stove was allocated one full page. The Star Windsor and the West Windsor stoves were each allocated a half page.

After collecting sales information about the three stove models, you discovered that Box Windsor stove sales have steadily decreased since 1991. Although the Box Windsor stove was the best-selling model during the 1980s, sales of Star Windsor stoves and West Windsor stoves increased steadily, outselling the Box Windsor. You believe that the space allocated to the Box Windsor stove should be reduced to a half page while the Star Windsor stove and the West Windsor stove should each have a full page.

You need to convince the marketing director to change the space allocation in the new catalog, so you are preparing a presentation for the next department meeting. In the presentation you plan to show four charts graphically illustrating the sales pattern of the Box Windsor, Star Windsor, and West Windsor stoves. You also plan to show a map of the United States illustrating sales of the Box Windsor by state.

SESSION **5.1**	*In this session you will learn about the variety of Excel chart types available to you and learn to identify the parts of a chart. You will also learn how to select non-adjacent ranges, how to create a 3-D pie chart, and how to select and activate a chart. Finally you will learn a number of techniques for improving your chart, including moving and resizing a chart, pulling a wedge from a pie chart, and changing chart patterns.*

Excel Charts

The sales figures are saved in a workbook named Concepts. You will generate the charts from the data in the worksheet.

To Start Excel, open the Concepts workbook, and rename it:

1. Start Excel as usual.

2. Open the Concepts workbook in the Tutorial.05 folder on your Student Disk.

You see the documentation worksheet. Notice that the contents portion of this sheet lists only three worksheets. You will use several new worksheets during this tutorial and then revise the Documentation sheet in the Tutorial Assignments. For now, you can type your name and the current date and then save the workbook under a new name.

1. Type your name and the current date in the appropriate cells in the Documentation sheet.

2. Save the workbook as Cast Iron Concepts. After you do so, the new filename, Cast Iron Concepts, appears in the title bar.

3. Click the **Sales Figures** tab to move to that sheet. See Figure 5-1.

Figure 5-1 ◄
Cast Iron
Concepts
workbook

new filename

total dollar volume
for each year

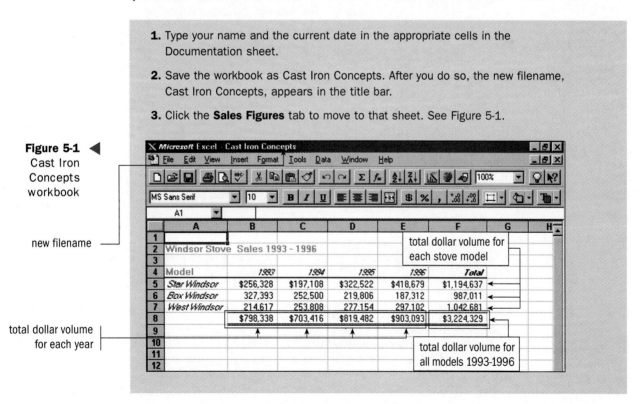

The worksheet shows the sales each Windsor stove model generated in the period 1993 through 1996. The total dollar volume during the four-year period for each model is in column F. The total dollar volume for each year is in row 8.

It is easy to visually represent this kind of worksheet data. You might think of these graphical representations as "graphs"; however, in Excel they are referred to as **charts**. Figure 5-2 shows the 15 **chart types** you can use to represent worksheet data. Of the 15 chart types, nine produce two-dimensional (2-D) charts and six produce three-dimensional (3-D) charts.

Figure 5-2 ◄
Excel chart
types

Icon	Chart Type	Purpose
	Area chart	Shows the magnitude of change over a period of time
	Bar chart	Shows comparisons between the data represented by each bar
	Column chart	Shows comparisons between the data represented by each column
	Line chart	Shows trends or changes over time
	Pie chart	Shows the proportion of parts to a whole
	Radar chart	Shows changes in data relative to a center point
	XY chart	Shows the pattern or relationship between sets of (x,y) data points
	Combination chart	Shows how one set of data corresponds to another set by super-imposing one chart type over another
	3-D Area chart	Shows the magnitude of each data series as a solid, three-dimensional shape
	3-D Bar chart	Similar to a 2-D Bar chart, but bars appear three-dimensional
	3-D Column chart	Shows three-dimensional columns and some formats show data on x-, y-, and z-axes
	3-D Line chart	Shows each chart line as a ribbon within a three-dimensional space
	3-D Pie chart	Shows the proportion of parts to a whole, with emphasis on the data values in the front wedges
	3-D Surface chart	Shows the interrelationship between large amounts of data
	Doughnut chart	Shows the proportion of parts to whole

Each chart type has several predefined **chart formats** that specify format characteristics such as gridlines, chart labels, axes, and so on. For example, the Area chart type has the five predefined formats shown in Figure 5-3. You can find more information on chart types and formats in the Microsoft Excel user's guide, in the Excel Help facility, and in the ChartWizard.

Figure 5-3 ◀
Predefined
formats for the
Area chart type

Predefined Chart Format	Format Characteristics
	Simple Area chart
	100% Area chart
	Area chart with drop lines
	Area chart with gridlines
	Area chart with labels

Figure 5-4 shows the elements of a typical Excel chart. Understanding the Excel chart terminology is particularly important so you can successfully construct and edit charts.

Figure 5-4 ◀
Excel chart
elements

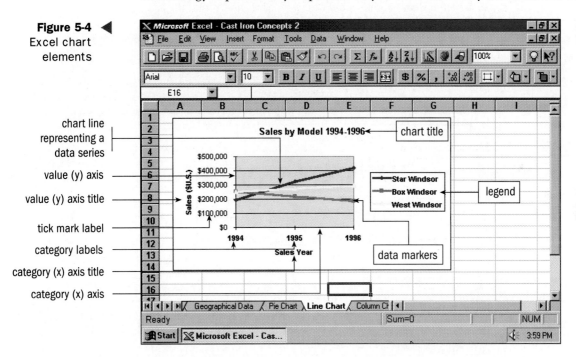

The **chart title** identifies the chart. The horizontal axis of the chart is called the **category axis** or the **x-axis**. The vertical axis is called the **value axis** or the **y-axis**. Each axis on a chart can have a title that identifies the scale or categories of the chart data; in Figure 5-4 the **x-axis title** is "Year" and the **y-axis title** is "Sales in U.S. Dollars."

A **tick mark label** shows the scale for the y-axis. Excel automatically generates this scale based on the values selected for the chart. The **category names** or **category labels**, usually displayed on the x-axis, correspond to the labels you use for the worksheet data.

A **data point** is a single value in a cell in the worksheet. A **data marker** is a bar, area, wedge, or symbol that marks a single data point on a chart. For example, the 1996 sales of the Star Windsor stove in cell E5 of the worksheet on your screen is a data point. The small square on the chart line in Figure 5-4 that shows the 1996 sales of the Star Windsor stove is a data marker.

A **data series** is a group of related data points, such as the Star Windsor sales shown in cells B5 through E5 on your worksheet. On a chart like the one in Figure 5-4, a data series shows as a set of data markers connected by a chart line.

When you have more than one data series, your chart will contain more than one set of data markers. For example, Figure 5-4 has three chart lines, each representing a data series. When you show more than one data series on a chart, it is a good idea to use a **legend** to identify which data markers represent each data series.

You want to show that the West Windsor and Star Windsor stove models generate a higher proportion of the total Windsor stove sales than the Box Windsor model. Because pie charts effectively show the relationship of parts to the whole, you decide to use a pie chart to show sales for each model as a percentage of total Windsor stove sales.

You know that pie charts and 3-D pie charts illustrate the same relationships, but you decide to create a 3-D pie chart because you think it looks more professional. Because you will create a number of charts, you decide to put each chart on a separate sheet. This will let you switch quickly from one chart to another, without scrolling up and down through numerous charts. In the next set of steps, you rename Sheet4 "Pie Chart."

To rename Sheet4:

1. Double-click the **Sheet4** tab to open the Rename Sheet dialog box.

2. Type **Pie Chart** in the Name box, then click the **OK** button. See Figure 5-5.

Figure 5-5 ◀
Renaming a
blank sheet

type the new sheet
name here

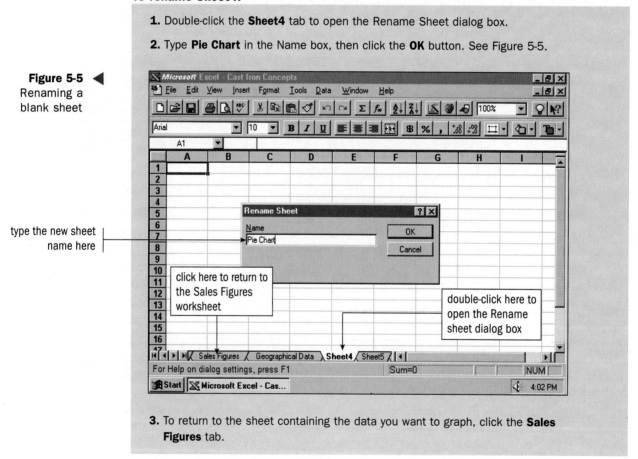

3. To return to the sheet containing the data you want to graph, click the **Sales Figures** tab.

Now you are ready to create a pie chart on the Pie Chart sheet.

Creating a 3-D Pie Chart

A **pie chart** represents one data series by displaying each data point as a wedge. The size of the wedge represents the proportion of the data point in the total circle, or "pie." When you create a pie chart, you generally specify two ranges. Excel uses the first range for the category labels and the second range for the data series. Excel automatically calculates the percentage for each wedge, draws the wedge to reflect the percentage, and gives you the option of displaying the percentage as a label on the completed chart.

A 3-D pie chart shows a three-dimensional view of a pie chart. The 3-D representation adds visual interest and emphasizes the data points in the front wedges or in any wedges that are pulled out, or "exploded," from the circle. Each wedge on an Excel 3-D pie chart can be colored or patterned, displayed with category labels, or labeled with its percentage relative to the whole pie.

You want to create a 3-D pie chart to show the percentage of sales generated by each Windsor stove model during 1996. To begin, you draw a sketch (like Figure 5-6) showing how you want the pie chart to look. The pie chart will have three wedges, one for each stove model. You want each wedge labeled with a stove model's name and its percentage of total sales. Because you won't know the percentages until Excel calculates them and displays them on the chart, you can put "__%" on your sketch to show where you want the percentages to appear.

Figure 5-6 ◀
Pie chart
sketch

labels for pie wedges
(category labels)

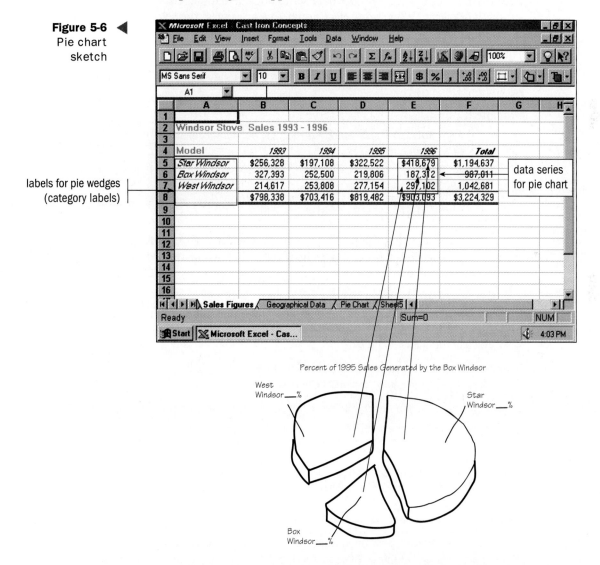

The sketch shows roughly what you want the chart to look like. It is difficult to envision exactly how a chart will look until you know how the data series looks when it is plotted; therefore, you don't need to incorporate every detail on the chart sketch. As you construct the chart, you can take advantage of Excel's editing capabilities to try different formatting options until your chart looks just the way you want it.

You refer back to your worksheet and note in the sketch that the data labels for the pie wedges are in cells A5 through A7 and the data points representing the pie wedges are in cells E5 through E7. You must select these two ranges to tell the ChartWizard what you want to chart, but you realize that these ranges are not next to each other on the worksheet. You know how to highlight a series of adjacent cells; now you need to learn how to select two separate ranges at once.

Selecting Non-adjacent Ranges

A **non-adjacent range** is a group of individual cells or ranges that are not next to each other. Selecting non-adjacent ranges is particularly useful when you construct charts because the cells that contain the data series and the data labels are often not side by side on the worksheet. When you select non-adjacent ranges, the selected cells in each range are highlighted. You can then format the cells, clear them, or use them to construct a chart.

REFERENCE window	**SELECTING NON-ADJACENT RANGES**
	■ Click the first cell or highlight the first range you want to select.
	■ Press and hold Ctrl while you click additional cells or highlight additional ranges.
	■ After you select all the cells you want to include, release [Ctrl].

To begin constructing the pie chart, you first select the range A5:A7, which contains the data labels. Then you hold down the Control key while highlighting the range E5:E7, which contains the data points.

To select range A5:A7 and range E5:E7 in the Sales Figures sheet:

1. Make sure the Sales Figures sheet is active. Highlight cells **A5** through **A7**, then release the mouse button.

2. Press and hold **Ctrl** while you highlight cells **E5** through **E7**. Release **Ctrl**. Two ranges are now highlighted: A5:A7 and E5:E7.

   TROUBLE? If you don't highlight the cells you want on your first try, click any cell to remove the highlighting, then go back to Step 1 and try again.

Now that you have selected the cells you want to use for the pie chart, you use the ChartWizard button to specify chart type, chart format, and chart titles.

To create the pie chart using the ChartWizard:

1. Click the **ChartWizard** button . The prompt "Drag in document to create chart" appears in the status bar. This prompt asks you to specify where you want the chart to appear in the worksheet.

2. Click the **Pie Chart** tab to select the sheet where you want the chart to appear.

3. Move the ✚ pointer to cell A1 to specify where the upper-left corner of the chart will appear.

4. Hold down the mouse button and drag the pointer to cell **F13** to outline the area where you want the chart to appear. Release the mouse button to display the ChartWizard - Step 1 of 5 dialog box. Now the dialog box appears over the Sales Figures sheet so you can correct the range address if necessary. See Figure 5-7.

Figure 5-7 ◀
ChartWizard -
Step 1 of 5
dialog box

sales data

address of the data
you want to chart

sales Figures sheet
is active

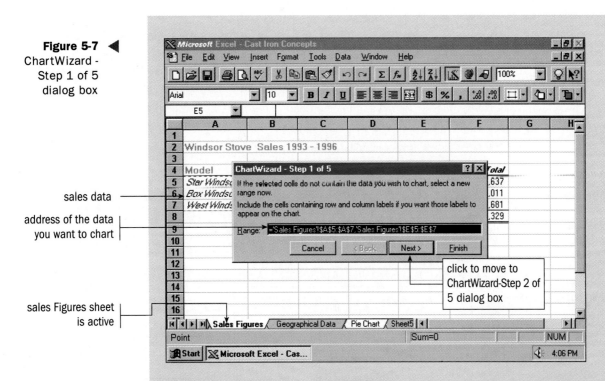

Make sure the range is ='Sales Figures'!$A$5:$A$7,'Sales Figures'!$E$5:$E$7. These cell references are the absolute references to the ranges you selected in the previous set of steps. Note that the cell references also include the name of the sheet where the cells are located. The exclamation mark (!) indicates an absolute sheet reference.

TROUBLE? If the range displayed on your screen is not correct, type the necessary corrections in the Range box.

5. Click the **Next >** button to display the ChartWizard - Step 2 of 5 dialog box.

6. Double-click the **3-D Pie** chart type to display the ChartWizard - Step 3 of 5 dialog box.

7. Double-click chart format **7** so your chart will show labels and percentages for each wedge. ChartWizard - Step 4 of 5 shows you a sample of the chart. See Figure 5-8.

Figure 5-8 ◀
Sample 3-D pie
chart

sample chart

wedge percentage

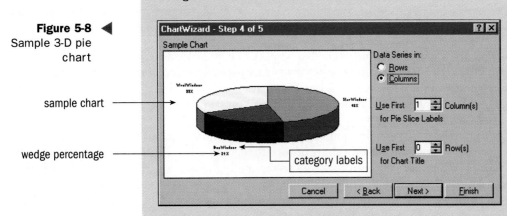

This looks right, so next you'll add a chart title.

8. Click the **Next >** button to display the ChartWizard - Step 5 of 5 dialog box.

9. Click the **Chart Title** box, then type **Percent of 1996 Sales Generated by the Box Windsor**. After a pause, Excel displays the new title in the Sample Chart box.

10. Click the **Finish** button to complete the chart. The new chart, along with the chart toolbar, appears in the Pie Chart sheet. Use the scroll bars, if necessary, to view the entire chart on the worksheet. See Figure 5-9.

TROUBLE? If your monitor is monochrome, the chart will be displayed in shades of gray instead of colors.

Figure 5-9 ◄
3-D pie chart positioned on worksheet

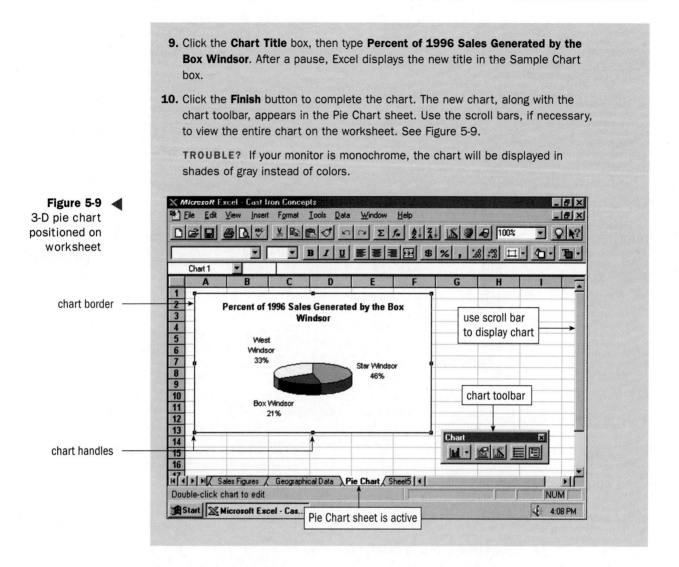

If your chart looks somewhat different from Figure 5-9, you might need to change its size, as explained later in this tutorial. For now, don't worry about the chart toolbar. You'll learn to use it later.

Selecting and Activating the Chart

The chart you created is an embedded object or an embedded chart. To modify an embedded chart, you need to either select it or activate it. To select a chart, simply click once anywhere within its borders. When the chart is selected, Excel displays handles, eight small black squares, along the chart border. You can drag these handles to change the chart's size.

You activate a chart by double-clicking anywhere within its borders. Usually, when the chart is activated, the thin chart border changes to a thick colored (or gray) line. If the chart is so big that you need to scrool to see it all, you may see the entire activated chart in a special chart window, with a title bar. Don't be concerned if you see one of your charts in a chart window; it simply means your chart is too big to fit in the worksheet window. Treat the chart window just as you would an activated chart with a thick border.

Activating a chart (also known as putting a chart in Edit mode) gives you access to the Chart commands on the menu bar. Also, when the chart is activated, you can double-click any part of the chart to open a Format dialog box. Let's experiment with some of these techniques now.

To practice selecting and activating the chart:

1. Make sure the Pie Chart sheet is active. Click anywhere outside the chart border to make sure the chart is not selected. The chart toolbar disappears; so do the square handles around the chart border.

2. Click once anywhere within the chart border to select the chart. The chart toolbar and the square handles on the chart border appear.

3. To activate the chart (or put it in Edit mode), double-click anywhere within the chart border. The chart border turns into a thick colored (or gray) line. Additional square handles might appear along the edge of the chart. The horizontal and vertical scroll bars disappear from the worksheet window. See Figure 5-10.

Figure 5-10 ◀
Chart in Edit mode

activated chart is ready to be edited ──

large black handles appear inside chart border ──

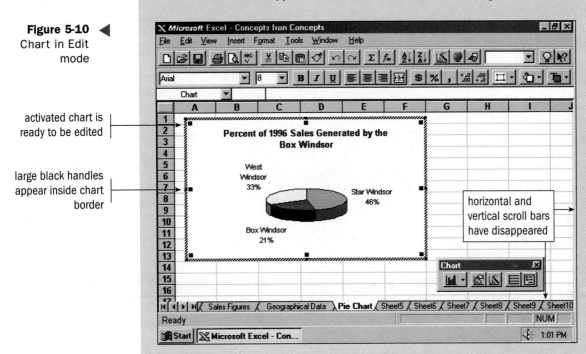

horizontal and vertical scroll bars have disappeared

TROUBLE? If you don't see the large black handles shown in Figure 5-10, try clicking the white area in the chart's lower-right corner. If you see the chart in a window with a menu bar, don't be concerned. Perform the following steps as if the chart were displayed within a thick border.

Now that the chart is in Edit mode (activated), you have access to the Chart commands on the menu bar.

4. Click **Format**. The Format menu displays the chart formatting options. Click **Format** again to close the Format menu.

5. To open the Format Chart Area dialog box, double-click anywhere on the white space in the chart border. The Format Chart Area dialog box shown in Figure 5-11 appears.

Figure 5-11 ◄
Format Chart
Area dialog box

if you see a different
title you double-
clicked the wrong part
of the chart

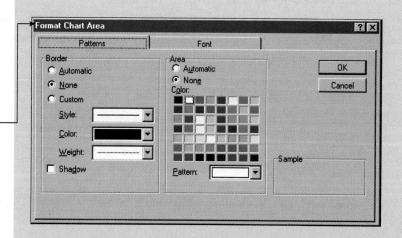

TROUBLE? If the dialog box has a slightly different title, don't worry—it simply means that you double-clicked on a part of the chart other than the white space. As a result, Excel displays the dialog box appropriate for that part of the chart.

6. Click the **Cancel** button to close the dialog box and return to the Pie Chart sheet.

7. Double-click anywhere outside the chart border to deactivate the chart. The chart border becomes a thin line, and the chart toolbar disappears.

Now that you're familiar with selecting and activating a chart, you can modify the pie chart.

Moving and Changing the Size of a Chart

When you use the ChartWizard to create a chart, you drag the pointer to outline the worksheet area where you want the chart to appear. If the area you outlined is not large enough, Excel positions the chart elements as best as it can, but the text on the chart might break in odd places. For example, in Figure 5-9 the chart title appears on two lines. You can increase the chart's size to eliminate this problem.

To change a chart's size, you first click the chart to select it. You can reposition the chart on the worksheet by clicking anywhere inside the chart border and dragging the chart to the new location. Let's practice moving the chart and changing its size.

To move and change the chart's size:

1. Click anywhere within the chart border to select the chart. Black handles appear on the chart border.

2. Position the pointer anywhere within the chart border, then hold down the mouse button and drag the chart two rows down. Release the mouse button to view the chart in its new position.

3. Position the pointer over a handle on the right-hand chart border. Hold down the mouse button and drag the border one column to the right. Release the mouse button to view the new chart size.

4. Adjust the size and position of your chart so it looks like Figure 5-12.

Figure 5-12 ◀
Adjusting the
chart's size and
position

title fits on one line
after chart is widened

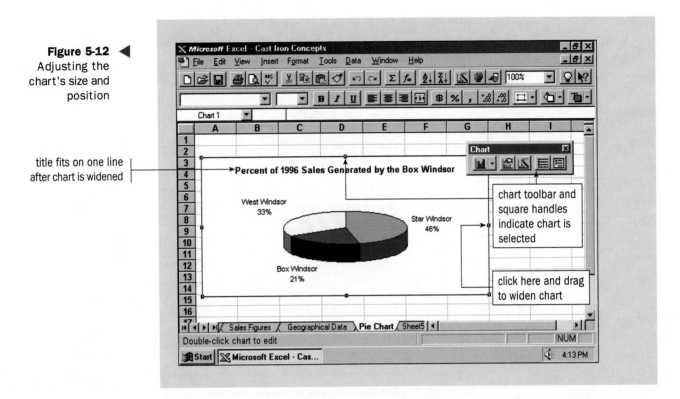

You decide to draw attention to the Box Windsor data by pulling out the wedge that represents its sales.

Pulling Out a Wedge of a Pie Chart

When the chart is in Edit mode, you can manipulate each of its parts. When you click a wedge of the pie chart, small black handles appear, showing that you selected the wedge. You can then drag the wedge out of the circle or pull it back into the circle. In this case, you want to pull out the wedge that represents sales for the Box Windsor stove.

To pull out the wedge that represents the Box Windsor stove sales:

1. Double-click within the border of the chart to activate it. The border changes to a thick colored (or gray) line.

2. Click the white space just inside the chart border to make sure the large black handles appear around the inside edge of the activated chart, as in Figure 5-10. These handles indicate that you selected the entire chart border.

3. Click anywhere on the pie to select it. One square handle appears on each pie wedge.

4. Now that you have selected the entire pie, you can select one part of it, the Box Windsor wedge. Position ⌖ over the wedge that represents Box Windsor sales, then click to select the wedge. Handles now appear on this wedge only. See Figure 5-13.

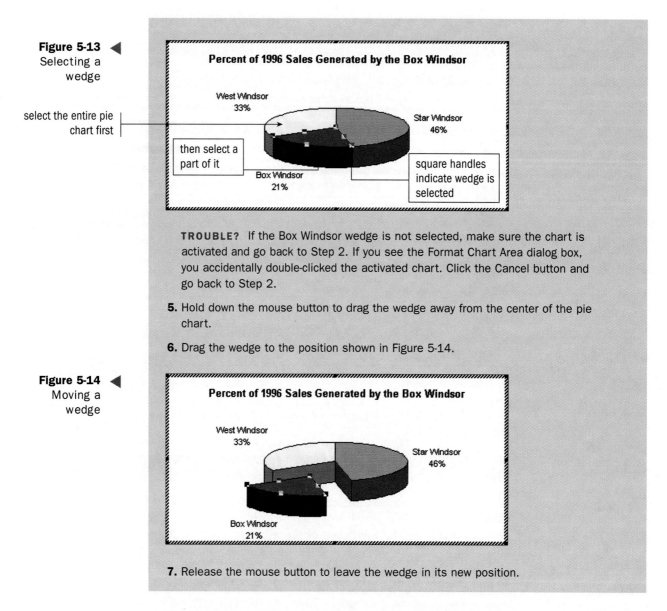

Figure 5-13 ◀
Selecting a
wedge

select the entire pie
chart first

Figure 5-14 ◀
Moving a
wedge

TROUBLE? If the Box Windsor wedge is not selected, make sure the chart is activated and go back to Step 2. If you see the Format Chart Area dialog box, you accidentally double-clicked the activated chart. Click the Cancel button and go back to Step 2.

5. Hold down the mouse button to drag the wedge away from the center of the pie chart.

6. Drag the wedge to the position shown in Figure 5-14.

7. Release the mouse button to leave the wedge in its new position.

The chart on your screen shows that the Box Windsor stove sales generated the smallest percentage of total Windsor stove sales in 1996. After looking over the chart, you decide to add patterns to the chart wedges for more visual interest.

Changing Chart Patterns

Patterns add visual interest to a chart, and they can be useful when your printer has no color capability. Although your charts appear in color on a color monitor, if your printer does not have color capability Excel translates colors to gray shades for the printout. It's difficult to distinguish some colors, particularly darker ones, from one another when Excel translates them to gray shades and then prints them. You can make your charts more readable by selecting a different pattern for each data marker.

To apply a pattern to a data marker, such as a wedge in a pie chart, activate the chart, select the data marker to which you want to apply a pattern, then select the pattern you want from the Patterns dialog box.

SELECTING A PATTERN FOR A DATA MARKER

REFERENCE window

- Make sure the chart is activated.
- Select the wedge, or column data marker, to which you want to apply a pattern.
- Click Format then click Selected Data Point to display the Format Data Point dialog box (or double-click the wedge or column marker to which you want to apply a pattern to display the Format Data Point dialog box).
- Click the Patterns tab, then click the Patterns list arrow to display a list of patterns.
- Click the pattern you want to apply, then click the OK button to close the dialog box.

You want to apply a dot pattern to the Box Windsor wedge, a horizontal stripe pattern to the Star Windsor wedge, and a grid pattern to the West Windsor wedge.

To apply patterns to the wedges:

1. Make sure the chart is activated.

2. If necessary, select the Box Windsor wedge to display the small black handles.

3. Double-click the **Box Windsor wedge** to display the Format Data Point dialog box.

   TROUBLE? If the dialog box you see has a different title, then you didn't select the wedge before double-clicking. Close the dialog box and go back to Step 2.

4. If necessary, click the Patterns tab, then click the **Pattern** list arrow to display the patterns.

5. Click the **sparse dot** pattern to select it. See Figure 5-15.

Figure 5-15 ◄
Format Data
Point dialog
box

Format Data Point
dialog box appears
when you double-click
an activated wedge

use horizontal stripe
pattern for the Star
Windsor wedge

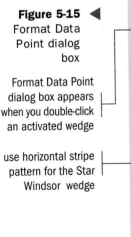
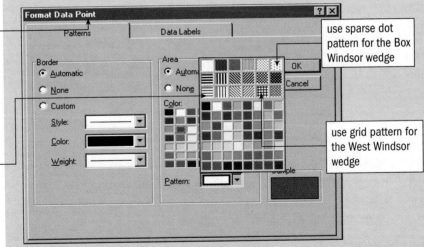

6. Click the **OK** button to close the dialog box and see the pattern.

7. Repeat Steps 2 through 6 to select a horizontal stripe pattern for the Star Windsor wedge, and again to select a grid pattern for the West Windsor wedge. After you select patterns for the Star Windsor and West Windsor wedges, your chart should look like Figure 5-16.

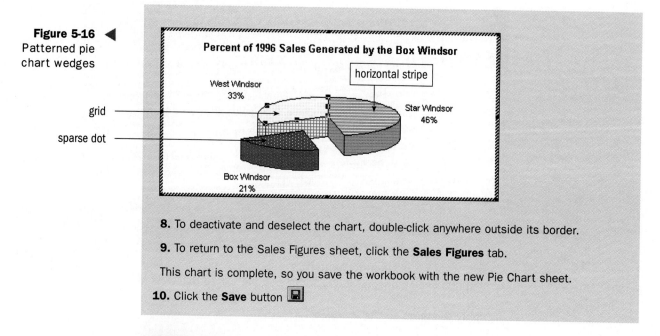

Figure 5-16 ◀
Patterned pie
chart wedges

Percent of 1996 Sales Generated by the Box Windsor

West Windsor
33%

horizontal stripe

Star Windsor
46%

grid

sparse dot

Box Windsor
21%

8. To deactivate and deselect the chart, double-click anywhere outside its border.

9. To return to the Sales Figures sheet, click the **Sales Figures** tab.

This chart is complete, so you save the workbook with the new Pie Chart sheet.

10. Click the **Save** button 🖫

Quick Check

1. Define the following terms:
   a. data point
   b. data marker
   c. data series
   d. non-adjacent range

2. Explain how to select the cells A1, C5, and D10 at the same time.

3. What type of chart shows the proportion of parts to a whole?

4. Describe how to put a chart in Edit mode.

5. List chart types that effectively show comparisons.

6. What do you need to do before you can move a chart?

7. Explain how to apply a dot pattern to a pie chart wedge.

SESSION 5.2

In this session you will learn how to create line and column charts, and practice revising the chart's data series. You will also learn how to add and edit chart text, add chart gridlines, format chart lines, use pictures, and enhance a chart title by adding color and a drop-shadow.

Creating a Line Chart

You want to show change in sales volume for each model during the period 1993 through 1996. You decide to create a line chart to illustrate this change. You begin by renaming a blank sheet, just as you did with the pie chart.

The first dialog box option, "Data Series in:," lets you specify whether the data series are in rows or columns. Looking at the sketch, you see that the data series are in rows. For example, the first line on the chart should plot Star Windsor sales in row 5: $256,328; $197,108; $322,522; and $418,679. The Rows option button is selected in the dialog box. This is correct, so you do not need to change this setting.

The second dialog box option, "Use first __ Row(s) for Category (X) Axis Labels," lets you specify whether you want to use any rows as category labels for the x-axis. The first row that you highlighted for the chart contains the values 1993, 1994, 1995, and 1996. You want to use these values as category labels, so you need to change the setting to 1. Before doing that, let's look at the last option in the dialog box.

The third dialog box option, "Use First __ Column(s) for Legend Text," lets you specify whether you want to use any columns for the legend text. The first column that you highlighted for the chart was column A, which contains the name of each stove model. You want to use labels in this column as legend text so the chart clearly shows which line represents the sales data for each stove. Excel automatically selects the first column for the legend text. You do not need to change the setting for this option.

You need to change the setting for the Category (X) Axis Labels, so that the values in the first row become x-axis labels instead of the first data series. Let's do that now.

To use the first row for x-axis labels:

1. Click the **up arrow** button for the Category (X) Axis Labels option to select **1** as the new setting. See Figure 5-19.

Figure 5-19 ◀
Revised sample
chart

now legend shows
three data series

x-axis labels from first
row of chart range

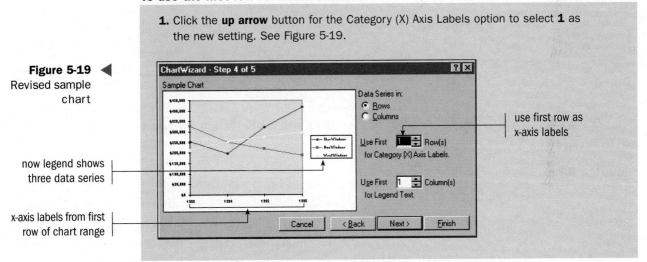

use first row as
x-axis labels

The revised chart looks good. The x-axis is labeled with years, the legend box contains labels for each stove model, and the chart displays one colored line for each stove model. Now you can complete the chart by adding the chart title and the x-axis title.

To add the chart title and x-axis title:

1. Click the **Next >** button to display the ChartWizard - Step 5 of 5 dialog box.

2. Click the **Chart Title** box, then type **Sales by Model 1993–1996** for the chart title, but don't press Enter. You also need to type the x-axis title.

   TROUBLE? If you inadvertently pressed Enter and the ChartWizard disappeared, don't worry about it now; just continue to Step 5.

3. Press **Tab** to move the pointer to the Category (X) box.

4. Type **Sales Year** and press **Enter** to complete the chart and display it on the Line Chart sheet. See Figure 5-20.

Figure 5-20 ◀
Completed line
chart

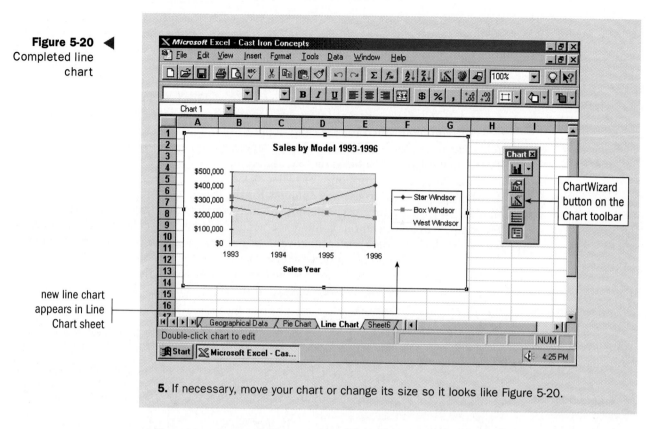

new line chart
appears in Line
Chart sheet

ChartWizard
button on the
Chart toolbar

5. If necessary, move your chart or change its size so it looks like Figure 5-20.

You are concerned because the chart shows a decline in sales of the Star Windsor between 1993 and 1994. You think you could make a stronger point if you include only the years 1994 through 1996 in the chart. But can you revise the chart without starting over?

Revising the Chart Data Series

After you create a chart, you might discover that you specified the wrong data range, or you might decide that your chart should display different data series. Whatever your reason, you do not need to start over in order to revise the chart's data series.

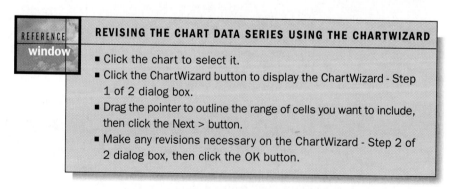

REFERENCE
window

REVISING THE CHART DATA SERIES USING THE CHARTWIZARD

■ Click the chart to select it.
■ Click the ChartWizard button to display the ChartWizard - Step 1 of 2 dialog box.
■ Drag the pointer to outline the range of cells you want to include, then click the Next > button.
■ Make any revisions necessary on the ChartWizard - Step 2 of 2 dialog box, then click the OK button.

You will use the ChartWizard to revise the data series for your line chart. This time, you'll use the ChartWizard button on the Chart toolbar. You want to show the sales for each stove during the period 1994 through 1996, instead of the period 1993 through 1996. Examining your worksheet, you see that you need to select range A4:A7 as legend text and range C4:E7 as the data series.

To revise the line chart:

1. If the line chart is not selected, click it to display the small black handles.

2. Click the **ChartWizard** button 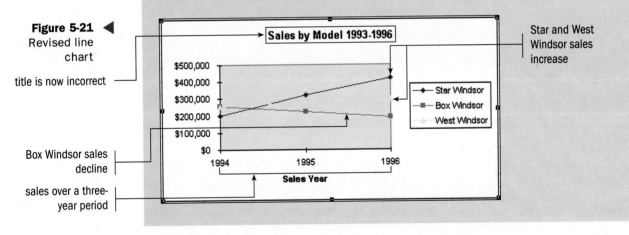 on the chart toolbar to display the ChartWizard - Step 1 of 2 dialog box on the Sales Figures sheet. Figure 5-20 shows the location of the ChartWizard button on the Chart toolbar.

3. Highlight cells **A4** through **A7** for the first range, then release the mouse button.

   TROUBLE? If the ChartWizard dialog box hides the range you need to highlight, drag the title of the dialog box to a new location.

4. Press and hold **Ctrl** while you highlight cells **C4** through **E7**.

5. Release the mouse button then release **Ctrl**.

6. Make sure the Range box displays

   ='Sales Figures'!$A$4:$A$7,'Sales Figures'!$C$4:$E$7, then click the **Next >** button to display the ChartWizard - Step 2 of 2 dialog box.

7. Verify that the sample chart shows three years on the x-axis. (You probably can't actually read the labels, but you should be able to tell if they're displayed.) Don't worry if the dates split onto two lines. If the chart doesn't look right, click the Back button to return to the previous dialog box and reselect the range.

8. Click the **OK** button to close the ChartWizard dialog box and return to the Line Chart sheet. See Figure 5-21.

Figure 5-21 ◄
Revised line chart

title is now incorrect

Star and West Windsor sales increase

Box Windsor sales decline

sales over a three-year period

The revised chart clearly shows that Box Windsor sales have decreased, while Star Windsor and West Windsor sales have increased. You notice that you now need to change the chart title to reflect your revisions.

Adding and Editing Chart Text

Excel classifies the text on your charts in three categories: label text, attached text, or unattached text. **Label text** includes the category names, the tick mark labels, the x-axis labels, and the legend. Label text often derives from the cells on the worksheet; you usually specify it using the ChartWizard or the Edit Series command on the Chart menu.

Attached text includes the chart title, x-axis title, and y-axis title. Although attached text appears in a predefined position, you can edit it and move it by clicking and dragging. To add attached text, use the Titles command on the Insert menu. To edit attached text, click the text, then type the changes.

Unattached text includes text boxes or comments that you type on the chart. You can position unattached text anywhere on the chart. To add unattached text to a chart, you use the Text Box tool.

As noted earlier, you need to change the chart title so it reflects the revised data series. To do this you must activate the chart, select the chart title, then change "1993" to "1994."

To revise the chart title:

1. Double-click the chart to activate it.

2. Click the chart title to select it and display the gray border and small black handles. See Figure 5-22.

Figure 5-22 ◀
Revising the
chart title

chart must be
activated before you
can select the
chart title

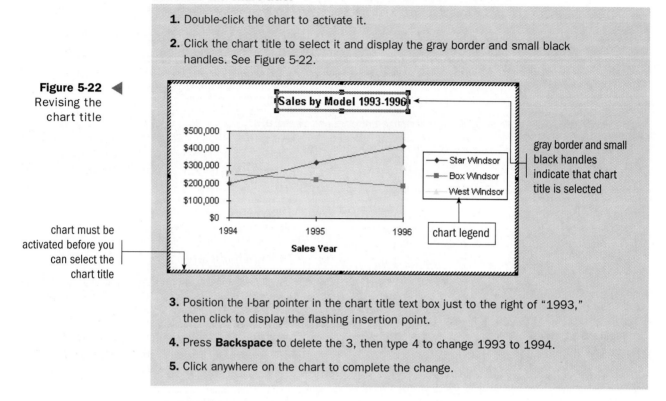

3. Position the I-bar pointer in the chart title text box just to the right of "1993," then click to display the flashing insertion point.

4. Press **Backspace** to delete the 3, then type 4 to change 1993 to 1994.

5. Click anywhere on the chart to complete the change.

Checking your original sketch, you notice that you forgot to include a y-axis title. You use the Titles command to add this title.

To add a y-axis title:

1. Make sure the chart is still activated.

2. Click **Insert** then click **Titles** to display the Titles dialog box.

3. Click the **Value (Y) Axis** option button to indicate that you want to add a y-axis title.

4. Click the **OK** button to close the Titles dialog box. Eight black handles and a gray border appear, surrounding the letter "Y" on the y-axis.

5. Type **Sales ($U.S.)**. Notice that the letters appear in the formula bar as you type.

6. Press **Enter** to add the y-axis title to the chart.

   TROUBLE? If you need to revise the y-axis title after you press Enter, make sure the title is selected, then type your revisions in the formula bar.

Now that the titles accurately describe the chart data, all you have left to do is format the chart labels.

Using Boldface for the Legend and Axis Labels

You can change any chart text's format using the Standard toolbar buttons or the Format menu. Each text item on a chart is an object; as with any object, you must click the object to select it before you can change it.

You look at the chart and decide that it will look better if you bold the legend text and the category labels along the x-axis.

To bold the legend text and the category labels:

1. Make sure the chart is still in Edit mode, then click the chart legend (shown in Figure 5-22) to select it and display square black handles.

2. Click the **Bold** button **B** to change the font in the chart legend to bold.

3. Click the x-axis, the bottom horizontal line of the chart. Two square handles appear on the x-axis.

4. Click **B** to change the x-axis text to bold.

After examining the chart, you decide to make several additional enhancements. First, you decide to display horizontal gridlines to make the chart easier to read.

Adding Horizontal Gridlines to a Chart

You can add horizontal gridlines to most 2-D and 3-D chart types. Gridlines stretch from one axis across the chart, providing a visual guide for more easily estimating the value or category of each data marker. You can specify gridlines when you select the format for your chart using the ChartWizard, or you can add gridlines later by activating the chart and using the Gridlines command from the Insert menu. You can also use the Gridlines button on the Chart toolbar.

To add horizontal gridlines to the chart:

1. Make sure the chart is still activated, then click the **Horizontal Gridlines** button 🗐 on the Chart toolbar. Horizontal gridlines appear on the chart. See Figure 5-23.

Figure 5-23 ◀
Adding
horizontal
gridlines

horizontal gridlines
added to line chart

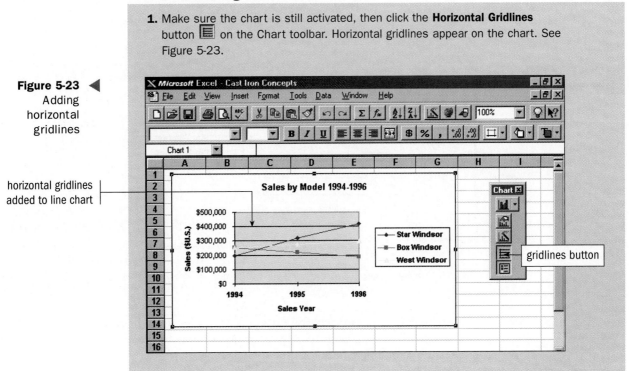

Next you want to improve the appearance of the lines that represent data on the chart.

Formatting Chart Lines

You can change the format or appearance of the lines and data markers on a chart. In this case, you want to make each chart line thicker. Excel provides a variety of line colors, line styles such as dashed lines and dotted lines, and line weights or thicknesses. Excel also provides a variety of data marker colors and styles, such as triangles, squares, and circles. As with any changes you make to a chart, you must activate the chart before you can change the appearance of its chart lines.

Each chart line is an object, so when you want to format a chart line, you must first select it to display the handles. After you select a chart line, you can apply formats using the Data Series dialog box.

To format the chart lines:

1. Make sure the chart is still in Edit mode, then click the blue line that represents the Star Windsor sales trend. When you select the line, handles appear. Also, the formula bar displays the address of cells containing each data point represented on the line.

   TROUBLE? If your monitor is monochrome, refer to Figure 5-24 for the blue line's location.

2. Click **Format**, click **Selected Data Series**, then click the **Patterns** tab in the Format Data Series dialog box.

3. Click the **Weight** box list arrow to display available line weights. Click the thickest line weight to select it.

4. Click the **OK** button to make the changes.

5. Repeat Steps 1 through 5, but select the pink line that represents Box Windsor sales.

6. Repeat Steps 1 through 5, but select the yellow line that represents West Windsor sales.

7. Click an empty area of the chart to deselect the line representing West Windsor sales. Your chart should look like Figure 5-24.

Figure 5-24 ◀
Completed line
chart

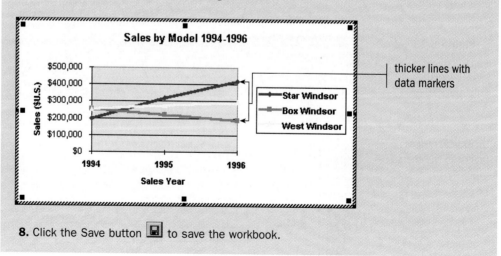

8. Click the Save button 🖫 to save the workbook.

Your new line chart supports your argument for allocating the Box Windsor stove less catalog space. Next, you want to drive your point home by creating a column chart that compares the total dollar sales for each model.

Creating a Column Chart

As you saw in Figure 5-2, Excel's **column chart** type uses vertical bars to represent data. You might want to call this a "bar chart," but another Excel chart type called a bar chart uses horizontal bars to represent data. Both the column chart and the bar chart are excellent choices to show comparisons. Constructing either chart type is easy with the ChartWizard.

You decide that you want to make a column chart to compare total sales of each stove model for the entire four-year period. Figure 5-25 shows a sketch of this chart. You examine your worksheet and note that data labels are located in column A. The data series for the column chart is in column F.

Figure 5-25 ◄
Column chart
sketch

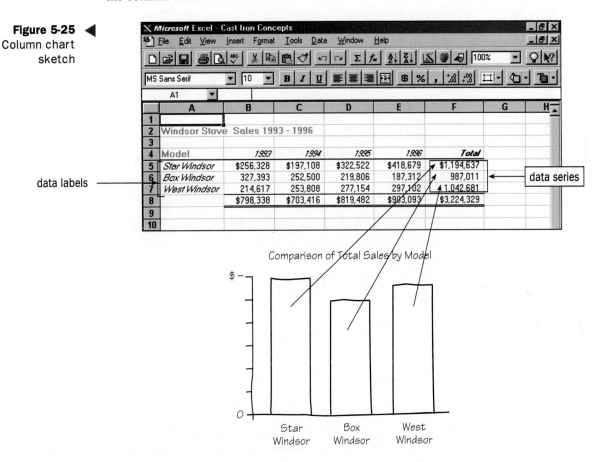

To create the column chart, you rename a blank sheet. Then you select non-adjacent ranges that contain the data labels and the data series.

To rename Sheet6 and then select non-adjacent ranges for the column chart:

1. Double-click the **Sheet6** tab to open the Rename Sheet dialog box.

2. Type **Column Chart** in the Name box, then click the **OK** button.

3. To return to the sheet containing the data you want to graph, click the Sales Figures tab.

4. Highlight cells **A5** through **A7**, which contain labels for the chart.

5. Press and hold **Ctrl** while you highlight cells **F5** through **F7**, which contain the data for the chart.

6. Release the mouse button and then release **Ctrl**.

Next, you use the ChartWizard to create a column chart in the Column Chart sheet.

To create the column chart:

1. Click the **ChartWizard** button .

2. Click the **Column Chart** tab to activate the sheet where you want to create the chart.

3. Drag the pointer from cell **A1** to cell **G16** to outline the area where the chart should appear. Release the mouse button and the ChartWizard - Step 1 of 5 dialog box appears.

4. Make sure the range is ='Sales Figures'!$A$5:$A$7,'Sales Figures'!$F$5:$F$7, then click the **Next >** button to display the ChartWizard - Step 2 of 5 dialog box.

5. Double-click the **Column** chart type to display the chart formats.

6. Double-click chart format 2. ChartWizard - Step 4 of 5 displays the sample chart.

You compare the sample chart to the sketch to make sure that the ChartWizard option buttons are set correctly. The chart looks as you expected, so you continue to the next step.

7. Click the **Next >** button to continue.

8. Click the **Chart Title** box, then type **Comparison of Total Sales by Model**.

9. Click the **Finish** button to complete the chart and view it on the worksheet. See Figure 5-26. Change your chart's size, if necessary, so it looks like the figure.

Figure 5-26 ◄
Column chart
embedded in
the worksheet

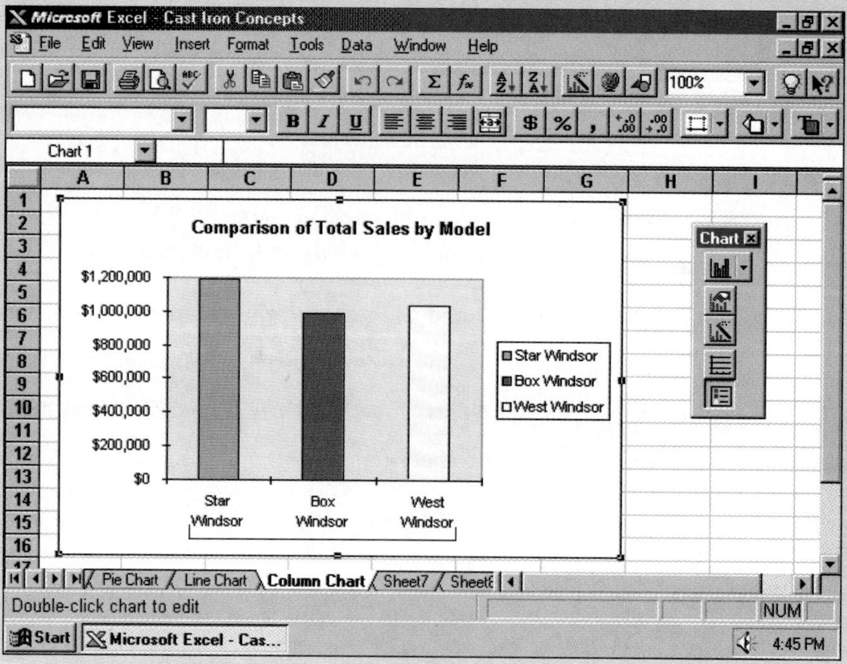

adjust chart size if
labels are not
formatted like this

Next, you decide to use a picture in your chart.

Using Pictures in a Column Chart

When the ChartWizard creates a column or bar chart, it uses a plain bar as the data marker. You can add visual impact to your charts by using pictures or graphical objects instead of a plain bar. You can stretch or shrink these pictures to show chart values, or you can create a stack of pictures to show chart values.

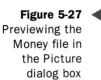

REFERENCE window

CREATING A PICTURE CHART

- Create a bar or column chart using the ChartWizard.
- Select all the bars or columns in the chart.
- Click Insert, then click Picture.
- Select the image file you want to use.
- Click OK.

Last month one of the graphic artists in the marketing department created a picture of a stack of money to use in an advertisement. You think it would be clever to use the picture as the data marker in your column chart. The picture is in the file Money on your Student Disk. To replace the plain bars with the picture, you need to select one column of the chart and use the Picture command on the Insert menu.

To insert the picture in the column chart:

1. Make sure you can see the entire chart on the screen, then double-click the column chart to activate it.

2. Click any column in the chart so all three columns display handles.

3. Click **Insert** then click **Picture**. The Picture dialog box opens.

4. If necessary, select the Tutorial.05 folder on your Student Disk.

5. In the filename box click **Money**. After a pause, the dialog box displays the selected image for you to preview, as in Figure 5-27.

Figure 5-27 ◄
Previewing the
Money file in
the Picture
dialog box

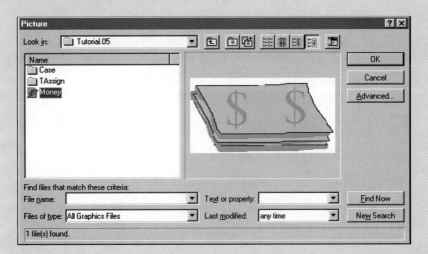

6. Click **OK** to insert the picture in the chart. The picture of money appears in each column. See Figure 5-28. Notice that each picture "stretched" to reflect different values.

Figure 5-28 ◀
Picture chart
with stretched
graphics

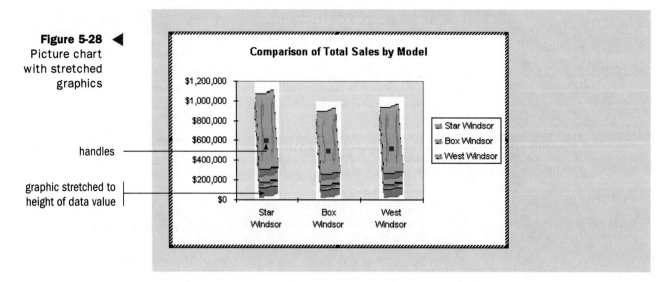

handles

graphic stretched to
height of data value

When you paste a picture into a bar or column chart, Excel automatically stretches the picture to show each bar's different values. Excel also provides a way to stack the pictures instead of stretching them.

Stretching and Stacking Pictures

Excel can either stretch or stack the picture or graphical object you use as the data marker on a column chart to represent the bar height. Some pictures stretch well; others become very distorted and detract from, rather than add to, the chart's impact. Use your artistic judgment to decide whether to stretch or stack pictures you use for data markers on your charts.

On your chart the money became too distorted when Excel stretched it, so you try stacking it instead.

To stack the data marker picture:

1. If the handles have disappeared from the columns, click any column in the chart to select all columns.

2. Click **Format**, click **Selected Data Series**, then click the **Patterns** tab in the Format Data Series dialog box.

3. Click **Stack**.

4. Click the **OK** button to apply the format. See Figure 5-29.

Figure 5-29 ◀
Picture chart
with stacked
graphics

stacked graphics ⟶

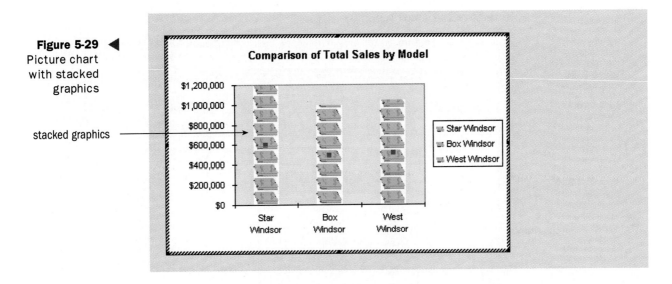

You look at the chart and see that the stacked graphics effectively show that the Box Windsor stove produced the lowest dollar volume of the three stove models. You notice that the chart title needs a box around it for emphasis.

Displaying the Title in a Colored Box with a Shadow

As mentioned earlier, the title chart is an object that you can select and then format using the menu options and toolbar buttons. To add emphasis to the title, you decide to fill the title area with green and then add a thick border around the title. To complete the title format, you create a shadow effect under the title box.

To display the title in a colored box with a shadow:

1. Click the title to select it and display the handles.

2. Click **Format**, click **Selected Chart Title**, then click the **Patterns** tab in the Format Chart Title dialog box.

3. Click the bright green box in the top row of the Color palette.

    TROUBLE? If your monitor is monochrome, select a light gray shade.

4. Click the **Weight** box list arrow in the Border section to display a list of border weights.

5. Click the thickest line in the list.

6. Click **Shadow** to display a shadow under the title.

7. Click the **OK** button to apply the format.

The chart looks better with its title emphasized. Now you notice that because all the column markers are the same color, the chart legend is not necessary. The x-axis labels sufficiently differentiate the columns. The easiest way to delete the chart legend is to use the Legend button on the Chart toolbar. If you look closely at the Legend button now, it appears to be indented, indicating that a legend is displayed. To remove the chart legend, simply click the Legend button.

To remove the chart legend:

1. Click the **Legend** button [icon]. The chart legend disappears. See Figure 5-30.

Figure 5-30 ◀
Completed
picture chart

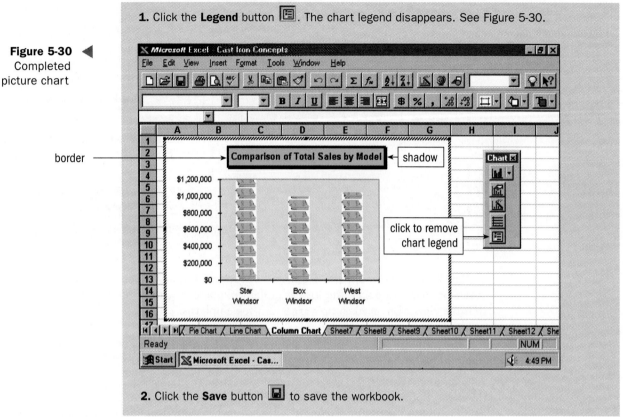

border →

2. Click the **Save** button [icon] to save the workbook.

Quick Check

1 A line chart is used to show _____.

2 Describe a situation in which you would use the first row of the chart range as x-axis labels.

3 Explain how to revise a chart's data series.

4 What are the three possible types of chart text? Give an example of each and explain how to edit them.

5 Describe two methods for adding gridlines to an existing chart.

6 What dialog box would you use to change the formatting of one line in a line chart?

7 How do a bar chart and a column chart differ?

8 Explain how to create a picture chart.

9 You remove a chart legend by
a. Selecting the legend and pressing [Delete].
b. Selecting the chart and clicking [icon].
c. Activating the legend and clicking Chart Legend on the menu bar.
d. Dragging the legend out of the chart border.

In this session you will create a 3-D column chart and learn how to rotate it. You also learn how to use Chart sheets and how to add a border to a chart. Finally, you will learn how to create and edit an Excel data map.

Creating a 3-D Column Chart

A 3-D column chart displays three-dimensional vertical bars plotted on either two or three axes. Excel provides the eight different formats for 3-D column charts shown in Figure 5-31.

Figure 5-31 ◀
Predefined formats for 3-D column charts

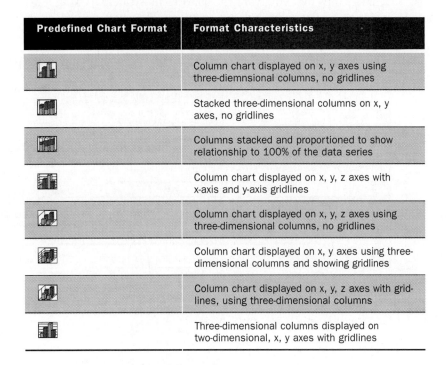

Predefined Chart Format	Format Characteristics
	Column chart displayed on x, y axes using three-diemnsional columns, no gridlines
	Stacked three-dimensional columns on x, y axes, no gridlines
	Columns stacked and proportioned to show relationship to 100% of the data series
	Column chart displayed on x, y, z axes with x-axis and y-axis gridlines
	Column chart displayed on x, y, z axes using three-dimensional columns, no gridlines
	Column chart displayed on x, y axes using three-dimensional columns and showing gridlines
	Column chart displayed on x, y, z axes with grid-lines, using three-dimensional columns
	Three-dimensional columns displayed on two-dimensional, x, y axes with gridlines

Formats 1, 2, 3, and 4 convey the same information as 2-D column charts but have the added visual appeal of three-dimensional columns. Like their 2-D counterparts, 3-D formats 1, 2, 3, and 4 use two axes: the horizontal x-axis and the vertical y-axis. Formats 5, 6, and 7 display the data on three axes: the x-axis in the front of the chart, the y-axis on the side of the chart, and a vertical axis called the z-axis.

The three-dimensional arrangement of data on a chart with three axes makes viewing the data in different ways easier. For example, suppose you want to compare the number of employees in a company who work in clerical to those who work in managerial positions. Suppose you are also interested in the number of males and females in clerical and managerial positions. Figure 5-32 shows a 2-D column chart and a 3-D column chart created using the same data range. Both charts were designed to compare the number of male, female, clerical, and managerial employees.

Figure 5-32 ◀
2-D and 3-D column charts

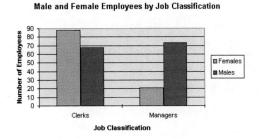

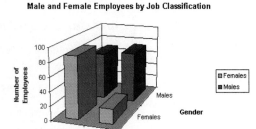

The 2-D chart in Figure 5-32 compares the number of males and females by job classification. Clearly there are more female clerical workers than males and fewer female managers. That more men work in managerial positions than in clerical positions is not as apparent in this chart. The 3-D column chart in Figure 5-32 shows comparisons based on both gender and job classification.

You want to create a 3-D column chart to compare sales data in two ways. You want it to show sales trends by model; for example, how the sales of Star Windsor changed from 1993 to 1996. You also wants the chart to show sales by year; for example, the relative sales of each model in 1996. You think that a 3-D column chart will make examining the sales data by year or by model easier.

Figure 5-33 shows a sketch of the 3-D column chart, along with a note about the two relationships that you want the chart to illustrate. Drawing a 3-D column chart by hand is not easy so the sketch is not complete. However, you try to show what will appear on the three graph axes.

Figure 5-33 ◄
3-D column
chart sketch

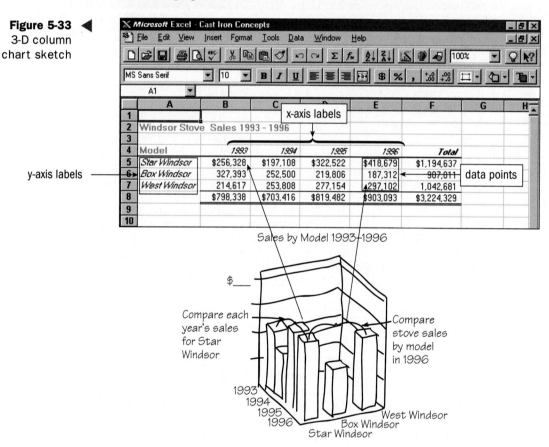

So far you've placed all your new charts on blank worksheets. This time you'll place your new chart on a **Chart sheet**, a special sheet that contains only one chart. It does not have the rows and columns you are used to seeing in a regular worksheet. When using a Chart sheet, you don't have to worry about selecting, positioning, and sizing the chart. Instead, Excel automatically sizes the chart to fill the sheet window. A Chart sheet always displays the Chart toolbar and the Chart menu; it's not necessary to activate the chart to edit it.

To create a 3-D column chart on a chart sheet:

1. To return to the sheet containing the data you want to graph, click the **Sales Figures** tab.

2. Highlight cells **A4** through **E7**, then release the mouse button.

3. Click **Insert**, point to **Chart**, then click **As New Sheet**.

Now you can continue with the ChartWizard dialog boxes, as usual.

4. In the first dialog box, make sure the range is ='Sales Figures'!$A$4:$E$7, then click the **Next >** button to display the ChartWizard - Step 2 of 5 dialog box.

5. Double-click the **3-D Column** chart type to display the ChartWizard - Step 3 of 5 dialog box.

6. Double-click chart format **6** to view the sample chart. See Figure 5-34.

Figure 5-34 ◄
Sample
3-D chart

values in row 4
plotted as first
data series

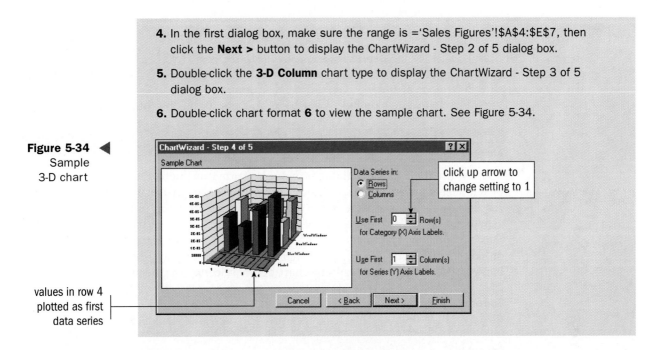

Compare the sample chart on your screen with the sketch in Figure 5-33. In the sample chart Excel used the values in row 4 as the first data series. You encountered this same problem when you created the line chart. You must tell Excel to use the values in row 4 (the first row of the chart range) as x-axis labels, not as a data series.

To tell Excel to use the values in row 4 as x-axis labels:

1. Click the up arrow button to change the Category (X) Axis Labels setting to 1.

Now the chart looks more like the sketch. Let's add the title to complete the chart.

2. Click the **Next >** button to continue to the next ChartWizard step.

3. Click the **Chart Title** box, type **Sales by Model 1993–1996**, and click the **Finish** button to complete the chart. The chart appears in a Chart sheet named Chart1, to the left of the Sales Figures sheet, as shown in Figure 5-35.

Figure 5-35 ◄
New chart in
Chart sheet

no gridlines in
chart sheet

Chart sheet tab

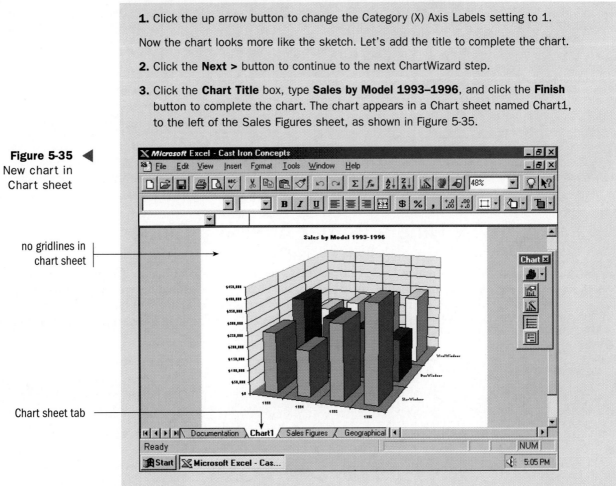

You decide to give the chart sheet a more descriptive name.

4. Double-click the **Chart1** tab and rename it 3-D Column Chart.

Notice that some bars hide other bars. You can fix this by rotating the chart.

Rotating a 3-D Column Chart

You can use the 3-D View dialog box on the Format menu to rotate a 3-D column chart by ten-degree increments, either clockwise or counterclockwise. By rotating the chart you can display the clearest view of the columns or draw attention to the data from a certain viewpoint. It's possible to do this by dragging one axis, but it's easy drag too far and skew the chart, making it difficult to read. In general, it's safer to use the 3-D View command on the Format menu. Because the Chart sheet always displays the chart menu and toolbar, you don't have to activate the chart before selecting the menu command.

To rotate the chart:

1. Click **Format** then click **3-D View** to display the Format 3-D View dialog box. See Figure 5-36.

Figure 5-36 ◀
Rotating
the 3-D
column chart

chart outline

Rotation box

clockwise button

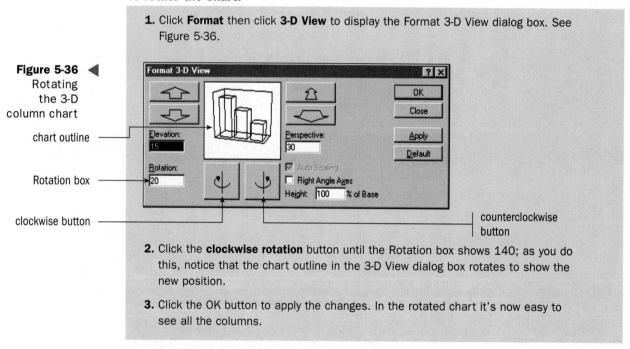

counterclockwise
button

2. Click the **clockwise rotation** button until the Rotation box shows 140; as you do this, notice that the chart outline in the 3-D View dialog box rotates to show the new position.

3. Click the OK button to apply the changes. In the rotated chart it's now easy to see all the columns.

Applying a Border Around a Chart

You can customize the border that appears around a chart by using the options in the Patterns dialog box. A border helps define a chart and makes it visually appealing. For good visual balance, the weight of the chart border should be equivalent to the weight of the chart elements—a chart with vividly colored columns and large, bold text elements should have a thicker border than a line chart with a lighter text font. You want to put a thick, black border around the 3-D column chart.

To place a black border around the chart:

1. Click any blank space in the upper-left corner of the chart. Eight handles appear inside the chart border indicating that the chart border is selected.

2. Click **Format**, click **Selected Chart Area**, then click the **Patterns** tab in the Format Chart Area dialog box.

3. Click the **Weight** box down arrow button, then click the thickest line.

4. Click the **OK** button to apply the changes.

5. Press **Esc** to deselect the chart border.

6. Click the **Save** button 🖫 to save the workbook. Your chart should match Figure 5-37.

Figure 5-37 ◄
Completed 3-D
column chart

thicker chart border ──────────→

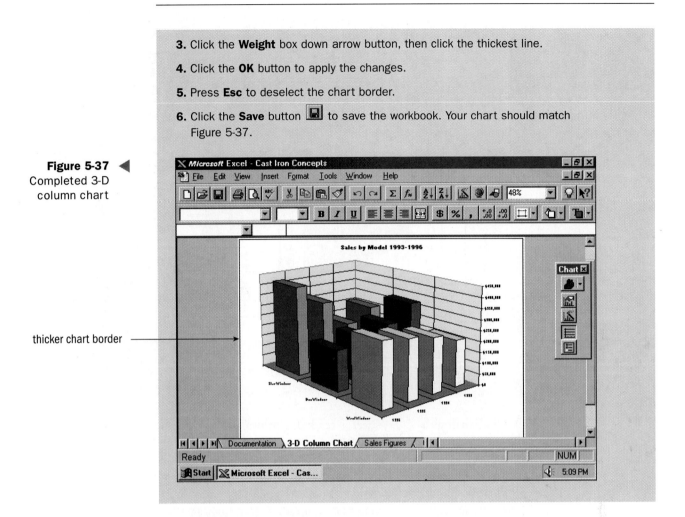

Previewing and Printing the Worksheet and Charts

You have four charts arranged vertically on four different sheets. How will the printed results look? Use the Print Preview button to find out.

To preview the 3-D Column chart before printing:

1. Make sure the 3-D Column Chart sheet is still on your screen.

2. Click the Print Preview button 🔍 to preview the chart. The chart appears in the Print Preview window, as shown in Figure 5-38.

Figure 5-38 ◀
Previewing a
Chart sheet

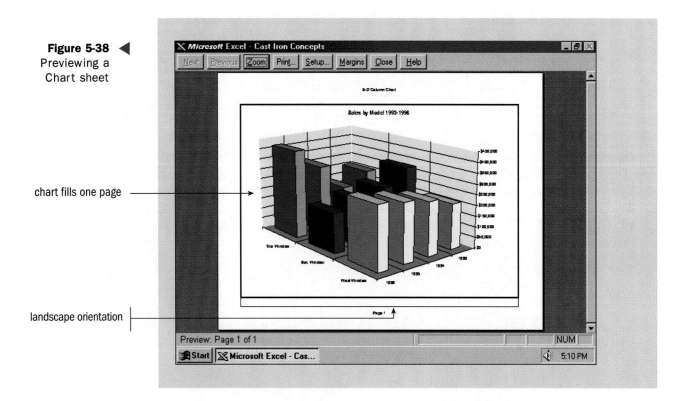

chart fills one page

landscape orientation

The chart on the Chart sheet is ready for printing. You don't need to change any setup options. Is the same true of charts on the regular worksheets? Find out by previewing the column chart.

To preview the column chart:

1. Click **Close** to close the Preview window.

2. Click the **Column Chart** tab. If necessary, use the arrows on the sheet tab scroll bar to display the sheet tabs as you need them.

3. Click the **Preview** button 🔲 to preview the worksheet. If necessary, click the **Next>** button to view the second page. (Don't worry if your chart doesn't fit on one page; you'll change the orientation to landscape next.) See Figure 5-39.

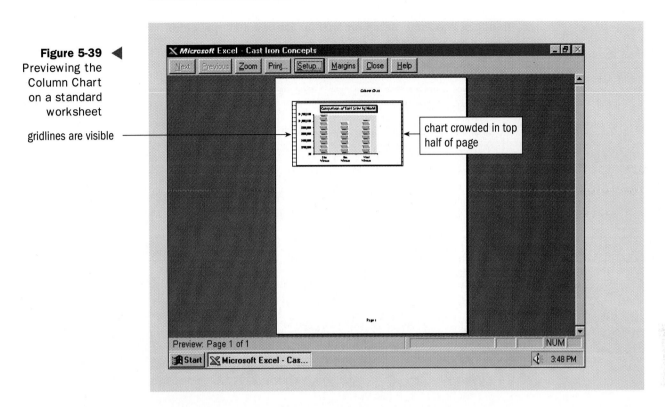

Figure 5-39
Previewing the
Column Chart
on a standard
worksheet

gridlines are visible

chart crowded in top
half of page

You need to adjust the chart on the standard worksheet in order to produce an attractive printout. You decide to use the scaling option in the Page Setup dialog box to enlarge the chart when it is printed. You also change the orientation to landscape.

To adjust the Page Setup options:

1. Click the **Setup** button at the top of the Print Preview dialog box, then click the **Page** tab to display the Page Setup dialog box.

2. Click **Landscape** to select landscape orientation.

3. In the Scaling box, change Adjust to: to **185%**.

4. Click the **Margins** tab.

5. Click the **Horizontally** box and click the **Vertically** box to put a check in each box.

6. Click the sheet tab.

7. If there's a check in the Gridlines box, remove it so gridlines will not appear on the printout.

8. If there's a check in the Row & Column Headings box, remove it so row and column headings will not appear on the printout.

9. Click the **OK** button to return to the print preview and view the result of the revised page setup settings.

   TROUBLE? If some chart text appears to be cut off, click the Zoom button to more accurately preview the output.

10. Click the **Close** button to return to the worksheet.

Now you will adjust settings for the remaining workbook sheets.

To adjust the Page Setup options for the remaining sheets:

1. Click the **Line Chart** tab. If necessary, use the scroll arrows on the sheet tab scroll bar to display the sheet tabs as you need them.

2. Click the **Print Preview** button, click the **Setup** button, then click the **Page** tab to display the Page Setup dialog box.

3. Click **Landscape** to select landscape orientation. In the Scaling box, change Adjust to: to **185%**.

4. Click the **Margins** tab.

5. Click the **Horizontally** box and click the **Vertically** box to put a check in each box.

6. Click the **sheet** tab.

7. If there's a check in the Print Gridlines box, remove it so gridlines will not appear on the printout.

8. If there's a check in the Row & Column Headings box, remove it so row and column headings will not appear on the printout.

9. Click the **OK** button to return to the print preview and view the result of the revised page setup settings, then click the Close button to return to the worksheet.

10. Repeat Steps 2 through 9 for the Pie Chart sheet and the Sales Figures sheet. Remember to use the scroll arrows on the sheet tab scroll bar to display the sheet tabs as you need them.

    TROUBLE? If you see pound signs (###) in the Preview window for the Sales Figures sheet, you may need to widen the worksheet columns slightly and change the Adjust to: percentage to 160%. If the Sales Figures worksheet is displayed on more than one page, change the Adjust to percentage to 160%.

You do not need to print the charts from this tutorial now. You will have an opportunity to print them when you do the Tutorial Assignments. Now you can save the workbook with the print specifications.

To save the workbook:

1. Click the **Save** button 🖫.

The four charts you've created should help convince the marketing director to reduce the Box Windsor catalog page by half. But just in case, you want to be prepared to suggest an alternative. You decide to create a map illustrating sales distribution by state for the Box Windsor. If the map clearly shows higher sales in one region than another, the marketing director may prefer to produce two versions of the catalog—one with a full-page Box Windsor ad (for the region with higher sales), and one with a half-page ad (for the region with lower sales).

Creating a Map

Excel's data mapping facility makes geographical data easier to understand. For instance, suppose you have population figures for Europe. You could easily create a map of Europe showing countries with total population of 0 to 10 million in dark green, 11 to 20 million in another shade of green, and so on.

Before you can create a map, your worksheet must contain at least two columns. One column must contain acceptable geographical names (for example, California) or two-character map codes that Excel can interpret as geographical locations (for example, CA for California). The other column must contain data used in calculations, for example, the net cost of operations in each state, or the quarterly revenue from European product sales.

The Geographical Data sheet in the Cast Iron Concepts workbook contains all the data you need to create your map.

To view the map data:

1. Click the **Geograpical Data** tab. The map data is arranged in two columns, as shown in Figure 5-40.

Figure 5-40 ◀
Geographical
Data sheet

one column contains
geographical names

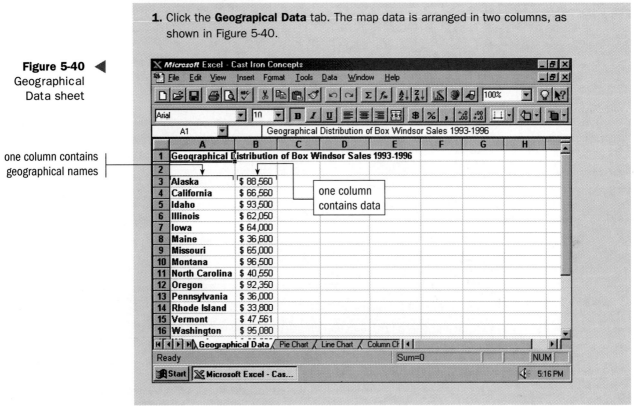

one column
contains data

To create a map, first select the range you want to map. Then start the MapWizard and use the techniques you used when you created a chart. Keep in mind that your map does not automatically reflect changes to your worksheet data. To update your map you need to click the Map Refresh button ⊞ in the upper-left corner of the map. (You'll have a chance to try this in the Tutorial Assignments.)

You'll create your map on the Geographical Data sheet.

To create your map:

1. Select the range **A3:B17**, then click the **Map tool** 🗺 The pointer changes shape to ✛. This pointer draws the map's border.

2. Position ✛ at the top of cell A21, then drag the pointer to the lower-right corner of cell G36 to select the range **A21:G36**. After a moment, the Multiple Maps Available dialog box appears. Your map includes data on Alaska, so you choose a map showing Alaska inset below the continental states.

3. Click **United States (AK & HI Inset)** then click **OK**. After a moment, the map and Data Map Control dialog box appear, as shown in Figure 5-41. You can use the Data Map Control dialog box to quickly change your map. You won't be using this dialog box now, so you can close it.

Figure 5-41 ◀
Newly created
map with
the Data
Map Control
dialog box

states differentiated
by shading

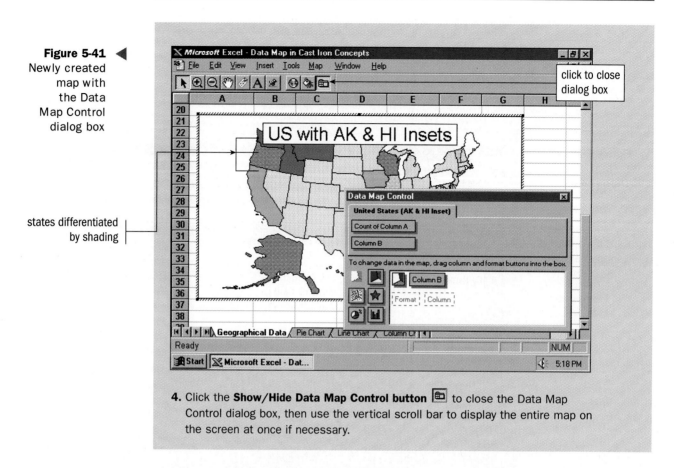

4. Click the **Show/Hide Data Map Control button** 🔲 to close the Data Map
Control dialog box, then use the vertical scroll bar to display the entire map on
the screen at once if necessary.

Just like a chart, the map is displayed in Edit mode with a thick border or in its own
window, along with the Mapping toolbar and menu.

Editing the Map Legend

After you create a map, you usually need to edit it to suit your particular needs. In this
case, the meaning of various patterns on the map is not clear. You decide to edit the map
legend so it displays more information. You also need to add a better legend title.

To edit the map legend:

1. Locate the **map legend** shown in Figure 5-42.

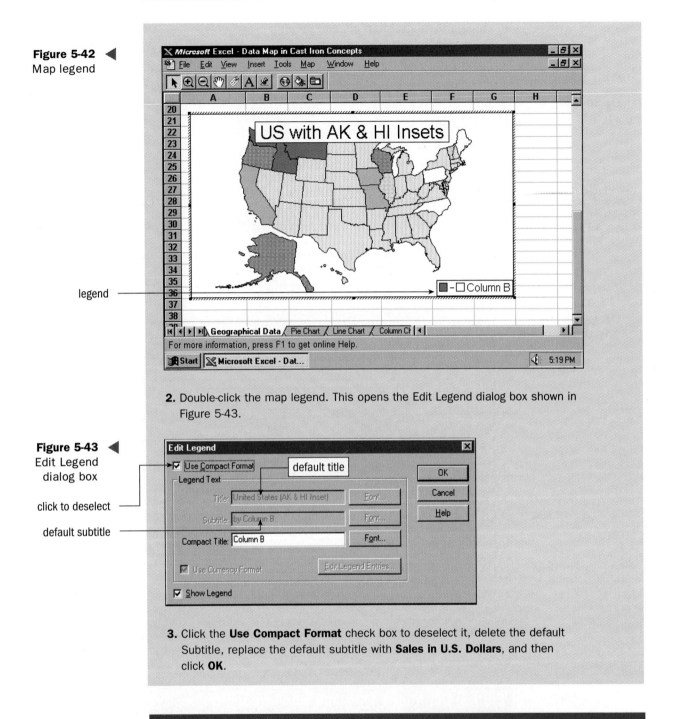

Figure 5-42 ◀
Map legend

legend ——

2. Double-click the map legend. This opens the Edit Legend dialog box shown in Figure 5-43.

Figure 5-43 ◀
Edit Legend dialog box

click to deselect ——

default subtitle ——

3. Click the **Use Compact Format** check box to deselect it, delete the default Subtitle, replace the default subtitle with **Sales in U.S. Dollars**, and then click **OK**.

Changing the Value Shading Options

The expanded legend indicates that states in solid gray have projected sales of $93,500 to $96,500, the states in darked checked gray have sales of $68,900 to $93,500, and so on. Numbers in parentheses indicate the number of states in each category. Notice that the intervals for each category are not equal. For instance, the light checked states have sales ranging from $40,600 to $64,000 (an interval of $23,400) whereas the dark gray states have an interval of only $3000.

To make the intervals the same for each category, you need to select Equal spread of values in the Value Shading Options dialog box. You'll do that next and at the same time change the color used for the map patterns.

To change the data intervals and colors:

1. Click **Map**, click **Value Shading Options**, then click the **Equal spread of values in each range** button in the Value Shading Options dialog box. See Figure 5-44.

Figure 5-44 ◀
Value Shading
Options dialog
box

Color list arrow

click to make the
intervals the same for
each category

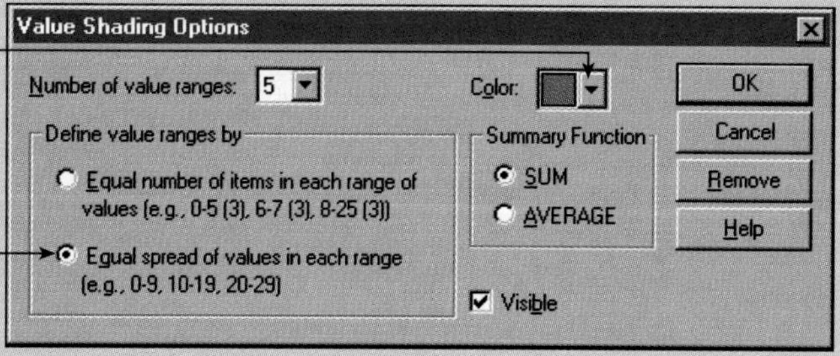

2. Click the **Color list** arrow, scroll the list and click the **violet-purple** box, located between the navy blue and sage green boxes, and then click **OK**. The revised map has sales figures grouped in intervals of roughly $15,700. See Figure 5-45.

Figure 5-45 ◀
Revised map

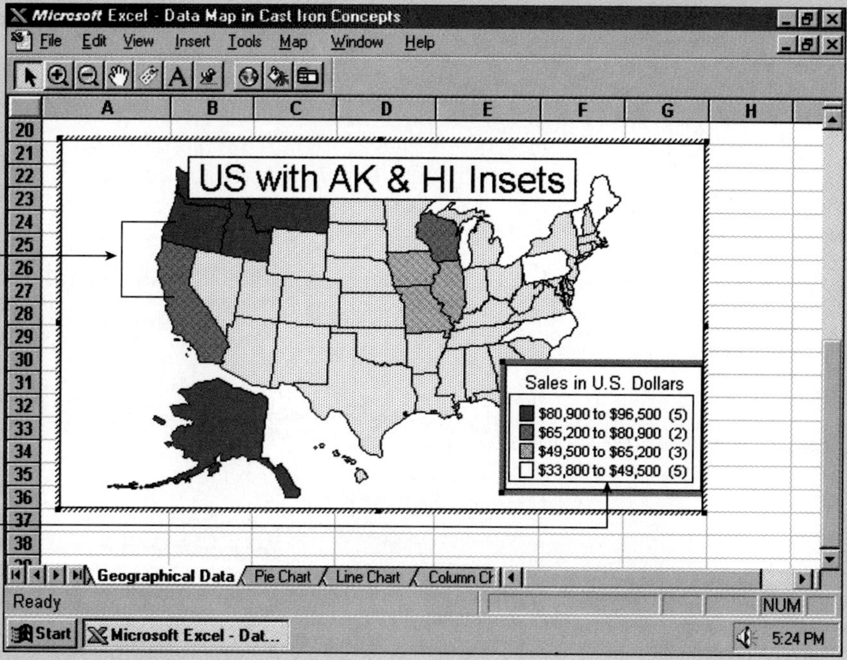

new color

sales figures grouped
in equal intervals

Editing the Map's Title and Background Color

Next, you decide to change the background color from green to a more attractive color. Finally, you want to give the map a meaningful title.

To edit the background color:

1. Right click the **map** to display the short-cut menu, then click **Features** to open the Map Features dialog box.

2. Make sure "United States (AK & HI Inset)" is selected, click the **Custom** button, click the **Custom** list arrow button to display a list of possible colors, scroll through the list, and click the light gray box located between the dark grey and red boxes. See Figure 5-46.

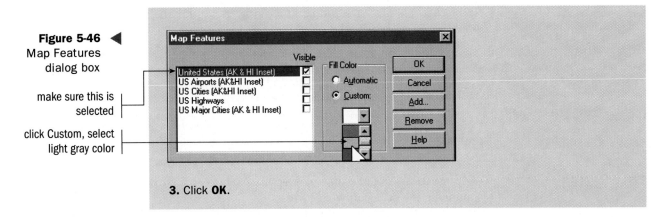

Figure 5-46 ◀
Map Features
dialog box

make sure this is
selected

click Custom, select
light gray color

3. Click **OK**.

The map is nearly finished. All that remains is to change the default title to something more meaningful.

To change the title and save your work:

1. Double click the map title, **US with AK & HI Insets**, use the cursor to select the text, press **Delete**, type **Box Windsor, 1993-1996,** and then press **Enter**.

2. Click **File** on the menu bar, then click **Save** to save your map.

Your map clearly illustrates that the Box Windsor sells best in the Western states. You'll want to emphasize this point in your upcoming meeting with the marketing director. You'll have a chance to print your map in the Tutorial Assignments.

For now you can close the workbook.

To close the workbook:

1. Close the workbook and exit Excel if you are not going to do the Tutorial Assignments now.

Tips for Creating Charts and Maps

Excel includes many additional chart and map types, formats, and options. The Tutorial Assignments and Case Problems at the end of this tutorial give you an opportunity to use some of these. Here are some hints that can help you construct charts and maps that effectively represent your data.

- Use a line chart, a 3-D line chart, an area chart, or a 3-D area chart to show trends or change over a period of time.

- Use a column chart, a bar chart, a 3-D column chart, or a 3-D bar chart to show comparisons.

- Use a pie chart or a 3-D pie chart to show the relationship or proportion of parts to a whole.

- Before you begin to create a chart, locate the cell ranges on the worksheet that contain the data series you want to chart and the cell range that contains the x-axis labels. Then draw a sketch showing the x-axis, the x-axis title, the x-axis category labels, the y-axis, the y-axis title, y-axis labels, and the data series.

- Design the chart so that viewers understand the main point at first glance. Too much detail can make a chart difficult to interpret.

- Chart consistent categories of data. For example, if you want to chart monthly income, do not include the year-to-date income as a data point.

- Every chart should have a descriptive title, a title for the x-axis, a title for the y-axis, and category labels.

- Put your chart on a standard worksheet if you want to include more than one sheet on a chart, or if you want to include worksheet data on the same sheet as the chart. Also, keep in mind that when a chart is on a standard worksheet you can size it to suit your needs.

- Put your chart on a Chart sheet to avoid resizing the chart or adjusting page setup settings.

- Before you create a map, make sure your data is arranged in at least two columns, with one column containing geographical names or abbreviations and the other containing the data you want to map.

- To divide your data into equal intervals on the map, use the Equal Spread of Values option in the Value Shading Options dialog box.

- Changes in worksheet data are not automatically reflected in a map, as they are with a chart. When you update the worksheet, you need to double-click the map and then click the Map Refresh button ▣ (in the upper-left corner of your map) to update your map.

Quick Check

1. What are the advantages of placing your charts on standard worksheets?

2. What are the advantages of placing your charts on Chart sheets?

3. Explain how to rotate a 3-D column chart.

4. What tab in the Format Chart Area dialog box would you use to edit the chart border?

5. A column chart is used to show _____.

6. How should you organize your worksheet if you want to create a map?

7. What does one column of your worksheet need to contain before you can create a map?

8. Explain how to make each color on the map correspond to the same interval of values.

9. Describe three changes you can make to a map in order to improve its appearance and make it easier to read.

Tutorial Assignments

You want to create a line chart that shows the change in total stove sales between 1993 and 1996. You also want to create another map illustrating the sales by state for both the Box Windsor and the Star Windsor. To do this:

1. Open the file Concepts2 in the TAssign folder for Tutorial 5.
2. Save the file under the new name Cast Iron Concepts 2 in the Tassign folder.
3. Type your name and the current date in the documentation sheet.
4. Rename the next blank sheet "Line Chart #2."
5. On the Sales Figures sheet highlight the non-adjacent ranges that contain the dates and the total sales.
6. Use the ChartWizard to create a chart positioned between rows 1 and 16 of the Line Chart #2 sheet.
7. Continue using the ChartWizard to select the Line chart type and format 2.
8. Use first row for the Category (X) Axis Labels at the prompt.
9. Enter "Total Stove Sales 1993–1996" as the chart title.

10. Activate the chart and make the chart line thicker.

11. Remove the chart legend.

12. Put a box around the chart's title.

13. Fill the title box with bright green color and put a shadow under it.

14. Select yellow for the chart's background color and put a thick border around the entire chart.

15. Bold all the text in the chart and adjust chart size, as necessary, so that the chart text is formatted correctly.

16. Revise the worksheet header so it includes your name, the filename, and the date.

17. Preview the new chart. Adjust the page setup options as necessary to the center the chart on the page, enlarged to the proper percentage, without gridlines.

18. Save the workbook, print your new chart, and then close the Cast Iron Concepts 2 workbook.

19. The charts you created in the Tutorial are part of a series and, as such, should share a standard format. To standardize the appearance of all charts in the Cast Iron Concepts workbook, open the workbook (which you created in the Tutorial) and repeat Steps 13 through 17 as necessary for each chart.

20. Revise the contents portion of the Documentation sheet to include any worksheets not currently listed.

21. Save your work and then print the charts and the Documentation sheet. Close the Cast Iron Concepts workbook.
    In the tutorial you created a map and used shading to illustrate one set of data values. You can illlustrate additional sets of values on a map by using patterns and markers. Try mapping two columns of data now to create a map that shows Box Windsor and Star Windsor sales by state.

22. Open the Cast Iron Concepts 2 workbook in the Tassign folder for Tutorial 5. (If you did not complete Steps 1 through 19 in the Tutorial Assignments, you can use the Concepts 2 workbook instead.)

23. In the Geographical Data sheet, select the range A3:C18, click the Map button, and create a map of the United States with Alaska and Hawaii insets. Place the map below the map data, on the same sheet.

24. The map currently is shaded to show Box Windsor sales figures. To display Star Windsor figures, you need to use the Data Map Control dialog box. Drag the Box Windsor button, in the white portion of the Data Map Control dialog box, to the grey tab at the top of the dialog box. This removes all shading on the map.

25. To display shading for Star Windsor values, drag the Star Windsor button to the white part of the Data Map Control dialog box. The Value Shading button appears next to the Star Windsor button, indicating that the Star Windsor values are illustrated on the map using shades of the default color.

26. To display a dot pattern on top of the shading to represent Box Windsor sales, drag the Box Windsor button to the second row of the white part of the dialog box (below the Star Windsor button, into the dotted rectangle labeled "Column"). The Dot Density button appears next to the Box Windsor button, indicating that the Box Windsor values are illustrated on the map by dots.

27. The dot pattern is difficult to interpret, so you decide to use a graduated symbol instead to represent Box Windsor sales. Drag the Graduated Symbol button (the star) to the Format box next to the Box Windsor button. The Graduated Symbol button replaces the Dot Density button. Circles of various sizes appear on the map, illustrating Box Windsor values.

28. Close the Data Map Control dialog box and save your work. Notice that the map now contains two legends, one for each set of values illustrated on the map.

29. Edit the Box Windsor legend. Use the compact format. Change the compact title to "Box Windsor Sales." Because the symbol is only intended to show relative sales, you don't need any more legend information.

30. Edit the Star Windsor legend. Do not use the compact format. Add a good title and delete the default subtitle. When you finish, drag the Box Windsor legend to the map's lower-right corner.

31. Edit the Value Shading Options to display an equal spread of values in each range. Change the shading color to a color other than grey. Change the background color to a color other than green. Replace the default map title with something more meaningful.

32. Click anywhere outside the map to deselect it. Now try changing the data values to see how this affects the map. Change the values for Alaska to 500 for both the Box Windsor and the Star Windsor.

33. Scroll back down the worksheet to display the map. Double-click the map to put it in Edit mode. To update the map to reflect the new data values for Alaska, click the Map Refresh button (the exclamation mark) in the map's upper-left corner. After a pause, the map displays the new value.

34. Click anywhere outside the map, then preview the worksheet. Change the page setup settings as necessary to produce an attractive printout.

35. Print your worksheet. If you have problems getting it to print, your computer or printer may not have enough memory. Try printing on a computer with 16 Megabytes of RAM or see your technical support person for instructions.

36. Revise the Documentation sheet to reflect your changes to the workbook. Then save and close the workbook.

Case Problems

1. Illustrating Production Data at TekStar Electronics You are executive assistant to the President of TekStar Electronics, a manufacturer of consumer electronics. You are compiling the yearly manufacturing reports and have collected production totals for each of TekStar's four European manufacturing plants. The workbook TekStar contains these totals. Now you need to create a 3-D pie chart showing the relative percentage of CD players each plant produced. You also need to create a map showing the number of VCRs each plant produced.

1. Open the workbook Tekstar in the Case folder for Tutorial 5 and add the necessary information to the Documentation sheet to create a complete summary of the workbook. Include information for the charts and map you will create in the following steps. Save the workbook as TekStar Electronics in the Case folder for Tutorial 5.

2. Use the ChartWizard to create the 3-D pie chart on a chart sheet. Use chart format 7 to show the plant name and the percentage of CD players that plant produced.

3. Name the Chart sheet 3-D Pie Chart.

4. Enter "Total CD Player Production" as the chart title.

5. Activate the chart and pull out the slice representing the French plant's CD player production.

6. Select patterns and colors for the chart to give it visual impact when it is printed.

7. Preview and print the chart sheet. Save your work.

To create a map showing VCR production at the four plants:

8. Select the range A5:B8 and then use the Map button to create a map of Europe in the same sheet, below the production totals. When the map is complete, close the Data Map Control dialog box.

9. Click the Zoom In button on the Map toolbar, and use the pointer to outline the four shaded countries. To zoom in even further, outline the shaded region again. (If you make a mistake, click View, then click Entire Map to redisplay the whole map. Then try again.)

10. Right-click the legend, then click Hide to remove the legend.
11. Click the Add Text button in the toolbar, position the pointer in the middle of France, and type "France: 18,500 units." Do the same for the remaining countries. Scroll up the worksheet as necessary to find the correct figures. If you're not sure which country is which, click the Map Labels button, and then move the pointer over the map to display labels for each country.
12. Edit the map to make it more attractive. Change the Value Shading colors and the background color. Add a better title.
13. Preview the worksheet and make any necessary page setup changes. Save the workbook.
14. Print the Production Totals worksheet. If you have a problem printing, your computer or printer may not have enough memory. Try using a computer with 16 Megabytes of RAM, or see your technical support person for assistance.

2. Showing Sales Trends at Bentley Twig Furniture You are a marketing assistant at Bentley Twig Furniture, a small manufacturer of rustic furniture. Bentley's major products are rustic twig chairs, rockers, and tables. Your boss, Jack Armstrong, has asked you to create a line chart showing the sales of the three best-selling products during the period 1993 through 1996.

You have collected the necessary sales figures, entered them in a worksheet, and are ready to prepare the line chart.

1. Open the workbook Twig (in the Case folder for Tutorial 5) and add the necessary information to the Documentation sheet to create a complete summary of the workbook. Include the information for the chart you will create in the following steps. Save the workbook as Bentley Twig Furniture in the Case folder for Tutorial 5.
2. Use the ChartWizard to prepare a line chart that shows the change in sales for the three best-selling items over the period 1993 through 1996. Create the chart on the Sales Figures sheet, below the sales data. Use chart format 2.
3. Enter "Total Unit Sales 1993–1996" as the chart title.
4. Size the chart as necessary so that all labels are displayed correctly.
5. Bold the x-axis and y-axis labels.
6. Change all lines to a heavier line weight and assign each line a different data marker.
7. Add a shadow border around the entire chart.
8. Adjust the chart's size and placement as needed.
9. Save the workbook with chart.
10. Preview your work and make any changes necessary to position the printed worksheet and chart for the best visual impact.
11. Print the worksheet and chart. Save your print settings.

3. Comparing Sales at Trail Ridge Outfitters You are working in the marketing department of Trail Ridge Outfitters, a manufacturer of camping equipment. Trail Ridge management is considering an expansion of its Canadian marketing efforts. You have been asked to prepare a chart showing the relative sales of major camping equipment items in the United States and Canada. You have prepared a simple worksheet containing the latest figures for Trail Ridge sales of camp stoves, sleeping bags, and tents in the U.S. and Canadian markets. You now want to prepare a 3-D column chart to illustrate relative sales in each market.

1. Open the workbook Trail (in the Case folder for Tutorial 5) and add the necessary information to the Documentation sheet to create a complete summary of the workbook. Include the information for the charts you will create in the following steps. Save the workbook as Trail Ridge in the Case folder for Tutorial 5.
2. Use the ChartWizard to create a 3-D column chart showing the relative sales in each market. Create the chart on a Chart sheet. Use 3-D column chart format 6.
3. Enter "'U.S. and Canadian Unit Sales" as the chart title.

4. Adjust the size of the chart so the labels are displayed correctly.
5. Rotate the chart so that the Canadian figures are clearly visible.
6. Put a shadowed box around the chart title.
7. Change the x-, y-, and z-axis labels to boldface text.
8. Preview the chart.
9. Print the Sales Figures worksheet and the chart.
10. Save your workbook.

4. Duplicating a Printed Chart or Map Look through books, business magazines, or textbooks for your other courses to find an attractive chart or map. Select one, photocopy it, and create a worksheet that contains the data displayed on the chart or map. You can estimate the data values plotted on the chart. Do your best to duplicate the chart or map you found. You might not be able to duplicate the chart fonts or colors exactly, but choose the closest available substitutes. When your work is complete, save it, preview it, and print it. Submit the photocopy of the original as well as the printout of the chart or map you created.

Managing Data with Excel

Analyzing Personnel Data

In this tutorial you will:

- Identify the elements of an Excel data list

- Sort data in a worksheet

- Query a list to find information

- Maintain a list with a data form

- Learn the difference between an internal and an external database

- Filter records

- Create PivotTables from internal and external databases using Microsoft Query

CASE

North State University

You are administrative assistant to Ralph Long, the dean of the College of Business at North State University. He frequently asks you to look up and summarize information about the College of Business faculty. To fulfill these requests more efficiently and accurately, you created an Excel worksheet that contains the names, academic rank, department, hire date, salary, and gender of each faculty member in the College of Business.

The College of Business has two academic departments: the Management department and the Accounting department. Each faculty member holds an academic rank, such as professor or associate professor. Most faculty members are hired as instructors or assistant professors. After a period of time, the faculty member might be promoted to associate professor and then to full professor. Faculty salaries usually reflect the faculty member's rank and length of service in the department.

SESSION

6.1

You already know how to use Excel to perform calculations using numeric data or values you entered into worksheet cells. In this tutorial you will learn how to use Excel to manage numeric and non-numeric data. You will discover how easy it is to sort the information on a worksheet, to add and delete data, and to search for specific information. You will also learn how to filter the information to display only rows meeting certain criteria.

Data Management with Excel

Data management refers to tasks required to maintain and manipulate a data collection. Data management tasks typically include entering data, updating current data, sorting data, searching for information, and creating reports. For long, complicated lists of information, you'd want to use data management software, such as Access or dBASE. But when working with a simple list, such as the Faculty database, Excel is the probably the better option because its Data commands are so easy to use.

To start Excel and open the Faculty workbook:

1. Start Excel as usual.

2. Open the Faculty workbook in the Tutorial.06 folder on your Student Disk.

3. Type your name and the current date in the Documentation sheet.

4. Save the workbook as Business Faculty.

5. Click the **Faculty** tab.

Your worksheet, shown as a split window view in Figure 6-1, lists information, or data, about faculty members in the College of Business. A data list like this is also called a database. The information about individual faculty members in rows 7 through 41 includes last name, first name, department, rank, hire date (START DATE), salary, and gender. The column titles in row 6 identify the information in each column. Each column in a database is known as a **field**. Each column heading is known as a **field name**. Each row in a database is known as a **record**.

Figure 6-1 ◀
Faculty
worksheet

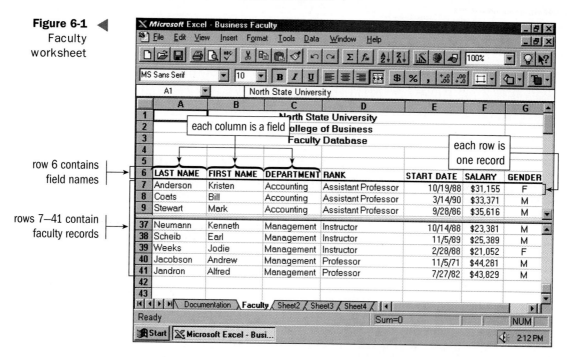

As you can see in Figure 6-1, each worksheet row contains information about one faculty member. Another way to envision a data list is as a set of cards or forms, like those shown in Figure 6-2. Here each card corresponds to one row (or record) on the Excel worksheet. Each entry line on a card corresponds to one column (or field) in the worksheet. As you progress through the tutorial, you will learn that you can view your data in rows and columns on the worksheet or in a format (called a data form) similar to a card file.

Figure 6-2 ◀
Card file
representation
of an Excel
database

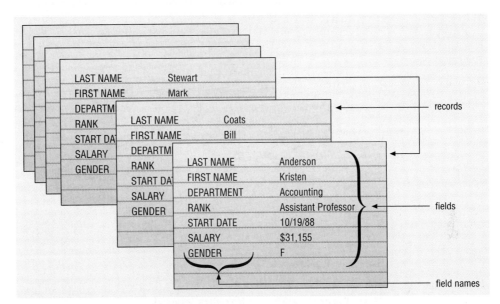

The dean asked you to provide him with a list of all faculty members in the College of Business, sorted alphabetically by last name. He also wants another list of all faculty members organized by rank with the faculty members sorted alphabetically by last name within each rank. You'll use Excel's Sort command to create these lists.

Sorting Data

When you sort a list, Excel rearranges the rows of the list according to the contents of one or more columns. For example, in your worksheet you could sort the rows alphabetically according to the information contained in the DEPARTMENT column. The result would be a list in which all rows containing information about faculty in the Accounting department would appear first, followed by all rows containing information about the Management faculty. If you sorted by department and then by rank, the result would be similar to Figure 6-3.

Figure 6-3 ◀
Faculty data
sorted by
department
and rank

assistant professor is
the first rank in each
department

sorted alphabetically
by department

North State University
College of Business
Faculty Database

LAST NAME	FIRST NAME	DEPARTMENT	RANK	START DATE	SALARY	GENDER
Anderson	Kristen	Accounting	Assistant Professor	10/19/88	$31,155	F
Coats	Bill	Accounting	Assistant Professor	3/14/90	$33,371	M
Stewart	Mark	Accounting	Assistant Professor	9/28/86	$35,616	M
Downs	Clifton	Accounting	Associate Professor	7/27/82	$34,887	M
Mikkola	Claudia	Accounting	Associate Professor	4/27/76	$34,281	F
Palermo	Sheryl	Accounting	Associate Professor	2/14/88	$33,617	F
Wolter	Christine	Accounting	Associate Professor	8/11/83	$32,918	F
Collins	Roger	Accounting	Head	8/11/91	$47,281	M
Ball	Robin	Accounting	Instructor	3/14/87	$23,723	F
Blackwell	Dean	Accounting	Instructor	11/12/92	$25,797	M
Bressette	Cheryl	Accounting	Instructor	7/27/87	$24,582	F
Jackson	Carole	Accounting	Instructor	3/14/92	$21,781	F
May	Jim	Accounting	Instructor	10/14/90	$26,881	M
Doepke	Cheryl	Accounting	Professor	12/14/78	$40,105	F
Nelsen	Beth	Accounting	Professor	9/12/77	$40,339	F
Nelson	Dale	Accounting	Professor	3/11/88	$42,578	M
Parker	Mathew	Accounting	Professor	10/11/74	$45,892	M
Smith	Tom	Accounting	Professor	7/16/72	$45,167	M
Smith	Alicia	Accounting	Professor	7/16/89	$37,955	F
True	David	Accounting	Professor	2/28/86	$41,181	M
Weaver	Robert	Accounting	Professor	8/11/76	$43,775	M
Bordeau	Katherine	Management	Assistant Professor	2/14/86	$30,311	F
Young	Jeff	Management	Assistant Professor	10/11/90	$31,513	M
Comensoli	Angela	Management	Associate Professor	4/27/78	$32,212	F
Fitzgerald	Edmond	Management	Associate Professor	11/12/90	$36,757	M
Lewis	Karl	Management	Associate Professor	5/22/79	$36,387	M
Smythe	Janice	Management	Associate Professor	3/17/86	$34,887	F
Rothenberger	James	Management	Head	10/11/90	$49,781	M
Hill	Trevor	Management	Instructor	6/11/90	$23,590	M
McKaye	Susan	Management	Instructor	7/28/89	$21,979	F
Neumann	Kenneth	Management	Instructor	10/14/88	$23,381	M
Scheib	Earl	Management	Instructor	11/5/89	$25,389	M
Weeks	Jodie	Management	Instructor	2/28/88	$21,052	F
Jacobson	Andrew	Management	Professor	11/5/71	$44,281	M
Jandron	Alfred	Management	Professor	7/27/82	$43,829	M

In Figure 6-3, the rows within the group of Accounting faculty are arranged alphabetically by rank, with the assistant professors listed first, the associate professors next, and so on. The same is true for the Management faculty rows.

To sort the data in an Excel worksheet, you highlight one cell within the list of data you want to sort. In this tutorial, you will always select the cell in the upper-left corner of the list (immediately under the column heading) because this cell is always visible on the screen. Excel automatically recognizes the rows of information as a collection of related data; it also recognizes the bold text at the top of the list as column headings. You use the Sort command on the Data menu to specify the columns by which you want to sort. If you have a problem with a sort, use the Undo command to restore the database to the way it was before the sort.

REFERENCE window

SORTING ROWS IN A DATA LIST

- Highlight any cell in the list.
- Click Data then click Sort to display the Sort dialog box. The Sort By box is active.
- Use the arrow button to display the list of column headings and select the column by which you want to sort.
- If you want to sort by a second column, click the Then By box and use the arrow button to select the desired column heading.
- If you want to sort by a third column, click the second Then By box and select the desired column heading.
- Click the OK button to sort the list.

Sorting Data by One Column

The dean wants a list of faculty members sorted alphabetically by last name. To prepare this list, you highlight any cell in the range A6:G41, which contains the column headings and information you want to sort. You then use the Sort dialog box to specify that Excel should sort by the contents of the LAST NAME column.

To sort the records alphabetically by last name:

1. Click cell **A7**, the cell in the upper-left corner of the list. Remember that Excel automatically recognizes the adjacent rows and columns as a data list.

2. Click **Data** then click **Sort** to display the Sort dialog box. Note that Excel automatically selects the entire data list (but not the column headings) when it displays this dialog box.

3. Click the **Sort By** arrow button to display the list of column headings. If LAST NAME is not already displayed in the Sort By box, select LAST NAME now.

4. Make sure the **Ascending** option button is selected. This tells Excel to arrange the rows alphabetically by last name from A to Z. (If you wanted to arrange the rows by last name from Z to A, you would click Descending.) Make sure the **Header Row** option is selected in the My List Has box. See Figure 6-4.

Figure 6-4 ◄
Specifying the
Sort key

Excel automatically
selects the entire list

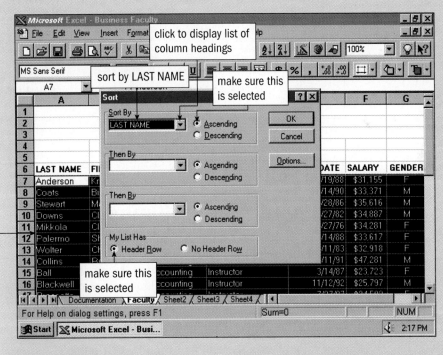

5. Click the **OK** button to sort the records alphabetically by last name.

6. If necessary, click any cell to remove the highlighting. Notice that the faculty members' last names are now in alphabetical order.

7. Preview the worksheet, adjust print settings as necessary, and then print it. Figure 6-5 shows the printed worksheet.

Figure 6-5
Printed list
sorted by
last name

North State University
College of Business
Faculty Database

LAST NAME	FIRST NAME	DEPARTMENT	RANK	START DATE	SALARY	GENDER
Anderson	Kristen	Accounting	Assistant Professor	10/19/88	$31,155	F
Ball	Robin	Accounting	Instructor	3/14/87	$23,723	F
Blackwell	Dean	Accounting	Instructor	11/12/92	$25,797	M
Bordeau	Katherine	Management	Assistant Professor	2/14/86	$30,311	F
Bressette	Cheryl	Accounting	Instructor	7/27/87	$24,582	F
Coats	Bill	Accounting	Assistant Professor	3/14/90	$33,371	M
Collins	Roger	Accounting	Head	8/11/91	$47,281	M
Comensoli	Angela	Management	Associate Professor	4/27/78	$32,212	F
Doepke	Cheryl	Accounting	Professor	12/14/78	$40,105	F
Downs	Clifton	Accounting	Associate Professor	7/27/82	$34,887	M
Fitzgerald	Edmond	Management	Associate Professor	11/12/90	$36,757	M
Hill	Trevor	Management	Instructor	6/11/90	$23,590	M
Jackson	Carole	Accounting	Instructor	3/14/92	$21,781	F
Jacobson	Andrew	Management	Professor	11/5/71	$44,281	M
Jandron	Alfred	Management	Professor	7/27/82	$43,829	M
Lewis	Karl	Management	Associate Professor	5/22/79	$36,387	M
May	Jim	Accounting	Instructor	10/14/90	$26,881	M
McKaye	Susan	Management	Instructor	7/28/89	$21,979	F
Mikkola	Claudia	Accounting	Associate Professor	4/27/76	$34,281	F
Nelsen	Beth	Accounting	Professor	9/12/77	$40,339	F
Nelson	Dale	Accounting	Professor	3/11/88	$42,578	M
Neumann	Kenneth	Management	Instructor	10/14/88	$23,381	M
Palermo	Sheryl	Accounting	Associate Professor	2/14/88	$33,617	F
Parker	Mathew	Accounting	Professor	10/11/74	$45,892	M
Rothenberger	James	Management	Head	10/11/90	$49,781	M
Scheib	Earl	Management	Instructor	11/5/89	$25,389	M
Smith	Tom	Accounting	Professor	7/16/72	$45,167	M
Smith	Alicia	Accounting	Professor	7/16/89	$37,955	F
Smythe	Janice	Management	Associate Professor	3/17/86	$34,887	F
Stewart	Mark	Accounting	Assistant Professor	9/28/86	$35,616	M
True	David	Accounting	Professor	2/28/86	$41,181	M
Weaver	Robert	Accounting	Professor	8/11/76	$43,775	M
Weeks	Jodie	Management	Instructor	2/28/88	$21,052	F
Wolter	Christine	Accounting	Associate Professor	8/11/83	$32,918	F
Young	Jeff	Management	Assistant Professor	10/11/90	$31,513	M

last names in
alphabetical order

The dean also requested a list of faculty data sorted alphabetically by rank and, within each rank, sorted alphabetically by last name.

Sorting by Two Columns

To prepare the second list for the dean, you sort the information using two columns. You use RANK as the Sort By entry in the dialog box and LAST NAME as the Then By entry in the dialog box. As a result of the sort, the records for all faculty members of a particular rank will be listed together; within each rank, the faculty member records will be sorted alphabetically by last name. As with all Data commands, you begin by selecting one cell in the list.

To sort faculty data by rank and then by last name:

1. Click cell **A7**.

2. Click **Data**, then click **Sort** to display the Sort dialog box.

3. Click the **Sort By** arrow button to display the list of column headings.

4. Click **RANK** to display it in the Sort By box.

5. Click the **Then By** arrow button to display the list of column headings.

6. Click **LAST NAME** to display it in the Then By box.

7. Click the **OK** button to sort the records first by rank and then by last name. If necessary, click any cell to remove the highlighting and view the newly sorted data.

8. Preview the worksheet, adjust print settings as necessary, and print it.

Your printed worksheet should look like Figure 6-6.

Figure 6-6 ◄
Printed list
sorted by rank
and last name

faculty in each rank
alphabetized by
last name

North State University
College of Business
Faculty Database

LAST NAME	FIRST NAME	DEPARTMENT	RANK	START DATE	SALARY	GENDER
Anderson	Kristen	Accounting	Assistant Professor	10/19/88	$31,155	F
Bordeau	Katherine	Management	Assistant Professor	2/14/86	$30,311	F
Coats	Bill	Accounting	Assistant Professor	3/14/90	$33,371	M
Stewart	Mark	Accounting	Assistant Professor	9/28/86	$35,616	M
Young	Jeff	Management	Assistant Professor	10/11/90	$31,613	M
Comensoli	Angela	Management	Associate Professor	4/27/78	$32,212	F
Downs	Clifton	Accounting	Associate Professor	7/27/82	$34,887	M
Fitzgerald	Edmond	Management	Associate Professor	11/12/90	$36,757	M
Lewis	Karl	Management	Associate Professor	5/22/79	$36,387	M
Mikkola	Claudia	Accounting	Associate Professor	4/27/76	$34,281	F
Palermo	Sheryl	Accounting	Associate Professor	2/14/88	$33,617	F
Smythe	Janice	Management	Associate Professor	3/17/86	$34,887	F
Wolter	Christine	Accounting	Associate Professor	8/11/83	$32,918	F
Collins	Roger	Accounting	Head	8/11/91	$47,281	M
Rothenberger	James	Management	Head	10/11/90	$49,781	M
Ball	Robin	Accounting	Instructor	3/14/87	$23,723	F
Blackwell	Dean	Accounting	Instructor	11/12/92	$25,797	M
Bressette	Cheryl	Accounting	Instructor	7/27/87	$24,582	F
Hill	Trevor	Management	Instructor	6/11/90	$23,590	M
Jackson	Carole	Accounting	Instructor	3/14/92	$21,781	F
May	Jim	Accounting	Instructor	10/14/90	$26,881	M
McKaye	Susan	Management	Instructor	7/28/89	$21,979	F
Neumann	Kenneth	Management	Instructor	10/14/88	$23,381	M
Scheib	Earl	Management	Instructor	11/5/89	$25,389	M
Weeks	Jodie	Management	Instructor	2/28/88	$21,052	F
Doepke	Cheryl	Accounting	Professor	12/14/78	$40,105	F
Jacobson	Andrew	Management	Professor	11/5/71	$44,281	M
Jandron	Alfred	Management	Professor	7/27/82	$43,829	M
Nelsen	Beth	Accounting	Professor	9/12/77	$40,339	F
Nelson	Dale	Accounting	Professor	3/11/88	$42,578	M
Parker	Mathew	Accounting	Professor	10/11/74	$45,892	M
Smith	Tom	Accounting	Professor	7/16/72	$45,167	M
Smith	Alicia	Accounting	Professor	7/16/89	$37,955	F
True	David	Accounting	Professor	2/28/86	$41,181	M
Weaver	Robert	Accounting	Professor	8/11/76	$43,775	M

Excel performed this sort by first alphabetizing the ranks in column D—in effect, grouping the records by rank. All assistant professors are grouped together, as are all associate professors, department heads, instructors, and professors. Within each rank, Excel sorted the records alphabetically by last name. For example, within the assistant professor rank, Anderson is listed first, followed by Bordeau.

When you use the Excel Sort command, you work with the data using the row and column format in which it appears on the worksheet. You'll often find it convenient to do other data management tasks using Excel's data form, which lets you view the data in a card file format.

Maintaining a List with Excel's Data Form

A **data form** is a dialog box that makes it easy to search for, view, edit, add, and delete rows (also known as records) in a list. A data form displays one record at a time, rather than the table of rows and columns you see on the worksheet.

You use the Form command now to display one record at a time. Just as you did when you sorted, you begin by clicking any cell in the range A6:G41.

To display a data form:

1. Click cell **A7**.

2. Click **Data** then click **Form** to display the data form. The first record in the list is displayed, as shown in Figure 6-7. Note that the dialog box title, "Faculty," matches the name of the active sheet.

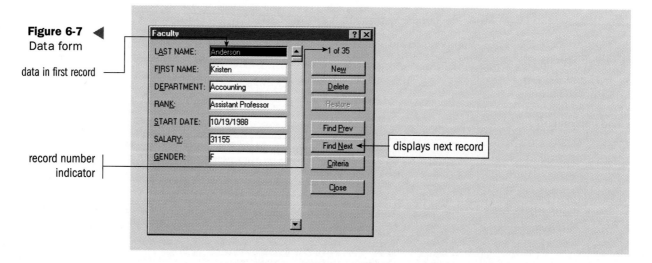

Figure 6-7
Data form

data in first record

record number
indicator

displays next record

You can use the data form to move through records until you find the one you want, or you can have Excel search for the specific record you want.

Manual Search

You can use the data form to manually scroll through the list one record at a time using the arrow buttons on the data form vertical scroll bar, or the Up Arrow and Down Arrow keys on the keyboard. You can also use the scroll box on the data form vertical scroll bar to move quickly to a particular record number.

The **record number indicator** in the upper-right corner of the data form indicates the number of the record displayed in the data form, and it shows the total number of records in the database. In Figure 6-7 the record indicator shows "1 of 35," indicating that the current record is the first record in the database and that there are 35 records in the database.

Take a moment to practice using the scroll arrow buttons and arrow keys to scroll through the database records.

To practice manually scrolling through the database:

1. Click the **down arrow** button at the bottom of the vertical scroll bar once, or press ↓ once to display the next record in the database. The record number indicator shows that record 2 of 35 is displayed. See Figure 6-8.

Figure 6-8
Record 2 of 35

record number
indicator

down arrow button

Faculty		? □ ×
LAST NAME:	Bordeau	2 of 35
FIRST NAME:	Katherine	New
DEPARTMENT:	Management	Delete
RANK:	Assistant Professor	Restore
START DATE:	2/14/1986	
SALARY:	30311	Find Prev
GENDER:	F	Find Next
		Criteria
		Close

2. Click the **down arrow** button once, or press ↓ once to display record 3 of 35.

3. Click the **up arrow** button once, or press ↑ once to scroll back to record 2 of 35.

> **4.** Drag the **scroll** box on the scroll bar until the record number indicator shows 18 of 35. Release the mouse button to display the contents of record 18.
>
> **5.** Drag the **scroll** box to the top of the scroll bar to display record 1 of 35.

With large data lists, manually locating specific rows, or records, can take time. The alternative is to have Excel automatically search for records in the database that match criteria you specify.

Criteria Search

You can use the Criteria button on the data form to have Excel search for a specific record or group of records. When you initiate a search, you specify the **search criteria,** or the instructions for the search. Excel starts from the current record and moves through the list searching for any records that match the search criteria. If it finds more than one match, Excel displays the first record that matches the search criteria. You use the Find Next button on the data form to display the next record that matches the search criteria. The Find Prev button displays the previous record that matches the search criteria.

The search is not case sensitive; that is, it does not matter if you type uppercase or lowercase letters when you enter the search criteria. For example, if you have a record with "Hill" as the last name, you can find it by entering "HILL" or "Hill" or "hill" as the search criteria.

REFERENCE window

SEARCHING FOR A RECORD USING THE DATA FORM
■ Click any cell in the data list.
■ Click Data then click Form to display the data form.
■ Make sure the data form displays the first record in the list so Excel starts searching at the beginning of the list.
■ Click the Criteria button.
■ Click the Clear button to clear any previous search criteria.
■ Enter the search criteria in the appropriate boxes. You can use uppercase or lowercase letters.
■ Click the Find Next button to display the next record that matches the search criteria.
■ Click the Find Prev button to display the previous record that matches the search criteria.

A criteria search is also called a **query** because you use a criteria search to find the answers to questions, or queries, about information in the database. Let's see how you might query the faculty database.

Suppose you want to find the date that Trevor Hill started working at the College of Business. You can use the Criteria button to have Excel search for the record of a faculty member with the last name "Hill." Then, when you find the record, you need only to look in the START DATE field to find out when he started.

To search for the record for Trevor Hill:

> **1.** Make sure the record number indicator says 1 of 35.
>
> **2.** Click the **Criteria** button to begin entering the criteria. Notice that some buttons change and the word "Criteria" appears in the upper-right corner of the dialog box.

3. Click the **LAST NAME** box, then type Hill. See Figure 6-9.

Figure 6-9 ◄
Entering search
criteria in the
data form

type "Hill" here

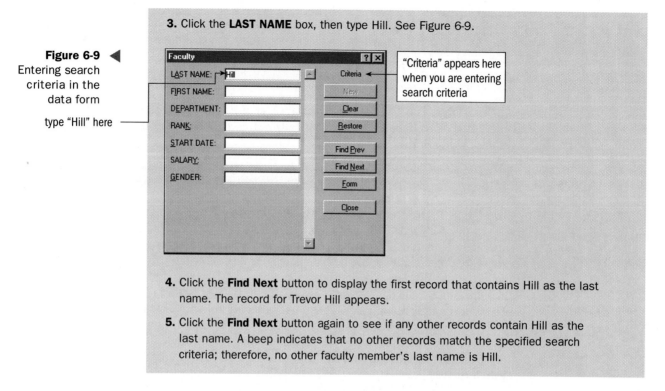

4. Click the **Find Next** button to display the first record that contains Hill as the last name. The record for Trevor Hill appears.

5. Click the **Find Next** button again to see if any other records contain Hill as the last name. A beep indicates that no other records match the specified search criteria; therefore, no other faculty member's last name is Hill.

You can see from the record in the data form that Trevor started on 6/11/1990.

Next, suppose that you need to find the names of the female faculty members with the rank of professor. For this query, you must enter two search criteria: RANK must be "Professor" and GENDER must be "F."

To view the records for all female professors:

1. Click the **up arrow** button at the top of the scroll bar to display record 1 of 35.

2. Click the **Criteria** button.

3. Click the **Clear** button to clear the previous search criteria.

4. Click the **RANK** box, then type Professor.

5. Click the **GENDER** box, then type **F**.

6. Click the **Find Next** button to view the record for the next female professor. Record 26 displays information for Cheryl Doepke, a professor in the Accounting department.

7. Click the **Find Next** button again to view the next record that matches the search criteria. Record 29 displays information for Beth Nelsen, a professor in the Accounting department.

8. Click the **Find Next** button again to view the next record. Record 33 displays information for Alicia Smith, a professor in the Accounting department.

9. Click the **Find Next** button again to view the next record. A beep indicates that no other records match the search criteria.

You now know that three females are professors in the College of Business—Cheryl Doepke, Beth Nelsen, and Alicia Smith.

Next, suppose that you want to find out which faculty members started at the university before 1/1/1975. You can use the less than symbol (<) to specify that you want to select faculty members whose start date is less than (earlier than) 1/1/1975.

To view the records for all faculty members who started before 1/1/1975:

1. Click the **up arrow** button at the top of the scroll bar to display record 1 of 35.

2. Click the **Criteria** button.

3. Click the **Clear** button to clear the previous search criteria.

4. Click the **START DATE** box, then type **< 1/1/1975** to search for all faculty members who started before 1/1/1975. See Figure 6-10.

Figure 6-10
Searching for
records by
start date

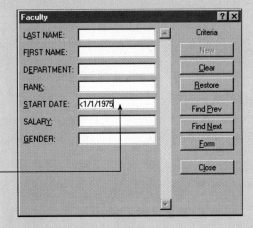

Excel will find all
records with start
dates before
1/1/1975

5. Click the **Find Next** button to view the record for the first faculty member who started before 1/1/1975. Record 27 displays information for Andrew Jacobson, who started in the Management department on 11/5/1971.

6. Click the **Find Next** button to view the record for the next faculty member who started before 1/1/1975. Record 31 displays information for Mathew Parker, who started in the Accounting department on 10/11/1974.

7. Click the **Find Next** button again to view the record for the next faculty member who started before 1/1/1975. Record 32 displays information for Tom Smith, who started in the Accounting department on 7/16/1972.

8. Click the **Find Next** button to view the record for the next faculty member who started before 1/1/1975. A beep indicates that no other records match the search criteria.

The dean mentions that on the way to work he heard part of a radio interview with a North State faculty member from the College of Business who recently won first place in a women's local 10K race. He remembers that her last name started with Ne, as in Nesbitt or Nelson. You offer to use your database to find out who won the race. Because you do not know the exact search criteria, you use a wildcard to replace part of the search criteria.

Using Wildcards

Excel's data form lets you use wildcards when you enter search criteria. A **wildcard** is a symbol that stands for one or more characters. The Excel data form recognizes two wildcards: the question mark and the asterisk.

The question mark (?) wildcard represents any single character. For example, if you didn't know if a faculty member's last name was spelled Nelsen or Nelson, you could specify Nels?n as the search criteria. The data form would display all records in which the last name started with Nels, followed by any single character, and ending with n.

The asterisk (*) wildcard represents any group of characters. For example, if you use Ne* as the search criteria for the last name field, Excel finds all records with last names that begin with Ne, regardless of the letters that follow. If you use *son as the search criteria for the last name field, Excel finds all records with last names that end with son, regardless of the letters beginning the last name.

You decide to use the asterisk wildcard to find all female faculty members whose last names start with the letters Ne.

To search for all female faculty members whose last names start with Ne:

1. Click the **up arrow** button at the top of the scroll bar to display record 1 of 35.

2. Click the **Criteria** button.

3. Click the **Clear** button to clear the previous search criteria.

4. Click the **LAST NAME** box, then type **Ne*** to select last names that start with Ne.

5. Click the **GENDER** box then type **F** to limit the search to female faculty members.

6. Click the **Find Next** button to view the record for the first female faculty member whose last name starts with Ne. The record for Beth Nelsen is displayed. Beth could be the person who won the 10K race.

7. Click the **Find Next** button again to view the next record that matches the search criteria. A beep indicates that no more records match the search criteria.

You found only one female faculty member whose last name starts with Ne, so Beth Nelsen must be the faculty member who won the women's 10K race.

Maintaining Data in a List

In addition to querying the list, you need to keep its data accurate by making changes, additions, or deletions. The process of keeping data accurate is often called **updating**.

In your in-basket you find a memo announcing that Jim May, an instructor in the Accounting department, has resigned and that Martin Stein has been hired as his replacement. You need to update your faculty list to delete the record for Jim May and add a record for Martin Stein.

Deleting Records

The Delete button on the data form lets you delete records in the database. To delete a record using the data form, you display the record, then click the Delete button. Excel removes deleted records from the worksheet.

REFERENCE window	**DELETING A RECORD USING THE DATA FORM**
	■ Click any cell within the list.
	■ Click Data then click Form to display the data form.
	■ Scroll or search through the records to display the record you want to delete.
	■ Click the Delete button.
	■ Click the OK button to delete the record.

You must locate the record for Jim May before you can delete it.

To locate and delete the record for Jim May:

1. Click the **up arrow** button at the top of the scroll bar to display record 1 of 35.

2. Click the **Criteria** button.

3. Click the **Clear** button to clear the previous query.

4. Click the **LAST NAME** box, then type **May** as the search criteria.

5. Click the **Find Next** button to display the first record that matches the search criteria. Jim May's record appears in the data form.

6. Click the **Delete** button.

7. When you see the message "Displayed record will be permanently deleted," click the **OK** button.

Excel deletes the row for Jim May from the worksheet. You will check the worksheet to verify the deletion after you add a new record and enter information for Martin Stein.

Adding New Records

The New button on the data form adds a new blank row, or record, to the bottom of the data list. If you want to keep your database in alphabetical order, you will need to sort it again after you add records.

REFERENCE window	**ADDING A RECORD USING THE DATA FORM**
	▪ Click any cell within the list.
	▪ Click Data then click Form to display the data form.
	▪ Click the New button.
	▪ Enter the information for the new record.
	▪ Click the Close button or scroll to another record to save the new record.

To add Martin Stein to the faculty database:

1. Click the **New** button to create a new record.

2. Type **Stein** in the LAST NAME box.

3. Press **Tab** to move to the FIRST NAME box, then type **Martin**.

4. Press **Tab** to move to the DEPARTMENT box, then type **Accounting**.

5. Press **Tab** to move to the RANK box, then type **Instructor**.

6. Press **Tab** to move to the START DATE box, then type **today's date** using the format MM/DD/YY (for example, 8/31/97).

7. Press **Tab** to move to the SALARY box, then type **20562**.

8. Press **Tab** to move to the GENDER box, then type **M**. Check that your form looks like Figure 6-11 before moving on to Step 9.

Figure 6-11 ◀
Adding a new
record

data for new record →

New button →

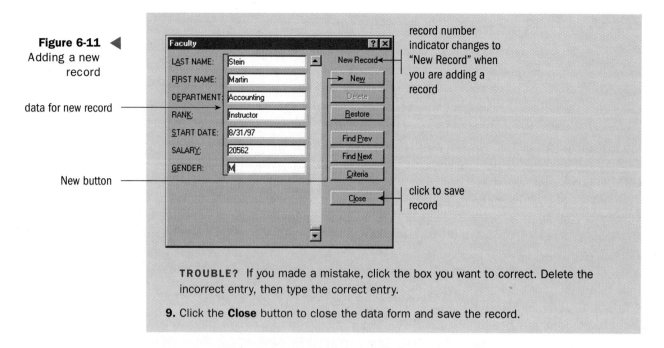

record number
indicator changes to
"New Record" when
you are adding a
record

click to save
record

> **TROUBLE?** If you made a mistake, click the box you want to correct. Delete the
> incorrect entry, then type the correct entry.
>
> **9.** Click the **Close** button to close the data form and save the record.

You want to verify that you deleted the record for Jim May and added the record for
Martin Stein; then you can save the worksheet.

To verify the changes to the list and then save the worksheet:

> **1.** Scroll the worksheet and make sure the record for Jim May is gone.
>
> **2.** Scroll to the bottom of the worksheet and verify that row 41 now contains the
> record for Martin Stein.
>
> **3.** Click the Save button 🖫.

After lunch the dean returns from a meeting regarding equal pay for male and female
faculty members. The dean wants to know if male and female faculty members in the
College of Business receive equivalent salaries. He asks you to calculate the average pay
for male and female faculty members in the College of Business.

You think about the dean's request and decide that you can first list all the information for female faculty, then use the AVERAGE function to calculate their average salary.
You will then list all the information for male faculty and calculate their average salary.

Filtering a List

In this tutorial you have manually scrolled through the list to find records, and you have
used the data form Criteria button to search for records matching specific search criteria.
When you use the data form, you can view only one record at a time, even if more than
one record matches the search criteria. If you want to see a list of all records that match
the search criteria, you must filter the list.

The Filter command on the Data menu temporarily hides rows that do not match your
search criteria. When Excel filters a list, the worksheet is in Filter mode. You can edit,
format, chart, and print your filtered list.

Excel offers two ways to filter a list. AutoFilter lets you filter a list quickly based on one simple criteria at a time. For example, you will use AutoFilter to display the records for all female faculty. Advanced Filter lets you use more complicated criteria or several different criteria at once. For example, you might use Advanced Filter if you want to display the records for all female faculty in the Accounting Department with salaries greater than $30,000. For now, you will only be concerned with AutoFilter. You will learn how to use Advanced Filter in the case problems at the end of this tutorial.

To use AutoFilter, simply click any cell within the list you want to filter. Then use the AutoFilter command on the Data menu to display arrow buttons on each column heading in the data list. You can use the arrow buttons to display lists of possible search criteria. Once you select a criteria, Excel displays only the rows that match your criteria. The row headings are displayed in blue as a reminder that you are seeing only part of the entire data list. The arrow button in the column you used as the search criteria also appears in blue. To display all rows in the list (not just those that match your search criteria), use the blue arrow button to select (All) as the search criteria. To remove the arrow buttons, click AutoFilter on the Data menu again.

REFERENCE window	FILTERING A LIST WITH AUTOFILTER
	■ Click any cell within the list you want to filter.
	■ Click Data, point to Filter, then click AutoFilter to display the arrow buttons on each column heading in the worksheet.
	■ Click the arrow button in the column you want to search to display a list of possible search criteria.
	■ Click the desired search criteria.
	■ Click Data, click Filter, then click AutoFilter again to remove the arrow buttons from the column headings.

Using AutoFilter

The dean wants you to find the average salary for female faculty members and for male faculty members. You want first to display the rows for female faculty members. As usual with Data commands, you begin by clicking any cell within the data list.

To display the list of female faculty members:

1. Click cell **A7**.

2. Click **Data**, point to **Filter**, then click **AutoFilter**. Arrow buttons appear on each column label on the worksheet.

3. Click the **arrow** button in the Gender column (column G) to display a list of possible criteria. See Figure 6-12.

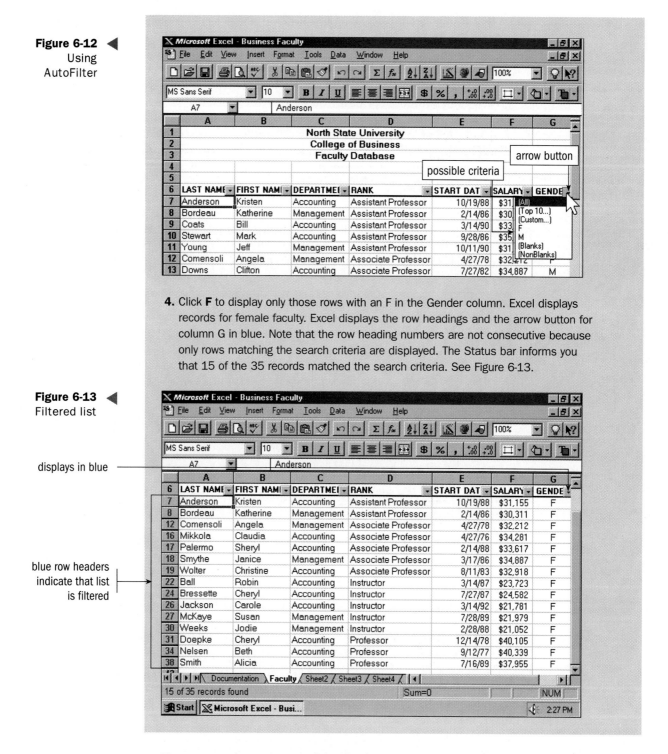

Figure 6-12
Using
AutoFilter

Figure 6-13
Filtered list

displays in blue

blue row headers
indicate that list
is filtered

4. Click **F** to display only those rows with an F in the Gender column. Excel displays records for female faculty. Excel displays the row headings and the arrow button for column G in blue. Note that the row heading numbers are not consecutive because only rows matching the search criteria are displayed. The Status bar informs you that 15 of the 35 records matched the search criteria. See Figure 6-13.

You want to keep a copy of the the female faculty records, so you copy these rows to a blank sheet, adjust column widths, and rename the sheet.

To copy the female faculty records to a blank sheet:

1. Highlight cells **A6** through **G38**.

2. Click the **Copy** button.

3. Click the **Sheet2** tab to display the blank **Sheet2**, then click cell **A1** to begin inserting rows there.

4. Click the Paste button [icon]. The female faculty records, along with the column headings, appear in the Sheet2 sheet. Note that Excel does not copy the AutoFilter arrow buttons from the Faculty sheet.

5. To format the columns so that all data is visible, click **Format**, point to **Column**, then click **AutoFit Selection**.

6. Click anywhere on the worksheet to remove the highlighting.

7. Rename Sheet2 **Female Faculty**. See Figure 6-14.

Figure 6-14 ◀
The Female
Faculty sheet

no arrow buttons
in column titles

row titles appear
in black

records copied here
and sheet renamed

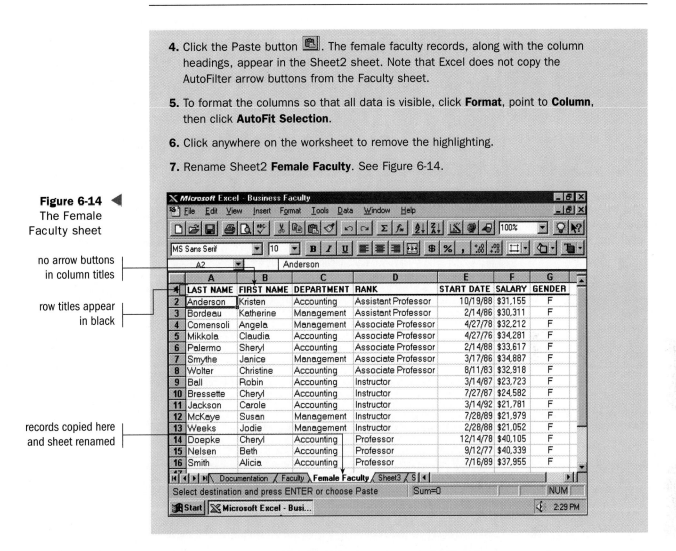

Now you can use the AVERAGE function to calculate the average salary for the female faculty members in the College of Business. You begin by entering the label "Average Salary."

To calculate the average salary for female faculty members in the College of Business:

1. Click cell **E17** because this is where you want to enter the label.

2. Type **Average Salary** and press **Enter**.

3. Click cell **F17** because this is where you want to enter the AVERAGE function.

4. Type **=AVERAGE(** to begin the formula. Don't forget to include the opening parenthesis.

5. Select cells **F2** through **F16**, the cells you want to average. When you see the range F2:F16 entered in the formula, release the mouse button.

6. Press **Enter** to complete the calculation and display the average salary.

The worksheet shows that the average salary for female faculty members in the College of Business is $30,726. Next, you notice that part of the "Average Salary" label has been cut off. You decide to format cells E17 and F17 to make them easier to read.

To format cells E17 and F17:

1. Click cell **E17**, then click the **Align Right** button 🗐 to display the entire label.

2. Highlight cells **E17** and **F17**, then click the **Bold** button 🄱. The label and average salary value appear in bold.

3. Click any cell to remove the highlighting. See Figure 6-15.

   TROUBLE? If you need to widen the Salary column to display the newly formatted average salary value, double-click the border between column headings F and G.

Figure 6-15 ◄
The formatted
Average Salary
label and value

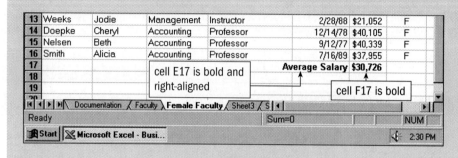

13	Weeks	Jodie	Management	Instructor	2/28/88	$21,052	F
14	Doepke	Cheryl	Accounting	Professor	12/14/78	$40,105	F
15	Nelsen	Beth	Accounting	Professor	9/12/77	$40,339	F
16	Smith	Alicia	Accounting	Professor	7/16/89	$37,955	F

cell E17 is bold and right-aligned

Average Salary $30,726

cell F17 is bold

Documentation / Faculty \ Female Faculty / Sheet3 / S

Ready   Sum=0   NUM

Start | Microsoft Excel - Busi...   2:30 PM

Now that you have created a separate worksheet for female faculty, you create a separate worksheet for male faculty. To do this, you simply change the search criteria from "F" to "M" in the Faculty sheet. Then you copy the records for male faculty to a separate sheet.

To display all records for male faculty members:

1. Click the **Faculty** tab to display the Faculty sheet with the AutoFormat arrow buttons. If necessary, click any cell to remove the highlighting.

2. Click the **blue arrow** button in the Gender column (column G) to display the list of possible search criteria.

   TROUBLE? If the column headings aren't visible, scroll the worksheet until they are visible.

3. Click **M** to hide the records for female faculty and display the records for male faculty.

Now you will copy the records for male faculty to a new sheet. You'll format the sheet and calculate the average salary, just as you did for female faculty records.

To copy male faculty records to a new sheet:

1. Highlight cells **A6** to **G41**, then click the **Copy** button 🖺.

2. Click the **Sheet3** tab to display the blank Sheet3, then click cell A1 to begin inserting rows there.

3. Click the **Paste** button 🖺. The male faculty records, along with column headings, appear in Sheet3.

4. To format the columns so all data is visible, make sure cells **A6** through **G21** are highlighted, click **Format**, point to **Column**, then click **AutoFit Selection**.

5. Click anywhere on the worksheet to remove the highlighting.

6. Rename Sheet3 **Male Faculty**.

Now you can use the AVERAGE function to calculate the average salary for the male faculty members in the College of Business. Once again, you begin by entering the label "Average Salary."

To calculate the average salary for male faculty members in the College of Business:

1. Enter **Average Salary** in cell E22.

2. Create a formula in cell F22 that averages the values in the range F2:F21.

3. Format cells E22:F22 as you did in the Female Faculty sheet.

   TROUBLE? If you need to widen the salary column to display the newly formatted average salary value, double-click the border between column headings F and G.

4. Return to the Faculty sheet and save the workbook with the new sheets.

The average salary for male faculty members, $36,551, in the College of Business is significantly higher than the average female salary of $30,726. You tell the dean the results of your calculations.

The dean thinks about the average salary figures for a while, then asks you if there is any way to determine the average salaries for males and females at each rank. The dean wants to compare the average salary of female instructors to the average salary of male instructors, the average salary of female assistant professors to the average salary of male assistant professors, and so on.

You know that you could calculate these figures by individually filtering data for male and female faculty members of each rank, then calculating their average salary. This, however, would be very time-consuming because you would need to copy the data and calculate the averages eight times. Instead, you decide to save time by using Excel's PivotTable Wizard to produce a table showing the average salaries for male and female faculty members at each rank.

Before you can create the PivotTable, you need to display all records in the data list.

To display all records in the data list:

1. Make sure the faculty worksheet is displayed.

2. Click the **blue arrow** button in the Gender column (column G) to display the list of possible search criteria.

3. Click **(All)** to display all records in the list.

4. Click **Data**, point to **Filter**, then click **AutoFilter** to remove the arrow buttons in the column headings.

5. Click the **Save** button 🖫 to save the workbook.

Quick Check

1. What is an Excel data list?

2. A row within a data list is often called a _____.

3. A column within a data list is often called a _____.

4. A data list is often called a _____.

5. The following list was sorted using three columns. Which column was used as the first column to sort by? Which column was used as the next column to sort by? Which column was used as the third column to sort by?

CLASS	LAST NAME	FIRST NAME
EN211	Baker	Joseph
EN211	Smith	Carol Ann
EN211	Smith	Jim
SP312	Andrews	Carole
SP312	Casselman	Timothy

6 Explain how to enter a new record using the data form.

7 Explain how to search for a record using the data form.

8 You can use the _____ wildcard to represent any group of characters.

9 Explain how to filter a list using AutoFilter.

SESSION 6.2

In this session you will learn how to create special tables, called PivotTables, based on data you sorted and selected. You will also learn how to bring data from another program into Excel. After you bring the data into Excel, you can manipulate it just as you would any Excel data list.

Using PivotTables

A **PivotTable** summarizes the contents of a database by automatically counting, averaging, or totaling the contents of selected fields. You could manually compile this information by doing a series of filters and calculations, but it's much easier to let the PivotTable Wizard do it for you. The PivotTable Wizard guides you through the steps for creating a PivotTable, just as the ChartWizard guided you through the steps for creating a chart. Following the PivotTable Wizard's directions, you specify the column headings (or fields) you want to include in the PivotTable and indicate the calculations you want to perform on each field.

REFERENCE window

GENERATING A PIVOTTABLE

- Make sure all rows in the data list are displayed.
- Click Data, then click PivotTable to start the PivotTable Wizard.
- Follow the PivotTable Wizard instructions to create a PivotTable on a separate sheet.
- Format and save the PivotTable.

You consider the information that the dean wants and create a PivotTable plan (Figure 6-16) and a PivotTable sketch (Figure 6-17). Your plan and sketch will help you work with the PivotTable Wizard to produce the PivotTable you want.

Figure 6-16 ◀
PivotTable plan

PivotTable Plan for Calculating Average Salaries

My Goal:
Create a table that compares female and male faculty salary averages for each academic rank.

What results do I want to see?
Average female salary for each rank.
Average male salary for each rank.
Overall average female salary.
Overall average male salary.
The average salary at each rank for males and females combined.

What information do I need?
The table rows will show the data for each RANK.
The table columns will show the data for each GENDER.
The table will show Grand Total values representing overall averages for faculty salaries.

What calculation method will I use for the values?
The SALARY values must be AVERAGED.

Figure 6-17 ◀
PivotTable
sketch

Average Salaries in the College of Business by Rank and Gender

	Female	Male	Grand Total
Assistant Professor	:	:	:
Associate Professor	:	:	:
Head	:	:	:
Instructor	:	:	:
Professor	:	:	:
Overall Average			

Now you are ready to create a PivotTable summarizing average faculty salaries. As with all Data commands, you begin by clicking any cell within the data list.

To create a PivotTable:

1. Click cell **A7**.

2. Click **Data** then click **PivotTable** to display the PivotTable Wizard - Step 1 of 4 dialog box. See Figure 6-18.

Figure 6-18 ◀
First PivotTable
dialog box

make sure this option
is selected

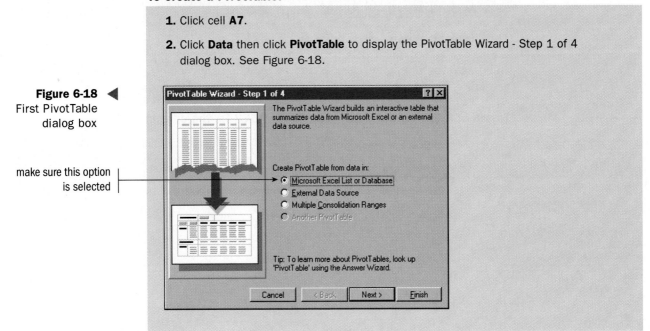

3. If necessary, click the Microsoft Excel List or Database option button to select it. This tells Excel that the data you want to use for the table is located in a Microsoft Excel workbook.

4. Click the **Next >** button to display the PivotTable Wizard - Step 2 of 4 dialog box. Excel automatically recognizes the range A6:G41 as the data list you want to use for the table. If your dialog box doesn't match the one in Figure 6-19, highlight cells A6 through G41 now.

Figure 6-19 ◀
Second
PivotTable
Wizard dialog
box

data list address

5. Click the **Next >** button to display the PivotTable Wizard - Step 3 of 4 dialog box shown in Figure 6-20.

Figure 6-20 ◀
Third PivotTable
Wizard dialog
box

field buttons

sample PivotTable

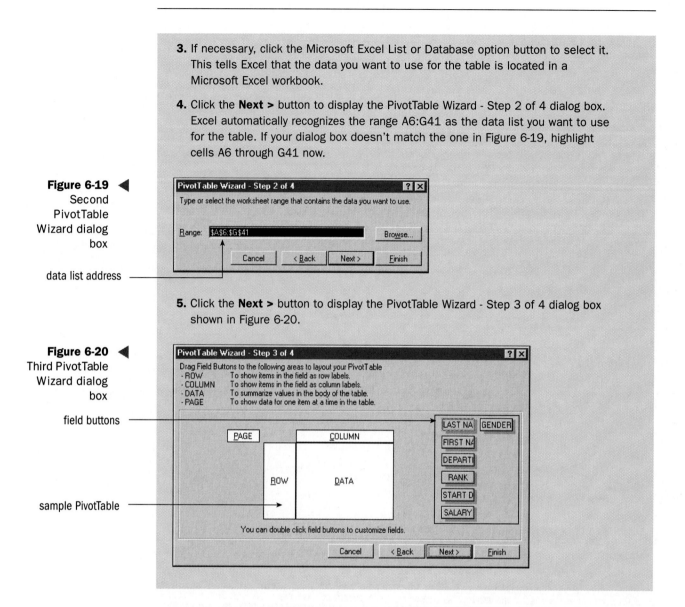

Adding Row and Column Labels

The PivotTable Wizard - Step 3 of 4 dialog box lets you select the field buttons you want to use for row and column labels in the PivotTable. You can click any field buttons on the right and drag them into the proper position on the sample PivotTable. Your sketch shows that row labels should list the faculty members' rank. Column labels should identify gender.

To select RANK for the row labels and GENDER for the column labels:

1. Click the **RANK** button and drag it to the ROW section of the sample PivotTable. When you release the mouse button, RANK appears in the row section of the sample PivotTable. See Figure 6-21.

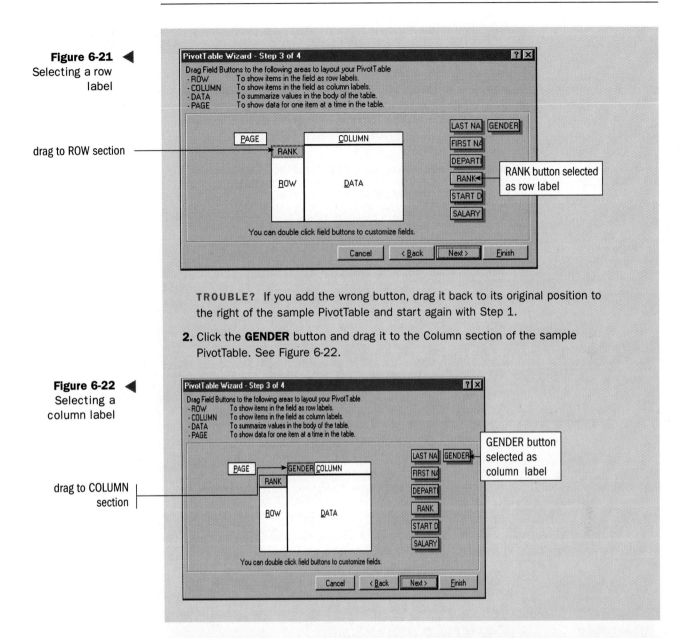

Figure 6-21 ◀
Selecting a row
label

drag to ROW section

Figure 6-22 ◀
Selecting a
column label

drag to COLUMN
section

TROUBLE? If you add the wrong button, drag it back to its original position to the right of the sample PivotTable and start again with Step 1.

2. Click the **GENDER** button and drag it to the Column section of the sample PivotTable. See Figure 6-22.

Selecting a Data Field for a PivotTable

The data fields you define for a PivotTable contain data you want to count, total, average, and so forth. You want to average faculty members' salaries. Following your plan, you select SALARY as the data field for the PivotTable.

To select the data field for the PivotTable:

1. Click the **SALARY** button to the right of the sample PivotTable and drag it to the Data section of the sample PivotTable. A Sum of SALARY button appears in the DATA section of the sample PivotTable.

Selecting a Calculation Method for a PivotTable

Unless you specify otherwise, the PivotTable Wizard automatically sums the values in the data field. If you want the PivotTable to perform a different calculation, such as counting or averaging, you must double-click the data field button and select the calculation method you want.

In this case, you are interested in average salary rather than total salary.

To select Average as the calculation method for the report:

1. Double-click the **Sum of SALARY** button to display the PivotTable Field dialog box.

2. Click **Average** in the Summarize by list box. See Figure 6-23.

Figure 6-23 ◀
Selecting a
calculation
method

click to select as the
calculation method

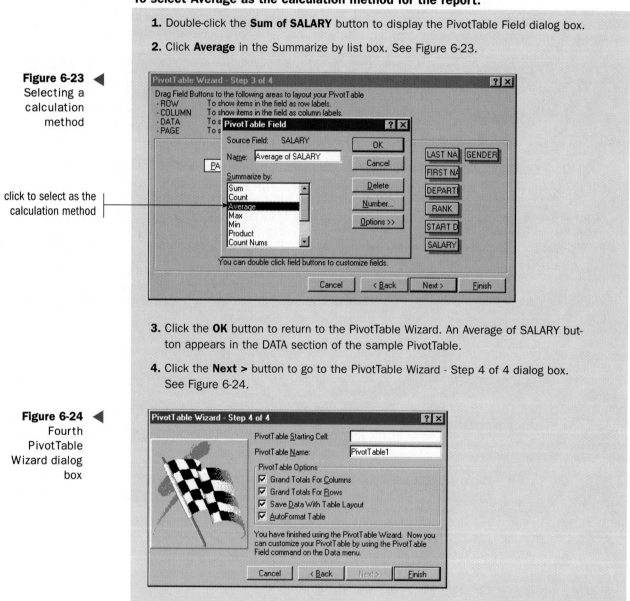

3. Click the **OK** button to return to the PivotTable Wizard. An Average of SALARY button appears in the DATA section of the sample PivotTable.

4. Click the **Next >** button to go to the PivotTable Wizard - Step 4 of 4 dialog box. See Figure 6-24.

Figure 6-24 ◀
Fourth
PivotTable
Wizard dialog
box

This final dialog box asks you where you what to place the new PivotTable. Unless you specify a worksheet cell, Excel places the PivotTable in a separate sheet. You decide to place the PivotTable in a separate sheet and accept the other default settings for the PivotTable.

To place the PivotTable in a separate sheet:

1. Click the **PivotTable Starting Cell** box, then click the **Sheet4** tab at the bottom of the screen. Sheet4! appears in the PivotTable Starting cell box. The dialog box is now displayed over the blank Sheet4.

2. Click cell **A3** in Sheet4. You want to begin the PivotTable here, instead of in cell A1, to leave room for a title. The dialog box on your screen should now match Figure 6-25.

   TROUBLE? If your PivotTable Starting Cell box doesn't match the one in the figure, delete the incorrect cell reference, and start again with Step 2.

Figure 6-25 ◄
Specifying the
starting cell

select cell A3 in
Sheet5

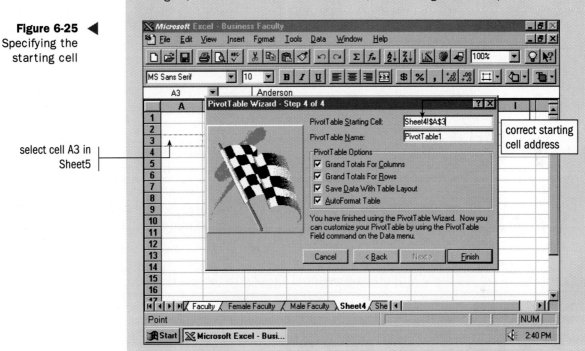

Completing a PivotTable

With the row category, column category, data field, and calculation method defined, you are ready to complete the PivotTable.

To complete the PivotTable:

1. Check that the PivotTable options in the Step 4 of 4 dialog box match Figure 6-25.

2. Click the **Finish** button. In a short time, the PivotTable appears in Sheet4 along with the Query and Pivot toolbar. See Figure 6-26.

Figure 6-26 ◄
Completed
PivotTable

completed PivotTable —————

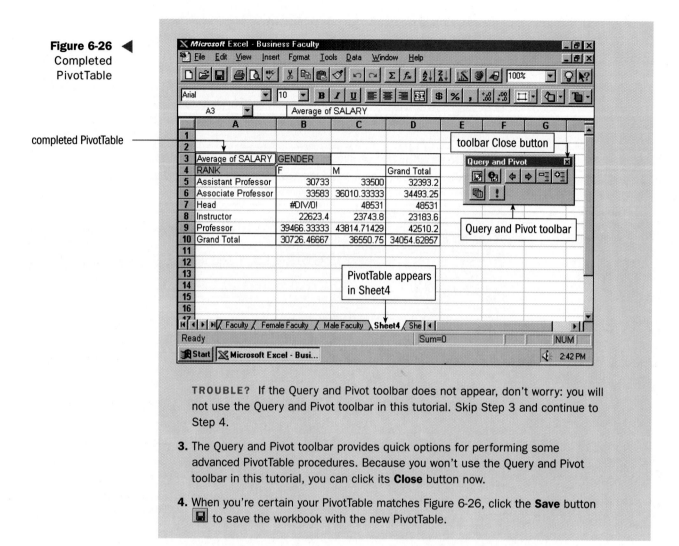

TROUBLE? If the Query and Pivot toolbar does not appear, don't worry: you will not use the Query and Pivot toolbar in this tutorial. Skip Step 3 and continue to Step 4.

3. The Query and Pivot toolbar provides quick options for performing some advanced PivotTable procedures. Because you won't use the Query and Pivot toolbar in this tutorial, you can click its **Close** button now.

4. When you're certain your PivotTable matches Figure 6-26, click the **Save** button 🖫 to save the workbook with the new PivotTable.

When you examine the PivotTable, you notice that cell B7 displays "#DIV/0!" This cell is supposed to show the average salary of female department heads, but in fact there are no female department heads. To calculate average salary for this cell, Excel totaled salaries of all female department heads ($0) and attempted to divide the total by the number of female department heads (0). Because dividing by zero is impossible, Excel displays the #DIV/0! message. You cannot delete this from the cell because it is part of the PivotTable.

The upper-left corner, cell A3, describes the calculation method used to create the table. Cells B3 and A4 contain the field buttons. After you create a PivotTable, you can easily modify it by dragging field headings to new positions or by double-clicking on column headings to display data in greater detail. You can also double-click on any data cell to display a filtered list of related records. Let's take a moment to explore some of these features now.

To explore some PivotTable features:

1. Make sure you saved the workbook in the previous set of steps.

2. Click cell **B3** and drag the **GENDER** button to the left side of cell A5, below the RANK button. As you drag, the pointer changes to 🔓. When you release the mouse button, Excel changes, or pivots, the layout of the PivotTable, as shown in Figure 6-27.

Figure 6-27 ◀
New PivotTable
layout

GENDER information
respositioned in
column A

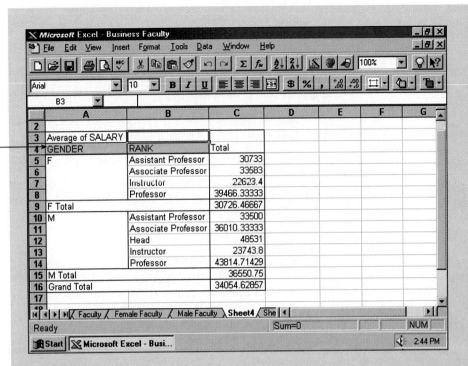

TROUBLE? If your table doesn't look like Figure 6-27, you may have moved the GENDER button too far to the right. Click the Undo button and then repeat Step 2.

3. Click the **Undo** button to restore the PivotTable's original layout. The Undo button is useful when the PivotTable doesn't turn out as you planned.

4. Double-click cell **B5**, located at the intersection of the Female column and the Assistant Professor row to display a list of all female assistant professors' records. The records for Kristen Anderson and Katherine Bordeau appear in a separate sheet. Click any cell to remove the highlighting. See Figure 6-28.

Figure 6-28 ◀
List of female
assistant
professors

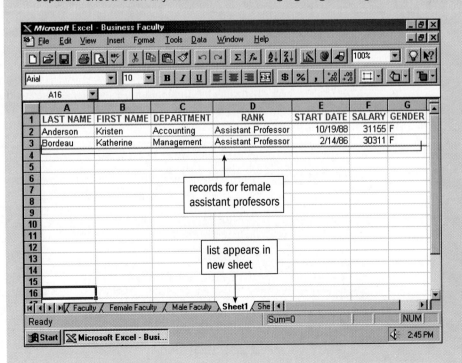

5. Click **Edit** then click **Delete Sheet** to delete the sheet with these records. When you see the message "Selected sheets will be permanently deleted. Continue?" click the **OK** button. Excel displays the PivotTable in Sheet4 again.

6. Try editing the contents of cells B5:D10. A dialog box informs you "Cannot change this part of a PivotTable."

7. Try editing the "Grand Total" labels in cells A10 or D4. A dialog box informs you "Cannot edit subtotal, block total, or grand total names."

8. Check to make sure your PivotTable matches the original layout in Figure 6-26.

 TROUBLE? If you made other modifications to your PivotTable and can't restore the PivotTable's original layout, close the workbook and then reopen it to view the original PivotTable in Sheet4.

The PivotTable includes the desired information, but the labels and format don't look like your sketch. To improve the PivotTable's appearance and make it easier to understand, you first add a title and change two column headings.

To add a title and change column headings:

1. Click cell **A1** then type **Average Salaries in the College of Business by Rank and Gender**.

2. Click cell **B4**, then type **Female**, and press →.

3. Type **Male** in cell C4 and press **Enter**.

Next, you use the AutoFormat command to improve the report format.

To improve the report format using AutoFormat:

1. Highlight cells **A3** through **D10**, then release the mouse button.

2. Click **Format** then click **AutoFormat** to display the AutoFormat dialog box.

3. Click **Accounting 3** in the Table Format box, then click the **OK** button to apply the format.

4. Click cell **A1**, then click the **Bold** button [B] to display the table title in bold. See Figure 6-29.

Figure 6-29 ◀
Formatted table

title in bold ——

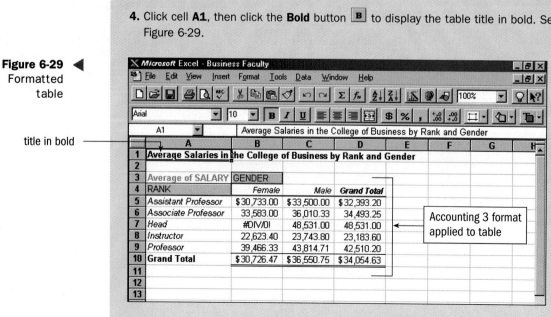

	A	B	C	D	E	F	G	H
1	Average Salaries in the College of Business by Rank and Gender							
2								
3	Average of SALARY	GENDER						
4	RANK	Female	Male	Grand Total				
5	Assistant Professor	$30,733.00	$33,500.00	$32,393.20				
6	Associate Professor	33,583.00	36,010.33	34,493.25				
7	Head	#DIV/0!	48,531.00	48,531.00				
8	Instructor	22,623.40	23,743.80	23,183.60				
9	Professor	39,466.33	43,814.71	42,510.20				
10	Grand Total	$30,726.47	$36,550.75	$34,054.63				
11								
12								
13								

Accounting 3 format applied to table

Now it is much easier to interpret the data. Cells B10 and C10 in the Grand Total row show overall average salaries for males and females. The average salary for females at all ranks is $30,726.47, while the average salary for males at all ranks is $36,550.75. Male and female salaries in columns B and C show that female faculty members at every rank earn less than their male counterparts.

To rename Sheet4, save the workbook, and then print the PivotTable:

1. Rename Sheet4 **Average Salary**.

2. Save the workbook with the newly formatted PivotTable.

3. Print the worksheet. Figure 6-30 shows the printed PivotTable.

Figure 6-30 ◀
Printed
PivotTable

Average Salaries in the College of Business by Rank and Gender				
Average of SALARY	**GENDER**			
RANK	*Female*	*Male*	*Grand Total*	
Assistant Professor	$30,733.00	$33,500.00	$32,393.20	
Associate Professor	33,583.00	36,010.33	34,493.25	
Head	#DIV/0!	48,531.00	48,531.00	
Instructor	22,623.40	23,743.80	23,183.60	
Professor	39,466.33	43,814.71	42,510.20	
Grand Total	$30,726.47	$36,550.75	$34,054.63	

The dean brings your PivotTable to his next meeting with the university's vice president. After some discussion, the vice president asks the dean to complete a salary analysis for faculty in all colleges and departments of North State University. The vice president gives the dean a disk containing a university-wide faculty database created, not with Excel, but with a database program called dBASE.

The dean calls and asks if you can create PivotTables from a dBASE file. You say that you will be able to access the dBASE file as an external database.

Internal and External Databases

Excel lets you work with both internal and external databases. An internal database is a data list that is part of the Excel worksheet you have open; an external database is not. It can be an Excel worksheet, an ASCII file, or file created with another application such as dBASE. An ASCII file is a standard file type for exchanging information between different computers. A dBASE file is created using dBASE or dBASE database management software.

The capability to access external databases is very useful, especially if you want to find or summarize information from large databases created on a mainframe computer or with the popular dBASE database management software.

Creating a PivotTable from an External Database

The PivotTable Wizard can generate a PivotTable from an internal database or an external database. This feature lets you analyze large databases created and maintained on a computer system other than your own or use databases created with software other than Excel. To access external databases, you must activate the MS Query add-in macro.

MS Query Add-In

An add-in adds features to the basic Excel spreadsheet command set installed with the software. The MS Query add-in modifies the Data menu, adding several new menu commands that give Excel the ability to work with external databases.

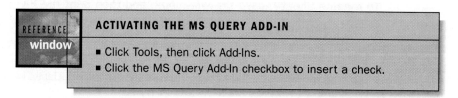

REFERENCE window

ACTIVATING THE MS QUERY ADD-IN

- Click Tools, then click Add-Ins.
- Click the MS Query Add-In checkbox to insert a check.

Many add-in macros, such as MS Query, are included with the Excel software. Although they are usually installed when Excel is installed, the person who installed Excel on your computer might have decided to save disk space by not installing the add-in macros. If you cannot activate the MS Query add-in in the next set of steps, see your instructor or technical support person for assistance.

You activate the MS Query add-in using the Add-Ins command on the Tools menu.

To activate the MS Query add-in:

1. Click **Tools** then click **Add-Ins** to display the Add-Ins dialog box.

2. If you don't see a check in the MS Query Add-In checkbox, click the **MS Query Add-In** checkbox now to display a check. See Figure 6-31.

Figure 6-31 ◀
Add-Ins dialog
box

click to display
a check

Add-Ins	? ☒
Add-Ins Available:	
☑ AccessLinks Add-In	OK
☐ Analysis ToolPak	Cancel
☐ Analysis ToolPak - VBA	
☐ AutoSave	Browse...
☑ MS Query Add-In	
☐ ODBC Add-In	
☑ Report Manager	
☑ Solver Add-In	
☐ Template Utilities	
☑ Template Wizard with Data Tracking	

AccessLinks Add-In
Lets you use Microsoft Access Forms and Reports on
Microsoft Excel data tables

TROUBLE? If you don't see the MS Query Add-In checkbox, see your instructor or technical support person for assistance.

3. Click the OK button to close the dialog box and return to the worksheet window.

Although the MS Query add-in macro does not appear to change the worksheet window, it does change the commands on the Data menu. Let's take a look.

To examine the changes in the Data menu:

1. Click **Data** to view the Data menu. Note the command Get External Data. The MS Query add-in macro added this command to the menu.

2. Click **Data** again to close the menu.

Using Microsoft Query

Now that the MS Query Add-In macro is active, you can use Microsoft Query to access information in the university-wide faculty database. MS Query is a powerful application that you can use with Excel and with other data management applications. The Get External Data command on the Data menu opens the MS Query application window. You can then use the MS Query commands to access data in external databases.

You can also open the MS Query window by using the PivotTable Wizard. You will use this method now as you create your PivotTable from information in the university-wide faculty database. You want to create the PivotTable in a separate sheet, so you begin by activating Sheet5.

To begin creating the university-wide faculty PivotTable:

1. Use the **sheet tab** scroll arrows, if necessary, to display the Sheet5 tab. Then click the **Sheet5** tab to display the blank Sheet5.

2. Click **Data** then click **PivotTable** to display the PivotTable Wizard - Step 1 of 4 dialog box.

3. Click the **External Data Source** option button, then click the **Next >** button to display the PivotTable Wizard - Step 2 of 4 dialog box.

4. Click the **Get Data** button. After a pause, the Microsoft Query application window appears with the Select Data Source dialog box open. See Figure 6-32.

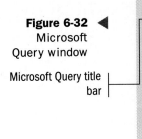

Figure 6-32
Microsoft
Query window

Microsoft Query title
bar

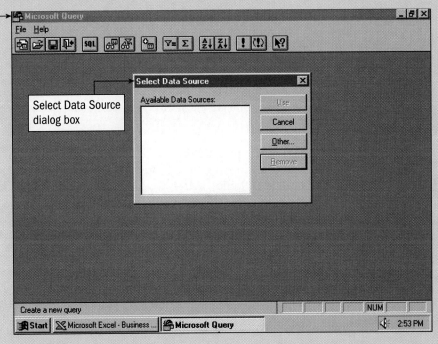

TROUBLE? If your MS Query window is not maximized, don't worry. You can maximize it later in this tutorial.

5. Click the **Other** button in the Select Data Sources dialog box to display the ODBC dialog box shown in Figure 6-33.

Figure 6-33 ◄
ODBC dialog
box

the university-wide
faculty database is a
dBase file

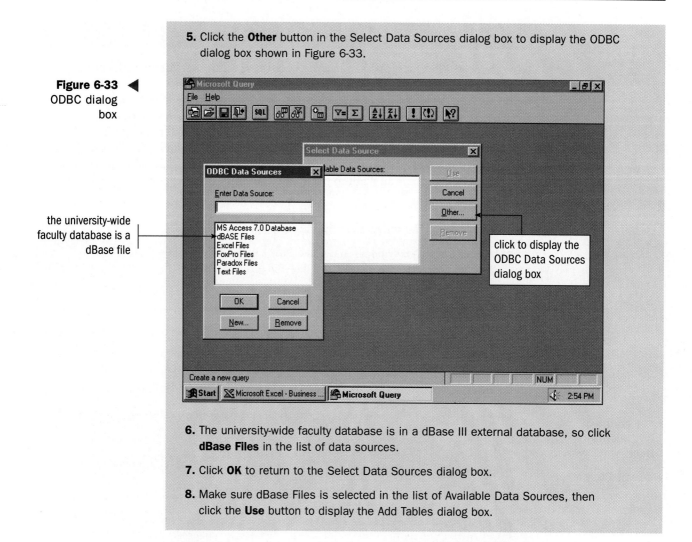

6. The university-wide faculty database is in a dBase III external database, so click **dBase Files** in the list of data sources.

7. Click **OK** to return to the Select Data Sources dialog box.

8. Make sure dBase Files is selected in the list of Available Data Sources, then click the **Use** button to display the Add Tables dialog box.

Now that you've specified the type of external data (a dBASE file), you need to choose the database file containing the records you want to display. In MS Query terms, a database file is called a "table." After you select a database file (or table), MS Query displays the field names (that is, the column headings) for the database. Then you can query the database to display the records you want to see. In this case, you want to see all records in the university-wide faculty database contained in the Univer.db file.

To display all records in the university-wide faculty database:

1. In the Drives box, select the drive containing your Student Disk. Then double-click the Tutorial.06 folder in the directories box if necessary.

2. In the **Table Name** list box, click **Univer.dbf**, then click the **Add** button.

3. Click the **Close** button to close the dialog box and view the field names in the MS Query window.

4. Maximize the **Query1** window. If necessary, maximize the MS Query window too. See Figure 6-34.

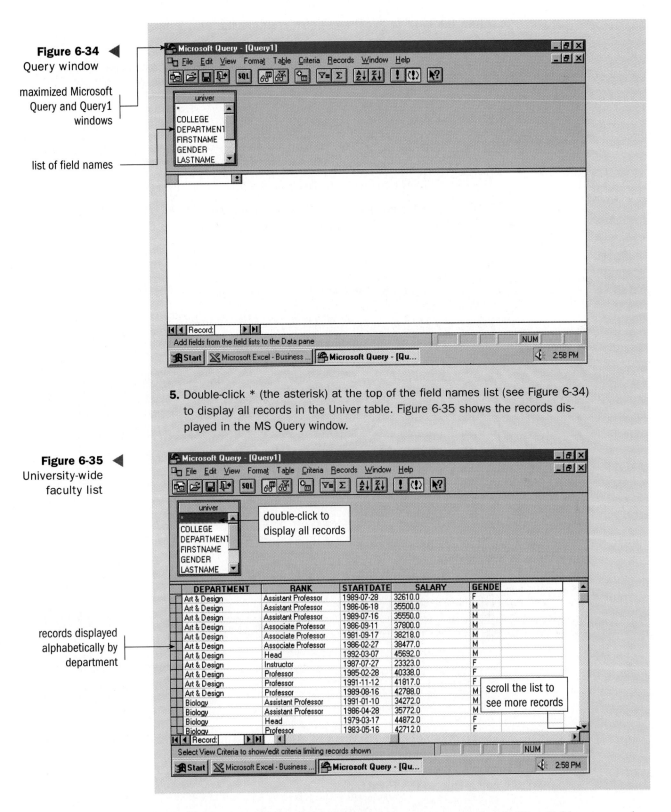

Figure 6-34 ◀
Query window

maximized Microsoft
Query and Query1
windows

list of field names

5. Double-click * (the asterisk) at the top of the field names list (see Figure 6-34) to display all records in the Univer table. Figure 6-35 shows the records displayed in the MS Query window.

Figure 6-35 ◀
University-wide
faculty list

records displayed
alphabetically by
department

Now that you have retrieved the data you want to use for the PivotTable, you need to return the data to Microsoft Excel. Then you can continue creating the PivotTable with the PivotTable Wizard. To do this, you use the Return Data to Microsoft Excel command on the File menu. The university-wide PivotTable you create will have the same layout as the College of Business PivotTable you created earlier. See your original sketch in Figure 6-17.

To return the data to Excel and finish creating the PivotTable:

1. Click **File** then click **Return Data to Microsoft Excel**. The Microsoft Query window closes and the PivotTable Wizard - Step 2 of 4 dialog box reappears in the Excel window. The message next to the Get Data button informs you that Excel retrieved the data.

2. Click the **Next >** button to display the PivotTable Wizard - Step 3 of 4 dialog box.

3. Drag the **RANK** button to the ROW section of the sample PivotTable. Then drag the **GENDER** button to the COLUMN section of the sample PivotTable.

4. Drag the **SALARY** button to the DATA section of the sample PivotTable.

5. Double-click the **Sum of SALARY** field button to display the PivotTable Field dialog box. Click **Average** in the Summarize by box, then click the **OK** button to return to the PivotTable Wizard - Step 3 of 4 dialog box.

6. Click the **Next >** button to display the PivotTable Wizard - Step 4 of 4 dialog box.

7. Click the **PivotTable Starting Cell** box, then click cell **A3** in Sheet5 to display Sheet5!$A$3 in the PivotTable Starting Cell box.

8. Click the **Finish** button to close the dialog box and view the completed PivotTable in the worksheet. See Figure 6-36.

Figure 6-36
Completed
PivotTable

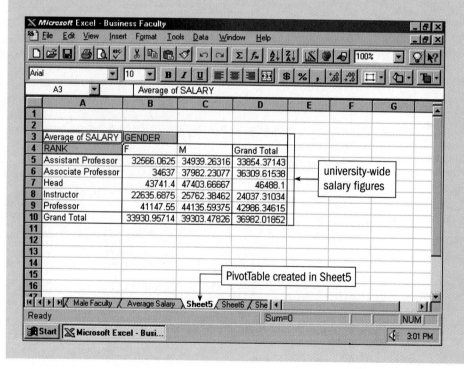

The PivotTable is almost complete. All that remains is to enter the appropriate title and column headings and format the PivotTable to make it easier to read.

To add a title to the PivotTable:

1. Click cell **A1** and type **North State University**.

2. Click cell **A2** and type **Average Salaries by Rank and Gender**.

3. Highlight cells **A1** through **D2**.

4. Click the **Center Across Columns** button to center the titles.

5. Click the **Bold** button **B** to display the titles in boldface.

Using your original sketch as a guide, you enter more informative column titles for the report.

To enter the column titles:

1. Click cell **B4**, then type **Female**, and press →.

2. Type **Male** in cell C4, and press **Enter**.

You decide to use AutoFormat to apply the Accounting 3 format.

To format the PivotTable:

1. Highlight cells **A3** through **D10**.

2. Click **Format**, then click **AutoFormat** to display the AutoFormat dialog box.

3. Click **Accounting 3** in the Table Format box, then click the **OK** button to apply the format.

4. Click any cell to remove the highlighting. See Figure 6-37.

Figure 6-37 ◀
The formatted
PivotTable

titles bolded and
centered

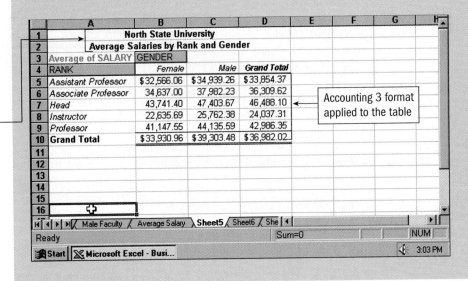

You rename Sheet5 and then save the workbook with the new PivotTable.

To rename Sheet5 and save the workbook:

1. Rename Sheet5 **Average Salary (Univ)**.

2. Click the **Save** button 🔲.

Finally, you preview the report, print a copy for the dean, and then close the workbook.

To preview and print the PivotTable and then close the workbook:

1. Click the **Print Preview** button 🔍 to preview the report.

2. Click the **Setup** button to display the Page Setup dialog box.

3. Click the **Margins** tab. If the Horizontally box is empty, click it to center the report between the right and left margins.

4. Click the **Sheet** tab. If necessary, click the **Cell Gridlines** box to remove the check.

5. Click the **OK** button to close the Page Setup dialog box and look at the revised print preview.

6. Click the **Print** button to display the Print dialog box.

7. Click the **OK** button on the Print dialog box to print the PivotTable shown in Figure 6-38.

Figure 6-38 ◀
Printed
university-wide
PivotTable

North State University Average Salaries by Rank and Gender			
Average of SALARY	**GENDER**		
RANK	*Female*	*Male*	*Grand Total*
Assistant Professor	$32,566.06	$34,939.26	$33,854.37
Associate Professor	34,637.00	37,982.23	36,309.62
Head	43,741.40	47,403.67	46,488.10
Instructor	22,635.69	25,762.38	24,037.31
Professor	41,147.55	44,135.59	42,986.35
Grand Total	$33,930.96	$39,303.48	$36,982.02

Now that you have printed the report, you need to revise the Documentation sheet to reflect changes you made in this Tutorial. Then you can close the workbook and exit Excel.

To revise the workbook documentation, close the workbook and exit Excel:

1. Click the **Documentation** tab and then update the **Sheet Contents**. Include all new sheet names, and describe the contents for each.

2. Add a one-sentence description of the workbook's purpose. Save the workbook.

3. Close the workbook.

4. Exit Excel if you are not going to do the Tutorial Assignments now.

The dean is very impressed with your work. The report provides exactly the information he needs for his meeting with the university's vice president.

Quick Check

1. Describe a situation in which you might want to create an Excel PivotTable. Explain how you could get the same information using other data management techniques.

2. Explain how to create a PivotTable.

3. What is the default calculation method for a PivotTable?

4. How does an external database differ from an internal database?

5. Which add-in is required to create a PivotTable for an external database?

6 What data source did you use in this tutorial?

7 In MS Query terms, what is another name for a database file?

8 What command do you use to return data to Miscrosoft Excel?

Tutorial Assignments

The dean has asked for more information about the College of Business faculty. To provide the answers he needs, complete the following:

1. Open the workbook Faculty2 (in the TAssign folder for Tutorial 6 on your Student Disk), and save it as Business Faculty 2. Type your name and date in the documentation sheet, then move to the Faculty sheet.

2. Use the New button on the data form to add the following information for a new faculty member. *Hint:* Remember to select any cell in the list before using commands on the Data menu.
   a. Last name = Gerety
   b. First name = Estelle
   c. Department = Management
   d. Rank = Assistant Professor
   e. Start date = Today's date
   f. Salary = 32454
   g. Gender = F

3. Use the data form to determine how many faculty members hold the rank of professor in the Management department.

4. Use the data form to determine how many female faculty members earn more than $35,000 per year.

5. Use the data form to determine how many faculty members hold the rank of associate professor in the College of Business.

6. Close the data form.

7. Use the AutoFilter command in the Data menu to display the arrow buttons in the column headings.

8. Select cell A7 in the LAST NAME column. Use the Sort Descending button to arrange the records in reverse alphabetical order (from Z to A) by last name. Print the sorted worksheet. Then use the Sort Ascending button to arrange the records in alphabetical order (from A to Z) by last name. Print the worksheet again.

9. Click the SALARY arrow button, and select (Custom...). Then use the Custom AutoFilter dialog box to display the rows where SALARY is greater than $40,105 or less than $30,311. Hint: Use the arrow buttons in the dialog box to select the appropriate symbols and salary figures. Also, make sure to select the Or option button.

10. Save the workbook and print the worksheet.

11. Use the Univer2 dBASE file (in the Tassign folder for Tutorial 6) and MS Query to create a PivotTable. You shouldn't have to select a data source this time in the Select Data Source dialog box. Instead, click dBASE Files - admin and then click Use. Display all records in the database, and then return them to Microsoft Excel. Your PivotTable should show the maximum salary (Max of Salary) by rank and gender. Place your Pivot Table on a blank sheet, leaving room for a title. Rename the PivotTable sheet using an appropriate name.

12. Format your PivotTable to produce an attractive printout. Add an appropriate title.

13. Preview the worksheet and adjust page settings as necessary.

14. Print the worksheet.

15. Revise the Documentation sheet to reflect changes to the workbook.

16. Save your workbook and close it.

Case Problems

1. Creating a List of Discontinued Inventory Items at OfficeMart Business Supplies You are an assistant buyer at OfficeMart Business Supplies, a retail business supply store. Your boss, Ellen Kerrigan, created an Excel workbook containing product and pricing information for inventory items purchased from each primary vendor.

Ellen is preparing her monthly order for EB Wholesale Office Supplies, one of OfficeMart's suppliers. She has asked you to print a list of all back-ordered EB Wholesale products so you can include them in the order. She would also like a list of all discontinued items so you can remove those items from the catalog.

1. Open the workbook Office (in the Case folder for Tutorial 6 on your Student Disk) and save it as EB Wholesale Office Supplies. Complete the Documentation sheet, then move to the Inventory sheet.
2. Use the AutoFilter command on the Data menu to insert the arrow buttons on the column headings.
3. Filter the list to display only records for back-ordered items. Refer to the status codes listed at the top of the worksheet.
4. Print records for back-ordered items (including the column headings).
5. Preview the worksheet and make any necessary formatting changes.
6. Print records for back-ordered items.
7. Filter the list again to display only records for discontinued items.
8. Print records for discontinued items.
9. Save the workbook.

2. Creating a Current Membership List for Shih Tzu Fanciers of America Jennifer Santarelli is the membership coordinator for the Shih Tzu Fanciers of America, a nonprofit organization for owners, fanciers, and breeders of Shih Tzu dogs. The organization maintains a membership list in dBASE format. The list includes the first name, last name, address, city, state, and zip code for approximately 1,000 current members.

The board of the Shih Tzu Fanciers of America (STFA) asked Jennifer to prepare a report on the current membership, showing the number of members in each state and the total current membership.

It's been some time since Jennifer used the database features in Excel. She has tried to create the report but has run into trouble, so she asks you to help her use the PivotTable Wizard to create the PivotTable.

1. Open a new workbook and activate the PivotTable Wizard.
2. Choose the External Data Source option, then in the PivotTable Wizard - Step 2 of 4 dialog box click the Get Data button to start MS Query.
3. You shouldn't have to select a data source in the Select Data Source dialog box. Instead, click dBASE Files - admin and then click Use.
4. In the Add Tables dialog box, select the file Member.dbf in the Case folder for Tutorial 6 on your Student Disk.

5. If you have trouble remembering how to use MS Query, you can display a set of Cue Cards that will guide you through any procedure. Click Help, then click Cue Cards. Use the MS Query Cue Card to learn what a query is. Begin by clicking the [>] button next to "See what a query is." Then follow the directions to learn more about queries. When you finish with the Cue Card, click its Close button to close it and return to the Query window.
6. Display all records in the Member.dbf database, and then return them to Microsoft Excel.
7. Select STATE as the ROW category. Do not select a column category.
8. Select STATE as the DATA field. Because STATE is a non-numeric field, the PivotTable Wizard automatically counts the number of records in each state.
9. Complete the PivotTable, using cell A3 in the blank sheet as the Starting Cell.
10. Add the title "Shih Tzu Fanciers of America, Current Membership by State," then format the PivotTable.

11. Preview the worksheet and use the Page Setup dialog box to center the PivotTable and print it at 85% (or less) of normal size. Make sure the PivotTable will print on one page.

12. Add a cell note to cell A1 to document the worksheet. Save the workbook as Membership by State in the Case folder for Tutorial 6 on your Student Disk.

13. Print the PivotTable.

3. Creating an Invitation List for Shih Tzu Fanciers of America The New Mexico Chapter of STFA is planning a Shih Tzu Fanciers picnic. They want to invite all STFA members in nearby states, and they asked Jennifer to send them a list of all current members in these states. Help Jennifer use Advanced Filter to filter the membership list and create a list of records for all members who live in the surrounding states. As you may recall, Advanced Filter lets you filter a list using several criteria at once. To use Advanced Filter you'll need to create a special range called a criteria range. You enter the critieria you want to use in your search in the criteria range. You begin by importing the external database into Excel.

1. Open a new workbook.

2. Use the Get External Data command on the Data menu to activate MS Query.

3. Select the external database Member.dbf from the Case folder for Tutorial 6 on your Student Disk. Display all records in the database, and then return the data to Microsoft Excel. When you see the Get External Data dialog box, make sure the Keep Query Definition and the Include Field Names options are selected. Use Sheet2, cell A1, as the destination.

4. Bold the labels in row 1 so Excel readily identifies them as column labels.

5. Create the criteria range by copying the column labels in cells A1:F1 and then pasting them in cells H1:M1.

6. Enter the criteria you want to use for your search. In this case, you want to find all records for New Mexico, Arizona, Colorado, and Texas. Enter NM in cell L2, AZ in cell L3, CO in cell L4, and TX in cell L5.

7. Click any cell in the data list, then use the Advanced Filter command on the Data menu to display the Advanced Filter dialog box.

8. Make sure the range address for the data list ($A$1:$F$1044) is displayed in the List Range box.

9. Enter the criteria range address by clicking the criteria range box and then selecting the criteria range (H1:M5) in the worksheet.

10. Make sure the Filter the list, in-place option box is selected, then click the OK button.

11. Use the Sort command on the Data menu to sort records by zip code and then by last name.

12. Copy the records to Sheet3, widen the columns using AutoFit Selection, then rename Sheet3 Mail List.

13. Redisplay all records in Sheet2 by clicking Data, clicking Filter, then clicking Show All.

14. Rename Sheet2 Membership List.

15. Save the workbook as Membership in the Case folder for Tutorial 6 on your Student Disk.

16. Preview and print the Mail List sheet. Hint: Print in landscape orientation and scale to 90% (or less) to fit complete records on each page.

17. Create a Documentation sheet in Sheet1.

18. Save the completed workbook.

4. Creating your Own Data List Think about information you use regularly that you would like to organize into an Excel data list. For example, consider creating a list of addresses, phone numbers and birthdays of your friends and family. Or perhaps a list of current and past courses, including total credits and grades.

Then do the following:

1. Enter your information in a new workbook, taking care to format it like an Excel datalist.

2. Use the techniques you learned in this tutorial to find answers to three questions about the information in your list. For example, you might create a PivotTable to find your average grade by department. Or you might use AutoFilter to find out which of your friends and family have January birthdays.

3. Create three printouts in all, and write the question the printout answers at the top of the page.

4. Document your workbook.

5. Save your new workbook in the Case folder for Tutorial 6.

Integrating Excel with Other Windows Programs

Preparing a Quarterly Sales Report

In this tutorial you will:

- Transfer or share data between programs using Object Linking and Embedding (OLE)

- Use Excel as both a source program (server) and destination program (client)

- Paste, link, and embed objects between Windows programs

- Update a linked Excel object

- Learn the importance of keeping linked files together

CASE

Analyzing Sales at J. J. Svensen

J. J. Svensen, a mail-order company, specializes in outdoor recreational clothing for hikers, campers, and skiers. Founded by the avid sportsman Jacob J. Svensen in the late 1940s, the company is owned and run by the Svensen family. Heather Svensen, Jacob's daughter, is president and C.E.O. Located in Boulder, Colorado, the company's line of merchandise is known and respected throughout the United States.

As the company's sales manager, you are responsible for preparing the quarterly sales report that is used to monitor the company's current performance. This important document includes sales figures for each type of product in the catalog. The final document will contain several paragraphs of text, the company logo, a chart analyzing sales information, and a complete list of items in the J. J. Svenson catalogue. Because the sales report circulates widely among management, you want it to look as professional as possible.

You will have to use more than one Windows program to create the sales report. You'll use Microsoft Excel to analyze sales data and create the chart. You'll also use Paint to provide the company logo. Finally, you'll use Microsoft WordPad, a word-processing program, to combine all elements of the report and print the final document. Figure 7-1 shows your plan for the sales analysis document.

Figure 7-1 ◀
Sales
document
sketch

document title

Excel worksheet

Excel chart

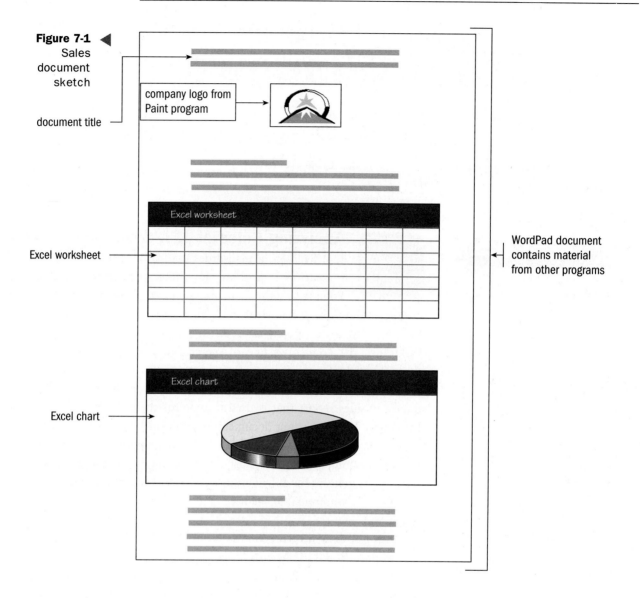

company logo from
Paint program

Excel worksheet

Excel chart

WordPad document
contains material
from other programs

SESSION

7.1

In this session you will learn about several methods for integrating Excel with other programs: pasting, linking, and embedding. You will also learn how to embed a Paint object in a WordPad document and then edit the object from within WordPad.

Each Program Has Its Purpose

Most programs are written to do one type of task efficiently. You can use **word-processing programs**, such as Word Perfect, Microsoft WordPad, and Microsoft Word, to create and edit memos, letters, and reports. In this tutorial, you'll use WordPad as the word processor because it is included with Windows 95. You should have it available regardless of what other word processor you normally use. The sales report you create in this tutorial is a WordPad document.

As you already know, **spreadsheet programs**, such as Microsoft Excel, are used for analyzing data, creating charts, and so on. Spreadsheets let you arrange an analysis as you want, and this lets you be creative when solving problems. In this tutorial, you will integrate catalog and sales information from Excel into the sales report in WordPad.

Graphics programs, such as Microsoft Paint and CorelDRAW, let you create a wide variety of graphic images. In this tutorial you'll use Microsoft Paint to add a graphic image (the company logo) to the report.

As you create your report, you will use several different methods to transfer or share data between programs.

Integrating Information Between Programs

One advantage of using Windows programs is that they make it easy to transfer and share data, information, and graphics between various programs. Three methods of doing this are embedding, linking, and pasting. The option you use will depend on what you want to accomplish.

The following section offers a general explanation of these data integration methods. You'll have a chance to try them out later in this tutorial. Don't worry if the explanations seem a little confusing at first. They'll make more sense once you actually begin transferring data between programs.

Embedding Objects

You can transfer data from one program into another using **Object Linking and Embedding (OLE).** An **object** is a package of data or information. Programs, such as Excel or WordPad, are considered objects, as are the workbooks or documents you create using these programs. OLE (pronounced oh-LAY) lets you copy an object from one program into another. For example, you could copy an image from Paint and embed it in a WordPad document. The program containing the original image is the **source,** or **server program,** and the program in which you place the copy is called the **destination,** or **client program.**

The copied object is **embedded** because it exists as a separate object within the document or worksheet in which it is embedded. The embedded copy has no connection to the source file, so changes to the original do *not* affect the copy in the destination program. Once embedded and saved, the copy becomes part of the destination file.

The advantage of embedding is that all information that belongs to a document is in one file. Suppose, for example, that you embed an Excel worksheet in a Word document. You can copy the Word document onto a disk and give it to your assistant. As long as he has Word and Excel on his computer, your assistant can read the Word document as well as the Excel workbook embedded in it. You do not need to give your assistant the original Excel workbook, because a copy of it is already embedded in the Word document. See Figure 7-2.

Figure 7-2 ◀
Embedding one
object in
another

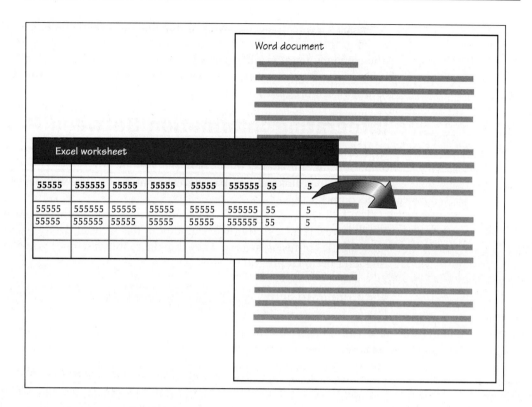

The disadvantage of embedding is that an embedded file can take a lot of disk space. When storage space is an issue, you may want to paste information instead. (You'll learn more about pasting information between programs in a moment.) Also, keep in mind that with embedded files the source and destination files are not connected. If you want changes in the source file to be made automatically in the destination file, you should use linking rather than embedding, as explained in the next section.

When you embed one object within another, you can directly access the source program by double-clicking the embedded object. This lets you edit the embedded object quickly and easily. For example, assume that you have an Excel chart embedded within a WordPad document, and that you have not yet started Excel. To edit the chart within the WordPad document, you simply double-click the chart. The chart appears in its own Excel window; the menus of the destination program (WordPad) switch to the menus of the source program (Excel). See Figure 7-3. You can edit the chart just as if you had started Excel and then opened a workbook containing the chart. You can click anywhere outside the embedded chart to return to the WordPad menus.

Figure 7-3
Editing an
embedded
Excel object

WordPad title bar

Excel menus
and tools

column headings

row headings

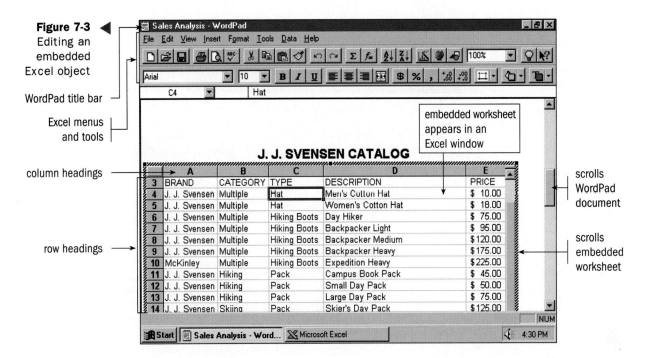

Keep in mind that not all programs use OLE. If the file you want to use was created in a program that does not support linking and embedding, you can still copy and paste information from that file, but you may have trouble embedding or linking it.

Linking Objects

Linking connects two or more files. After you link files, any changes you save in the source document will automatically be made in the destination file. For example, suppose you link a sales chart in an Excel workbook to a memo saved as a Word document. Then, after receiving new information, you revise the chart in the Excel workbook. After you save these changes in Excel, the same revisions will appear in the Word document the next time you open it. See Figure 7-4. It's important to remember that changes in the source file will not always be reflected in the destination file until you save the source file. As with embedded objects, you can double-click a linked object to directly access the source program's tools and menus.

The great advantage of linking is the ability to update several files at once. The chief disadvantage is that links between files are easily broken if you move or rename the files. For example, suppose you give your assistant the Word file on a disk, but forget to include the Excel file it's linked to. In this case Windows can not maintain the links between the two files. Your assistant *would* be able to open the Word file and view the latest version of the Excel worksheet in it. But subsequent changes to the Excel worksheet would not appear in the Word document. You'll learn more about this in the Tutorial Assignments at the end of this Tutorial, where you'll experiment with separating linked files.

Figure 7-4
Linking an
object from one
program to
another

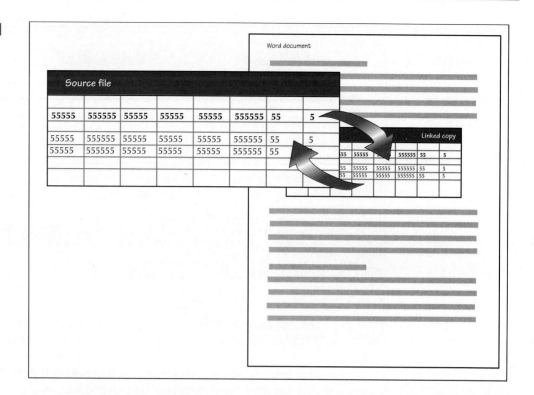

Pasting

You can **copy and paste** (or cut and paste) material—usually text, numbers, or illustrations—from one program into another the same way you copy and paste material within a program. For example, you can copy a column heading from an Excel worksheet and paste it in a WordPad document. If your program has no linking or embedding capabilities, copy and paste is likely to be the only way you can transfer data. Even if linking and embedding capabilities are available in your application, you might choose to paste if you want to move an entire text file to a different application.

While copy and paste can be very useful, it has some drawbacks. For one thing, the Paste command usually inserts information as simple text, without formatting from the original file. As you'll see later in this tutorial, when you simply paste an Excel range into another program, you lose most of the range's formatting. Also keep in mind that the Paste command does not establish links between files. If you want to revise data in one application, and have the changes reflected in a copy in another application, you should link rather than paste. See Figure 7-5.

Figure 7-5 ◀
Pasting
material from
one program
into another

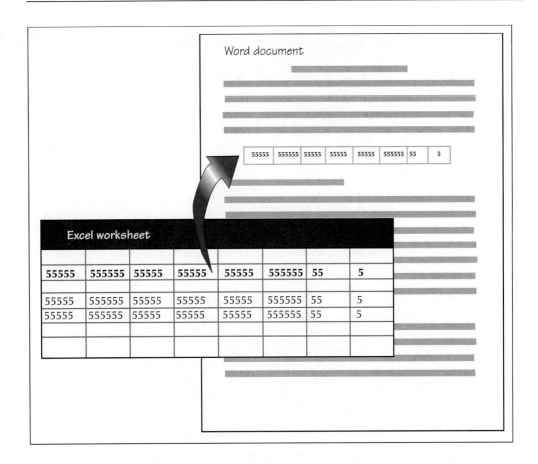

By now you should be familiar with the basics of copying and pasting. You will, however, have a chance to practice pasting in the Case Problems.

Choosing the Right Option

At first you may have trouble deciding which data transfer method you want to use: pasting, embedding, or linking. In general, the right method depends on what you want to accomplish. Figure 7-6 summarizes some common situations.

Figure 7-6 ◀
Common
integration
methods

Task	Method	Notes
Insert a copy of one object within another, without connecting the source and destination files	Embedding	Double-clicking the copy displays the source program's tools and menus
Insert a copy of one file within another and ensure that changes in the source file will also appear in the copy	Linking	Double-clicking the copy displays the source program's tools and menus
Transfer text without regard to maintaining original formatting	Cut and Paste, or Copy and Paste	

Don't be confused by the fact that you generally use copy and paste commands to embed and link objects. When you copy an object (such as a chart) and then switch to the source program, the paste commands in the source program either give you an opportunity to embed or link the object, or else automatically embed the object. (Exactly what happens depends on the program you use.) If you merely copy some text and then switch to the source program, the paste command only allows you to perform a simple paste (without links to the source program).

Embedding a Paint Object

According to your document plan, your sales report will contain a logo that has been created in Paint. Because you may want to make changes to the logo from within WordPad, you'll embed the logo in the sales report. (You might want to go back and reread the previous sections after you finish this tutorial, and are more familiar with the basics of embedding, linking, and pasting.) The text of the report has already been saved for you in a WordPad document.

To start WordPad:

1. Start Windows as usual.

2. Make sure your Student Disk is in the disk drive.

3. Click the **Start** button 🟦Start, point to **Programs**, then point to **Accessories.** See Figure 7-7.

Figure 7-7 ◀
Start Menus

your list of programs
may vary

point to Start,
then Programs,
then Accessories

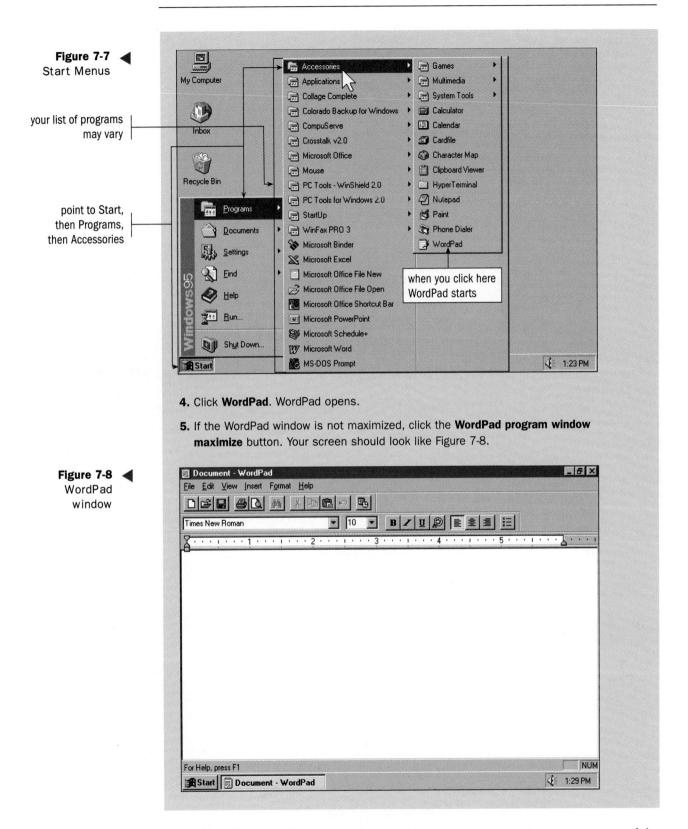

4. Click **WordPad**. WordPad opens.

5. If the WordPad window is not maximized, click the **WordPad program window maximize** button. Your screen should look like Figure 7-8.

Figure 7-8 ◀
WordPad
window

Because Windows 95 programs have standard menu systems, you can use many of the menu commands that you learned for Excel. As Figure 7-9 shows, you open a file in WordPad using either the Open command on the File menu or the Open tool 🖼, exactly as you do in Excel. WordPad gives filenames the .doc extension. Unless you specify otherwise, WordPad saves files in Word 6.0 format.

Figure 7-9
WordPad
File menu

commands are
similar to Excel
file menu

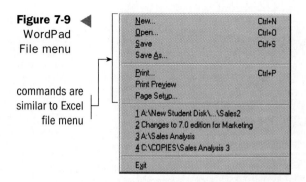

New...	Ctrl+N
Open...	Ctrl+O
Save	Ctrl+S
Save As...	
Print...	Ctrl+P
Print Preview	
Page Setup...	
1 A:\New Student Disk\...\Sales2	
2 Changes to 7.0 edition for Marketing	
3 A:\Sales Analysis	
4 C:\COPIES\Sales Analysis 3	
Exit	

You can use the File menu now to open the report and save it under a new name.

To open the Sales document file and save it as Sales Analysis:

1. Click **File** then click **Open** to display the Open dialog box.

2. Click the **Look in** list arrow, then click **3½ Floppy (A:)** in the list of drive names.

3. Double-click the **Tutorial.07** folder to display that folder name in the Look in box, as shown in Figure 7-10.

Figure 7-10
Open dialog
box

the document opens
when you double-click
its name

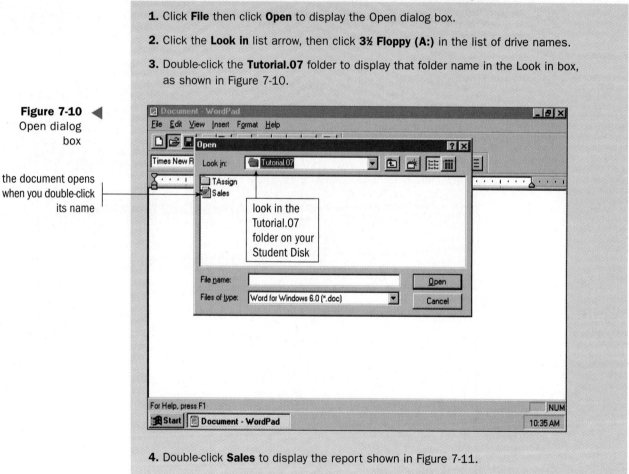

look in the
Tutorial.07
folder on your
Student Disk

4. Double-click **Sales** to display the report shown in Figure 7-11.

Figure 7-11
Sales
document

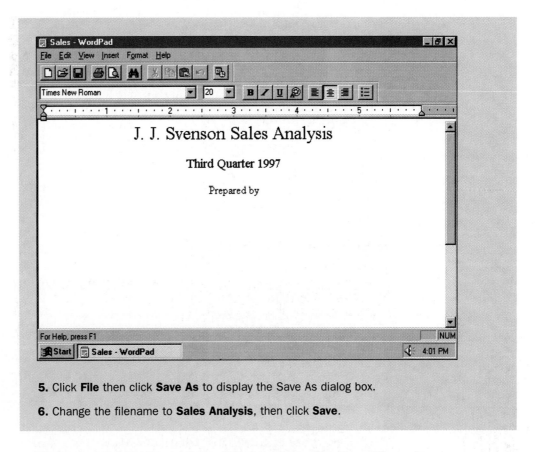

5. Click **File** then click **Save As** to display the Save As dialog box.

6. Change the filename to **Sales Analysis**, then click **Save**.

The company logo is stored in a Windows Paint file. You will use the copy and paste commands to embed the graphic in the report. Begin by starting Paint and opening the file containing the logo.

To start Paint and open the file containing the logo:

1. Click the **Start** button [Start], point to **Programs**, then point to **Accessories**.

2. Click **Paint**. Paint opens. The WordPad window is minimized to a button on the Taskbar.

3. If the Paint window is not maximized, click the **Paint window maximize** button. Paint appears as shown in Figure 7-12.

Figure 7-12 ◀
Paint window

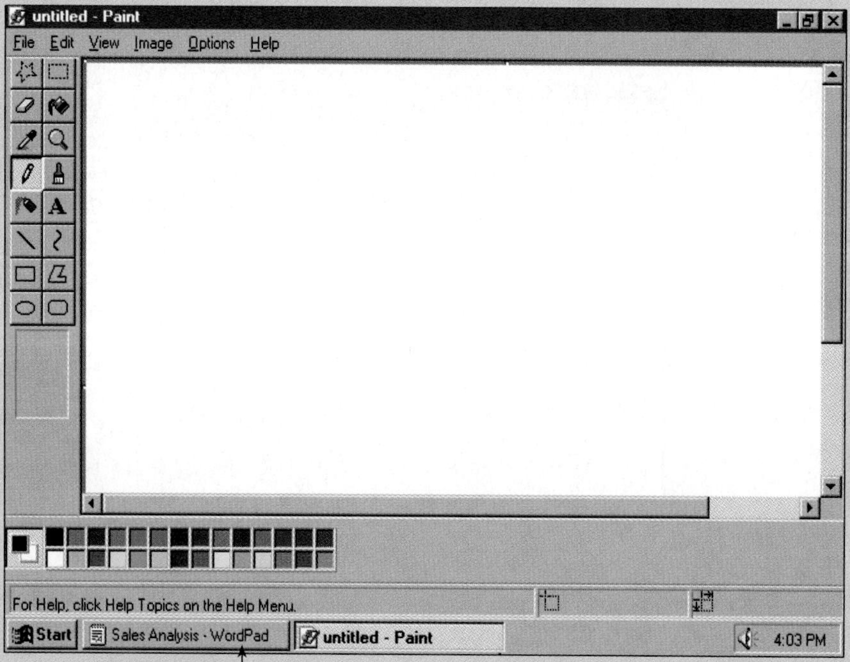

WordPad window
minimized to a button
on the Taskbar

4. Click **File** then click **Open** to display the Open dialog box.

5. If necessary, click the **Look in list** arrow, click **3 ½ Floppy (A:)** in the list of drive names, then double-click the **Tutorial.07** folder to display that folder name in the Look in box.

6. Double-click **Logo** to display the company logo shown in Figure 7-13.

Figure 7-13 ◀
Company logo

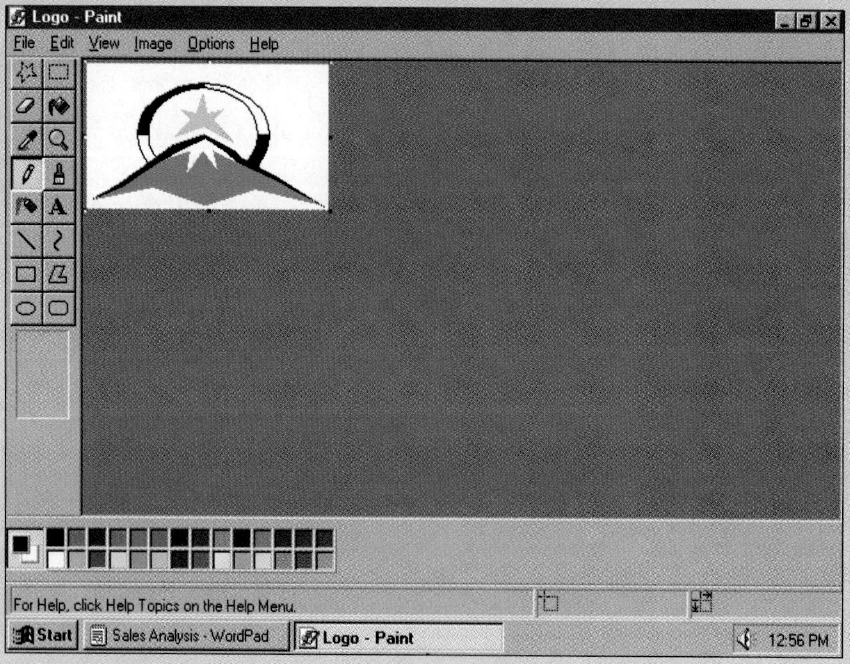

Now that you've found the logo you can copy it and paste it in the WordPad document.

To copy and paste the logo:

1. Click **Edit** then click **Select All**.

2. Click **Edit** then click **Copy**.

3. Click the **Sale Analysis - WordPad** button in the Taskbar. The WordPad window appears.

4. Click at the end of the line that reads **Prepared by**, type your name, and then press **Enter** twice to move the insertion pointer to the second blank line below the heading.

5. Click **Edit** then click **Paste** to paste the company logo in the report.

6. Click anywhere outside the company logo to remove the small black boxes (called handles) along its borders. The report now looks like Figure 7-14.

Figure 7-14 ◀
Company logo
embedded in
report

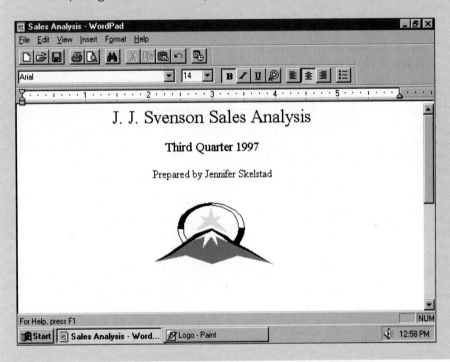

Now that you have embedded the logo in the report, you can close the Paint window.

To close the Paint window:

1. Click the **Logo - Paint** button in the Taskbar to return to the Paint window.

2. Click the **Paint** close button to close the Paint window.

3. If the WordPad window is not active, click the **WordPad** button in the Taskbar to switch to the WordPad window.

Editing an Embedded Object

When you paste a graphic image from Paint, Windows treats the image as an object and embeds it in the destination program document using OLE. Recall that an embedded object is *not* linked to the original—changes to the original object will *not* affect the embedded copy.

REFERENCE window	**EDITING AN EMBEDDED OBJECT USING OLE**
	▪ Double-click the embedded object.
	▪ Edit the object using the source program's commands and tools.
	▪ When you finish editing the object, click outside the object's borders to return to the source program's commands and tools.
	▪ Save the destination file.

After you close Paint, you notice that the colors of the company logo are not right for the sales report. You decide to edit the embedded logo from within WordPad.

To edit the embedded picture obejct:

1. Double-click **the company logo**. After a moment, Paint menus and tools appear within the WordPad window. The logo appears with its own vertical and horizontal scroll bars. Notice the small black handles on the border of the WordPad window. Keep in mind that you can drag handles to resize an embedded object the same way as you would resize an Excel chart. See Figure 7-15.

Figure 7-15
Using OLE to activate Paint tools and menus

Paint menus and tools appear in the WordPad window

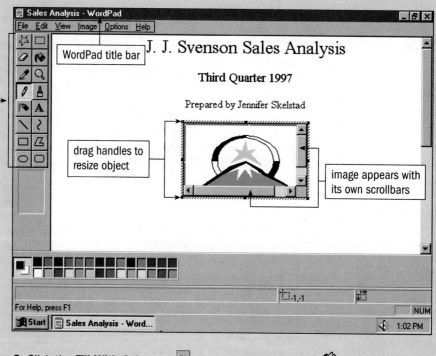

2. Click the **Fill With Color** tool [icon]. The pointer changes to [icon] when you move it over the logo.

3. In the color palette at the bottom of the Paint window, click the **brown** square (the third square from the left in the top row), then position the pointer as shown in Figure 7-16.

Figure 7-16 ◀
Editing
company logo

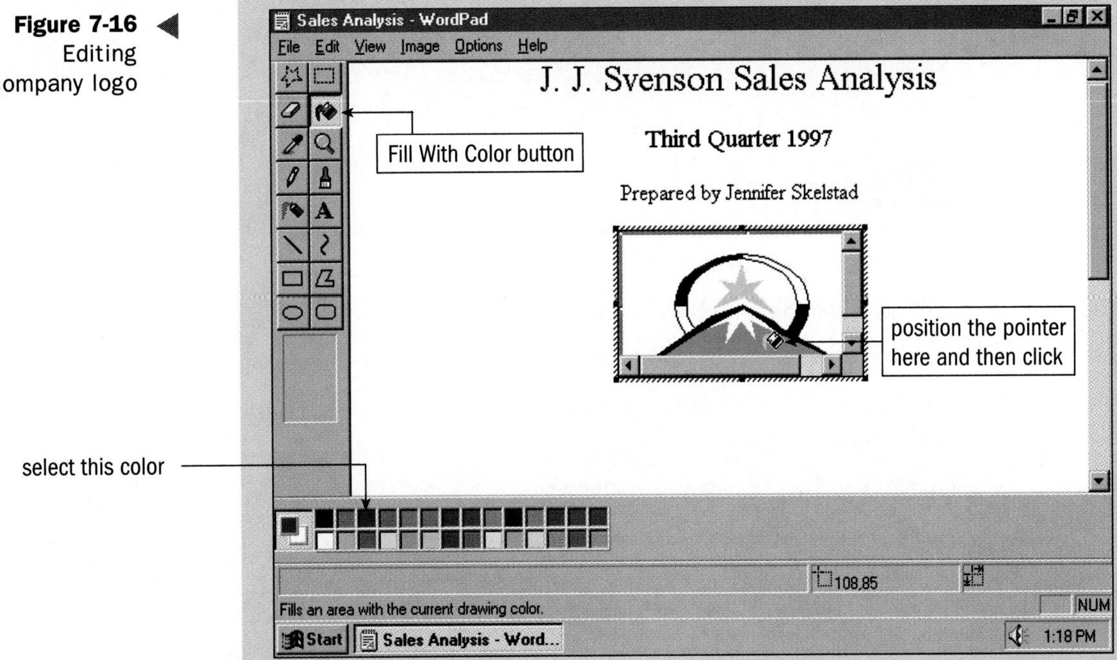

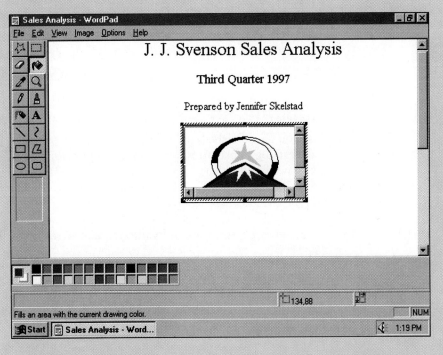

TROUBLE? If your monitor is monochrome, choose a gray square to match the shading in the logo.

4. Click the mouse button. Brown color fills the mountain portion of the logo. See Figure 7-17.

Figure 7-17 ◀
Edited logo

TROUBLE? If your screen doesn't match Figure 7-17 (for example, if the entire logo turns brown instead of just part of it), click Edit, then click Undo, then do step 3 again. Before you click the logo, make sure you position the entire pointer within the portion of the logo you want to fill with color.

5. Click anywhere outside the borders of the logo to display the WordPad menus and tools. The edited logo appears in the WordPad document.

6. Click **File** then click **Save** to save your edits.

Quick Check

1. What does the acronym "OLE" stand for?

2. How do embedding and linking differ?

3. Describe what happens when you double-click an embedded object in WordPad.

4. When sharing data between programs with OLE, what is a source program and what is a destination program?

5. What is a server and what is a client?

6. Define "object" and give four examples.

7. Describe two situations in which you might want to share data among programs.

Now that you have completed Session 7.1, you can exit the program or continue on to the next session.

SESSION

7.2

In this session you will learn how to embed an Excel range in a WordPad document, how to edit an embedded Excel object, how to link an Excel workbook to a WordPad document, and how to paste a Paint image into an Excel workbook. Finally, you will review the necessity of keeping linked files together.

Embedding an Excel Range

Now that you have finished inserting and editing the company logo, you turn your attention to the catalog information you want the report to include. This information is stored in an Excel workbook. When you copy it from the workbook to your Sales Analysis document, you'll use Excel as the Source program and WordPad as the destination program.

Let's open the Excel workbook now.

To start Excel, open the Catalog workbook and save it with a new name:

1. With WordPad still open, start Excel as usual.

2. Open the file **Catalog** in the Tutorial.07 folder on your Student Disk. See Figure 7-18.

Figure 7-18 ◀
Catalog
workbook

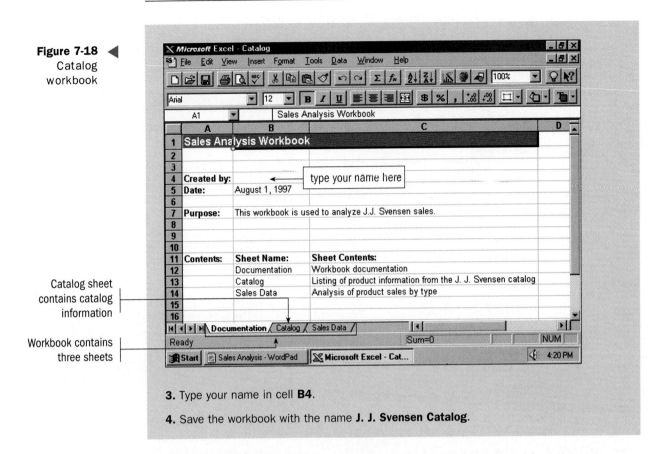

Catalog sheet
contains catalog
information

Workbook contains
three sheets

3. Type your name in cell **B4**.

4. Save the workbook with the name **J. J. Svensen Catalog**.

Notice the three worksheets in your workbook: Documentation, Catalog, and Sales Data. The Documentation worksheet contains the workbook documentation, and the Catalog worksheet contains the catalog information. The Sales Data worksheet contains the most recent sales figures for the third quarter.

Pasting a Range as an Excel Worksheet

You are ready to copy the catalog information and embed it into your WordPad document. You begin by displaying the sheet containing the material you want to copy.

To copy the catalog information to the Sales Analysis document:

1. Click the **Catalog** sheet tab to show the catalog information in this worksheet. Figure 7-19.

Figure 7-19 ◄
J. J. Svensen
catalog
information

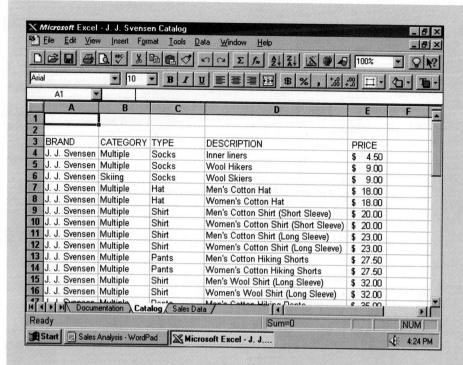

2. Select the range **A3:E51**

3. Click the **Copy** tool 🗐 . Now that you have copied the catalog list to the Windows Clipboard, you can paste it in the WordPad document.

4. In the Taskbar, click the **Sales Analysis - WordPad** button. The WordPad window opens.

5. Scroll down the document until you see the bold heading **J. J. SVENSEN CATALOG**, then click to the right of the word **CATALOG**.

6. Press **Enter** twice to move to the second line under the heading.

7. On the menu bar, click **Edit** then click **Paste** (do *not* click Paste Special).

8. Scroll up the document until you see the **J. J. SVENSEN CATALOG** heading. Figure 7-20 shows the catalog list as it appears in the document.

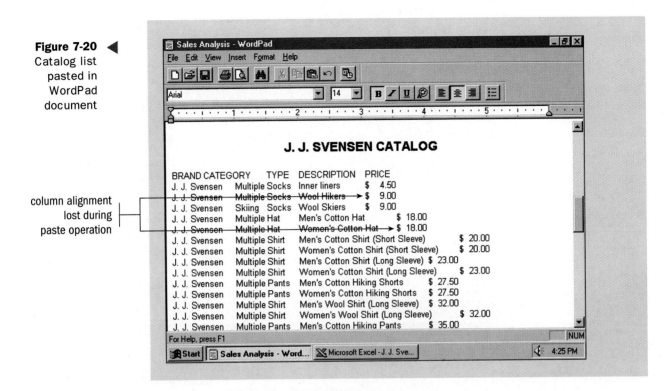

Figure 7-20
Catalog list
pasted in
WordPad
document

column alignment
lost during
paste operation

You successfully pasted all the catalog information in your sales report. In the process, however, you lost most of the formatting information, and as a result the columns no longer align properly. This is because the Paste command you used treated the copied material as simple text, not as an embedded range. You decide to try again using a different Paste option, but first you undo your last step.

To repaste the catalog list into the document:

1. On the WordPad menu, click **Edit** then click **Undo**. WordPad deletes the copy of the catalog list.

2. Click **Edit** again then click **Paste Special**. The Paste Special dialog box shown in Figure 7-21 appears.

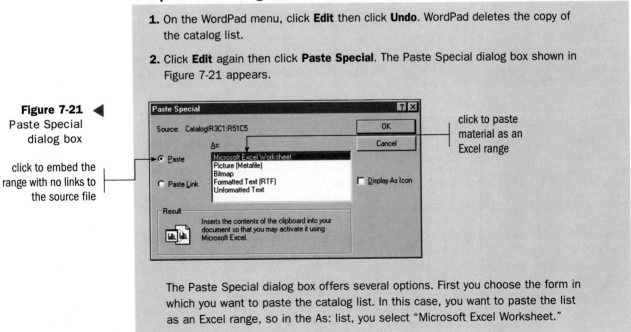

Figure 7-21
Paste Special
dialog box

click to embed the
range with no links to
the source file

click to paste
material as an
Excel range

The Paste Special dialog box offers several options. First you choose the form in which you want to paste the catalog list. In this case, you want to paste the list as an Excel range, so in the As: list, you select "Microsoft Excel Worksheet."

Next, you choose between the Paste and the Paste Link option buttons. If you choose Paste Link, you could update the catalog in the original Excel workbook and then have it automatically updated in the WordPad document. This doesn't seem necessary because the catalog list won't be revised in the near future. So you choose the default option, Paste, which embeds the Excel range in the document, but does not link it to the original Excel workbook.

3. Make sure the Paste option button is selected, then in the As: list, make sure Microsoft Excel Worksheet is selected.

4. Click **OK**. After a pause, the Excel range appears in the document.

5. Scroll up the document until you can see the **J. J. SVENSEN CATALOG** heading. The catalog information appears in the document, as shown in Figure 7-22. This time columns are properly aligned. A border with small black handles surrounds the catalog list, indicating that it is not simply text, but rather an object embedded in the document.

Figure 7-22 ◀
Catalog list pasted as an Excel worksheet range

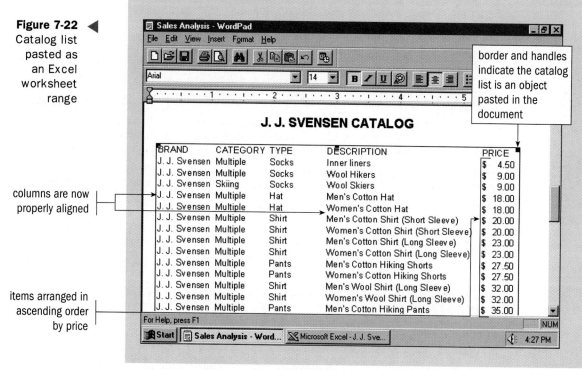

The format of the catalog list looks good, but you notice that the catalog items are arranged in ascending order by price. You would prefer to have them arranged alphabetically by type. You decide to edit the embedded object using the source program's tools and menus.

Editing an Embedded Excel Object

You edit an embedded Excel object in the same way you edited the embedded company logo. That is, you simply double-click the object to display the source program's menus and tools.

To edit the embedded Excel worksheet:

1. Double-click within the border of the catalog list. The catalog list appears in an Excel window, complete with row and column headings, all within the WordPad window.

2. Use the WordPad scroll bar (on the far right side of the window) to scroll up until you can see the **J. J. SVENSEN CATALOG** heading. The embedded worksheet looks like Figure 7-23. Now you can sort the catalog list alphabetically by type, using the Excel Sort tools.

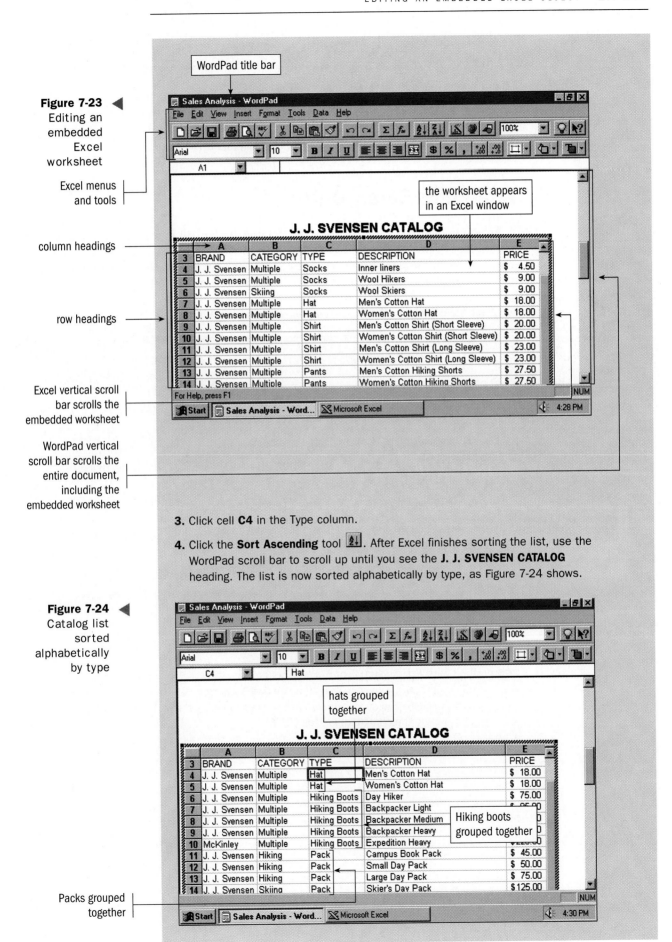

Figure 7-23
Editing an
embedded
Excel
worksheet

WordPad title bar

Excel menus
and tools

the worksheet appears
in an Excel window

column headings

row headings

Excel vertical scroll
bar scrolls the
embedded worksheet

WordPad vertical
scroll bar scrolls the
entire document,
including the
embedded worksheet

3. Click cell **C4** in the Type column.

4. Click the **Sort Ascending** tool . After Excel finishes sorting the list, use the WordPad scroll bar to scroll up until you see the **J. J. SVENSEN CATALOG** heading. The list is now sorted alphabetically by type, as Figure 7-24 shows.

Figure 7-24
Catalog list
sorted
alphabetically
by type

hats grouped
together

Hiking boots
grouped together

Packs grouped
together

5. Click anywhere outside the Excel window to return to the WordPad tools and menus. The catalog list appears with gridlines within the Sales Analysis document.

6. Click **File** then click **Save** to save your changes.

You successfully edited the embedded Excel range from within WordPad. The changes you just made have no affect on the original Excel file in the source program. You'll have a chance to verify this later in this tutorial.

Analyzing Sales Data

As you know from your sales analysis document plan, all that remains now is to analyze the sales data using the Excel Chart Wizard. After you create the chart, you'll paste it with links in the Sales Analysis document. That way, the chart will be automatically updated along with the sales figures. You begin by returning to the Excel window.

To chart sales data in the J. J. Svensen Catalog workbook:

1. Click the **Microsoft Excel** button in the Taskbar to return to the Excel window.

2. If necessary, maximize the J.J. Svensen Catalog window.

3. Click outside the selected range to remove the highlighting, then scroll up the worksheet to examine the catalog information. Notice that the sorting you performed in the WordPad document did not affect the original Excel file.

4. Click the **Sales Data** tab to display that sheet.

5. Select the range **A3:B9** then click **the ChartWizard** tool 🖾. The pointer changes to ⁺ⁱ.▪️.

6. Drag the pointer to outline the range **A12:F24**.

7. Check the ChartWizard - Step 1 of 5 dialog box to make sure you selected the correct range, then click **Next**.

8. In the ChartWizard - Step 2 of 5 dialog box, click **3-D Pie** then click **Next**.

9. In the ChartWizard - Step 3 of 5 dialog box, click type **7** if it is not already highlighted, then click **Next**.

10. Check the ChartWizard - Step 4 of 5 dialog box to make sure the sample chart looks like you expected, then click **Next**.

11. In the ChartWizard - Step 5 of 5 dialog box, make sure the **No** radio button is selected, type **J. J. Svensen Third Quarter Sales by Type** in the Chart Title box, then click **Finish**. The chart appears in the worksheet, as shown in Figure 7-25. (You might see the chart toolbar, too.)

Figure 7-25 ◀
Completed
chart

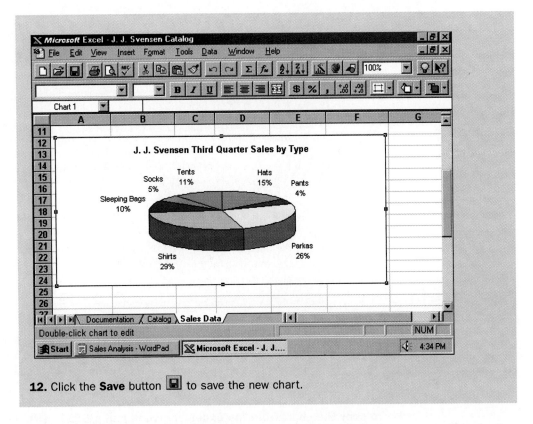

12. Click the **Save** button 🖫 to save the new chart.

The completed chart clearly illustrates each type of product's percentage of total sales. All you need to do now is paste it into your WordPad document.

Using OLE to Link Files

You could use the Paste command on the Edit menu to paste the chart into the report. Doing this would embed the chart in the report without links to the original data. But because sales figures are routinely updated, it's better to create a link between the numbers in your report and the numbers in the Excel worksheet. Then if you update the numbers in the worksheet the chart in the report will be updated automatically. You'll do this using OLE to link your Excel workbook file to your WordPad file.

Remember that OLE uses a source program as the source of material that is copied to a document in a destination program. When you use linking, changes made in the original file are reflected in the copy. As with embedded material, OLE lets you activate the source program in order to edit linked data.

You will use the Copy and Paste Special commands to link the chart to the sales report. The information you want is on the Sales Data worksheet of an Excel workbook, which means that Excel is the source program. You will paste the information into a WordPad document; that means WordPad is the destination program.

REFERENCE window

USING EXCEL AS A SOURCE PROGRAM FOR A WINDOWS WORDPAD DOCUMENT

- Start Excel and open or create the workbook you want to link.
- Start WordPad and open or create the document in which you will place the linked material.
- Switch to Excel and select the range in the Excel workbook that you want to link to the WordPad document.
- Click the Copy button to copy the information to the Clipboard.
- Switch to WordPad and position the insertion pointer where you want the linked material to be placed.
- Click Edit, then click Paste Special.
- In the Paste Special dialog box, click the appropriate option in the As: list (usually "Microsoft Excel Worksheet"). To embed the material without links, click the Paste option button. To link the material to the original Excel workbook (that is, to the source program), click the Paste Link option button.

You want to place the chart under the heading "Sales Percentages" in your report. You copy the material from the Excel workbook, return to WordPad, move the insertion point where you want the chart to appear, and then use the Paste Special command to insert the chart in the WordPad document.

To copy the chart from the Excel workbook and paste it with links in the WordPad document:

1. Make sure the chart is still selected, as indicated by black handles around the chart border. If the chart is not selected, click it once.

2. Click the **Copy** button to copy the chart to the Clipboard. Now that you've copied the data, you can return to the WordPad window and paste the data into the sales report.

3. In the Taskbar, click the **Sales Analysis - WordPad** button to open the WordPad window.

4. Scroll down the document until you see the heading **Sales Percentages**, click at the end of the word **Percentages**, and then press **Enter** twice to position the cursor in the second blank line under the heading.

5. Click **Edit** then click **Paste Special**. The Paste Special dialog box opens.

6. Click **Paste Link**. Notice the explanation of the Paste Link option in the Result box.

7. Make sure Microsoft Excel Chart is selected in the As: list, then click **OK**. The dialog box closes.

8. Click anywhere outside the chart border. The chart is copied from the Clipboard into the document as a linked worksheet object, as Figure 7-26 shows.

Figure 7-26 ◀
Chart pasted
into WordPad
document

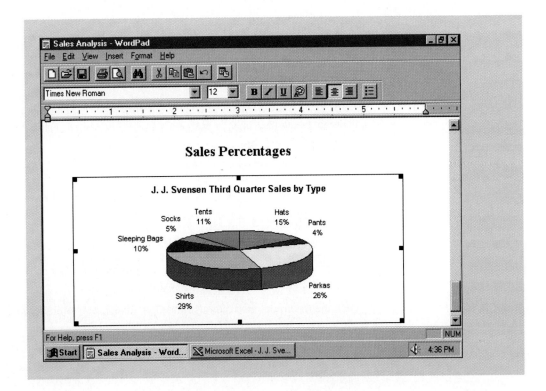

You just created a link between your report and the Excel J. J. Svensen Catalog work-book via Object Linking and Embedding (OLE). Next time you update and save the data in your Excel workbook, the changes will show up in your WordPad document.

Later on, you plan to add some paragraphs to your Sales Analysis document that point out the high percentage of sales of shirts and parkas. But for now, you decide to save the Sales Analysis document and exit WordPad.

To save the Sales Analysis document and exit WordPad:

1. Click the **Save** button 🖫.

2. Click **File** then click **Exit**. You return to the Excel window.

Testing Links

As you have learned, once you link files, changes made in the source (server) file are reflected in the destination (client) file. However, the opposite is *not* true. If you try to edit a linked object from within the destination file, Windows opens the original file in the source program for you to edit instead. For example, if you double-clicked the linked chart in your WordPad document in order to edit it, the Excel window would appear on top of the WordPad window, with the J. J. Svensen Catalog file open. (If Excel wasn't already running, it would start automatically.) Then you would have to edit the chart from within Excel. The changes you made would automatically appear in the linked chart in your WordPad document.

You've just received the final sales figure for the third quarter, showing that the sales of hats have declined, so you need to update the figures in the Sales Data sheet of the J. J. Svensen Catalog workbook. When you do so, you'll see how the Sales Analysis WordPad document is automatically updated to reflect these changes.

To update the sales figures:

1. If necessary, maximize the J. J. Svensen Catalog window.

2. In the Sales Data sheet, click cell **B3**, type **350000**, and then press **Enter**. The chart adjusts to reflect new sales data.

3. Scroll down the worksheet to display the entire chart. Notice that the Hats percentage, which was 15%, is now 9%.

4. Click the **Save** tool 🖫 to save your work.

Now you can open your WordPad document again to make sure this change was made in the linked chart.

To open the WordPad document and check the linked chart:

1. Click the **Start** button 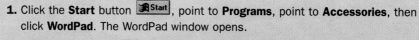, point to **Programs**, point to **Accessories**, then click **WordPad**. The WordPad window opens.

2. Click the **Open** tool 🖼, then use the Open dialog box to open the Sales Analysis document in the Tutorial.07 folder on your Student Disk.

3. Scroll down the document to display the chart. The pie chart slice representing the sales for hats reflects the changes made to the Excel workbook, as Figure 7-27 shows.

Figure 7-27 ◀
Linked chart
was updated
automatically

Hats percentage is
now 9%, as it is in the
Excel workbook

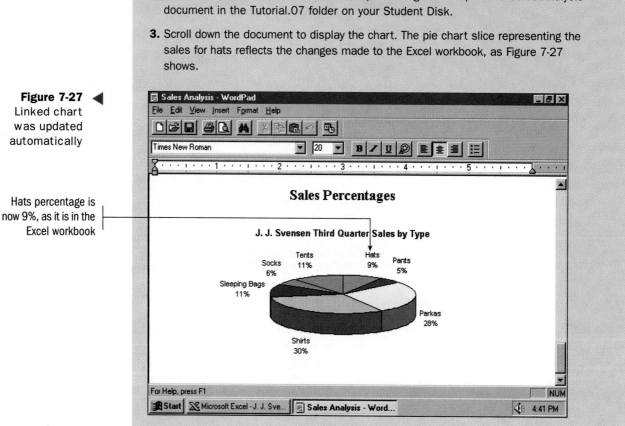

You can now be confident that every change you make to the sales data in your Excel workbook will be reflected in your sales analysis. (In the assignments at the end of this Tutorial you'll have a chance to update links between files that are already open.) You exit WordPad and return to the Excel window. (You'll have an opportunity to print the WordPad document in the Tutorial Assignments at the end of this chapter.)

To exit WordPad:

> **1.** Click **File** then click **Exit**. You return to the Excel window. Notice that it is not necessary to save changes to the WordPad document. The changes to the chart were automatically saved when you saved the revised Excel workbook.

Using Excel as a Destination Program and Paint as a Source Program

In the previous section you used Excel as a source program. When you embed and link OLE objects from other programs in an Excel workbook, you use Excel as a destination program. For example, you could embed a Paint image in an Excel workbook. Then, you could simply double-click the image in the Excel workbook to edit it, using the tools and menus of the source program, Paint.

Keep in mind, however, that although you can almost always paste objects with links from Excel into other Windows programs, it's not always possible to paste objects with links from other programs into Excel. You can't, for example, link an Excel workbook as the destination for a Paint file, so that every change you make to the Paint file is automatically made in the Excel file. Instead, you need to embed the Paint object in the Excel workbook, and then, if necessary, edit the object from within Excel.

When you paste a graphic object in an Excel workbook, you can choose to paste it in one of three formats: Bitmap, Picture, Bitmap Image Object. The **Bitmap** and **Picture** formats are useful if you are concerned about producing high quality printouts. However, both formats take more disk space than the Bitmap Image Object (with the Bitmap taking the most). Also, these formats don't allow you to edit the graphic using the source program's tools and menus. For these reasons, it's usually best to use the **Bitmap Image Object** format, which takes the minimum amount of disk space and lets you edit the graphic from within Excel.

REFERENCE window

USING EXCEL AS A DESTINATION PROGRAM FOR A WINDOWS PAINT GRAPHIC IMAGE

- Start Paint and open or create the graphic image you want to link.
- Start Excel and open or create the worksheet where you will place the linked material.
- Switch to Paint and select the image that you want to link to the Excel worksheet.
- Click Edit, then click Copy to copy the image to the Clipboard.
- Switch to Excel and click the cell in the upper-left corner of the range where you want to insert the image.
- Click Edit, then click Paste Special.
- Click Bitmap Image Object in the Paste Special dialog box.
- Click OK.
- Use handles to resize the image if necessary.
- Save the Excel workbook.

Next, you decide to add the J. J. Svensen company logo to your workbook. That way the logo will be handy later when you want to use it as a graphic on other worksheets. This time you'll use a revised version of the logo, with all the correct colors.

To add the revised company logo to the workbook:

1. Click the **Start** button to open Paint, and then maximize the Paint window, if necessary.

2. Open the file **2ndLogo**, located in the Tutorial.07 folder on your Student Disk.

3. Click **Edit** then click **Select All**.

4. Click **Edit** then click **Copy**.

5. Click the **Microsoft Excel** button in the Taskbar. The Excel window appears.

6. Click the **Documentation sheet** tab, then click cell **A18**.

7. Click **Edit** then click **Paste Special**. The Paste Special dialog box shown in Figure 7-28 opens.

Figure 7-28 ◀
Paste special
dialog box

pasting with links ——

lets you edit picture
object using Paint
tools and menus

useful if you need
high quality printouts

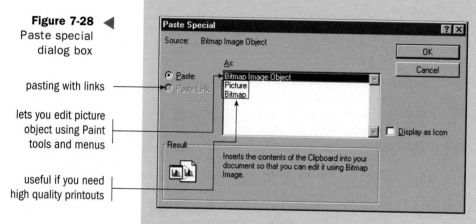

8. Make sure Bitmap Image Object is selected in the As: list, then click **OK**. The company logo appears in the Documentation sheet, Figure 7-29 shows.

9. Click anywhere outside the logo to deselect it.

Figure 7-29 ◀
Paint graphic
pasted as
Bitmap Image
Object

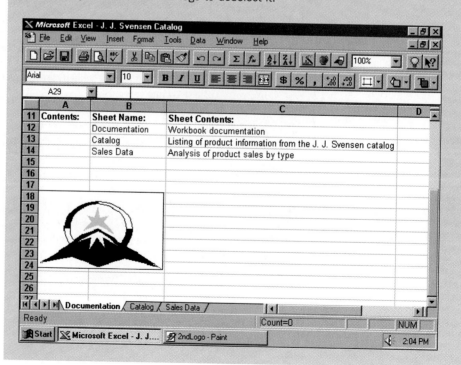

Now that you have embedded the logo in your Excel workbook, you can edit it anytime you want from within Excel, using the Paint tools and menus. You are finished with Paint for now, so you close it. You are also finished using your workbook, so you can close Excel.

To close Paint and save and close the workbook:

1. Click the **Paint** button in the taskbar to display the Paint window.

2. Click **File** then click **Exit** to close Paint. You return to the Excel window.

3. Click the **Save** tool 🖫 to save the workbook. Click **File** then click **Exit** to close the workbook and exit Excel.

Keeping Linked Files Together

You learned earlier in this tutorial that moving or renaming linked files can disrupt the links between them. (When you use embedding the destination file contains a complete copy of the source file, so you don't have to worry about maintaining a connection between two separate files.) To prevent problems with links, it's best to keep linked files in the same folder. This is a good idea for two reasons.

First of all, keeping linked files in the same folder will prevent you from accidentally separating them. If you need to give the linked files to someone else, you can simply copy the entire folder to the disk. For example, if you wanted to give a copy of your report to Heather, you would have to include:

■ Sales Analysis, the WordPad file containing a chart linked to an Excel workbook

■ J. J. Svensen Catalog, the workbook containing the chart

To make sure both of these files are included, you could simply copy the Tutorial.07 folder to a disk and give it to Heather.

Once you move the files to a disk, you may need to tell Windows 95 exactly where the files are located, so that the links can function properly—a process known as **updating links.** In general, updating links is much easier if you keep linked files in the same folder because you're less likely to get confused about exactly where a file is located. If you're not sure what files an Excel workbook is linked to, you can use the Links command on the Edit menu to open the Links dialog box. There you'll find information on links between the current workbook and any other files. You'll have a chance to use the Links dialog box in the Assignments at the end of this tutorial.

You have completed the first draft of your report. You'll add some additional explanatory text later. In the meantime, you take the linked files on disk to Heather.

Quick Check

1. Explain why column alignment was not properly maintained the first time you tried to paste the Excel range into the WordPad document.

2. If you edit an embedded object from the destination program, will the same changes automatically be made to the file in the source program? Why or why not?

3. When pasting a Paint image into an Excel workbook, which format should you use to ensure that you can edit the image in the future: Bitmap, Picture, or Bitmap Image Object?

4. If you were to e-mail someone the J. J. Svensen workbook, which contains an embedded copy of a Paint image, would you need to send along the original Paint file? Why or why not?

5 If you were to e-mail someone the Sales Analysis document, which contains a linked copy of an Excel chart, would you need to send along the original Excel workbook? Why or why not?

6 Describe a situation in which you use Excel as a destination program.

7 Describe a situation in which you use Excel as a source program.

Tutorial Assignments

Now that Heather has looked at the first draft of your report and made some suggestions, you're ready to create your final draft. The finished report will include a list of all staff at J. J. Svenson and a numerical analysis of sales by region. It will also include introductory paragraphs for the catalog list and the Sales Percentages chart. Finally, you need to replace the current logo with a revised version.

1. Start Excel and then start WordPad.
2. In the WordPad window, open the file Sales2 in the TAssign folder for Tutorial 7.
3. Save the file as Sales Analysis 2 in the TAssign folder for Tutorial 7, and then review the document. Notice that the introductory paragraphs for the catalog list and the Sales Percentages chart are already included. But you still need to format them properly.
4. Type your name after "Prepared by" and then scroll down to the heading "J. J. Svensen Catalog." Now you can use the WordPad formatting buttons (most are identical to Excel formatting buttons) to format the text. Use the cursor to select the paragraph in bold beneath the heading. Click the Bold button and the Align Left button to align the text on the left, in regular type. Use the Font list arrow to select Times New Roman. (If that font is not available to you, choose another). Use the Font Size box to select 11-point type.
5. Follow the same procedure to format the paragraph under the "Sales Percentages" heading.
6. Add the heading "J. J. Svensen Sales Representatives" under the Sales Percentages chart and format it appropriately, aligning text on the left.
7. Use the Taskbar to switch to the Excel window. Then open the file Catalog2 in the TAssign folder for Tutorial 7, and save it as J. J. Svensen Catalog 2 in the same folder. In the Documentation sheet, type your name in cell B4 and the current date in cell B5 Notice that a fourth worksheet, Sales by Staff, is listed on the Documentation sheet.
8. Click the Sales by Staff tab to display that sheet. Copy the range A4:B11 and then return to the WordPad window. Paste the range into the document as text. (Use the Paste command rather than the Paste Special command.) Align the list of sales representatives on the left, and adjust spacing or formatting to make the list look professional.
9. Add the heading "Sales by Region" below the list of sales representatives. Center the heading and format it appropriately.
10. Return to the Sales by Staff sheet in the Excel window. Select the range C3:D11 and then use the PivotTable command on the Data menu to analyze the sales data by region. In the Step 3 of 4 dialog box, drag the Third Quarter Sales button to Data box, and drag the Region button to the row box. Make cell A13 the starting cell for the PivotTable.
11. Copy the PivotTable and paste it with links into the WordPad document as a Microsoft Excel worksheet. Insert the PivotTable under the heading "Sales by Region."

12. Scroll up the WordPad window to display the company logo. Click the logo to display handles around it, and then press Delete to delete it from the document. Now you'll insert the revised logo as an object. Instead of opening Paint, copying the logo, and then inserting it in the document, use the Object command on the Insert menu. In the Insert Object dialog box, click the Create from File radio button. Click Browse, select the file 3rdLogo in the TAssign folder for Tutorial 7, click Insert, and then click OK. The new logo (with a different-colored mountain) appears in your worksheet as an embedded object. To verify that it is an embedded object, double-click it to display the Paint tools and menus. Click once outside of the selected object to return to your WordPad document.

Now you decide to replace the logo in the Excel workbook with the revised version in the WordPad document. To do this, you'll use a special OLE feature, called Drag and Drop, which lets you use the mouse, rather than menu commands, to transfer objects between programs. To begin, you need to tile the Excel and WordPad windows so that both are visible at the same time.

13. Use the Resizing button on the WordPad and Excel windows to display both windows at once. Drag the window borders so that the WordPad window fills the left side of the screen and the Excel window fills the right side.

14. In the Excel window, display the documentation sheet, scroll to display the current logo, and delete it. In the WordPad window, scroll to display the logo, and click it if necessary to display its handles. Press Ctrl, then press the mouse button again, and hold it down as you drag the pointer to the Excel window. When the logo's grey outline is correctly positioned in the workbook, release the mouse button. A copy of the revised logo drops into the worksheet.

After looking over the Sales by Staff worksheet, you notice that the data for two representatives is wrong. You'll correct that problem now. Then you'll see how Windows automatically updates the linked PivotTable in the WordPad document.

15. Maximize the Excel window and go to the Sales by Staff sheet. The sales data for Melissa Conklin and Robert Constanza are reversed. To correct this error, type 330000 in cell D4 and 545900 in cell D5.

16. Highlight the PivotTable, then click the Refresh Data button ![icon] on the Query and Pivot toolbar to update the PivotTable. (If you don't see the Query and Pivot toolbar, use the Toolbars command on the View menu to display it.) The new total for the East region should be $931,500. When you're finished revising the worksheet, save your changes.

17. Display and maximize the WordPad window. Scroll until you see the PivotTable. It matches the one in the workbook it's linked to.

18. Looking over the PivotTable, you think the Region names would look better in bold. You double-click the object to use the tools and menus of the source program (Excel). Because the PivotTable is a linked object, you return to the source program. Select the range A15:A18 and then click the Bold button. Save your changes and then return to the WordPad document to review your changes.

The sales report is finished. All that remains is to test the links between the WordPad document and the Excel workbook. You already know that the PivotTables in the two files are properly linked. What about the Sales Percentages chart in the WordPad document? In the tutorial you pasted it in the WordPad document with links to an Excel workbook. But as you know, the rather fragile links between files can be disrupted if you move or rename the files.

19. Return to the Excel workbook and display the Sales Data sheet. Change the Sales figures for Hats from $350,000 to $1,000,000, and watch Excel update the chart. Now return to the WordPad window and display its Sales Percentages chart. Does it reflect your changes to the Excel workbook? Select the Sales Percentages chart and then use the Links command on the Edit menu to open the Links dialog box. Notice that the highlighted link (for the Sales Data chart) is listed as update automatic, indicating that the chart should have updated automatically. Click the Update Now button to update the chart manually. Now notice that the highlighted link is listed as unavailable. Why? Did you do something earlier in the Tutorial Assignments to disrupt the link between the chart and its source document?

20. Rather than repairing the link (a complicated process), you decide to break it. Click Break Link and then click Yes to confirm your decision. Close the Links dialog box. The chart remains in the document as a picture object instead of a linked or embedded Excel chart. To confirm this, double-click the chart. What happens?

21. Print the Sales by Staff sheet and then the Sales Data sheet. When you finish printing, change the sales figure for Hats (in the Sales Data sheet) back to $350,000, save the workbook, close it, and exit Excel.

22. Save the Sales Analsis 2 document. Then use the Print button on the WordPad toolbar to print it. You may need to insert or delete blank lines between sections to avoid unattractive page breaks. If you have Microsoft Word 6.0, you might find it easier to close WordPad, reopen the document in Word, use CtrlEnter to insert page breaks where necessary, and then print the report.

23. Copy the Sales Analysis 2 document to a disk, and give it to a classmate. What happens when she tries to open Sales Analysis 2, now that it's separated from the files it's linked to? What happens when she double-clicks the linked chart?

Case Problems

1. Reporting Income at Crawdad Fishing Supplies Joseph Simpson of Crawdad Fishing Supplies is responsible for reporting financial results to upper-level management. He prepared an Excel workbook that contains the company's yearly income statement and is ready to write his report using WordPad. He asked you to help him link his worksheet to his report.

1. Open the workbook Crawdad (in the Case folder for Tutorial 7 on your Student Disk) and save it as Crawdad Fishing Supplies.

2. On the Documentation sheet, type your name and the current date. If necessary, adjust column widths, and then save your changes.

To create a report in WordPad:

3. Start WordPad and maximize the WordPad window if necessary.

4. Copy the titles for the report from cells A1:A2 on the Titles sheet in the Excel workbook and paste them at the top of the WordPad document.

5. Use the Center and Bold buttons and the Font Size list arrow to format the titles appropriately.

6. In your report, use OLE to paste the income statement (from the Income Statement worksheet) with links in the WordPad document.

7. Write a one-paragraph report analyzing the income statement. Discuss the variations in revenues, expenses, and net income during the four quarters.

8. Save the report as Crawdad Financial Results in the Case folder for Tutorial 7 on your Student Disk.

9. Print the report. If you have Microsoft Word, you might find it easier to close WordPad, reopen the document in Word, insert page breaks, and then print the report.

10. Exit WordPad.

Joseph has also asked you to create a picture of a fishing boat for the company's logo. After you create the logo, he wants you to add it to the Crawdad Fishing Supplies workbook.

To create a picture and place it in the workbook:
1. Return to Excel.
2. Use the Worksheet command on the Insert menu to insert a new worksheet in the workbook. Name the worksheet Art.

3. Create an embedded Paint picture object on the new worksheet:
   a. Click Insert, then click Object to open the Object dialog box.
   b. If necessary, click the Create New tab in the Object Type list box, click Paintbrush Picture, and then click OK. After a moment, you see the Paint tools and menus in the Excel window.
   c. Create a boat logo in Paint. Feel free to experiment and use the Paint Help system to guide you if necessary.
   d. To return to the Excel menus and tools, click anywhere outside the Paint object's border.
4. To resize the Paint object, click the logo to display handles on its borders, then drag the handle in the lower-right corner until the logo fills the range A1:F15
5. Save the workbook.
6. Print the Artwork sheet in landscape orientation. Do not print row and column borders or gridlines. Center your printout horizontally and include a right-aligned header with your name, the filename, the sheet name, and the date. Do not use a footer. The printout should fit on its own page.
7. Save the workbook again and then close it.
8. On a piece of paper, list all the data transfer methods you used in this case. Explain why you used each method, as well as any possible alternatives. Submit the list and your printouts to your instructor.

2. Ordering Parts at Shinohara Electronics You've just started a new job at Shinohara Electronics, a manufacturer of consumer electronic products. You are responsible for maintaining adequate inventory of parts used in the manufacturing process. Most parts are available from more than one vendor. Your supervisor has asked you to study how part orders are distributed among vendors to discover any patterns in Shinohara's parts purchases. After the analysis is complete, you need to write a report describing your results.
1. Open the workbook Parts (in the Case folder for Tutorial 7 on your Student Disk), and save it as Shinohara Parts Purchases.
2. On the Documentation sheet, type your name and the current date. If necessary, adjust column widths, and then save your changes.
3. Switch to the Inventory Analysis worksheet, and click cell A6
4. Create a PivotTable showing how many of each part have been purchased from each supplier:
   a. Start the PivotTable Wizard and create the PivotTable from a Microsoft Excel list.
   b. In the PivotTable Wizard - Step 3 of 4 dialog box drag the Vendor button to the Row box, and the Part ID # button to the Column box. Drag the Quantity button to the Data box to create a PivotTable that sums the quantities for each part.
   c. Make cell E5 in the Inventory Analysis sheet the starting cell for the PivotTable.
5. Save the workbook.
6. Start WordPad and maximize the WordPad window.
7. Write a report that introduces the analysis in the PivotTable.
8. Use OLE to paste the PivotTable in the report from the Inventory Analysis worksheet. Be sure to link the PivotTable in the WordPad document to the original in the Excel workbook.
9. Save the report as Shinohara Inventory Analysis.
10. Exit WordPad.

Your supervisor has just given you some revised information for the Inventory Analysis worksheet.

11. Return to Excel and change the value in cell C12 from 500 to 50,000.

12. Highlight the PivotTable, then click the Refresh data button [!] in the Query and Pivot toolbar to update the PivotTable, and then save your workbook.

13. Start WordPad again and open the Shinohara Inventory Analysis document. Does the PivotTable in the WordPad document reflect the changes in the Excel workbook? Why or why not?

14. Print a copy of the report. If you have Microsoft Word, you might find it easier to close WordPad, reopen the document in Word, insert page breaks, and then print the report.

15. Return to Excel and print the Inventory Analysis sheet in landscape orientation. Do not print row and column borders or gridlines. Center your printout horizontally and include a right-aligned header with your name, the filename, the sheet name, and the date. Do not use a footer. The printout should fit on its own page.

16. Close the workbook.

17. Assume your supervisor wants a copy of your report on disk. What would you include on the disk and why?

3. Tracking Shipments at Redmond-Wheeler Express You are the new accounts manager at Redmond-Wheeler Express, an express shipping company located in the Pacific Northwest. As part of your job, you are responsible for tracking shipments and sending invoices to clients. Your supervisor, Mario, has asked you to prepare a report on the company's top five clients. Mario plans to review your report on his laptop tomorrow, during a flight to Chicago. For the sake of convenience, he would like you to include your report in the Excel Workbook that already contains the relevant invoice data. That way he'll only have to bring along one file, without worrying about maintaining links between multiple files.

1. Open the workbook Express (in the Case folder for Tutorial 7) and save it as Redmond-Wheeler Express.

2. On the Documentation sheet, type your name and the current date. If necessary, adjust column widths, and then save your changes.

3. Switch to the Analysis worksheet. The PivotTable in this sheet is based on the data in the Invoice Data worksheet.

4. In the Analyis sheet, select the range A2:C5 (It's easiest to click on cell C5 first, and then drag to A2)

5. Use the ChartWizard to create a column chart illustrating the number of two-day shipments versus the number of overnight shipments. Place the chart in the Analysis sheet, next to the PivotTable.

6. Edit the chart as necessary to make it look professional.

7. Save the workbook.

8. Now that you've finished analyzing the data, you can write your report. To begin, switch to the Report worksheet.

9. Click cell B2.

10. Click Insert then click Object to open the Object dialog box. Scroll the Object Type list, select WordPad Document, and then click OK. After a pause, the WordPad tools and menus appear in the Excel window. A blank WordPad document appears in the worksheet, beginning in cell A1 Don't be concerned if the WordPad document does not fill the worksheet area. The document window expands to accommodate the text you type. Or, if you prefer, you can use the handles to resize the object.

11. In the WordPad document, write a brief report that introduces the analysis in the PivotTable and column charts. If necessary, refer to data in the Invoice Data sheet. Use the WordPad formatting tools to make the report look professional.

12. Click anywhere outside the document border to deselect it.

13. Preview and print the Report sheet and the Analysis sheet. Adjust the Page Setup settings to make your printouts look as attractive as possible.
14. Save your workbook and then close it.
15. Submit your workbook file and printouts to your instructor.

4. Reporting Travel Information to the Yellow Jersey Bicycle Club At a recent meeting of Yellow Jersey, your local biking club, you and other members discussed the possibility of organizing a two-week European tour. You volunteered to investigate the cost of air fare. After spending some time on the phone with travel agents, you compiled the information shown in Figure 7-30.

Figure 7-30 ◀

Destination	Air Fare
Rome	$675
London	$620
Paris	$780
Munich	$730
Berlin	$725
Milan	$650
Amsterdam	$615
Prague	$815
Seville	$820

Write a report in WordPad explaining your findings. Include the list of air fares as an Excel data list. Print two copies of the report, one with the air fare list sorted alphabetically by destination and one sorted in ascending order by air fare. Finally, use Paint to create an attractive logo to include in your report.

1. Open WordPad.
2. Type the text of your report (except for the air fare list), pointing out the three cheapest fares. Add an appropriate heading and then format your report so that it looks professional.
3. Open Paint and create a logo for the Yellow Jersey Bicycle Club and save it as Bike Logo in the Case Folder for Tutorial 7.
4. Paste the logo into the WordPad document.

5. Use the Object command on the Insert menu to insert an Excel worksheet into the document:
   a. Click Insert then click Object to open the Object dialog box. Scroll the Object Type list, select Microsoft Excel Worksheet, and then click OK. After a pause, an Excel worksheet appears in the WordPad window.
   b. Enter the air fare information from Figure 7-30 in the worksheet. Drag the worksheet border handles as necessary to increase or decrease its size. Try not to leave any blank cells visible.
   c. Format the worksheet data appropriately.

6. Use the Sort Ascending button to sort the list alphabetically by destination, then click anywhere outside the worksheet borders to deselect it.
7. Save the report as Air Fare in the Case folder for Tutorial 7.
8. Review your report, and make any necessary changes. Then print your report.
9. Double-click the Excel worksheet object to redisplay the Excel tools and menus. This time sort the list in ascending order by air fare.
10. Save the WordPad document again, then print it. If you have Microsoft Word, you might find it easier to close WordPad, reopen the document in Word, insert page breaks, and then print the report.
11. Submit the WordPad file and printouts to your instructor.

Answers to Quick Check Questions

SESSION 1.1

1 A spreadsheet can be used for cash flow analysis, budgeting, decision making, cost estimating, inventory management and financial reporting.

2 A spreadsheet is used for analyzing and evaluating information.

3 cell

4 open

5 active cell

6 split

7 Save As

8 d

SESSION 1.2

1 Position the pointer in the upper-left corner of the area you want to chart. Drag the pointer to highlight all the cells you want to chart. Make sure to include row and column titles. Click the ChartWizard button. Drag the pointer to outline the area in the worksheet where you want the chart to appear. Follow the ChartWizard instructions to complete the chart.

2 Save

3 range

4 page break

5 The Print dialog box setting for "Page(s) from:__ to:__" lets you specify which page you want to start from and which page you want to print to. To print only page 2, print from page 2 to page 2.

6 a. Save button b. Print button c. Undo button d. Redo button e. Excel title bar f. vertical scrollbar g. menu bar and title bars h. active cell i. AutoCalculate box j. sheet tabs k. Taskbar

7 label

8 values

9 function

10 formula

11 cell reference

12 a. multiplication b. subtraction c. addition d. division

13 a. label b. value c. value d. formula e. value f. formula g. formula h. label i. formula j. label k. label

14 Select the range containing the values you want to sum. View the sum in the AutoCalculate box in the status bar.

SESSION 2.1

1 Save As

2 After you type the first few letters of a label AutoComplete will detect a potential match in the column and display that label in the active cell. To accept Excel's suggestion, you can simply press [Enter]. To ignore it, continue typing the new label.

3 planning, building, testing, documenting

4 a. 20 b. 10 c. 9 d. 15

5   You can type the cell reference or you can use the mouse or arrow keys to select each cell.

6   relative

7   They adjust to reflect their new position in the worksheet.

8   Type the first two or three items in the series, select the range containing the entries, then drag the fill handle.

SESSION 2.2

1   The AutoSum button automatically creates formulas that contain the SUM function. Excel looks at the cells adjacent to the active cell, guesses which cells you want to sum, and displays a formula that contains a "best guess" about the range you want to sum. To use AutoSum, click the cell where you want to enter the formula, click the AutoSum button, press the Enter key to accept the formula or you can drag the mouse over a different range of cells to change the range in the formula.

2   1 is a useful test value because it allows you detect errors immediately.

3   [Del]

4   AutoFormat

5   Clearing a cell deletes the contents and/or formatting. Deleting a cell actually removes the entire cell from the worksheet.

6   Click any cell in the row above which you want to insert the new row. Or highlight a range of rows above which you want to insert new rows. Click Insert and then click Rows. Excel inserts one row for every row in the highlighted range. The rows are inserted above the highlighted range. (To insert a column substitute "column" for "row" in the preceding instructions.)

7   test values

8   Number signs indicate the column is too narrow to display the entire cell entry.

SESSION 2.3

1   Protect Document command

2   a. automatically sums a range of values b. checks spelling in the worksheet c. undoes your previous action d. redoes your previous action

3   A template is a version of a worksheet that includes titles and formulas, but no data values. Excel templates are stored with an .XLT extension rather than the .XLS extension used for workbooks. In the Open dialog box, the icon for a template is differentiated from the icon for a workbook by a thin yellow line at the top of the icon. When you open a template, Excel copies it from the disk to RAM and displays the template on your screen You fill in the template with values, as you would with any worksheet When you save this workbook, Excel prompts you for a new filename so you do not overwrite the template. Excel then saves the completed workbook under the new filename.

4   You can correct the spelling using Excel s suggestion or type in your own correction. You can also tell Excel to ignore the word. Finally, you can add the word to Excel's dictionary.

5   locked

6   Workbook documentation provides the information necessary to use and modify the workbook. Documentation can take the form of: worksheet plans, worksheet sketches, formula printouts, cell notes, documentation sheets.

7   Click the cell where you want to insert a cell note. Click Insert, then click Note... to display the Cell Note dialog box. Type the cell note, then click OK. To display the cell note, place the pointer over the cell.

SESSION 3.1

1   a. 13% b. $ 0.13

2   AutoFormat is easy to use, but the predefined formats might not be suitable for every worksheet. When you select your own formats (instead of using AutoFormat), you can format an individual cell or a range of cells.

3 format menu; shortcut menu; toolbar

4 The cell is formatted to display two decimal places, with a comma. The cell displays the cell entry with formatting. The formula bar displays the actual entry.

5 See Figure 3-6.

6 Data can be aligned on the left, the right, or centered.

7 As a general rule, you should center column titles, format columns of numbers so the decimal places are in line, and leave columns of text aligned on the left.

8 Double click the column-header border; drag the column-header border; right-click the column-header to display the shortcut menu and then select Column Width; click Format, click Column, then click Width; click Format, click Column, then click AutoFit Selection.

9 Sometimes the data is difficult to read.

10 Do not attach borders to cells in the data zone.

SESSION 3.2

1 Click the Drawing button on the Standard toolbar.

2 Click the Drawing button on the Standard toolbar.

3 Right-click any toolbar, then click the name of the toolbar you want to add or remove.

4 A text box is always displayed on the worksheet. A cell note appears only when you place the pointer over the cell to which it is attached.

5 shapes, arrows, text boxes

6 select

SESSION 3.3

1 a. Labels at the top of columns identifying the information in that column b. Attributes of a font, such as regular, italic, bold, and bold italic c. Also called a macro automatically performs a sequence of tasks or commands such as menu selections, dialog box selections, or keystrokes d. The process of changing the appearance of the data in the cells of the worksheet e. Words and symbols that produce dates, times, and filenames that you might want to include in a header or footer f. Additions to a font such as underline, color, etc. g. Text that appears at the top of every printed worksheet page h. Text that appears at the bottom of every printed worksheet page i. Letters such as A, B, etc. that appear at the top of every worksheet column.

2 Visual Basic module

3 Open the workbook in which it is stored.

4 Click Tools, click Macro, click the desired macro, then click Run.

5 Proper orientation; gridlines off; correct headers and footers; worksheet centered on page; row/column headings turned off

6 portrait

7 header

8 See figure 3-32.

9 Open the Page Setup dialog box. On the Margins tab, click the Horizontally and Vertically check boxes to display checks in them.

10 A printout of worksheet formulas is a good form of documentation.

SESSION 4.1

1

Function Name	What it does	Syntax	Example
MAX	Finds the largest number.	MAX(number1,number2,...)	=MAX(B5:B16)
MIN	Finds the smallest number.	MIN(number1,number2,...)	=MIN(B5:B16)
AVERAGE	Calculates the average, or the arithmetic mean.	AVERAGE(number1,number2,...)	=AVERAGE(B5:B15)
PMT	Calculates periodic payments on loans.	PMT (rate, nper, pv, fv, type)	=PMT(11%/12, 36, 5000)

2   Check your answers using the Function Wizard.

3   A function is a calculation tool that performs a predefined operation. In other words, a function is a type of formula.

4   The AVERAGE function sums the values in a range and then divides by the number of nonblank cells. Cells containing zeros are considered nonblank cells.

5   The MAX and MIN functions prevent you from having to search through a long list to find the largest or smallest number.

6   The Function Wizard dialog box reminds of the function s syntax and prompts you for each argument.

7   =PMT(.0875/12, 30*12, 150000)

8   =PMT(.08/12, 48, 10000)

SESSION 4.2

1   =IF(A9="Bonus", 100, 0)

2   =IF(B5>=800000, "Over Budget", "Budget OK")

3   You should use an absolute reference when you don t want a cell reference to change when you copy the formula. For example, when calculating loan payments you may enter the interest rate in one cell. All formulas referring to that cell should use absolute references for that cell.

4   It has no arguments.

5   Excel attempted to divide by zero, which is not possible.

6   F4

SESSION 5.1

1   a. A single value in a cell b. A bar, area, wedge, or symbol that marks a single data point on a chart c. A group of related data points d. A group of individual cells or ranges that are not next to each other.

2   Click the first cell or highlight the first range you want to select. Press and hold [Ctrl] while you click additional cells or highlight -additional ranges. When you have selected all the cells you want to include, release [Ctrl].

3   Pie chart

4   Double-click within the border of a selected chart.

5   See figure 5-2.

6   Select it.

7   Make sure the chart is activated. Select the wedge, or column data marker, to which you want to apply a pattern. Click Format, then click Selected Data Point... to display the Format Data Point dialog box. Or, double-click the wedge or column marker to which you want to apply a pattern to display the Format Data Point dialog box. Click the Patterns tab, then click the Patterns list arrow to display a list of patterns. Click the pattern you want to apply, then click the OK button to close the dialog box.

SESSION 5.2

1 Trends or changes over time.

2 When data is arranged in rows, with column titles in the first row of the chart range.

3 Click the chart to select it. Click the ChartWizard button to display the ChartWizard - Step 1 of 2 dialog box. Drag the pointer to outline the range of cells you want to include in the revised chart, then click the Next > button. Make any revisions necessary on the ChartWizard - Step 2 of 2 dialog box, then click the OK button.

4 Label text includes the category names, the tick mark labels, the x-axis labels, and the legend text. Label text is often derived from the cells on the worksheet and is usually specified or edited using the ChartWizard or the Edit Series command on the Chart menu. Attached text includes the chart title, the x-axis title, and the y-axis title. To edit attached text, you click the text, then type the changes. Unattached text includes text boxes or comments that you type on the chart. To edit unattached text, you click the text, then type the changes

5 Use the Gridlines button on the Chart toolbar; or use the Gridlines command on the Insert menu.

6 Selected Data Series dialog box.

7 Bar chart uses horizontal bars. A column chart uses vertical columns.

8 Create a bar or column chart using the ChartWizard. Select all the bars or columns in the chart. Click Insert, then click Picture. Select the image file you want to use. Click OK.

9 b

SESSION 5.3

1 Put your chart on a standard worksheet if you want to include more than one chart on a sheet, or if you want to include worksheet data on the same sheet as the chart. Also, when a chart is on a standard worksheet you can size it to suit your needs.

2 Put your chart on a chart sheet to avoid having to resize the chart or adjust page setup settings.

3 Use the 3-D View command on the Format menu. Change the setting in the Rotation box by clicking the rotation buttons.

4 Patterns tab

5 comparisons

6 Data should be arranged in at least two columns, with one column containing acceptable geographical names or codes, and the other containing the data you want to map.

7 Geographical names or codes.

8 Select Equal spread of values in the Value Shading Options dialog box.

9 Adjust the Value Shading Options; add a meaningful title; edit the legend.

SESSION 6.1

1 A collection of information arranged in columns and rows.

2 record

3 field

4 database

5 The list was sorted first by Class, then by Last Name, and then by First Name.

6 Click any cell within the list. Click Data, then click Form... to display the data form. Click the New button. Enter the information for the new record. Click the Close button or scroll to another record to save the new record.

7 Click any cell in the data list. Click Data, then click Form to display the data form. Make sure the data form displays the first record in the list so Excel starts searching at the beginning of the list. Click the Criteria button. Click the Clear button to clear any previous search criteria. Enter the search criteria in the appropriate boxes. You can use uppercase or lowercase. Click the Find Next button to display the next record that matches the search criteria. Click the Find Prev button to display the previous record that matches the search criteria.

8 Use * (an asterisk) to represent any group of characters. Use ? (a question mark) to represent any one character.

9 Click any cell within the list you want to filter. Click Data, click Filter, then click AutoFilter to display the arrow buttons on each column heading in the worksheet. Click the arrow button in the column you want to search to display a list of possible search criteria. Click the desired search criteria.

SESSION 6.2

1 You could create a PivotTable to calculate the number of graduates for each department. You could manually calculate these figures by filtering the data to show lists of graduates for each department, and then counting the number in each filtered list.

2 Make sure all the rows in the data list are displayed. Click Data, then click PivotTable to start the PivotTable Wizard. Follow the PivotTable Wizard instructions to create a PivotTable on a separate sheet. Format and save the PivotTable.

3 Sum

4 An external database is not a part of the open Excel workbook.

5 MS Query

6 dBASE

7 table

8 Return Data to Microsoft Excel, on the File menu

SESSION 7.1

1 Object Linking and Embedding

2 An embedded object is not connected to the source file. A linked object is. When changes are made in the source file, the changes are reflected in the linked copy.

3 After a pause, the screen changes to the tools and menus of the embedded object's source program.

4 The source program is the program an object originates from. For example, in the Sales Report, Paint is the source program for the company logo. The destination program is the program that receives something from the source program. For example, WordPad is the destination program for the company logo.

5 A server is the same as a source program. A client is the same as a destination program.

6 An object is a package of data or information. Some examples of objects are: WordPad, Excel, an Excel worksheet, a WordPad document, an image created in Paint, and an Excel chart.

7 Use your imagination and try to think of a situations that are different from the one presented in the tutorial.

SESSION 7.2

1 The Excel range was pasted as text, and not as an Excel worksheet.

2 No. An embedded object has no links to the source file.

3 Bitmap Image Object

4 No. The embedded object is a complete copy. It has no links to the source file.

5 If you want the person receiving the files to be able to update the Excel workbook, and have the changes reflected automatically in the Sales Analysis document, then, yes, you do need to send along the Excel workbook file.

6 Use your imagination, and try to think of a situation that is different from the one described in the tutorial.

7 Again, try to think of a situation that is different from the one described in the tutorial.

Index

Task Reference

TASK	PAGE #	RECOMMENDED METHOD	NOTES
AutoCalculate, use	EX 34	Select a range, then view the sum of the selected values in the AutoCalculate box in the lower right portion of the worksheet window. To select a different function, right-click the AutoCalculate box and select the desired function.	
AutoComplete, use	EX 51	To accept Excel's AutoComplete suggestion, press [Enter]. Otherwise, continue typing a new label.	You must be entering labels in contiguous cells in a column for AutoComplete to function.
AutoFill, activate	EX 54	Drag fill handle to highlight the cells to be filled.	
AutoFilter, activate	EX 221	Click any cell in the list you want to filter. Click Data, point to Filter, then click AutoFilter	
AutoFormat, activate	EX 70		See Reference Window "Using AutoFormat."
AutoSum button, activate	EX 73	Click the cell where you want the sum to appear. Click [Σ]. Make sure the range address in the formula is the same as the range you want to sum.	
Border, add	EX 104		See Reference Window "Adding a Border."
Border, remove	EX 104		See Reference Window "Removing a Border."
Cancel action		Press [Esc].	
Cell contents, clear	EX 74		See Reference Window "Clearing Cells."
Cell contents, copy using the Copy command		Highlight the cell or range you want to copy, then click [image].	
Cell contents, copy using fill handle	EX 62		See Reference Window the "Copying Cell Contents with the Fill Handle."
Cell note, add	EX 79		See Reference Window "Adding a Cell Note."
Cell note, display	EX 79	Position the pointer over the cell containing the text note.	
Cell references, edit	EX 149		See Reference Window "Editing Cell Reference Types."
Chart border	EX 192		

Task Reference

TASK	PAGE #	RECOMMENDED METHOD	NOTES
Chart title, add	EX 180	Activate the chart. Click Insert, click Titles, click the chart title box to display a check, then click the OK button. Highlight the word "Title" in the chart title, press [Del], then type the desired title.	
Chart, activate	EX 169	Double-click anywhere within the chart border.	Activating a chart is also known as putting the chart in edit mode.
Chart, add or remove gridlines	EX 170	Select the chart. Click ▤ on the Chart toolbar.	
Chart, adjust size	EX 170	Select the chart and drag handles	
Chart, applying a pattern to a data marker	EX 173		See Reference Window "Selecting a Pattern for a Data Marker."
Chart, creating picture chart	EX 185		See Reference Window "Creating a Picture Chart."
Chart, delete		Select the chart. Click Edit, then click Cut.	
Chart, move	EX 170	Select the chart and drag it to a new location	
Chart, revising using the ChartWizard	EX 178		See Reference Window "Revising the Chart Data Series Using the ChartWizard."
Chart, rotating a 3-D chart	EX 192	Activate a 3-D chart. Click Format, then click 3-D View. Type the values you want in the Rotation and Elevation boxes.	It's possible to drag the corner of the chart, but be careful not to drag too far.
Chart, select	EX 169	Click anywhere within the chart border.	
ChartWizard, activate	EX 27		See Reference Window "Creating a Chart with ChartWizard."
Clipboard contents, paste into a range		Click 🖻.	
Colors, applying to a range of cells	EX 106		See Reference Window "Applying Patterns and Color."
Column width, adjust	EX 53		See Reference Window "Changing Column Width."
Column, select entire		Click column heading.	
Data Form, adding a record	EX 219		See Reference Window "Adding a Record Using the Data Form."

Task Reference

TASK	PAGE #	RECOMMENDED METHOD	NOTES
Data Form, deleting a record	EX 218		See Reference Window "Deleting a Record Using the Data Form."
Data Form, searching for a record	EX 215		See Reference Window "Searching for a Record Using the Data Form."
Data list, filter	EX 221		See Reference Window "Filtering a List with AutoFilter."
Data list, retrieving external data	EX 237	Select the sheet where you want the new data to appear. Click Data, then click Get External Data to activate MS Query. Select the desired data source in the Select Data Source dialog box. Click Use. (If necessary, click Other to display a list of possible data sources.) Select the desired data file in the Add Tables dialog box. Click Add. Double-click the asterisk in the list of field names to display all the records. Click File, then click Return Data to Microsoft Excel.	
Data List, sorting rows	EX 210		See Reference Window "Sorting Rows in a Data List."
Embedded Object, edit	EX 260		See Reference Window "Editing an Embedded Object Using OLE."
Excel, exit	EX 39	Click the File, then click Exit.	You can also click the Excel close button
Excel, start	EX 5	Click the Start button, then click Programs, if necessary click Microsoft Office, and then click Microsoft Excel.	
Font, select	EX 95	Highlight the cell or range you want to format. Click the Font list arrow in the toolbar, then click the desired font.	
Font, size	EX 96	Highlight the cell or range you want to format. Click the Font Size list arrow in the toolbar, then click the desired font size.	
Footer, edit	EX 117	In the Print Preview window, click the Setup button. Then click the Header/Footer tab in the Page Setup dialog box. Click the Footer list arrow button to choose a preset footer, or click the Custom Footer button and edit the existing footer in the Footer dialog box.	To open the Page Setup dialog box from the worksheet window, click Page Setup on the File menu.
Format Painter button, activate	EX 101	Select the cell or range of cells with the format you want to copy. Click , then select the cell or range of cells you want to format.	

Task Reference

TASK	PAGE #	RECOMMENDED METHOD	NOTES
Format, bold	EX 95	Highlight the cell or range you want to format. Click **B**.	The Bold button toggles on and off.
Format, center in cell	EX 98	Highlight the cell or range you want to format. Click ▤.	The Center button toggles on and off.
Format, currency	EX 99	Select the cell or range of cells you want to format. Click Format, then click Cells. Click the Number tab, click Currency in the Category box, then click the desired options.	
Format, date	EX 147	Select the cell or range of cells you want to format. Click Format, then click Cells. Click the Number tab, click Date in the Category box, then click the desired options.	
Format, italic	EX 96	Highlight the cell or range you want to format. Click *I*.	The Italic button toggles on and off.
Format, left-align	EX 98	Highlight the cell or range you want to format. Click ▤.	The Align Left button toggles on and off.
Format, percentage	EX 102	Select the cell or range of cells you want to format. Click Format, then click Cells. Click the Number tab, click Percentage in the Category box, then click the desired options.	
Format, right-align	EX 98	Highlight the cell or range you want to format. Click ▤.	The Align Right button toggles on and off.
Format, underline	EX 96	Highlight the cell or range you want to format. Click **U**.	The Underline button toggles on and off.
Formula, enter	EX 61		See Reference Window "Entering a Formula."
Formulas, display	EX 120	Click Tools, then click Options. Click the View tab, then click the Formulas box in the Windows Options box to display a check.	
Function Wizard, activate	EX 133		See Reference Window "Using the Function Wizard."
Function, AVERAGE	EX 136		See Reference Window "Using AVERAGE to Calculate the Average of the Numbers in a Range of Cells."
Function, enter	EX 134		See Reference Window "Typing Functions Directly in a Cell."
Function, IF	EX 144		See Reference Window "Using the IF Function to Specify the Conditions."

Task Reference

TASK	PAGE #	RECOMMENDED METHOD	NOTES
Function, MAX	EX 134		See Reference Window "Using MAX to Display the Largest Number in a Range of Cells."
Function, MIN	EX 135		See Reference Window "Using MIN to Display the Smallest Number in a Range of Cells."
Function, PMT	EX 139		See Reference Window "Using PMT to Calculate a Monthly Payment."
Function, SUM	EX 63		See Reference Window "Entering the SUM Function."
Gridlines, add or remove from printout	EX 118	In the Print Preview window, click the Setup button. Then click the Sheet tab in the Page Setup dialog box. In the Print box, insert a check in the Gridlines box to add gridlines, delete the check to remove gridlines.	To open the Page Setup dialog box from the worksheet window, click Page Setup on the File menu.
Header, edit	EX 117	In the Print Preview window, click the Setup button. Then click the Header/Footer tab in the Page Setup dialog box. Click the Header list arrow to select a preset header, or click the Custom Header button to edit the existing header in the Header dialog box.	To open the Page Setup dialog box from the work sheet window, click Page Setup on the File menu.
Help button, activate	EX 36		See Reference Window "Using the Help Button."
Help Topics dialog box, activate	EX 37	Click Help, then click Microsoft Excel Help Topics. To search for a specific topic, follow the directions on the Index tab. To find the answer to a question, follow the directions on the Answer Wizard tab.	
Links between files, maintain	EX 272	Open the source file, make and save any necessary changes. Open the linked destination file to make sure the updates appear there automatically.	If links between files aren't functioning properly, use the Links command on the destination program's Edit menu to display helpful information in the Links dialog box.
Macro, run	EX 122	Click Tools, then click Macro. Select macro name, then click Run.	Macros are also known as "Visual Basic modules."
Manual page break, add		Select the cell where you want to start a new page. Click Insert, then click Page Break.	
Manual page break, remove		Select any cell directly below a horizontal page break or to the right of a vertical page break. Click Insert, then click Remove Page Break.	

Task Reference

TASK	PAGE #	RECOMMENDED METHOD	NOTES
Map, activate	EX 199	Double-click inside the map border.	Activating a map is also known as putting it in edit mode.
Map, change background color	EX 200	Select the map, click Map, then click Features. Use the Custom list arrow button to select a color.	
Map, change data intervals	EX 199	Select the map, click Map, then click Value hading Options. To make the intervals the same for each category, click Equal spread of values in each range.	
Map, change value shading colors	EX 199	Select the map, click Map, then click Value Shading Options. Use the Color list arrow to select a color.	
Map, create	EX 197	Select map data, click [icon]. If necessary, select the desired map in the Multiple Maps Available dialog box.	Map data must be arranged in at least 2 columns, one containing geographical names or codes, and the other containing data you want to map.
Map, edit legend	EX 199	Double-click map legend, then adjust settings in the Edit Legend dialog box. Remove the check in the Use Compact Format box to display a complete legend.	
Map, edit title	EX 200	Select the map, double-click its title, use the cursor to select it and then press [Del]. Type the new title and press [Enter].	
Map, select	EX 199	Click the map to display handles on its border.	
MS Query Add-In, activate	EX 236		See Reference Window "Activating the MS Query Add-In."
Non-adjacent ranges, selecting	EX 166		See Reference Window "Selecting Non-adjacent Ranges."
Paint image, embed in Excel workbook	EX 273		See Reference Window "Using Excel as Destination Program for a Windows Paint Graphic Image.
Paint, exit	EX 275	Click File, click Exit.	
Paint, start	EX 274	Click the Start button, click Programs, click Accessories, then click Paint.	
Patterns, applying to a range of cells	EX 106		See Reference Window "Applying Patterns and Color."

Task Reference

TASK	PAGE #	RECOMMENDED METHOD	NOTES
PivotTable, generating from an Excel data list	EX 226		See Reference Window "Generating a PivotTable."
PivotTable, generating from an external data source	EX 235	Make sure all rows in the data list are displayed, then click any cell in the list. Click Data, then click PivotTable to activate the PivotTable Wizard. In the Step 1 of 4 dialog box, make sure the External Data Source option is selected. In the next dialog box, follow the instructions for activating MS Query and retrieving the external data.	
Print Formulas macro	EX 123		See "Tips for Using the Print Formulas Macro."
Print Preview window, open	EX 115	Click 🔍.	
Printout, center	EX 118	In the Print Preview dialog box, click the Setup button. Then click the Margins tab, then click the Horizontally and/or Vertically check boxes to display checks.	To open the Page Setup dialog box from the worksheet window, click Page Setup on the File menu.
Printout, landscape (sideways) orientation	EX 116	In the Print Preview window, click the Setup button. Then click the Page tab in the Page Setup dialog box, then click the Landscape option button in the Orientation box.	To open the Page Setup dialog box from the worksheet window, click Page Setup on the File menu.
Printout, portrait (normal) orientation	EX 116	In the Print Preview window, click Setup. Then click the Page tab in the Page Setup dialog box, then click the Portrait option button in the Orientation box.	To open the Page Setup dialog box from the worksheet window, click Page Setup on the File menu.
Protection, activating	EX 83		See Reference Window "Protecting Cells."
Protection, deactivating		Click Tools, click Protection, then click Unprotect Sheet . If you previously entered a password, enter the password in the Unprotect Sheet dialog box.	
Range, highlight	EX 26	Position pointer on the first cell of the range. Press and hold the mouse button and drag the mouse through the cells you want, then release the mouse button.	
Range, paste as a linked Excel worksheet in a destination document	EX 270	Select the Excel range you want to paste, go to the destination document, click Edit, then click Paste Special. Make sure the Paste Link button is selected, then click make sure Microsoft Excel Worksheet is selected in the As: list.	

Task Reference

TASK	PAGE #	RECOMMENDED METHOD	NOTES
Range, paste as an embedded Excel worksheet in a destination document	EX 270	Select the Excel range you want to paste, go to the destination document, click Edit, then click Paste Special. Make sure the Paste button is selected, then click make sure Microsoft Excel Worksheet is selected in the As: list.	
Range, select			See Highlight a range.
Row or column, delete	EX 68	Click the heading(s) of the row(s) or column(s) you want to delete, click Edit, then click Delete.	
Row or column, insert	EX 68		See Reference Window "Inserting a Row or Column."
Row, select entire		Click row heading.	
Sheet tab, rename	EX 56	Double-click the sheet tab. Type the new sheet name in the Rename Sheet dialog box.	
Sheet, activating		Click the sheet tab for the desired sheet.	
Sheet, copy		Press and hold [Ctrl]. Click the sheet tab, then position the pointer where you want the tab of the copied sheet to appear. Release the mouse button, and then [Ctrl].	
Sheet, move		Drag the sheet tab to the desired location.	
Sheet, move or copy to another workbook		Click Edit, then click Move or Copy Sheet. Select the workbook you want to move or copy the sheet to in the To Book box. Indicate where you want the sheet to appear in the workbook in the Before box. Click Create a Copy if you want to Copy the sheet instead of removing it from its original location.	
Shortcut menu, activate	EX 94	Select the cells or objects to which you want to apply the command, click the right mouse button, then select the command you want.	
Spelling command, activate	EX 81	Click cell A1, then click [icon].	See Reference Window "Using the Spelling Button."
Split the worksheet window	EX 20	Drag the horizontal or vertical split box to the desired position.	
Split window, move to	EX 20	Click the window.	
Template, save workbook as	EX 85	Create a workbook, click File, then click Save As. Click Template in the Save as type list box. Select the desired drive and folder in the Save in box. Type the name you want for the template in the File name box.	

Task Reference

TASK	PAGE #	RECOMMENDED METHOD	NOTES
Text box, add	EX 110		See Reference Window "Adding a Text Box and Comment."
Text, center across columns	EX 98	Highlight a range—include the text you want to center and at least one cell in each of the columns across which you want to center the text. Click [icon].	The Center Across Columns button toggles on and off.
Toolbar, add or remove	EX 108		See Reference Window "Activating and Removing Toolbars."
Undo command, activate	EX 18	Click [icon].	Don't confuse the Undo button with the Redo button.
Window, maximize	EX 7	Click the window's maximize button.	
Window, minimize		Click the window's minimize button.	
WordPad, exit	EX 271	Click File, click Exit.	
WordPad, start	EX 254	Click the Start button, click Programs, click Accessories, then click WordPad.	
Workbook, open	EX 11		See Reference Window "Opening a Workbook."
Workbook, save with a new name	EX 22		See Reference Window "Saving a Workbook with a New Filename."
Workbook, save with same name	EX 30	Click [icon].	
Worksheet window, remove split	EX 21	Click Window, then click Remove Split.	
Worksheet, close	EX 39	Click File, then click Close.	You can also click the worksheet Close button.
Worksheet, print	EX 24	Click [icon] to print without adjusting any print options. Use the Print command on the File menu to adjust options.	See Reference Window "Printing a Worksheet."
Worksheet, select entire		Click the rectangle at the intersection of the column and row headings, in the upper-left corner of the worksheet.	